SNIFF
SNIFF

空 知 英 秋

Hideaki Sorachi

There's a rumor going around that new copies of the *Gin Tama* graphic novels apparently have a vinegary smell. Even you, yes you, standing in the store reading this book without buying it, give it a good sniff if you don't believe me. See! ...Oh, Mr. Salesperson, this person here is rubbing off his nose oil in this manga! Please make this person take responsibility and buy it now that it's all smudged up!

V
R
R
R
R
R
R

Hideaki Sorachi was born on May 25, 1979 and grew up in Hokkaido, Japan. His ongoing series, *GIN TAMA*, became a huge hit when it began running in the pages of Japan's *Weekly Shonen Jump* in 2004. A *GIN TAMA* animated series followed soon after, premiering on Japanese TV in April 2006. Sorachi made his manga debut with the one-shot story *DANDELION!*

GIN TAMA VOL. 7
The SHONEN JUMP ADVANCED Manga Edition

STORY & ART BY HIDEAKI SORACHI

Translation/Matthew Rosin, Honyaku Center Inc.
English Adaptation/Gerard Jones
Touch-up Art & Lettering/Avril Averill
Cover Design/Sean Lee
Interior Design/Aaron Cruse
Editor/Mike Montesa

Editor in Chief, Books/Alvin Lu
Editor in Chief, Magazines/Marc Weidenbaum
VP of Publishing Licensing/Rika Inouye
VP of Sales/Gonzalo Ferreyra
Sr. VP of Marketing/Liza Coppola
Publisher/Hyoe Narita

Published by VIZ Media, LLC
P.O. Box 77010
San Francisco, CA 94107

SHONEN JUMP ADVANCED Manga Edition
10 9 8 7 6 5 4 3 2 1
First printing, July 2008

THE WORLD'S MOST
CUTTING-EDGE MANGA

SHONEN JUMP
ADVANCED
www.shonenjump.com

VIZ MEDIA
www.viz.com

Vol. 7

You Always Remember the Things that Matter the Least

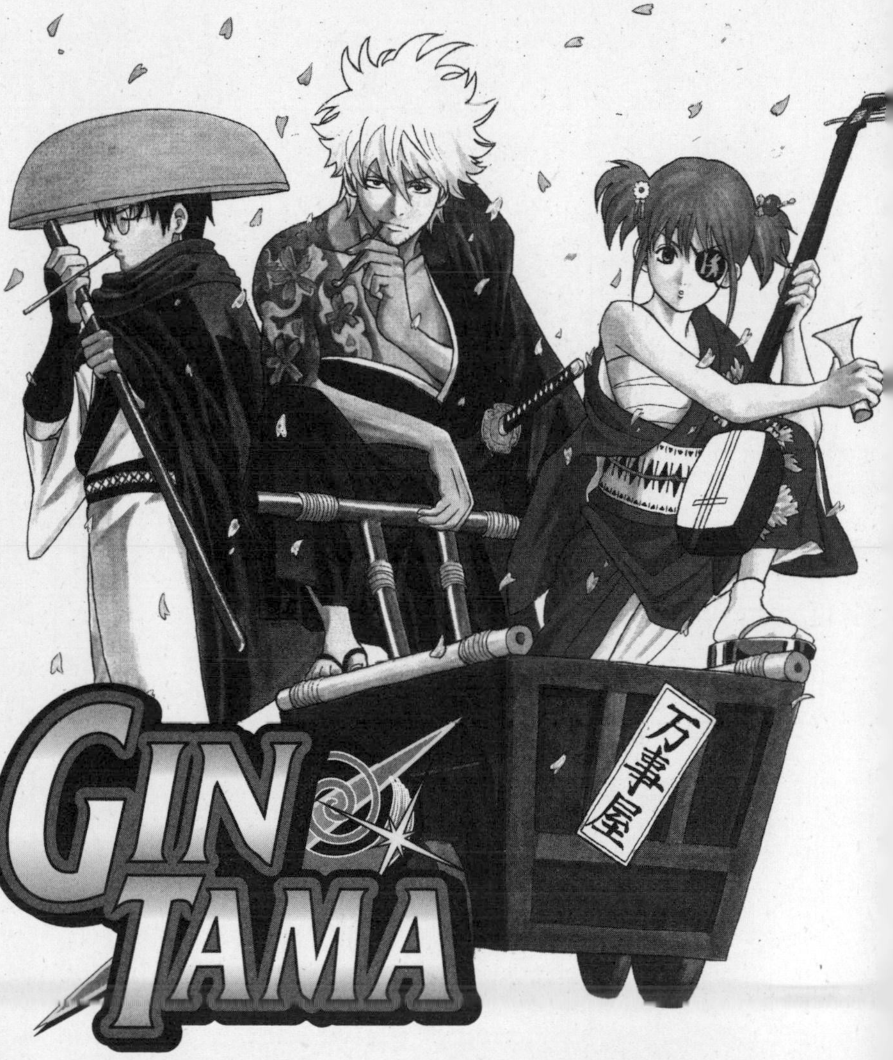
GIN TAMA
万事屋

STORY & ART BY

HIDEAKI SORACHI

Cast of Characters

Yorozuya Members

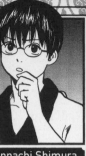

Shinpachi Shimura

Works under Gintoki in an attempt to learn the samurai spirit, but has been regretting his decision recently. Also president of idol singer Tsu Terakado's fan club.

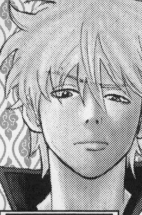

Gintoki Sakata

The hero of our story. He needs to eat something sweet periodically or he gets cranky. He commands a powerful sword arm but is one step away from diabetes. A former member of the exclusionist faction that seeks to eliminate the space aliens and protect the nation.

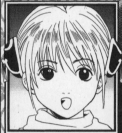

Kagura

A member of the "Yato Clan," the most powerful warrior race in the universe. Her voracious appetite and often inadvertent comic timing are unrivalled.

Shinsengumi Soldiers

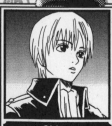

Okita

The most formidable swordsman in the Shinsengumi. His jovial attitude hides an utterly black heart. He wants to take over as the Vice-Chief.

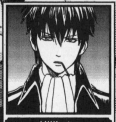

Hijikata

Vice-Chief of the Shinsengumi, Edo's elite Delta Force police unit. His cool demeanor turns to rage the moment he draws his sword. The pupils of his eyes always seem a bit dilated.

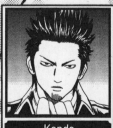

Kondo

Chief of the Shinsengumi, and trusted by all its soldiers. Also stalking Shinpachi's elder sister Otae.

Other Characters

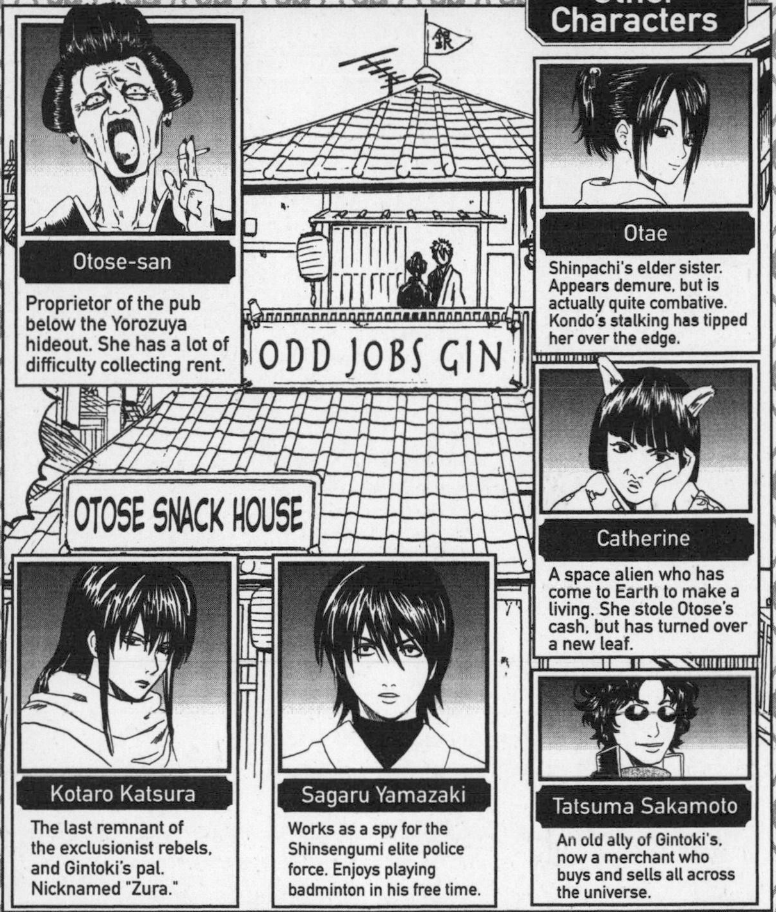
Otose-san
Proprietor of the pub below the Yorozuya hideout. She has a lot of difficulty collecting rent.
ODD JOBS GIN
Otae
Shinpachi's elder sister. Appears demure, but is actually quite combative. Kondo's stalking has tipped her over the edge.
OTOSE SNACK HOUSE
Catherine
A space alien who has come to Earth to make a living. She stole Otose's cash, but has turned over a new leaf.
Kotaro Katsura
The last remnant of the exclusionist rebels, and Gintoki's pal. Nicknamed "Zura."
Sagaru Yamazaki
Works as a spy for the Shinsengumi elite police force. Enjoys playing badminton in his free time.
Tatsuma Sakamoto
An old ally of Gintoki's, now a merchant who buys and sells all across the universe.

The story thus far

In an alternate-universe Edo (Tokyo), extraterrestrials land in Japan and the new government issues an order outlawing swords. The samurai, who have reached the pinnacle of power and prosperity, fall into rapid decline.

Twenty years hence, only one samurai has managed to hold onto his fighting spirit: a somewhat eccentric fellow named Gintoki "Odd Jobs Gin" Sakata. A lover of sweets and near diabetic, our hero sets up shop as a *yorozuya*—an expert at managing trouble and handling the oddest jobs.

Joining "Gin" in his business is Shinpachi Shimura, whose sister Gintoki saved from the clutches of nefarious debt collectors. After a series of unexpected circumstances, the trio meets a powerful alien named Kagura, who becomes—after some arm-twisting—a part-time team member.

While hunting for mushrooms, the Yorozuya are attacked by a giant bear, battle a crooked gambling boss, play cupid (unsuccessfully, of course), turn back an invasion of super-cockroaches, and unveil a phony religious cult. Let's hope something actually *happens* this time...

WHAT THIS MANGA'S FULL OF
vol. 7

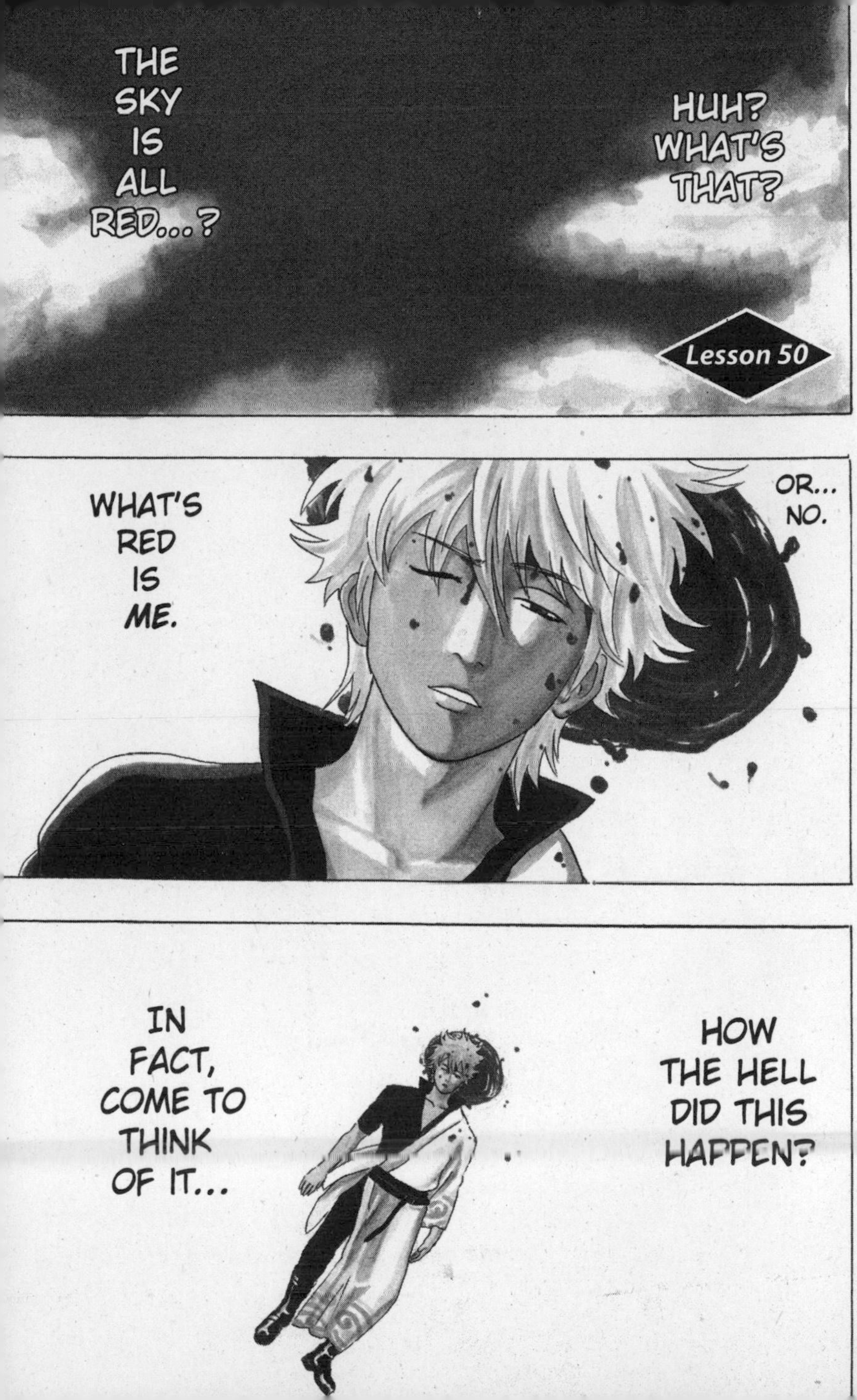
HUH? WHAT'S THAT?
THE SKY IS ALL RED...?
Lesson 50
OR... NO.
WHAT'S RED IS ME.
HOW THE HELL DID THIS HAPPEN?
IN FACT, COME TO THINK OF IT...

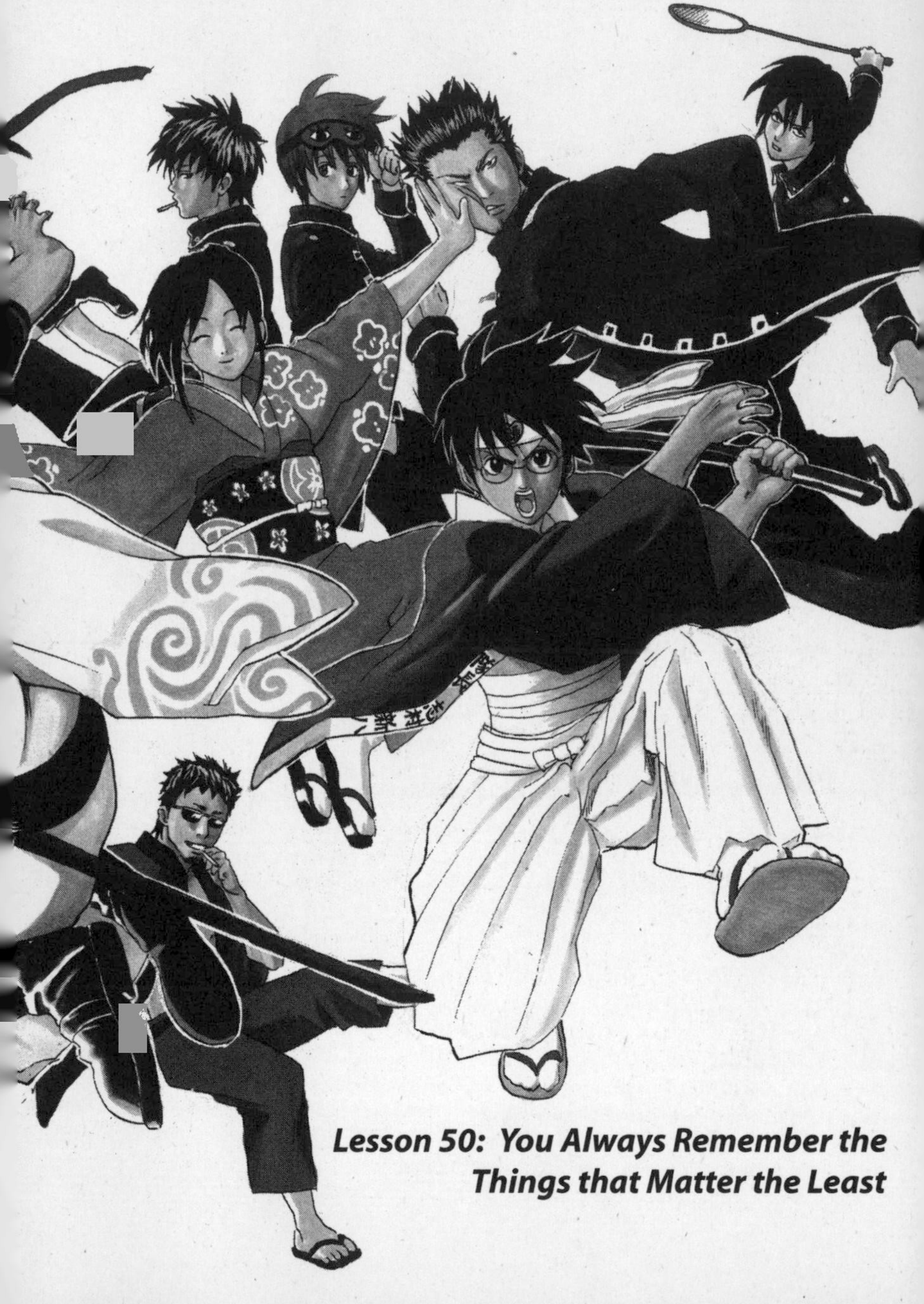

Lesson 50: You Always Remember the Things that Matter the Least

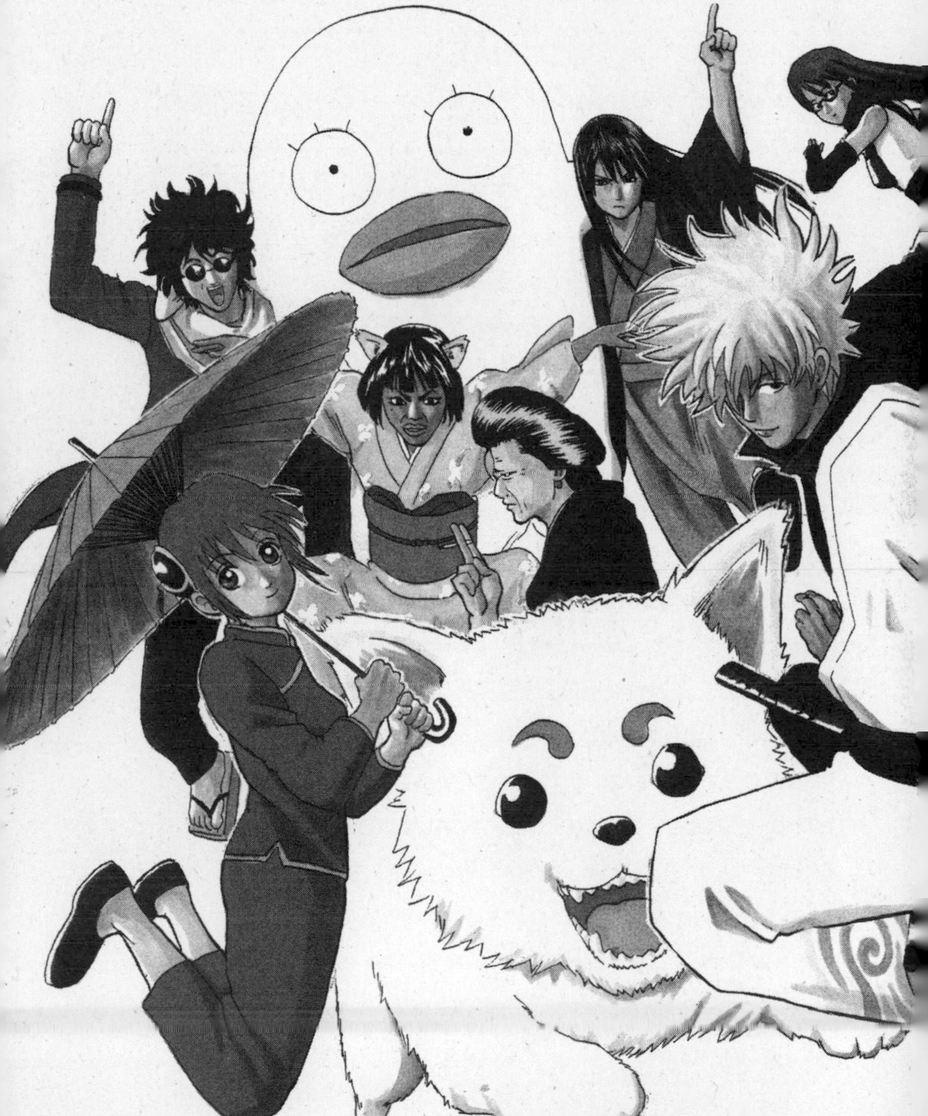

Thanks for buying Gin Tama 7. Back when 6 came out, I was wandering through a bookstore and there was this kid who was buying a copy. I thought about telling him, "Hey, I'm the guy who drew that. You want me to sign it for you?" But I decided not to.

I mean, what if he said, "No way Sorachi-sensei is gonna look like you! Get a job, you bum!" Can't go and spoil the dreams of young people, you know. I'm only 5'4", and I kind of look like Tetsuya Takeda, the actor/songwriter. Not exactly skinny and cool-looking. Anyway, if you happen to be reading this while standing in a bookstore, take a look around. If you see a guy who looks like a smirking Tetsuya Takeda...well, it's probably Tetsuya Takeda...

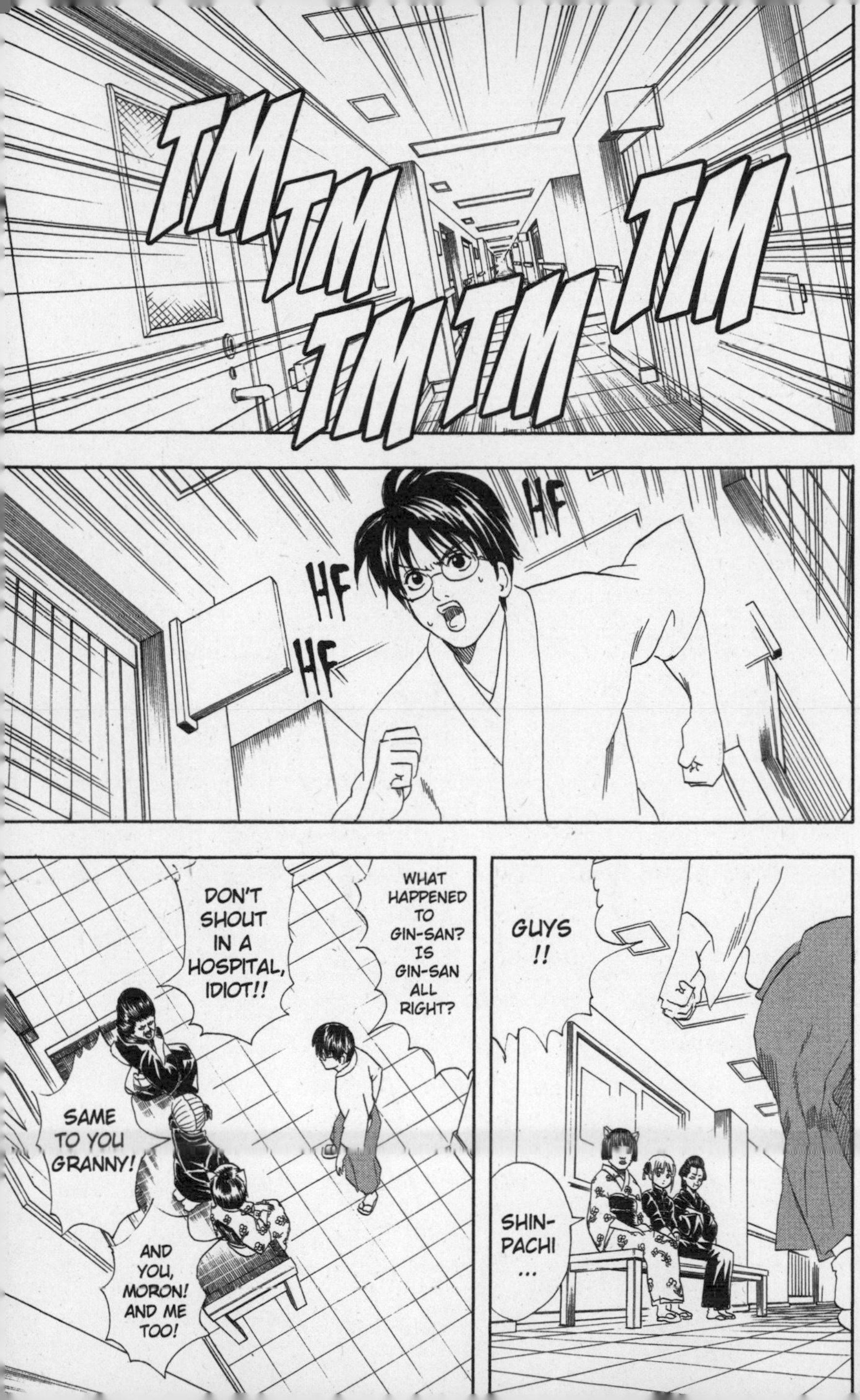
TM
TM
TM-TM
TM
HF
HF
HF
GUYS!!
SHIN-PACHI...
WHAT HAPPENED TO GIN-SAN? IS GIN-SAN ALL RIGHT?
DON'T SHOUT IN A HOSPITAL, IDIOT!!
SAME TO YOU GRANNY!
AND YOU, MORON! AND ME TOO!

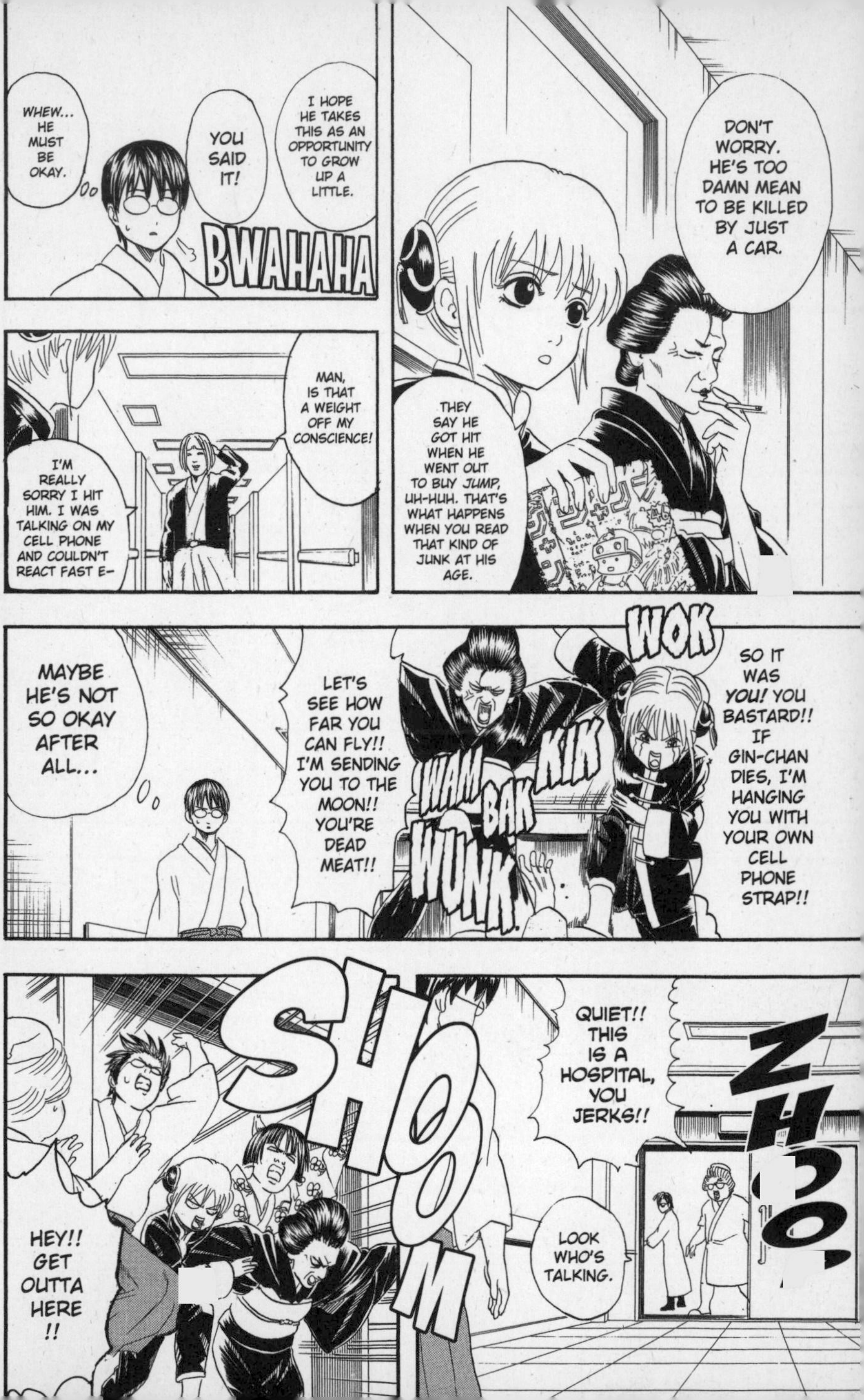
DON'T WORRY. HE'S TOO DAMN MEAN TO BE KILLED BY JUST A CAR.
THEY SAY HE GOT HIT WHEN HE WENT OUT TO BUY JUMP, UH-HUH. THAT'S WHAT HAPPENS WHEN YOU READ THAT KIND OF JUNK AT HIS AGE.
I HOPE HE TAKES THIS AS AN OPPORTUNITY TO GROW UP A LITTLE.
YOU SAID IT!
BWAHAHA
WHEW... HE MUST BE OKAY.
MAN, IS THAT A WEIGHT OFF MY CONSCIENCE!
I'M REALLY SORRY I HIT HIM. I WAS TALKING ON MY CELL PHONE AND COULDN'T REACT FAST E-
SO IT WAS YOU! YOU BASTARD!! IF GIN-CHAN DIES, I'M HANGING YOU WITH YOUR OWN CELL PHONE STRAP!!
WOK
LET'S SEE HOW FAR YOU CAN FLY!! I'M SENDING YOU TO THE MOON!! YOU'RE DEAD MEAT!!
KIK
WAM
BAK
WUNK
MAYBE HE'S NOT SO OKAY AFTER ALL...
ZHOO
QUIET!! THIS IS A HOSPITAL, YOU JERKS!!
LOOK WHO'S TALKING.
SHOOM
HEY!! GET OUTTA HERE !!

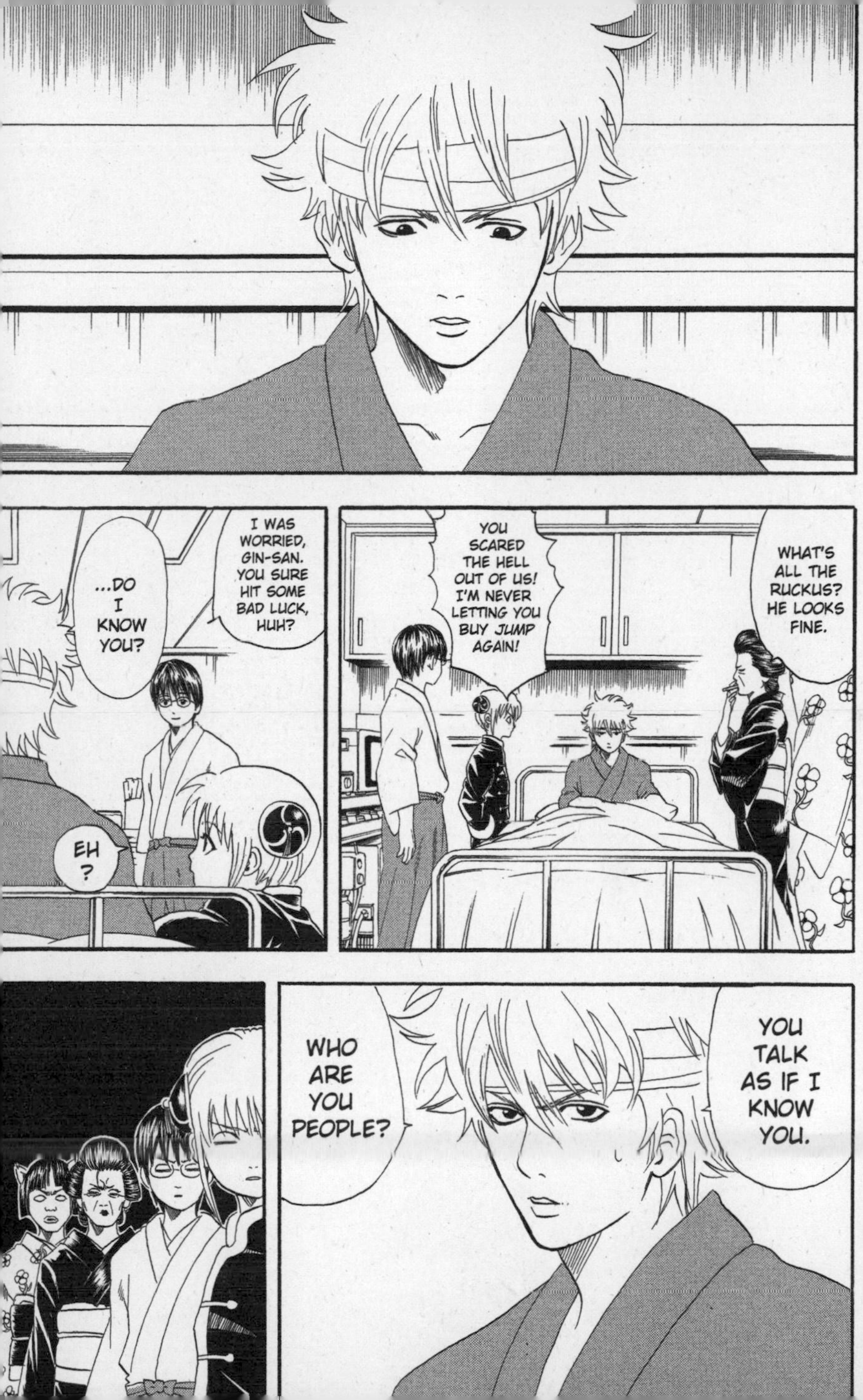
WHAT'S ALL THE RUCKUS? HE LOOKS FINE.
YOU SCARED THE HELL OUT OF US! I'M NEVER LETTING YOU BUY JUMP AGAIN!
I WAS WORRIED, GIN-SAN. YOU SURE HIT SOME BAD LUCK, HUH?
...DO I KNOW YOU?
EH?
YOU TALK AS IF I KNOW YOU.
WHO ARE YOU PEOPLE?

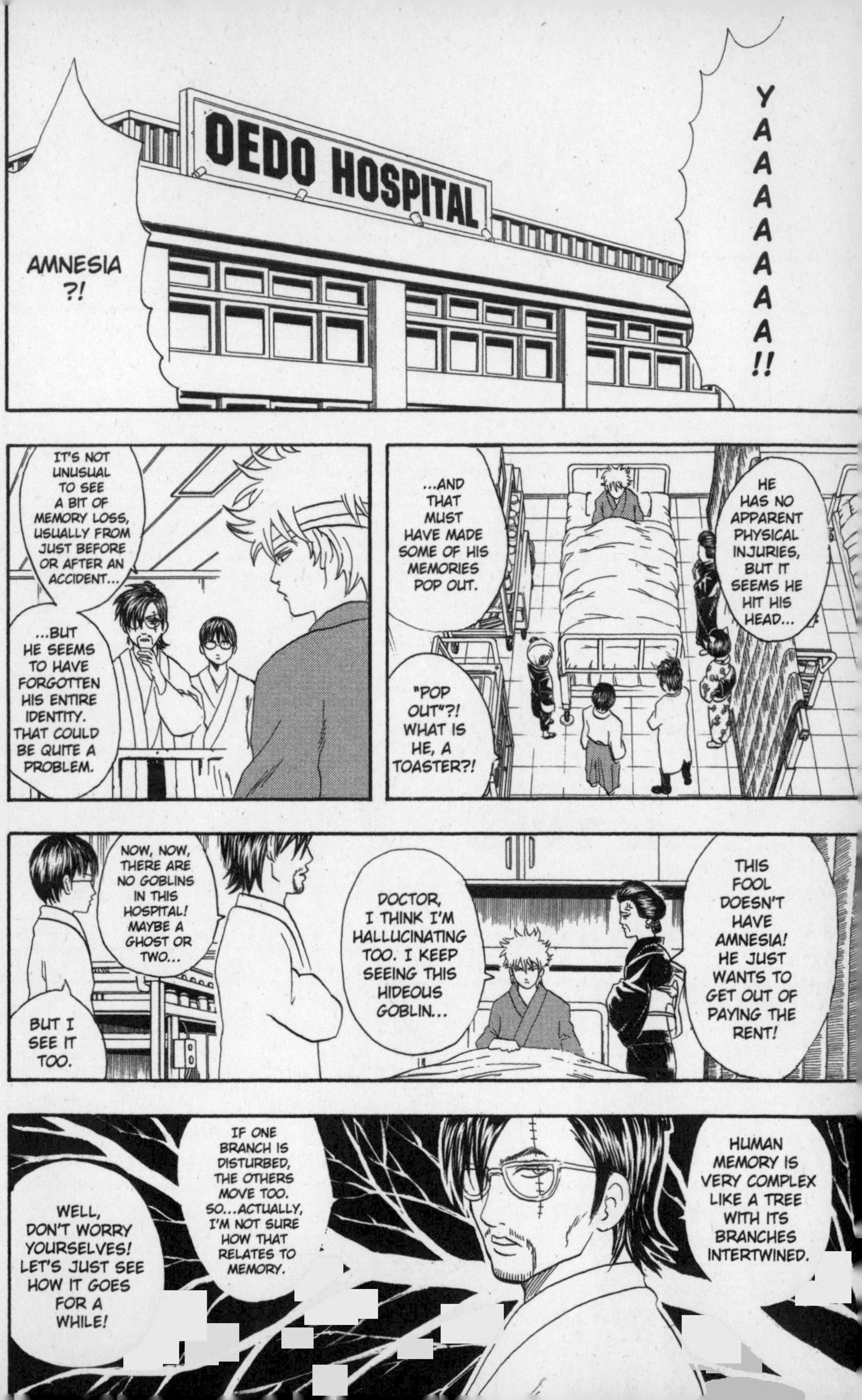
YAAAAAAA!!
AMNESIA ?!
HE HAS NO APPARENT PHYSICAL INJURIES, BUT IT SEEMS HE HIT HIS HEAD...
...AND THAT MUST HAVE MADE SOME OF HIS MEMORIES POP OUT.
"POP OUT"?! WHAT IS HE, A TOASTER?!
IT'S NOT UNUSUAL TO SEE A BIT OF MEMORY LOSS, USUALLY FROM JUST BEFORE OR AFTER AN ACCIDENT...
...BUT HE SEEMS TO HAVE FORGOTTEN HIS ENTIRE IDENTITY. THAT COULD BE QUITE A PROBLEM.
THIS FOOL DOESN'T HAVE AMNESIA! HE JUST WANTS TO GET OUT OF PAYING THE RENT!
DOCTOR, I THINK I'M HALLUCINATING TOO. I KEEP SEEING THIS HIDEOUS GOBLIN...
NOW, NOW, THERE ARE NO GOBLINS IN THIS HOSPITAL! MAYBE A GHOST OR TWO...
BUT I SEE IT TOO.
HUMAN MEMORY IS VERY COMPLEX LIKE A TREE WITH ITS BRANCHES INTERTWINED.
IF ONE BRANCH IS DISTURBED, THE OTHERS MOVE TOO. SO...ACTUALLY, I'M NOT SURE HOW THAT RELATES TO MEMORY.
WELL, DON'T WORRY YOURSELVES! LET'S JUST SEE HOW IT GOES FOR A WHILE!

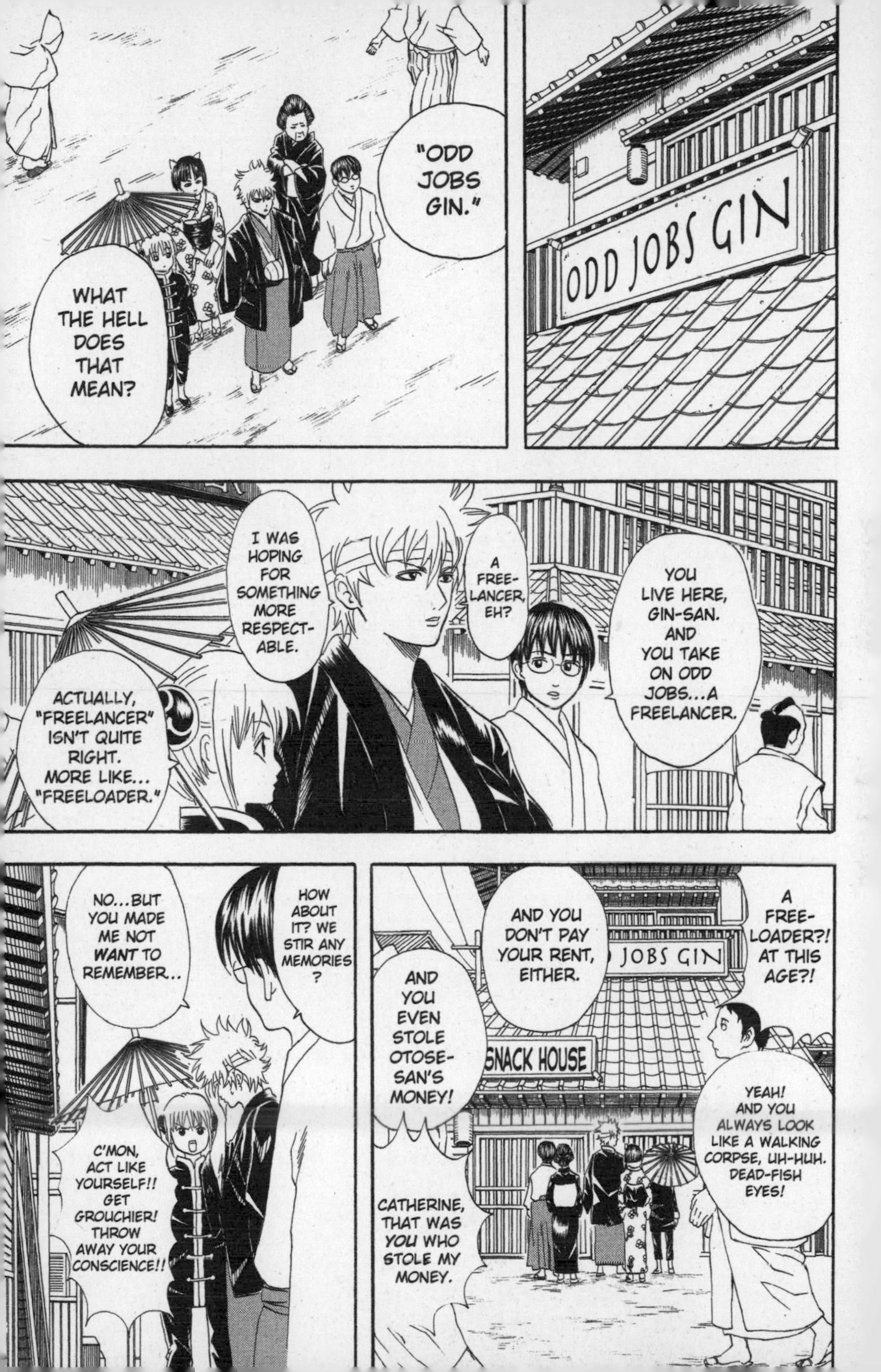
ODD JOBS GIN
"ODD JOBS GIN."
WHAT THE HELL DOES THAT MEAN?
YOU LIVE HERE, GIN-SAN. AND YOU TAKE ON ODD JOBS...A FREELANCER.
A FREE-LANCER, EH?
I WAS HOPING FOR SOMETHING MORE RESPECT-ABLE.
ACTUALLY, "FREELANCER" ISN'T QUITE RIGHT. MORE LIKE... "FREELOADER."
A FREE-LOADER?! AT THIS AGE?!
AND YOU DON'T PAY YOUR RENT, EITHER.
SNACK HOUSE
YEAH! AND YOU ALWAYS LOOK LIKE A WALKING CORPSE, UH-HUH. DEAD-FISH EYES!
AND YOU EVEN STOLE OTOSE-SAN'S MONEY!
CATHERINE, THAT WAS YOU WHO STOLE MY MONEY.
HOW ABOUT IT? WE STIR ANY MEMORIES?
NO...BUT YOU MADE ME NOT WANT TO REMEMBER...
C'MON, ACT LIKE YOURSELF!! GET GROUCHIER! THROW AWAY YOUR CONSCIENCE!!

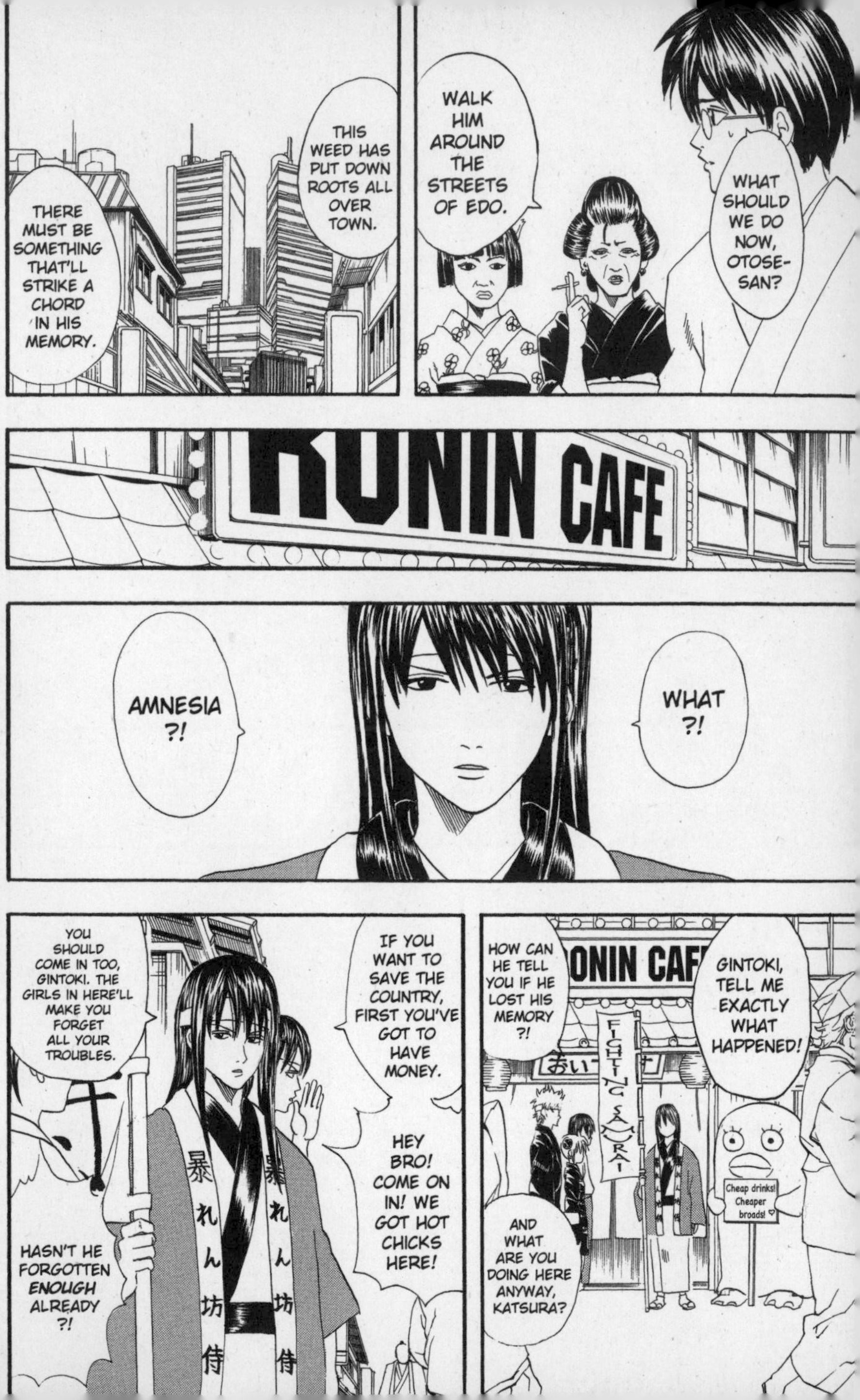
WHAT SHOULD WE DO NOW, OTOSE-SAN?
WALK HIM AROUND THE STREETS OF EDO.
THIS WEED HAS PUT DOWN ROOTS ALL OVER TOWN.
THERE MUST BE SOMETHING THAT'LL STRIKE A CHORD IN HIS MEMORY.
RONIN CAFE
WHAT?!
AMNESIA?!
GINTOKI, TELL ME EXACTLY WHAT HAPPENED!
HOW CAN HE TELL YOU IF HE LOST HIS MEMORY?!
ONIN CAF
FIGHTING SAMURAI
Cheap drinks! Cheaper broads! ♡
AND WHAT ARE YOU DOING HERE ANYWAY, KATSURA?
IF YOU WANT TO SAVE THE COUNTRY, FIRST YOU'VE GOT TO HAVE MONEY.
YOU SHOULD COME IN TOO, GINTOKI. THE GIRLS IN HERE'LL MAKE YOU FORGET ALL YOUR TROUBLES.
暴れん坊侍
暴れん坊侍
HEY BRO! COME ON IN! WE GOT HOT CHICKS HERE!
HASN'T HE FORGOTTEN ENOUGH ALREADY?!

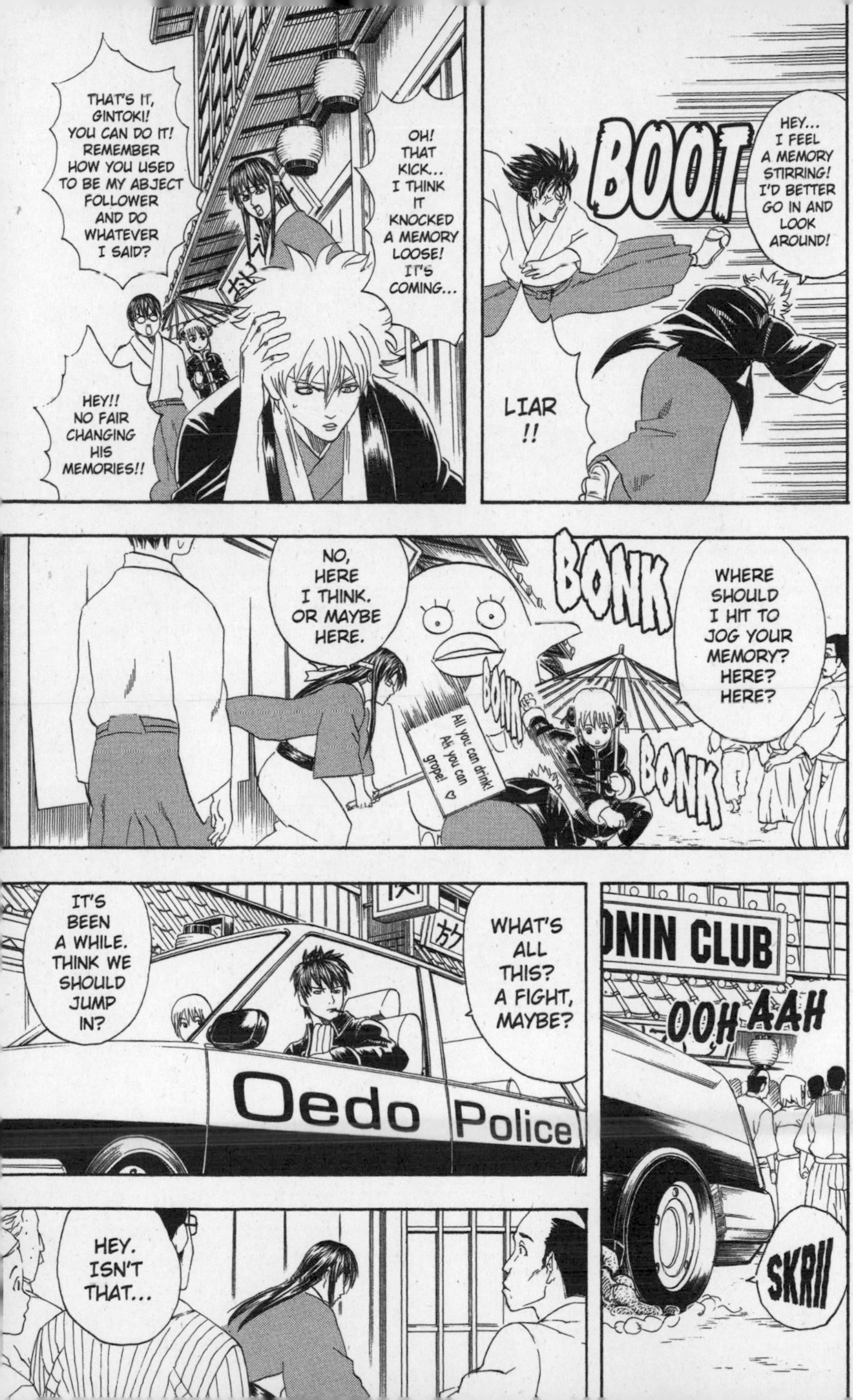
BOOT
HEY... I FEEL A MEMORY STIRRING! I'D BETTER GO IN AND LOOK AROUND!
LIAR !!
OH! THAT KICK... I THINK IT KNOCKED A MEMORY LOOSE! IT'S COMING...
THAT'S IT, GINTOKI! YOU CAN DO IT! REMEMBER HOW YOU USED TO BE MY ABJECT FOLLOWER AND DO WHATEVER I SAID?
HEY!! NO FAIR CHANGING HIS MEMORIES!!
WHERE SHOULD I HIT TO JOG YOUR MEMORY? HERE? HERE?
BONK
BONK
BONK
NO, HERE I THINK. OR MAYBE HERE.
All you can drink! All you can grope! ♡
ONIN CLUB
OOH AAH
SKRII
WHAT'S ALL THIS? A FIGHT, MAYBE?
IT'S BEEN A WHILE. THINK WE SHOULD JUMP IN?
Oedo Police
HEY. ISN'T THAT...

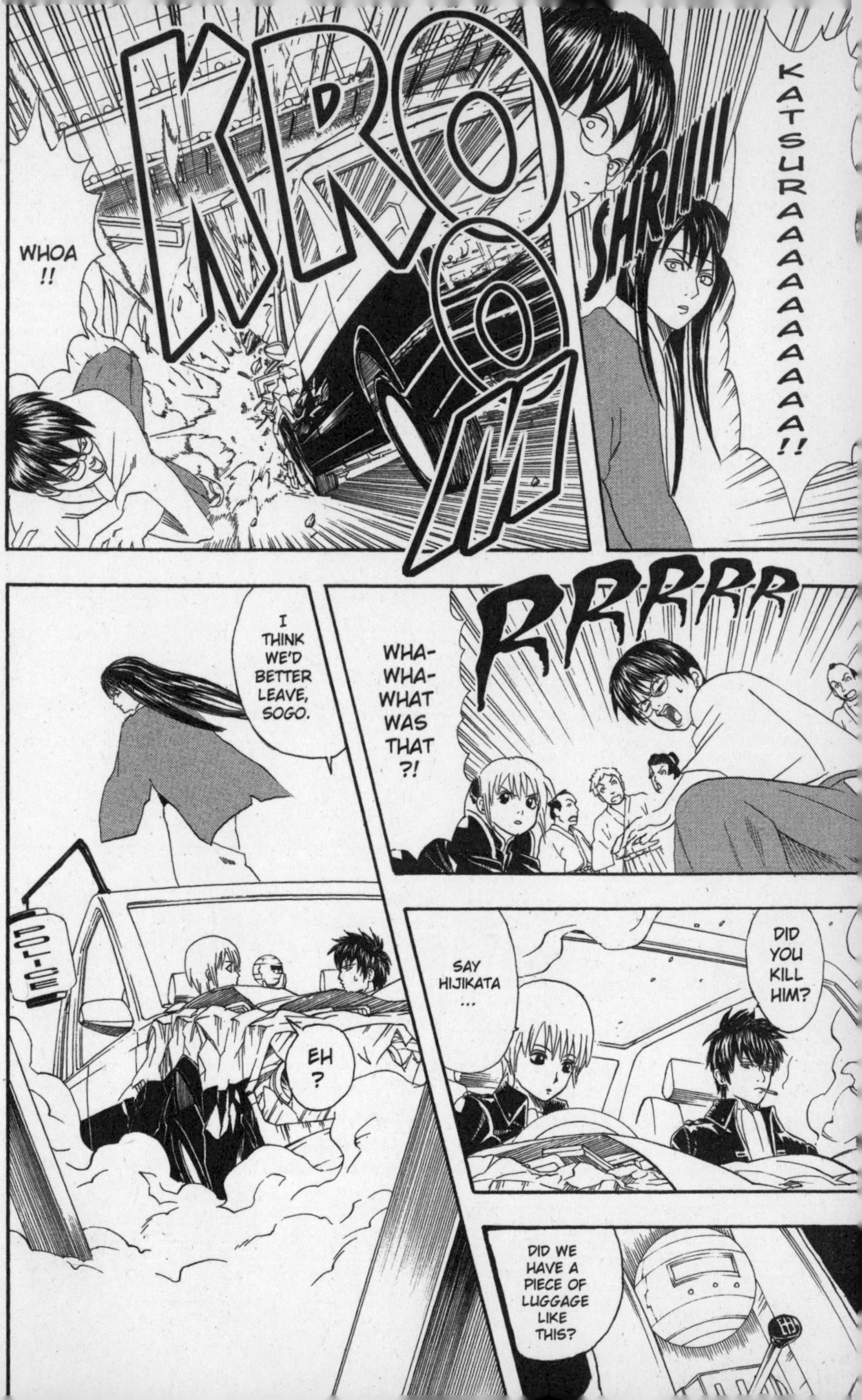
KATSURAAAAAAAAAA!!
SHRI!!!
KROOM
WHOA !!
RRRRR
WHA-WHA-WHAT WAS THAT ?!
I THINK WE'D BETTER LEAVE, SOGO.
DID YOU KILL HIM?
SAY HIJIKATA ...
DID WE HAVE A PIECE OF LUGGAGE LIKE THIS?
EH ?
POLICE

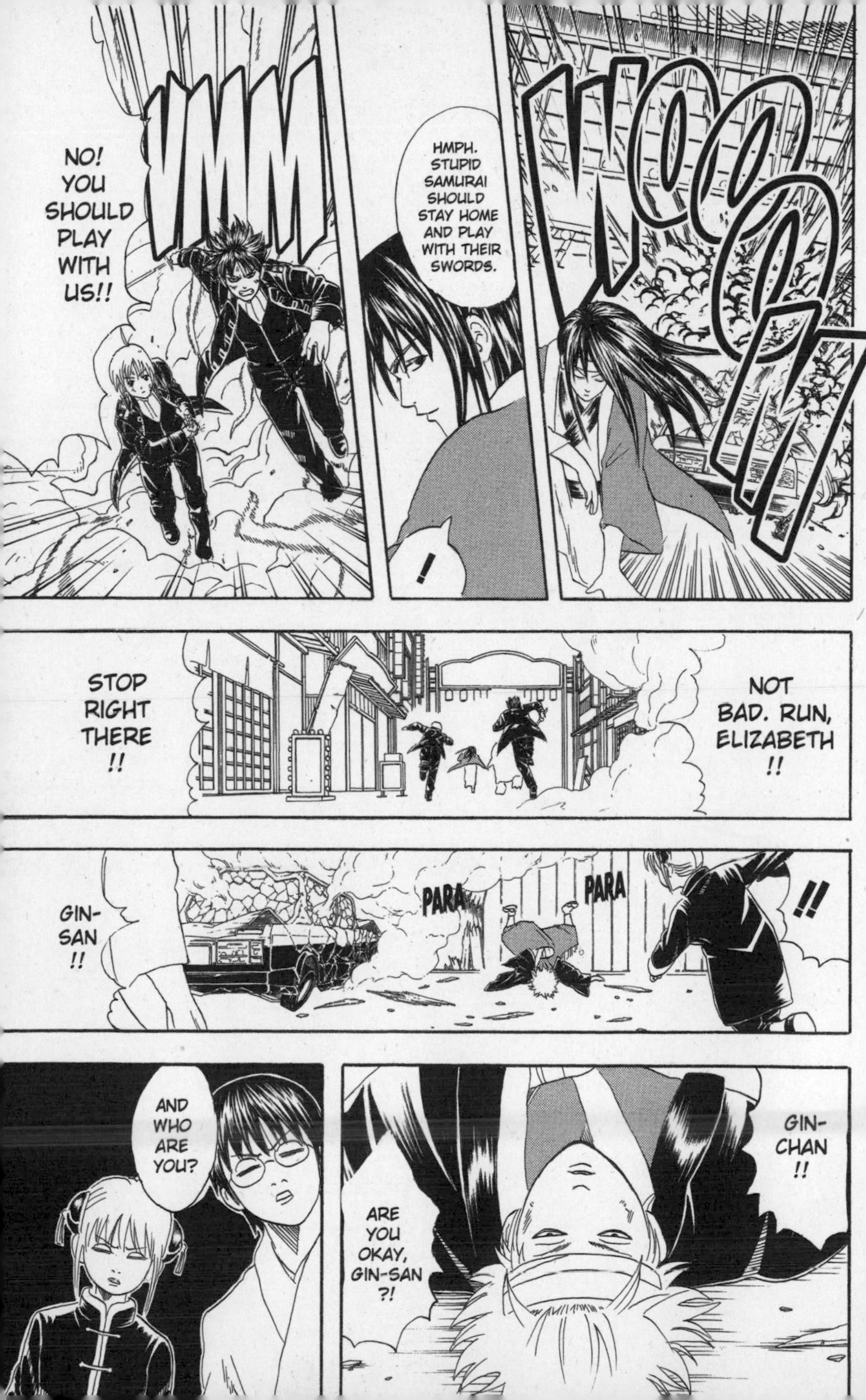
WOOOM
HMPH. STUPID SAMURAI SHOULD STAY HOME AND PLAY WITH THEIR SWORDS.
!
VMM
NO! YOU SHOULD PLAY WITH US!!
NOT BAD. RUN, ELIZABETH!!
STOP RIGHT THERE!!
!!
PARA
PARA
GIN-SAN!!
GIN-CHAN!!
ARE YOU OKAY, GIN-SAN?!
AND WHO ARE YOU?

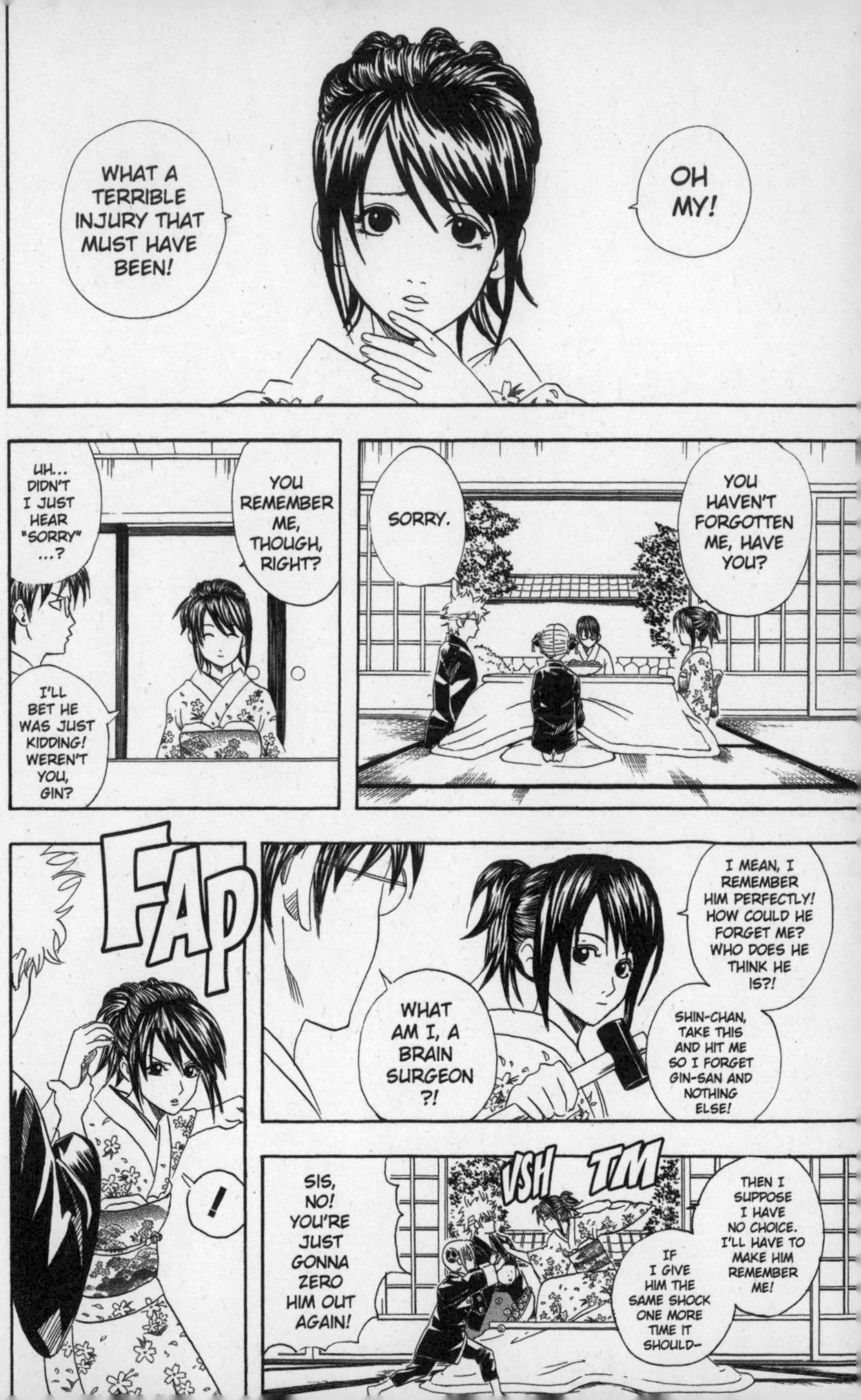
OH MY!
WHAT A TERRIBLE INJURY THAT MUST HAVE BEEN!
YOU HAVEN'T FORGOTTEN ME, HAVE YOU?
SORRY.
YOU REMEMBER ME, THOUGH, RIGHT?
UH... DIDN'T I JUST HEAR "SORRY" ...?
I'LL BET HE WAS JUST KIDDING! WEREN'T YOU, GIN?
I MEAN, I REMEMBER HIM PERFECTLY! HOW COULD HE FORGET ME? WHO DOES HE THINK HE IS?!
SHIN-CHAN, TAKE THIS AND HIT ME SO I FORGET GIN-SAN AND NOTHING ELSE!
WHAT AM I, A BRAIN SURGEON ?!
VSH
TM
THEN I SUPPOSE I HAVE NO CHOICE. I'LL HAVE TO MAKE HIM REMEMBER ME!
IF I GIVE HIM THE SAME SHOCK ONE MORE TIME IT SHOULD–
SIS, NO! YOU'RE JUST GONNA ZERO HIM OUT AGAIN!
FAP
!

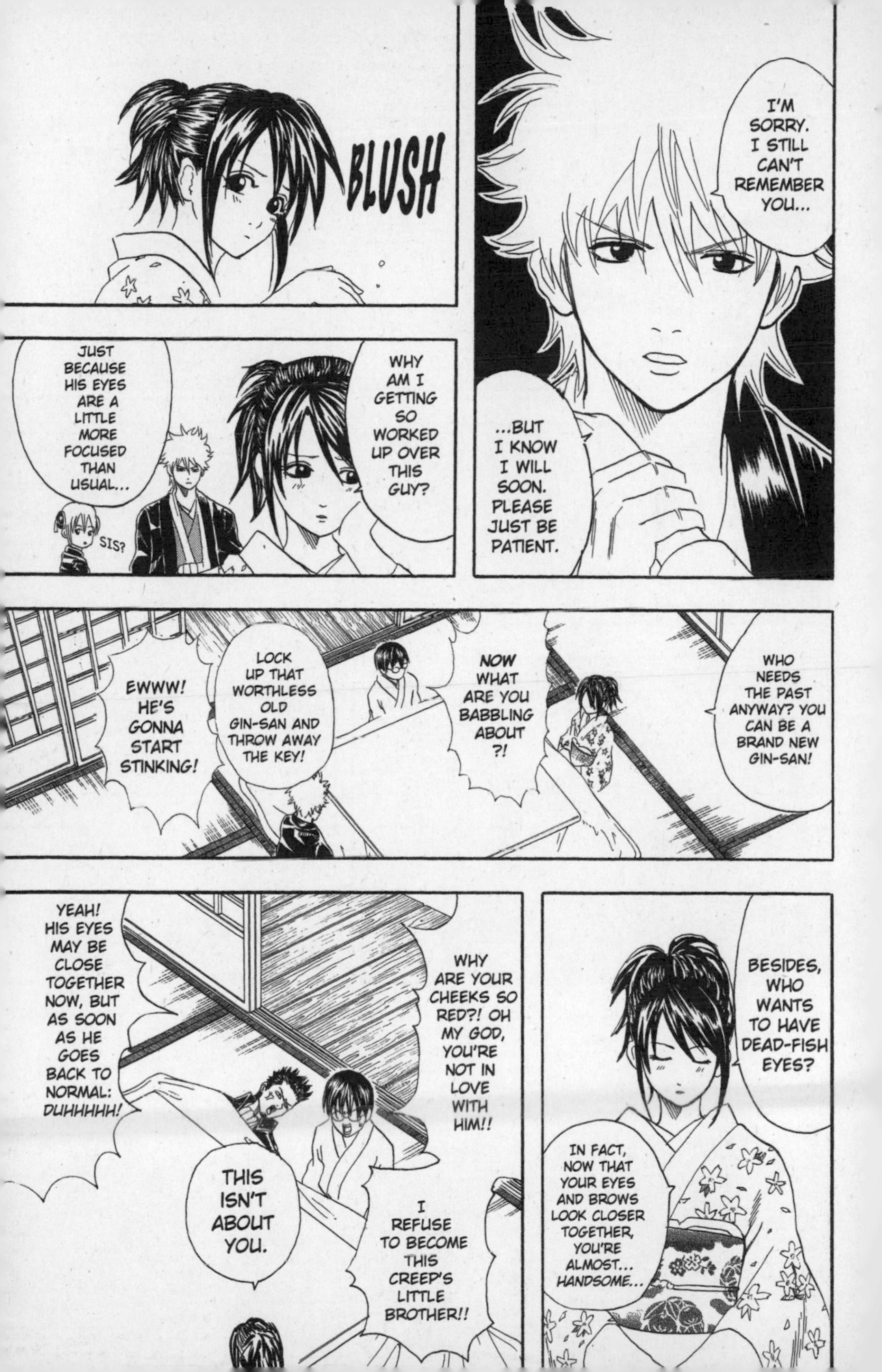
I'M SORRY. I STILL CAN'T REMEMBER YOU...
...BUT I KNOW I WILL SOON. PLEASE JUST BE PATIENT.
BLUSH
WHY AM I GETTING SO WORKED UP OVER THIS GUY?
JUST BECAUSE HIS EYES ARE A LITTLE MORE FOCUSED THAN USUAL...
SIS?
WHO NEEDS THE PAST ANYWAY? YOU CAN BE A BRAND NEW GIN-SAN!
NOW WHAT ARE YOU BABBLING ABOUT?!
LOCK UP THAT WORTHLESS OLD GIN-SAN AND THROW AWAY THE KEY!
EWWW! HE'S GONNA START STINKING!
BESIDES, WHO WANTS TO HAVE DEAD-FISH EYES?
IN FACT, NOW THAT YOUR EYES AND BROWS LOOK CLOSER TOGETHER, YOU'RE ALMOST... HANDSOME...
WHY ARE YOUR CHEEKS SO RED?! OH MY GOD, YOU'RE NOT IN LOVE WITH HIM!!
YEAH! HIS EYES MAY BE CLOSE TOGETHER NOW, BUT AS SOON AS HE GOES BACK TO NORMAL: DUHHHHH!
I REFUSE TO BECOME THIS CREEP'S LITTLE BROTHER!!
THIS ISN'T ABOUT YOU.

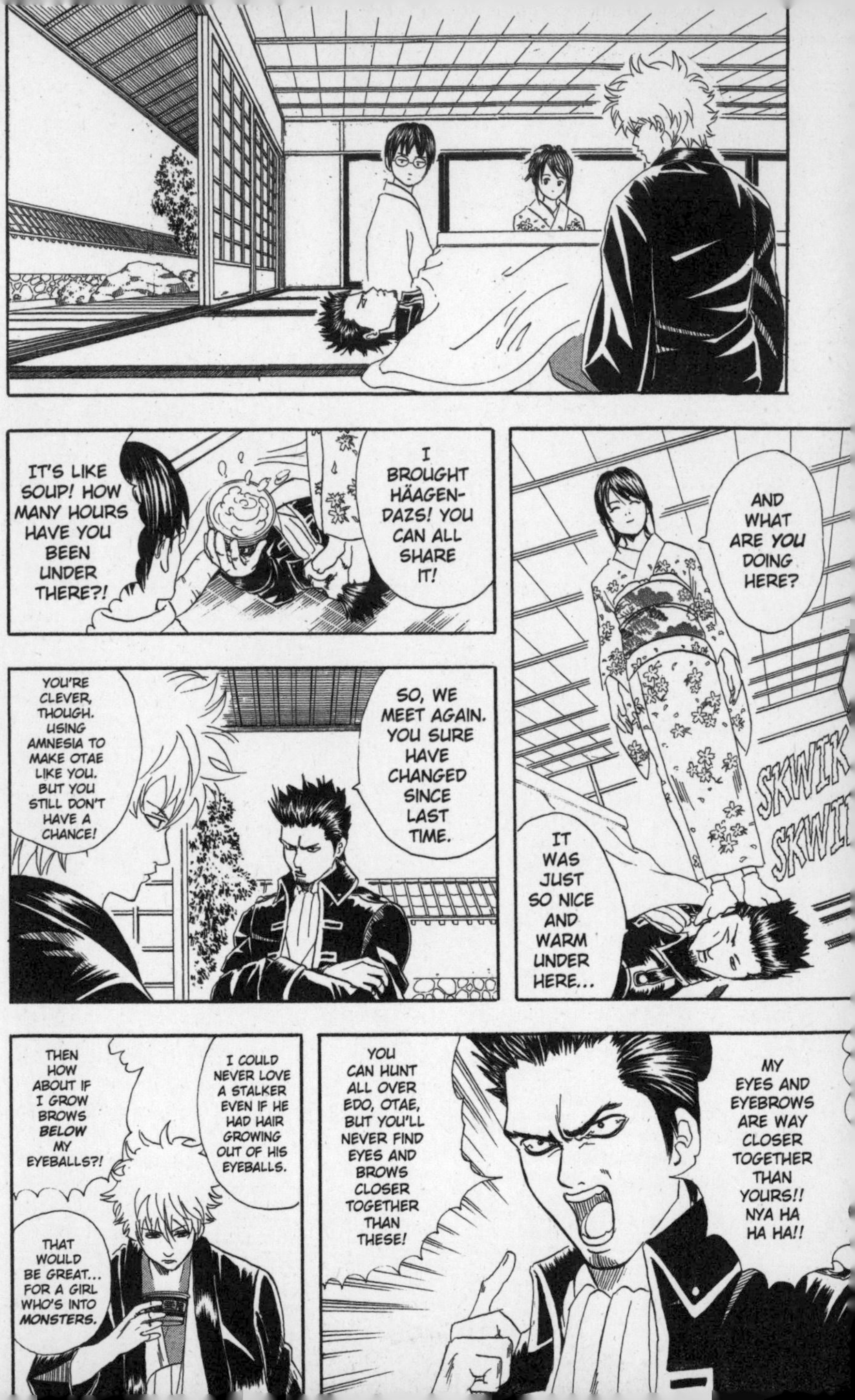
AND WHAT ARE *YOU* DOING HERE?
SKWIK
SKWI
IT WAS JUST SO NICE AND WARM UNDER HERE...
I BROUGHT HÄAGEN-DAZS! YOU CAN ALL SHARE IT!
IT'S LIKE SOUP! HOW MANY HOURS HAVE YOU BEEN UNDER THERE?!
SO, WE MEET AGAIN. YOU SURE HAVE CHANGED SINCE LAST TIME.
YOU'RE CLEVER, THOUGH. USING AMNESIA TO MAKE OTAE LIKE YOU. BUT YOU STILL DON'T HAVE A CHANCE!
MY EYES AND EYEBROWS ARE WAY CLOSER TOGETHER THAN YOURS!! NYA HA HA HA!!
YOU CAN HUNT ALL OVER EDO, OTAE, BUT YOU'LL NEVER FIND EYES AND BROWS CLOSER TOGETHER THAN THESE!
I COULD NEVER LOVE A STALKER EVEN IF HE HAD HAIR GROWING OUT OF HIS EYEBALLS.
THEN HOW ABOUT IF I GROW BROWS *BELOW* MY EYEBALLS?!
THAT WOULD BE GREAT... FOR A GIRL WHO'S INTO *MONSTERS*.

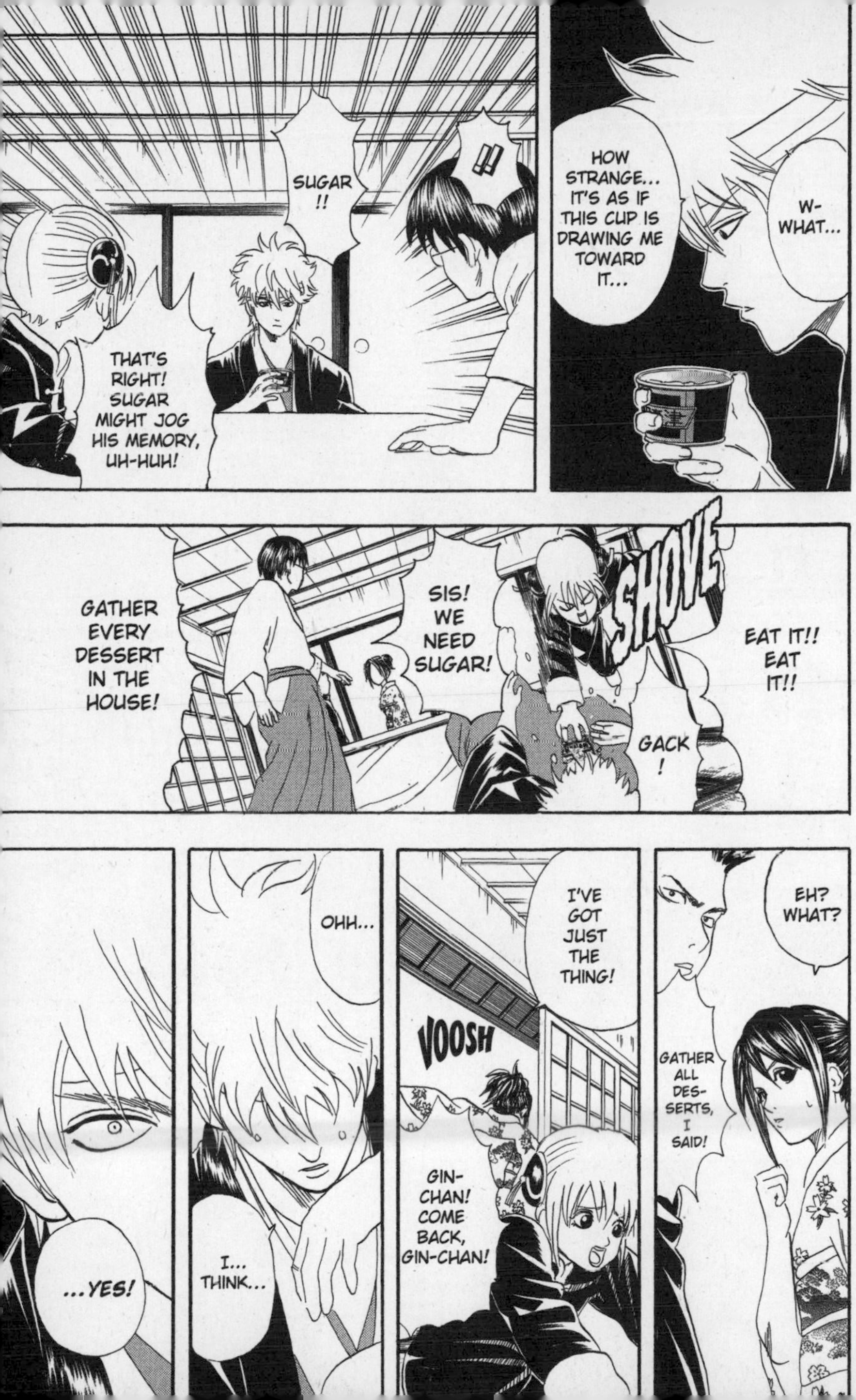
W-WHAT...
HOW STRANGE... IT'S AS IF THIS CUP IS DRAWING ME TOWARD IT...
!!
SUGAR !!
THAT'S RIGHT! SUGAR MIGHT JOG HIS MEMORY, UH-HUH!
SHOVE
EAT IT!! EAT IT!!
GACK !
SIS! WE NEED SUGAR!
GATHER EVERY DESSERT IN THE HOUSE!
EH? WHAT?
GATHER ALL DES-SERTS, I SAID!
I'VE GOT JUST THE THING!
VOOSH
GIN-CHAN! COME BACK, GIN-CHAN!
OHH...
I... THINK...
...YES!

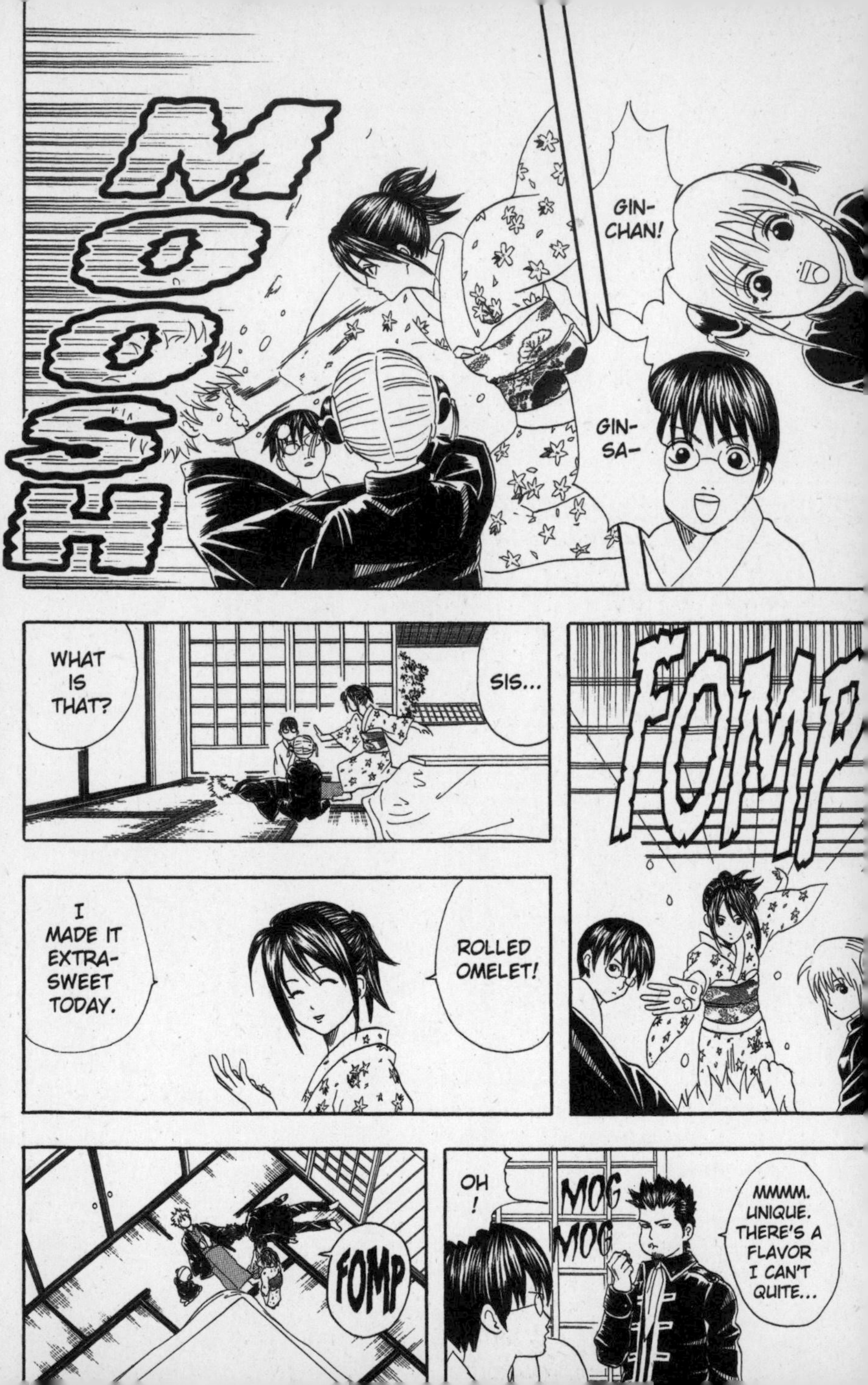
GIN-CHAN!
GIN-SA-
WOOSH
FOMP
SIS...
WHAT IS THAT?
ROLLED OMELET!
I MADE IT EXTRA-SWEET TODAY.
MMMM. UNIQUE. THERE'S A FLAVOR I CAN'T QUITE...
MOG MOG
OH!
FOMP

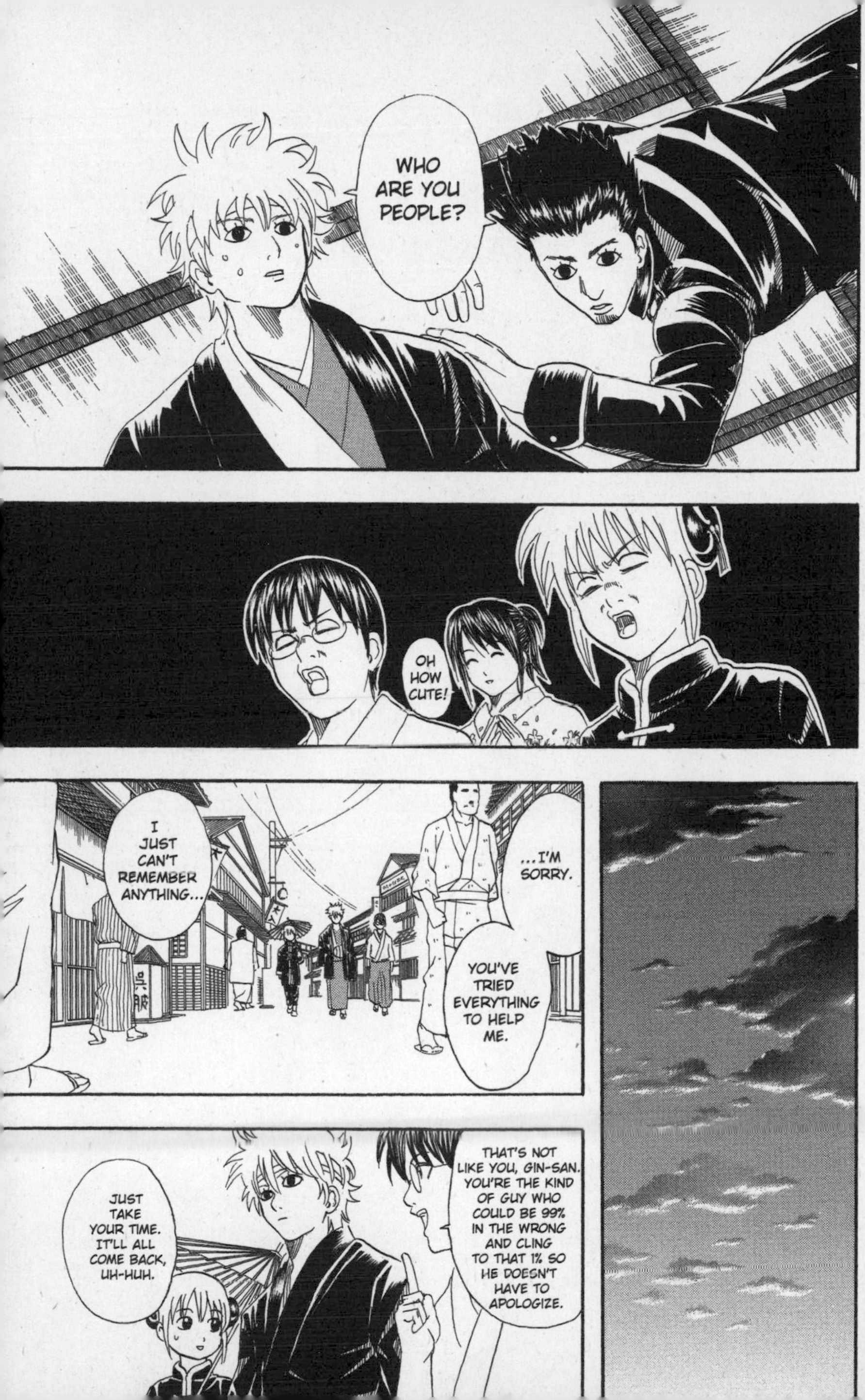
WHO ARE YOU PEOPLE?
OH HOW CUTE!
...I'M SORRY.
YOU'VE TRIED EVERYTHING TO HELP ME.
I JUST CAN'T REMEMBER ANYTHING...
THAT'S NOT LIKE YOU, GIN-SAN. YOU'RE THE KIND OF GUY WHO COULD BE 99% IN THE WRONG AND CLING TO THAT 1% SO HE DOESN'T HAVE TO APOLOGIZE.
JUST TAKE YOUR TIME. IT'LL ALL COME BACK, UH-HUH.

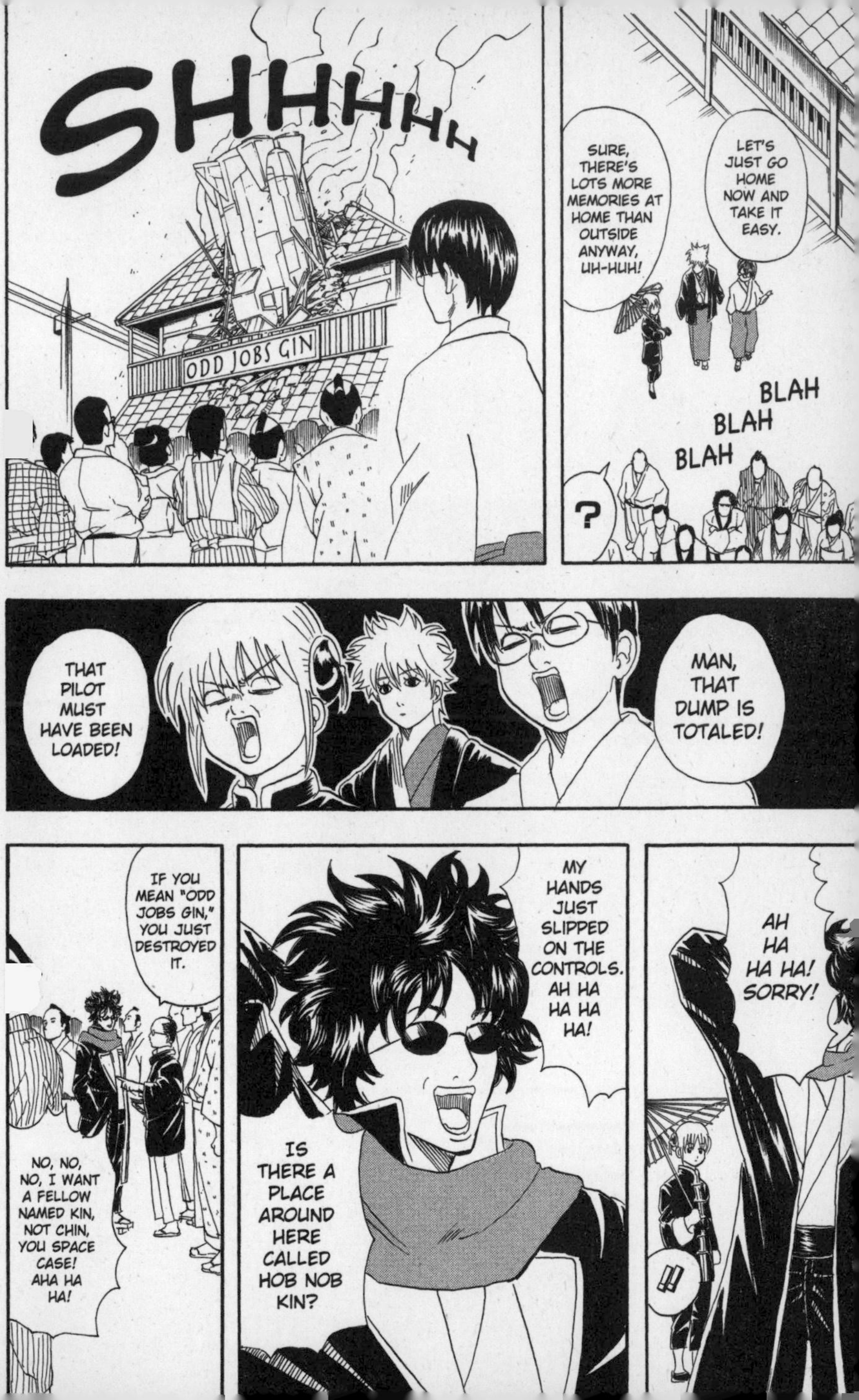
LET'S JUST GO HOME NOW AND TAKE IT EASY.
SURE, THERE'S LOTS MORE MEMORIES AT HOME THAN OUTSIDE ANYWAY, UH-HUH!
BLAH BLAH BLAH
?
SHHHHHH
ODD JOBS GIN
MAN, THAT DUMP IS TOTALED!
THAT PILOT MUST HAVE BEEN LOADED!
AH HA HA HA! SORRY!
!!
MY HANDS JUST SLIPPED ON THE CONTROLS. AH HA HA HA HA!
IS THERE A PLACE AROUND HERE CALLED HOB NOB KIN?
IF YOU MEAN "ODD JOBS GIN," YOU JUST DESTROYED IT.
NO, NO, NO, I WANT A FELLOW NAMED KIN, NOT CHIN, YOU SPACE CASE! AHA HA HA!

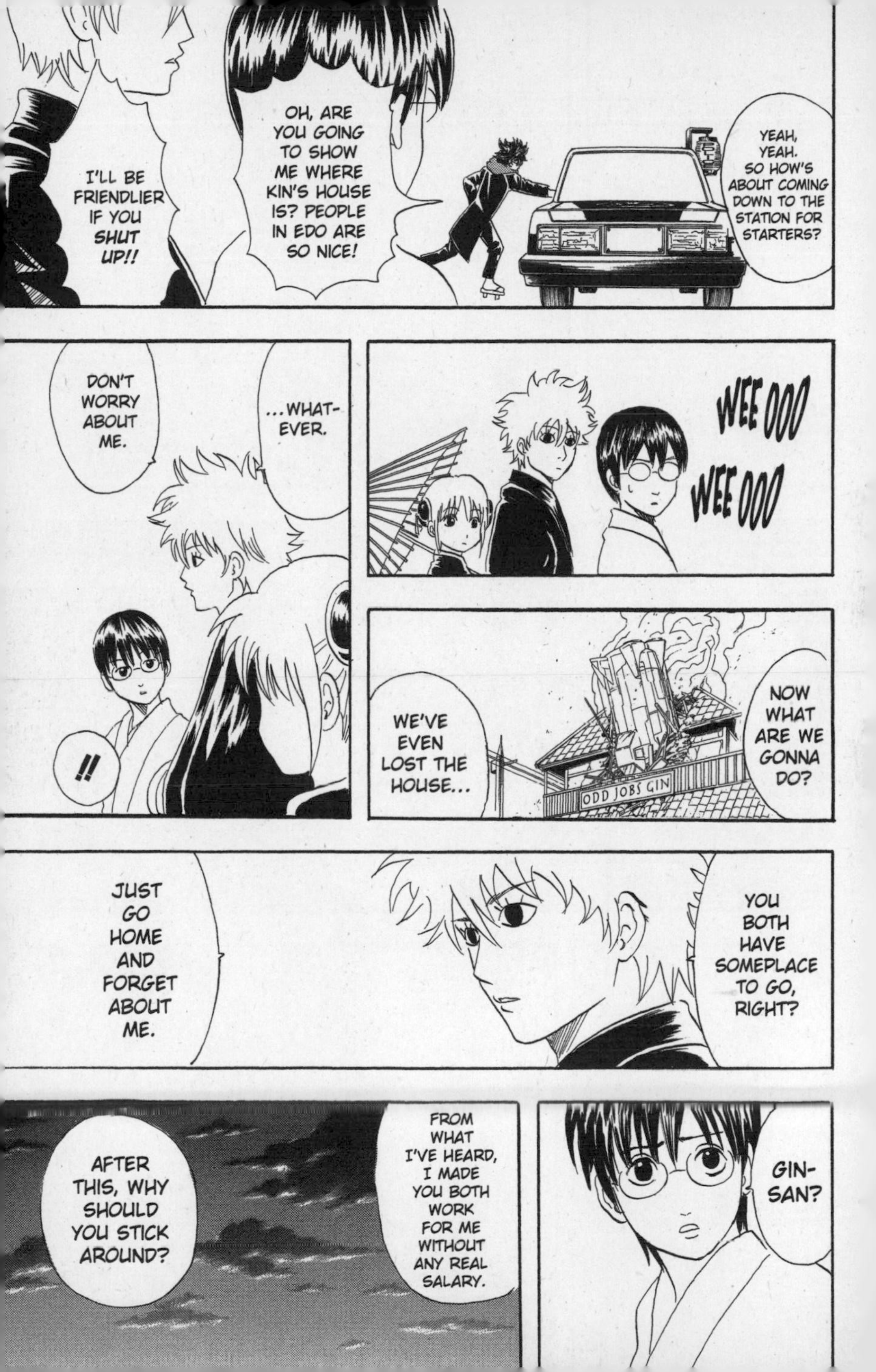
YEAH, YEAH. SO HOW'S ABOUT COMING DOWN TO THE STATION FOR STARTERS?
OH, ARE YOU GOING TO SHOW ME WHERE KIN'S HOUSE IS? PEOPLE IN EDO ARE SO NICE!
I'LL BE FRIENDLIER IF YOU SHUT UP!!
WEE OOO
WEE OOO
NOW WHAT ARE WE GONNA DO?
WE'VE EVEN LOST THE HOUSE...
ODD JOBS GIN
...WHAT-EVER.
DON'T WORRY ABOUT ME.
!!
YOU BOTH HAVE SOMEPLACE TO GO, RIGHT?
JUST GO HOME AND FORGET ABOUT ME.
GIN-SAN?
FROM WHAT I'VE HEARD, I MADE YOU BOTH WORK FOR ME WITHOUT ANY REAL SALARY.
AFTER THIS, WHY SHOULD YOU STICK AROUND?

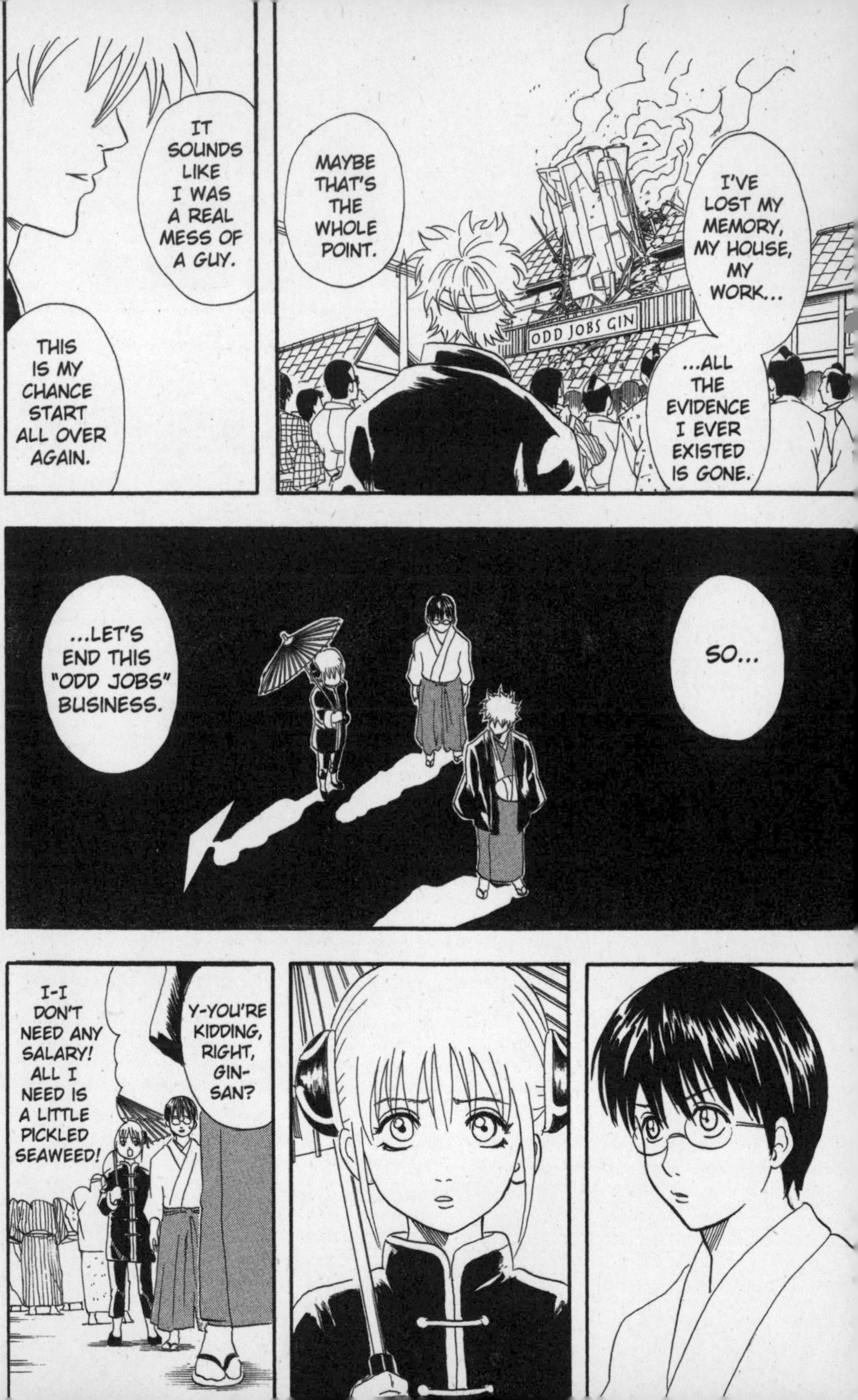
ODD JOBS GIN
I'VE LOST MY MEMORY, MY HOUSE, MY WORK...
...ALL THE EVIDENCE I EVER EXISTED IS GONE.
MAYBE THAT'S THE WHOLE POINT.
IT SOUNDS LIKE I WAS A REAL MESS OF A GUY.
THIS IS MY CHANCE START ALL OVER AGAIN.
SO...
...LET'S END THIS "ODD JOBS" BUSINESS.
Y-YOU'RE KIDDING, RIGHT, GIN-SAN?
I-I DON'T NEED ANY SALARY! ALL I NEED IS A LITTLE PICKLED SEAWEED!

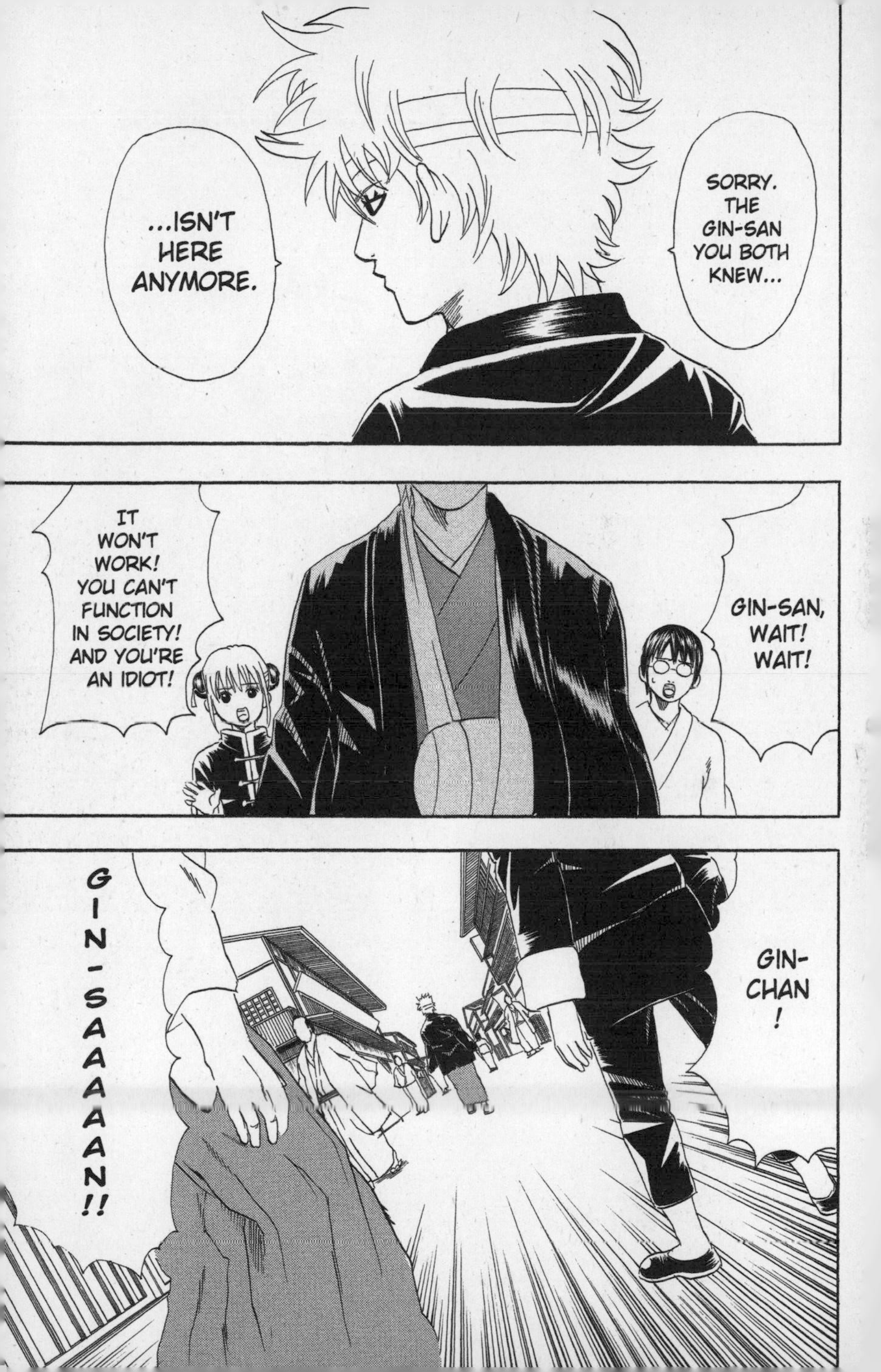
SORRY. THE GIN-SAN YOU BOTH KNEW...
...ISN'T HERE ANYMORE.
GIN-SAN, WAIT! WAIT!
IT WON'T WORK! YOU CAN'T FUNCTION IN SOCIETY! AND YOU'RE AN IDIOT!
GIN-CHAN!
GIN-SAAAAAAN!!

Gin-Sensei's Class

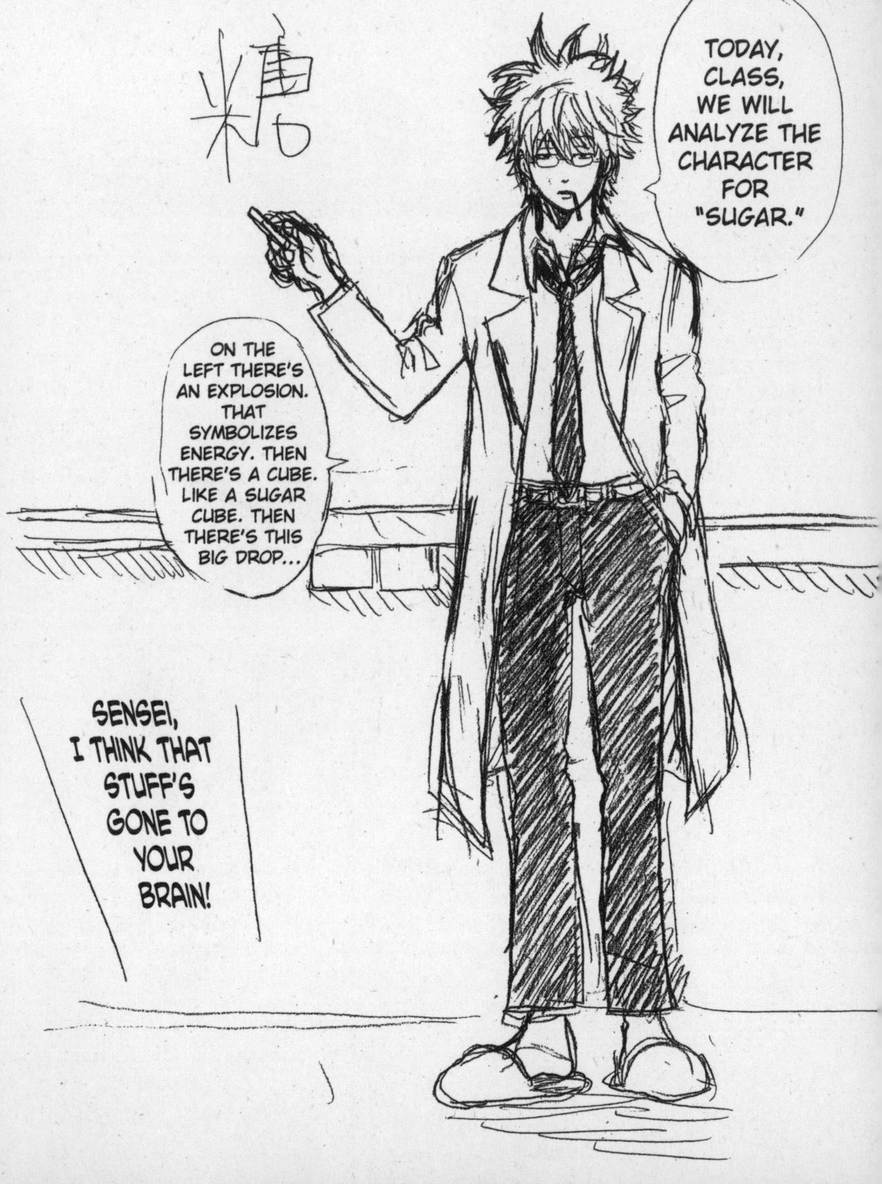
糖
TODAY, CLASS, WE WILL ANALYZE THE CHARACTER FOR "SUGAR."
ON THE LEFT THERE'S AN EXPLOSION. THAT SYMBOLIZES ENERGY. THEN THERE'S A CUBE. LIKE A SUGAR CUBE. THEN THERE'S THIS BIG DROP...
SENSEI, I THINK THAT STUFF'S GONE TO YOUR BRAIN!

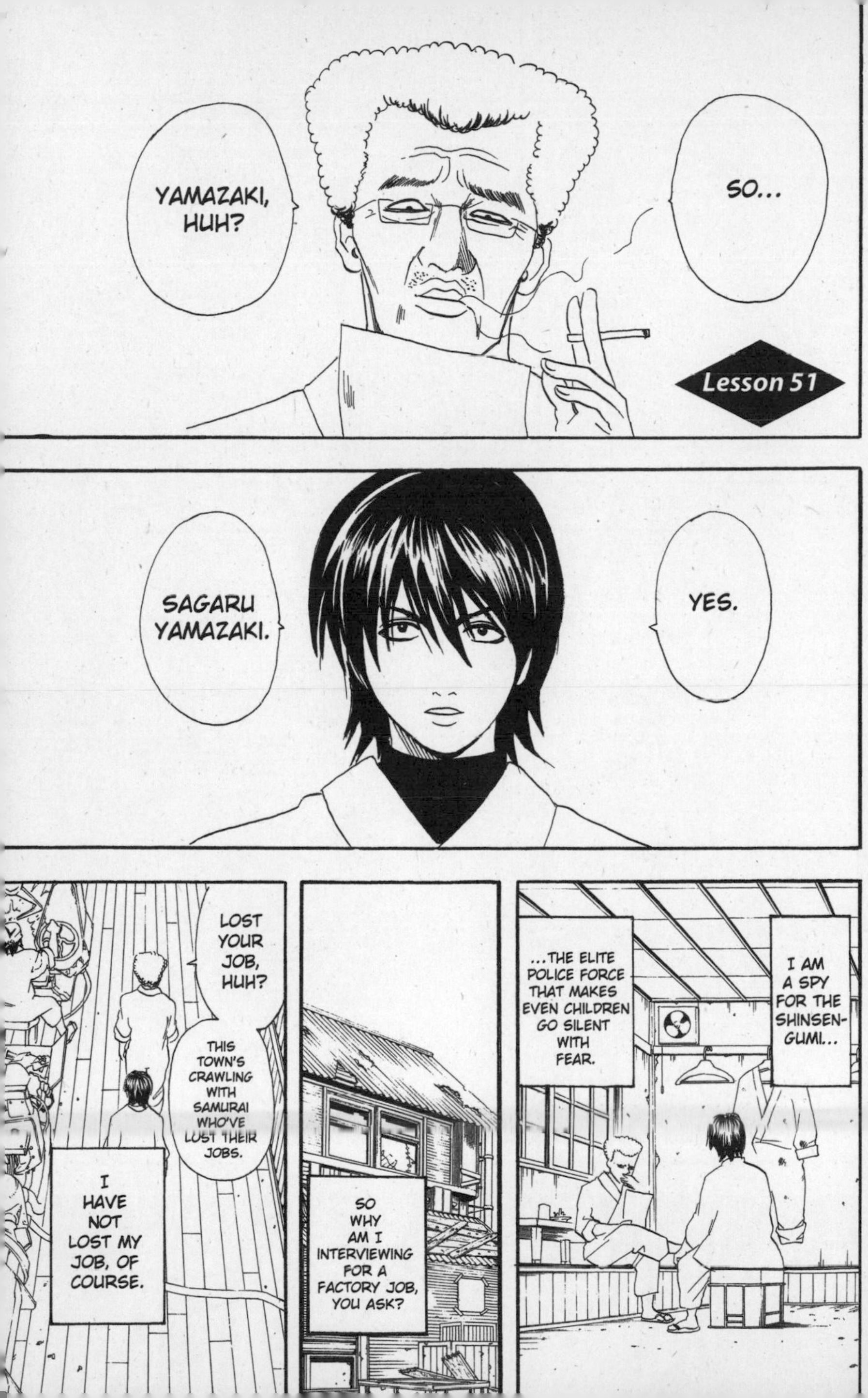
SO...
YAMAZAKI, HUH?
Lesson 51
YES.
SAGARU YAMAZAKI.
I AM A SPY FOR THE SHINSEN-GUMI...
...THE ELITE POLICE FORCE THAT MAKES EVEN CHILDREN GO SILENT WITH FEAR.
SO WHY AM I INTERVIEWING FOR A FACTORY JOB, YOU ASK?
LOST YOUR JOB, HUH?
THIS TOWN'S CRAWLING WITH SAMURAI WHO'VE LOST THEIR JOBS.
I HAVE NOT LOST MY JOB, OF COURSE.

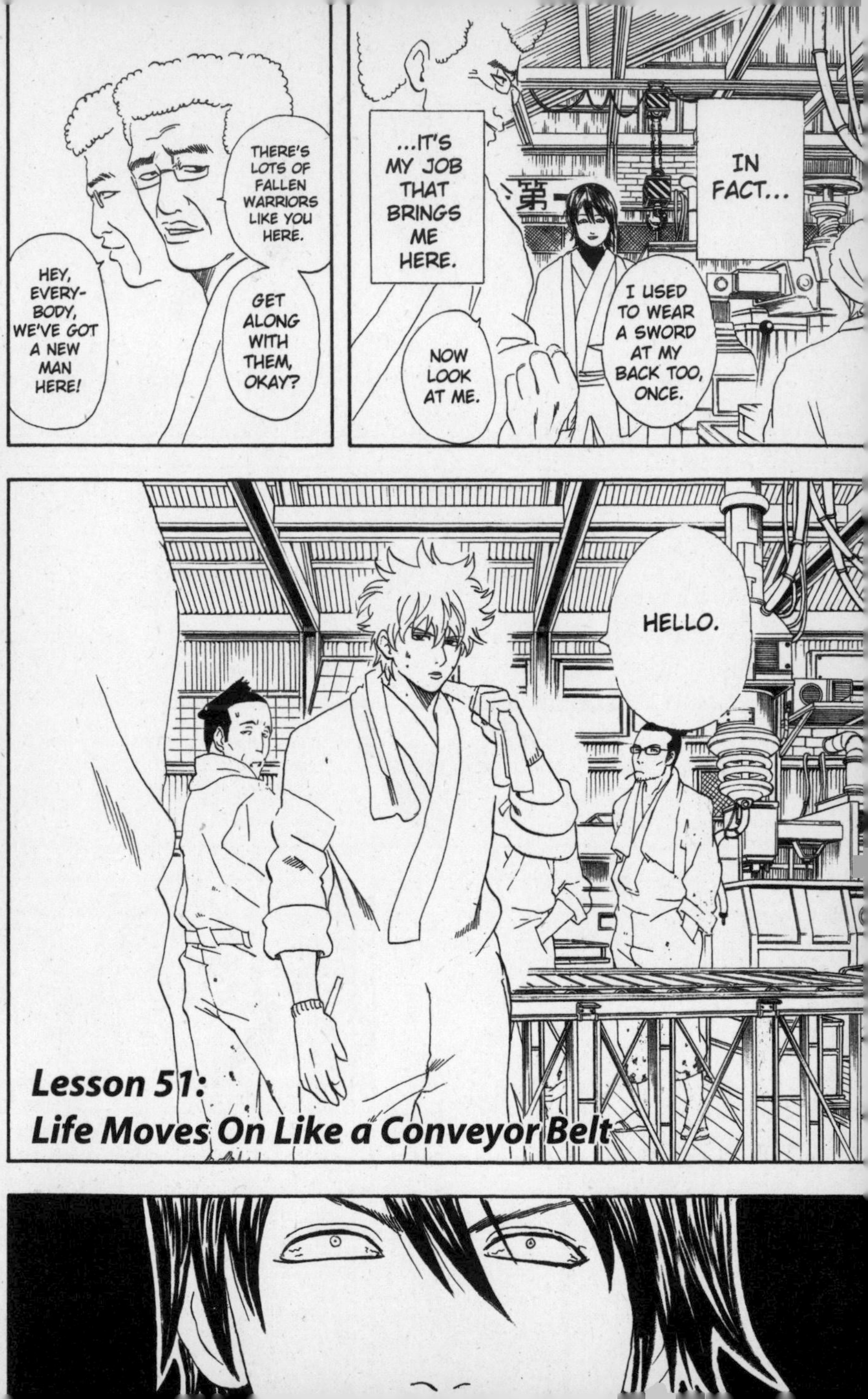
IN FACT...
I USED TO WEAR A SWORD AT MY BACK TOO, ONCE.
NOW LOOK AT ME.
...IT'S MY JOB THAT BRINGS ME HERE.
THERE'S LOTS OF FALLEN WARRIORS LIKE YOU HERE.
GET ALONG WITH THEM, OKAY?
HEY, EVERYBODY, WE'VE GOT A NEW MAN HERE!
HELLO.
Lesson 51:
Life Moves On Like a Conveyor Belt

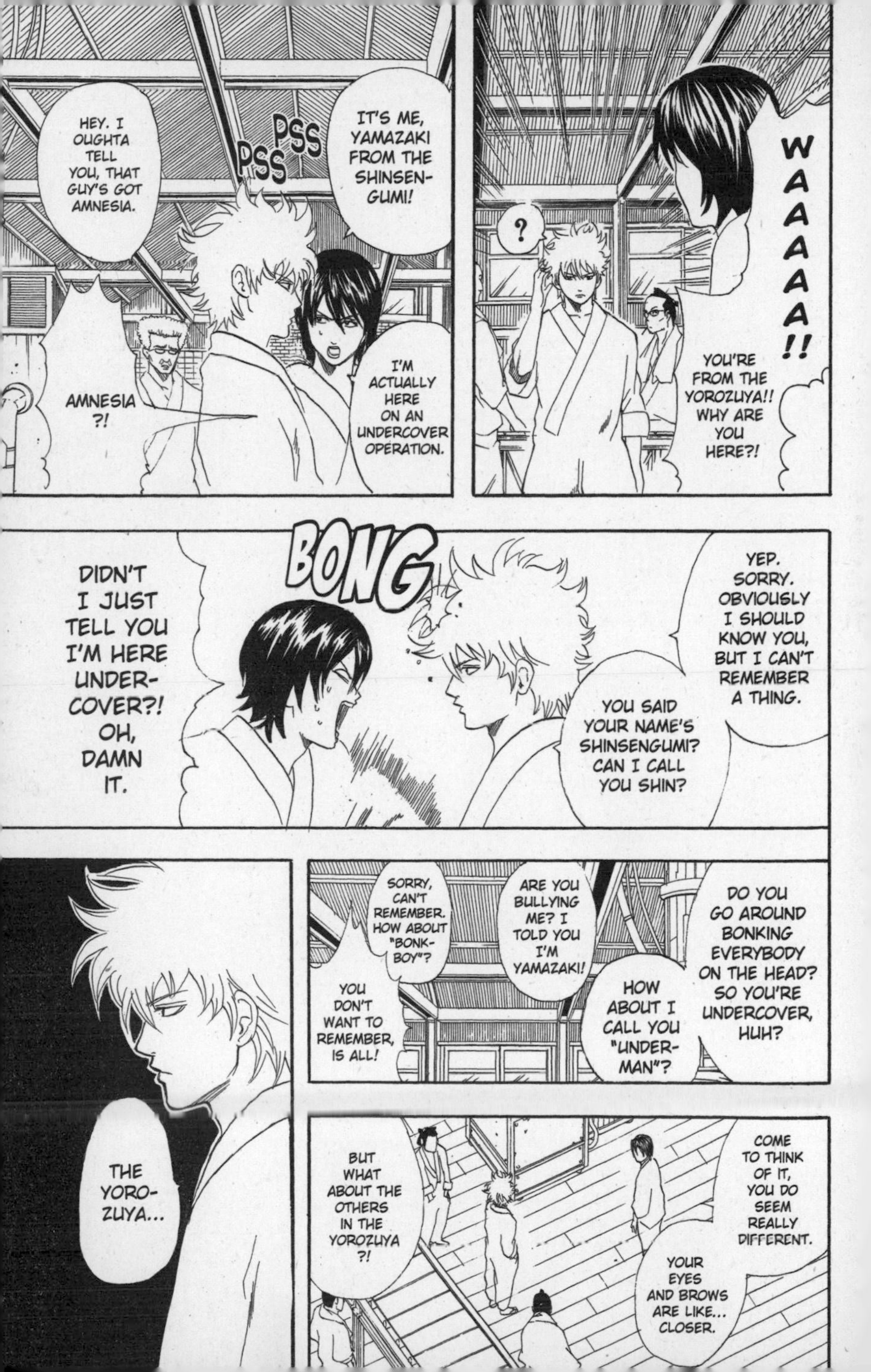
WAAAAAA!!
YOU'RE FROM THE YOROZUYA!! WHY ARE YOU HERE?!
?
IT'S ME, YAMAZAKI FROM THE SHINSEN-GUMI!
PSS PSS
HEY. I OUGHTA TELL YOU, THAT GUY'S GOT AMNESIA.
I'M ACTUALLY HERE ON AN UNDERCOVER OPERATION.
AMNESIA ?!
YEP. SORRY. OBVIOUSLY I SHOULD KNOW YOU, BUT I CAN'T REMEMBER A THING.
YOU SAID YOUR NAME'S SHINSENGUMI? CAN I CALL YOU SHIN?
BONG
DIDN'T I JUST TELL YOU I'M HERE UNDER-COVER?! OH, DAMN IT.
DO YOU GO AROUND BONKING EVERYBODY ON THE HEAD? SO YOU'RE UNDERCOVER, HUH?
ARE YOU BULLYING ME? I TOLD YOU I'M YAMAZAKI!
HOW ABOUT I CALL YOU "UNDER-MAN"?
SORRY, CAN'T REMEMBER. HOW ABOUT "BONK-BOY"?
YOU DON'T WANT TO REMEMBER, IS ALL!
COME TO THINK OF IT, YOU DO SEEM REALLY DIFFERENT.
YOUR EYES AND BROWS ARE LIKE... CLOSER.
BUT WHAT ABOUT THE OTHERS IN THE YOROZUYA ?!
THE YORO-ZUYA...

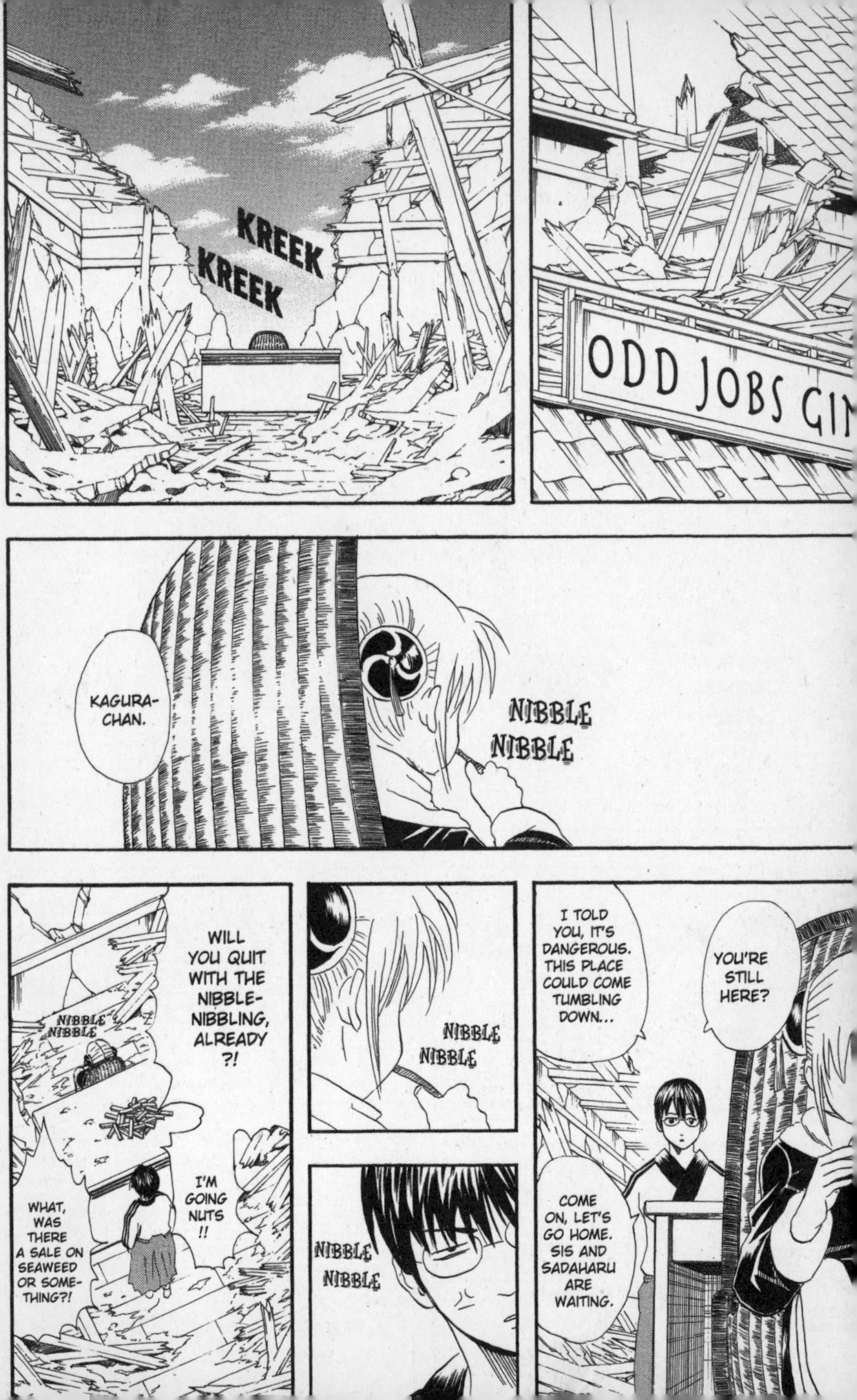

ODD JOBS GIN
KREEK
KREEK
NIBBLE
NIBBLE
KAGURA-CHAN.
YOU'RE STILL HERE?
I TOLD YOU, IT'S DANGEROUS. THIS PLACE COULD COME TUMBLING DOWN...
COME ON, LET'S GO HOME. SIS AND SADAHARU ARE WAITING.
NIBBLE
NIBBLE
NIBBLE
NIBBLE
WILL YOU QUIT WITH THE NIBBLE-NIBBLING, ALREADY?!
I'M GOING NUTS!!
NIBBLE
NIBBLE
WHAT, WAS THERE A SALE ON SEAWEED OR SOME-THING?!

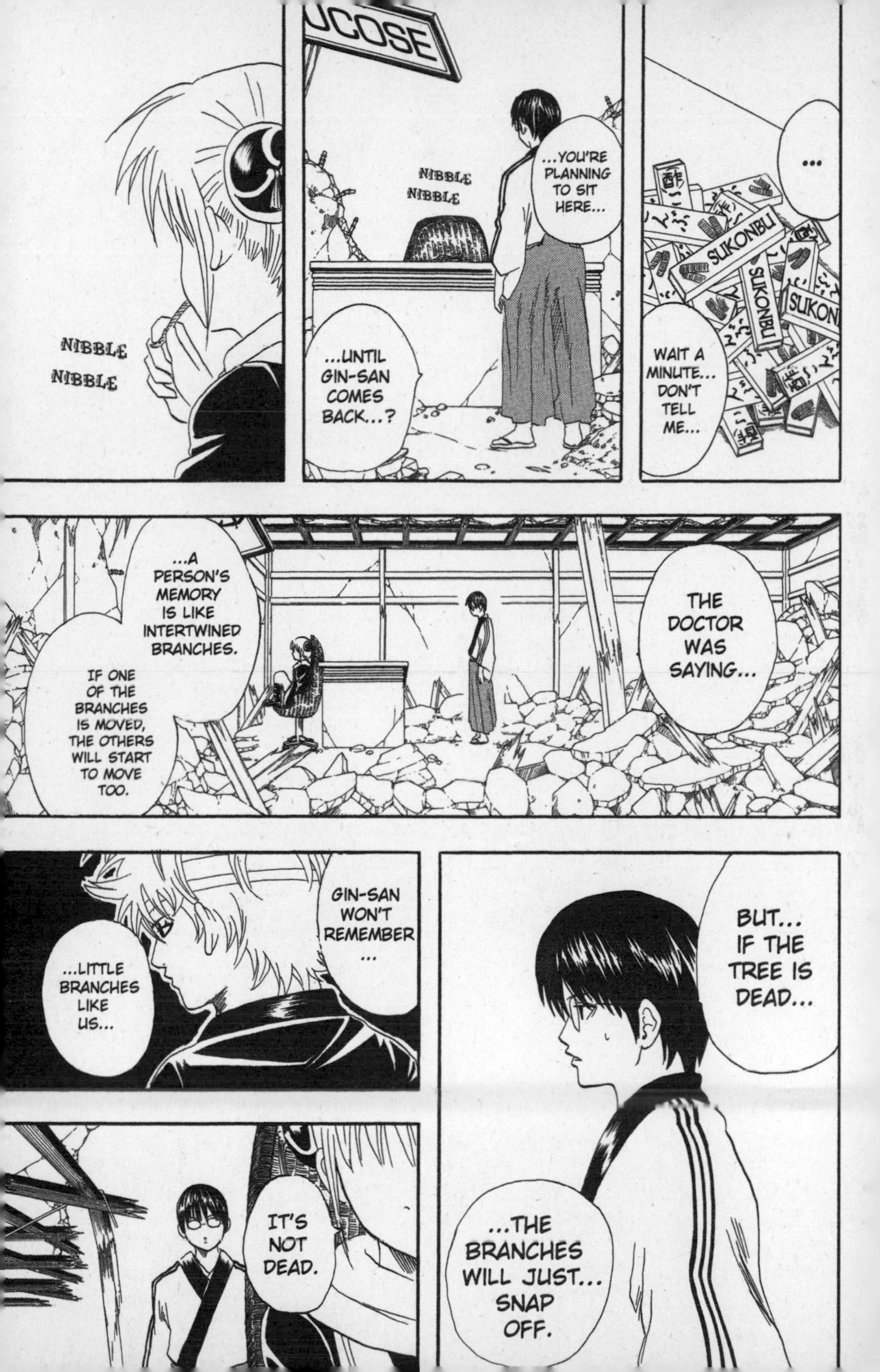
...
SUKONBU
SUKONBU
WAIT A MINUTE... DON'T TELL ME...
UCOSE
...YOU'RE PLANNING TO SIT HERE...
NIBBLE NIBBLE
...UNTIL GIN-SAN COMES BACK...?
NIBBLE NIBBLE
THE DOCTOR WAS SAYING...
...A PERSON'S MEMORY IS LIKE INTERTWINED BRANCHES.
IF ONE OF THE BRANCHES IS MOVED, THE OTHERS WILL START TO MOVE TOO.
BUT... IF THE TREE IS DEAD...
...THE BRANCHES WILL JUST... SNAP OFF.
GIN-SAN WON'T REMEMBER ...
...LITTLE BRANCHES LIKE US...
IT'S NOT DEAD.

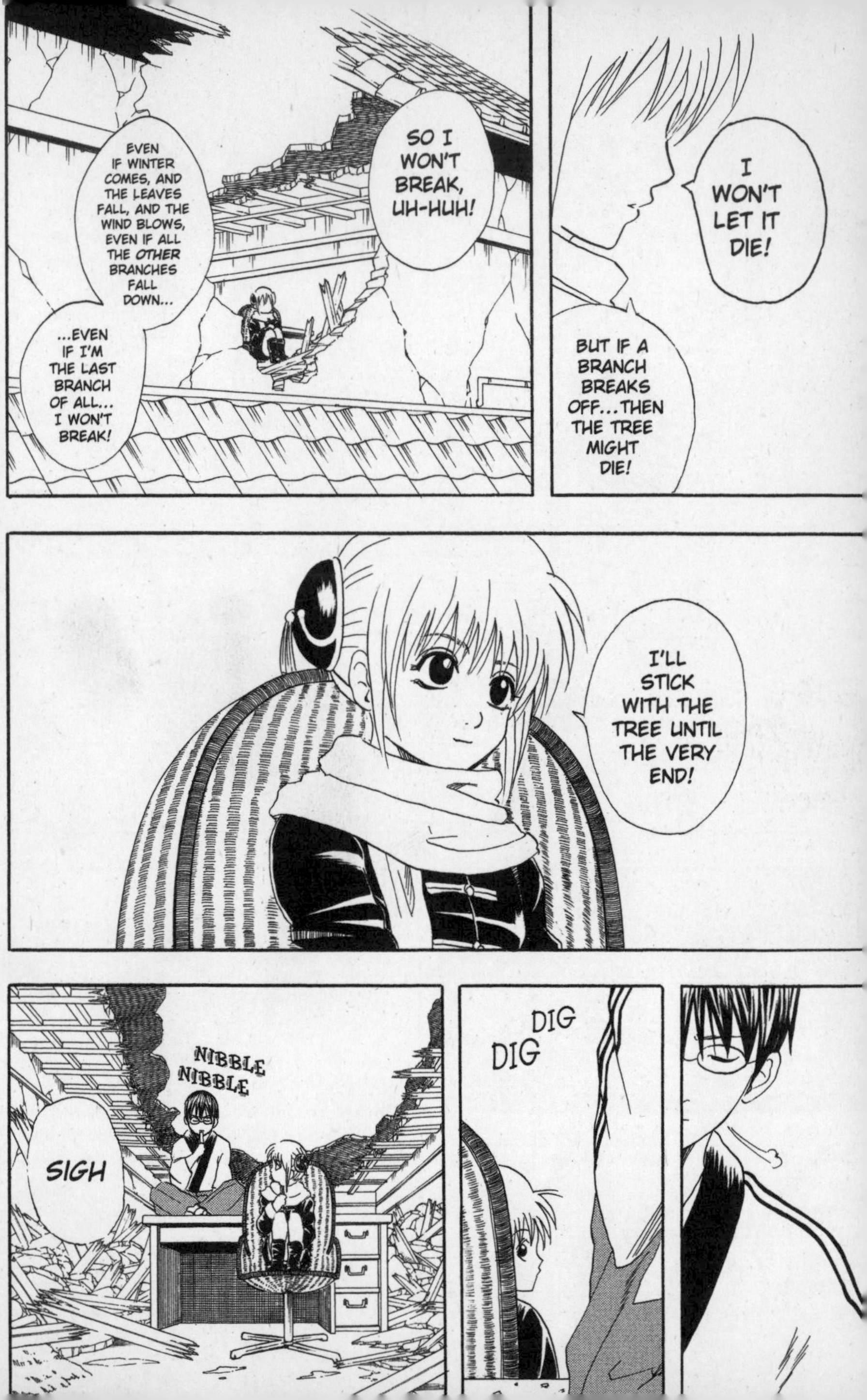
I WON'T LET IT DIE!
BUT IF A BRANCH BREAKS OFF...THEN THE TREE MIGHT DIE!
SO I WON'T BREAK, UH-HUH!
EVEN IF WINTER COMES, AND THE LEAVES FALL, AND THE WIND BLOWS, EVEN IF ALL THE *OTHER* BRANCHES FALL DOWN...
...EVEN IF I'M THE LAST BRANCH OF ALL... I WON'T BREAK!
I'LL STICK WITH THE TREE UNTIL THE VERY END!
DIG DIG
NIBBLE NIBBLE
SIGH

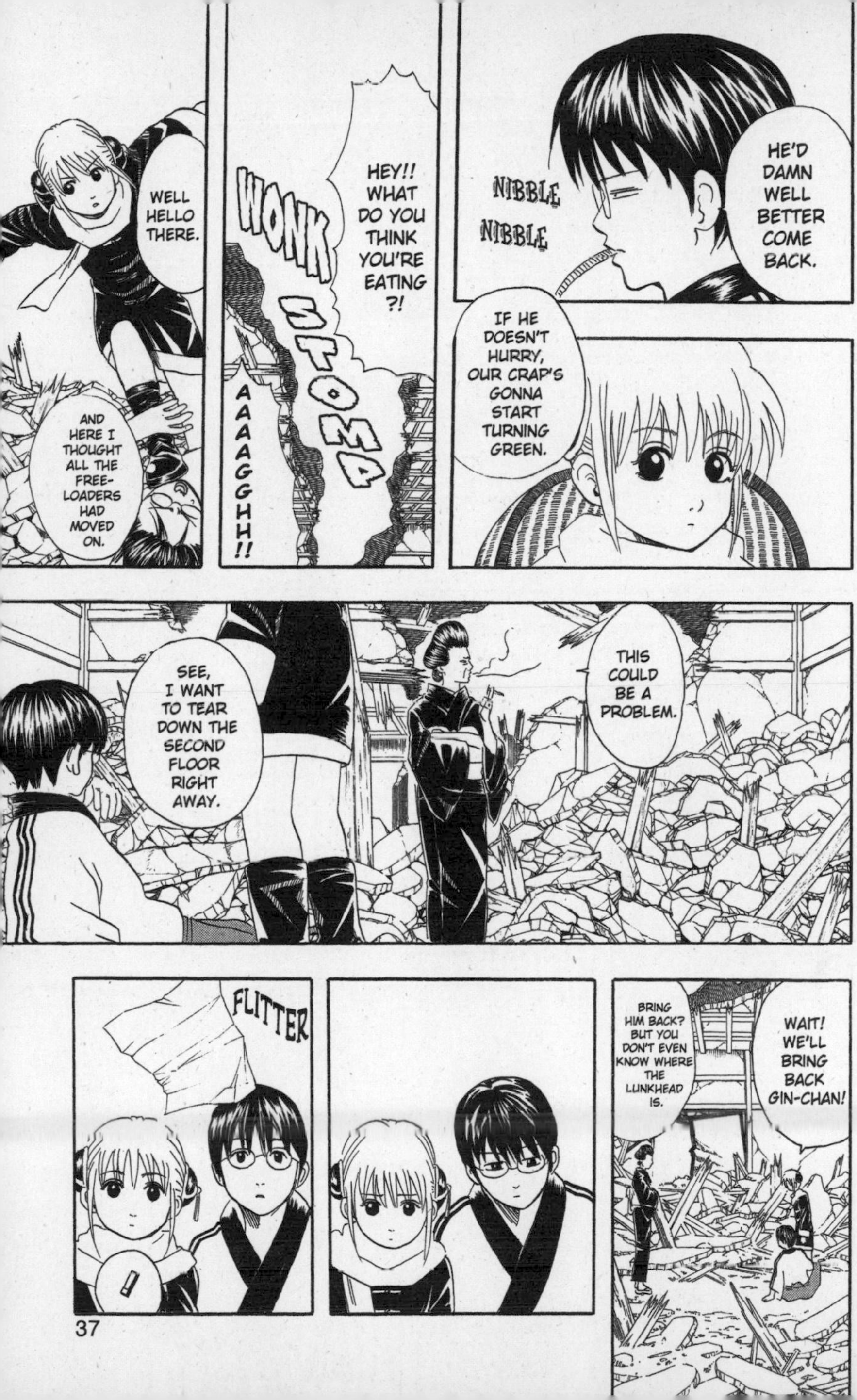
HE'D DAMN WELL BETTER COME BACK.
NIBBLE
NIBBLE
IF HE DOESN'T HURRY, OUR CRAP'S GONNA START TURNING GREEN.
HEY!! WHAT DO YOU THINK YOU'RE EATING ?!
WONK
STOMP
AAAAAGGHH!!
WELL HELLO THERE.
AND HERE I THOUGHT ALL THE FREE-LOADERS HAD MOVED ON.
THIS COULD BE A PROBLEM.
SEE, I WANT TO TEAR DOWN THE SECOND FLOOR RIGHT AWAY.
WAIT! WE'LL BRING BACK GIN-CHAN!
BRING HIM BACK? BUT YOU DON'T EVEN KNOW WHERE THE LUNKHEAD IS.
FLITTER
!

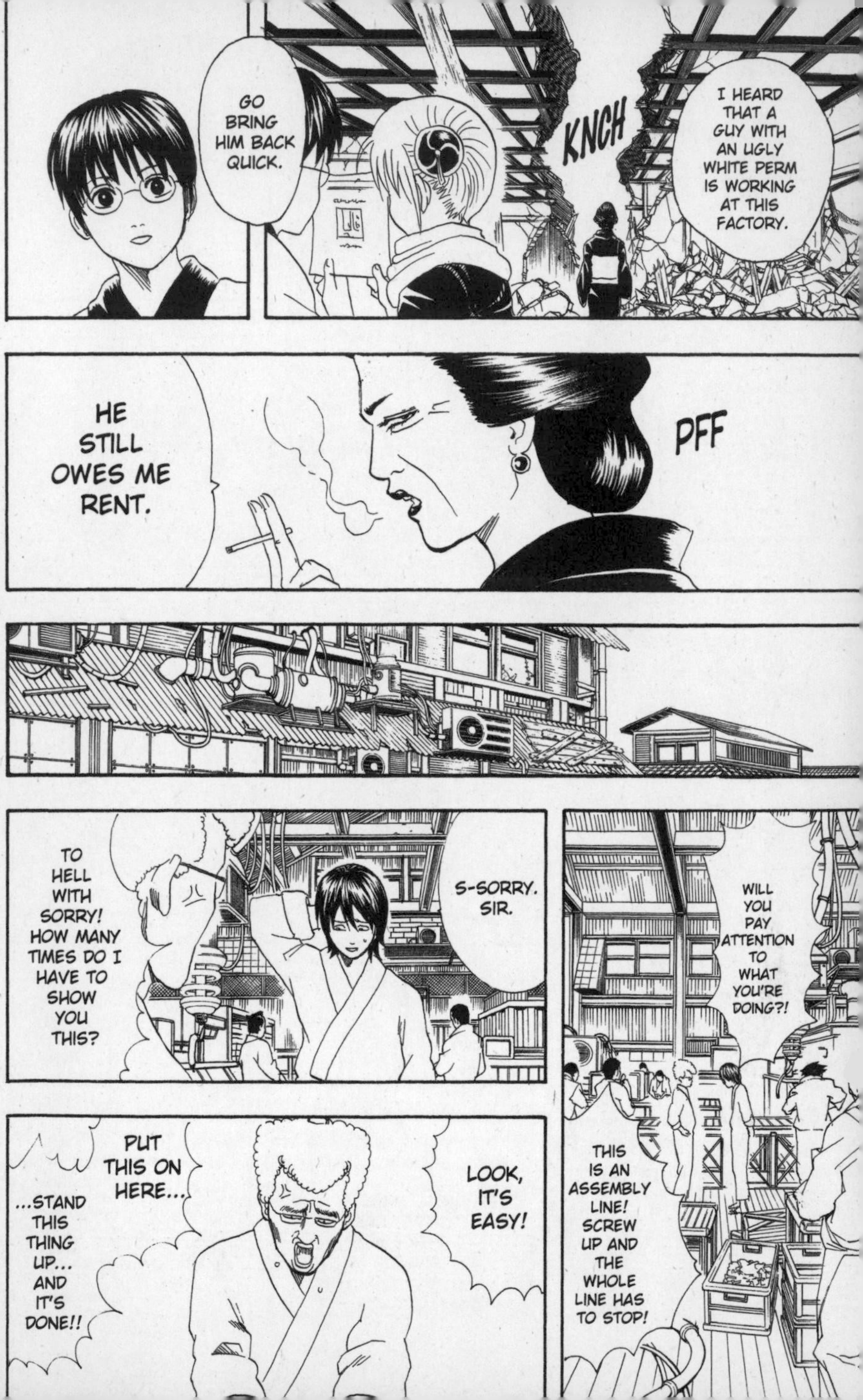
I HEARD THAT A GUY WITH AN UGLY WHITE PERM IS WORKING AT THIS FACTORY.
KNCH
GO BRING HIM BACK QUICK.
PFF
HE STILL OWES ME RENT.
WILL YOU PAY ATTENTION TO WHAT YOU'RE DOING?!
THIS IS AN ASSEMBLY LINE! SCREW UP AND THE WHOLE LINE HAS TO STOP!
S-SORRY. SIR.
TO HELL WITH SORRY! HOW MANY TIMES DO I HAVE TO SHOW YOU THIS?
LOOK, IT'S EASY!
PUT THIS ON HERE...
...STAND THIS THING UP... AND IT'S DONE!!

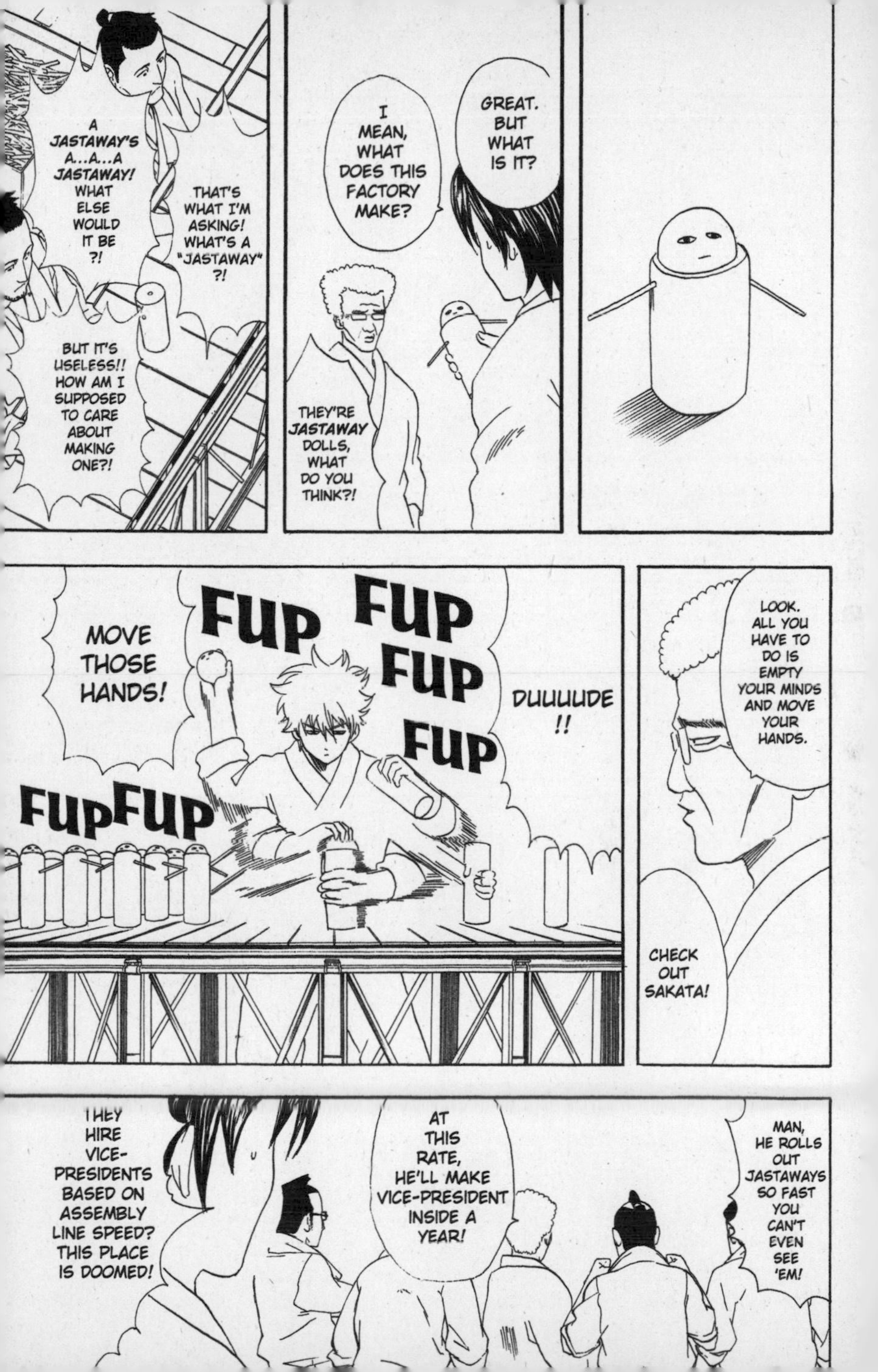
GREAT. BUT WHAT IS IT?
I MEAN, WHAT DOES THIS FACTORY MAKE?
THEY'RE JASTAWAY DOLLS, WHAT DO YOU THINK?!
THAT'S WHAT I'M ASKING! WHAT'S A "JASTAWAY"?!
A JASTAWAY'S A...A...A JASTAWAY! WHAT ELSE WOULD IT BE?!
BUT IT'S USELESS!! HOW AM I SUPPOSED TO CARE ABOUT MAKING ONE?!
LOOK. ALL YOU HAVE TO DO IS EMPTY YOUR MINDS AND MOVE YOUR HANDS.
CHECK OUT SAKATA!
DUUUUDE!!
FUP FUP FUP
FUP
MOVE THOSE HANDS!
FUPFUP
MAN, HE ROLLS OUT JASTAWAYS SO FAST YOU CAN'T EVEN SEE 'EM!
AT THIS RATE, HE'LL MAKE VICE-PRESIDENT INSIDE A YEAR!
THEY HIRE VICE-PRESIDENTS BASED ON ASSEMBLY LINE SPEED? THIS PLACE IS DOOMED!

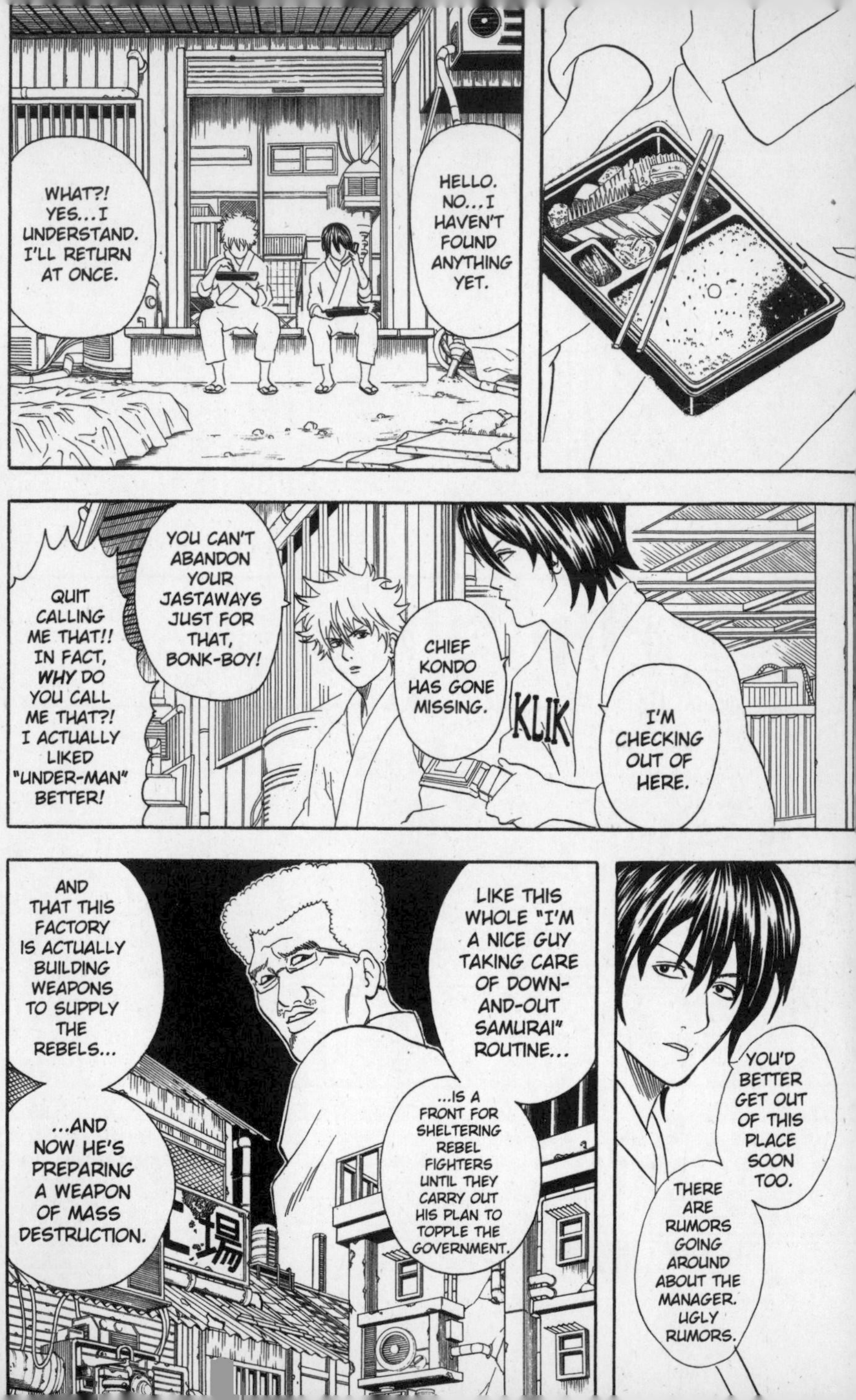
HELLO. NO...I HAVEN'T FOUND ANYTHING YET.
WHAT?! YES...I UNDERSTAND. I'LL RETURN AT ONCE.
I'M CHECKING OUT OF HERE.
KLIK
CHIEF KONDO HAS GONE MISSING.
YOU CAN'T ABANDON YOUR JASTAWAYS JUST FOR THAT, BONK-BOY!
QUIT CALLING ME THAT!! IN FACT, WHY DO YOU CALL ME THAT?! I ACTUALLY LIKED "UNDER-MAN" BETTER!
YOU'D BETTER GET OUT OF THIS PLACE SOON TOO.
THERE ARE RUMORS GOING AROUND ABOUT THE MANAGER. UGLY RUMORS.
LIKE THIS WHOLE "I'M A NICE GUY TAKING CARE OF DOWN-AND-OUT SAMURAI" ROUTINE...
...IS A FRONT FOR SHELTERING REBEL FIGHTERS UNTIL THEY CARRY OUT HIS PLAN TO TOPPLE THE GOVERNMENT.
AND THAT THIS FACTORY IS ACTUALLY BUILDING WEAPONS TO SUPPLY THE REBELS...
...AND NOW HE'S PREPARING A WEAPON OF MASS DESTRUCTION.

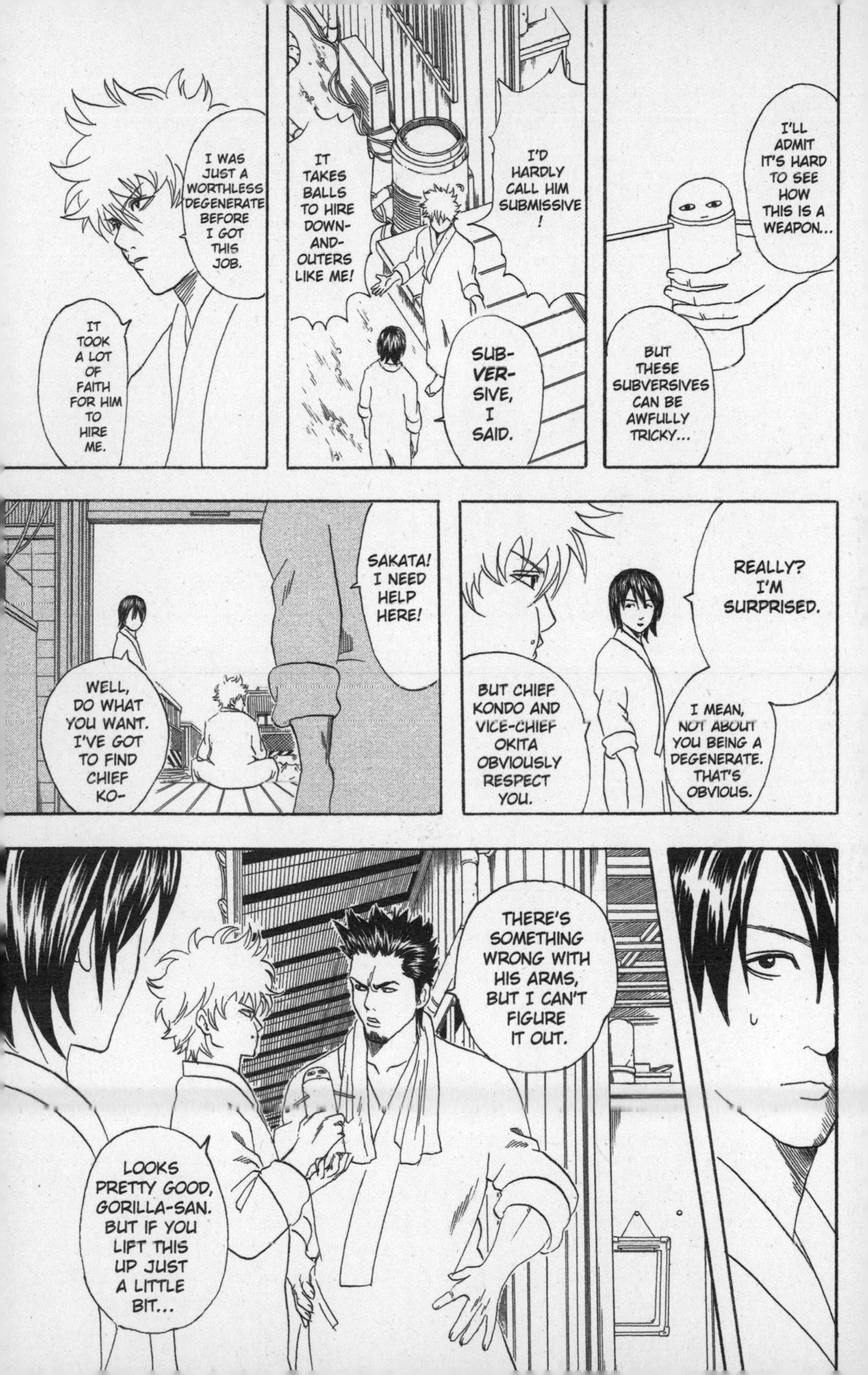
I'LL ADMIT IT'S HARD TO SEE HOW THIS IS A WEAPON...
BUT THESE SUBVERSIVES CAN BE AWFULLY TRICKY...
I'D HARDLY CALL HIM SUBMISSIVE!
IT TAKES BALLS TO HIRE DOWN-AND-OUTERS LIKE ME!
SUB-VER-SIVE, I SAID.
I WAS JUST A WORTHLESS DEGENERATE BEFORE I GOT THIS JOB.
IT TOOK A LOT OF FAITH FOR HIM TO HIRE ME.
REALLY? I'M SURPRISED.
I MEAN, NOT ABOUT YOU BEING A DEGENERATE. THAT'S OBVIOUS.
BUT CHIEF KONDO AND VICE-CHIEF OKITA OBVIOUSLY RESPECT YOU.
SAKATA! I NEED HELP HERE!
WELL, DO WHAT YOU WANT. I'VE GOT TO FIND CHIEF KO-
THERE'S SOMETHING WRONG WITH HIS ARMS, BUT I CAN'T FIGURE IT OUT.
LOOKS PRETTY GOOD, GORILLA-SAN. BUT IF YOU LIFT THIS UP JUST A LITTLE BIT...

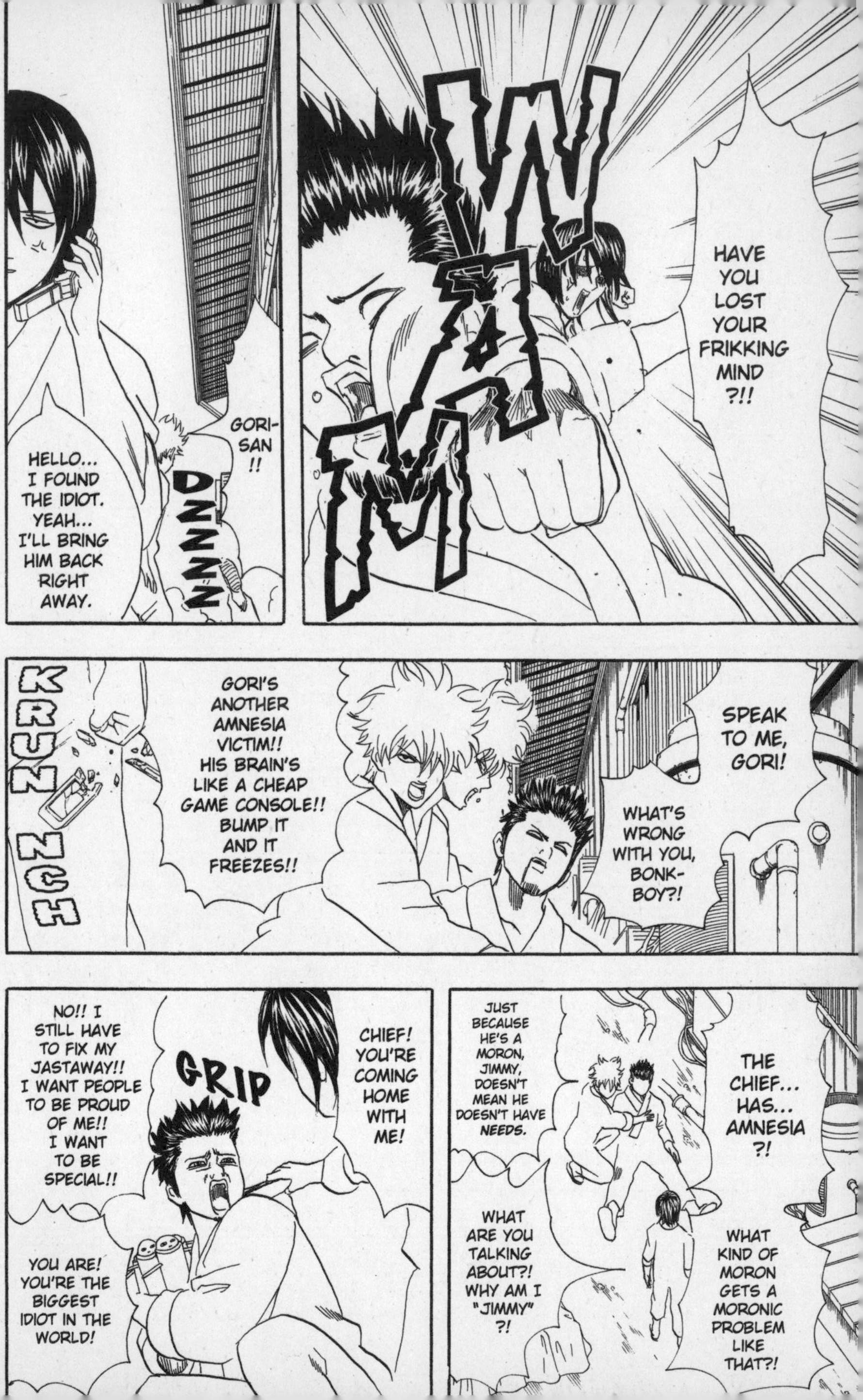
HAVE YOU LOST YOUR FRIKKING MIND ?!!
WHAM
GORI-SAN !!
DZZZZ
HELLO... I FOUND THE IDIOT. YEAH... I'LL BRING HIM BACK RIGHT AWAY.
SPEAK TO ME, GORI!
WHAT'S WRONG WITH YOU, BONK-BOY?!
GORI'S ANOTHER AMNESIA VICTIM!! HIS BRAIN'S LIKE A CHEAP GAME CONSOLE!! BUMP IT AND IT FREEZES!!
KRUNCH
THE CHIEF... HAS... AMNESIA ?!
WHAT KIND OF MORON GETS A MORONIC PROBLEM LIKE THAT?!
JUST BECAUSE HE'S A MORON, JIMMY, DOESN'T MEAN HE DOESN'T HAVE NEEDS.
WHAT ARE YOU TALKING ABOUT?! WHY AM I "JIMMY" ?!
CHIEF! YOU'RE COMING HOME WITH ME!
GRIP
NO!! I STILL HAVE TO FIX MY JASTAWAY!! I WANT PEOPLE TO BE PROUD OF ME!! I WANT TO BE SPECIAL!!
YOU ARE! YOU'RE THE BIGGEST IDIOT IN THE WORLD!

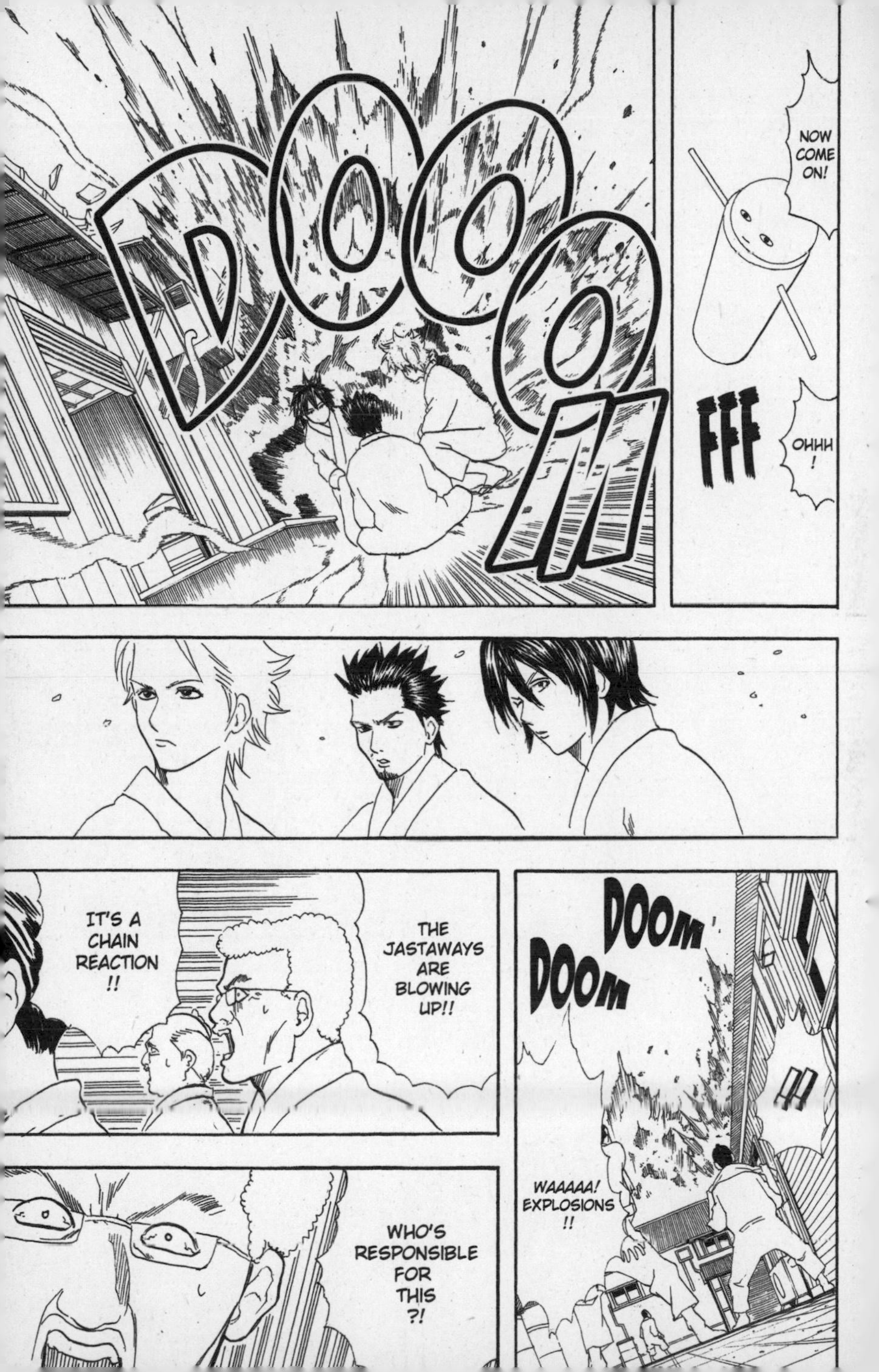
NOW COME ON!
OHHH!
FFF
DOOOM
DOOM
DOOM
WAAAAA! EXPLOSIONS!!
THE JASTAWAYS ARE BLOWING UP!!
IT'S A CHAIN REACTION!!
WHO'S RESPONSIBLE FOR THIS?!

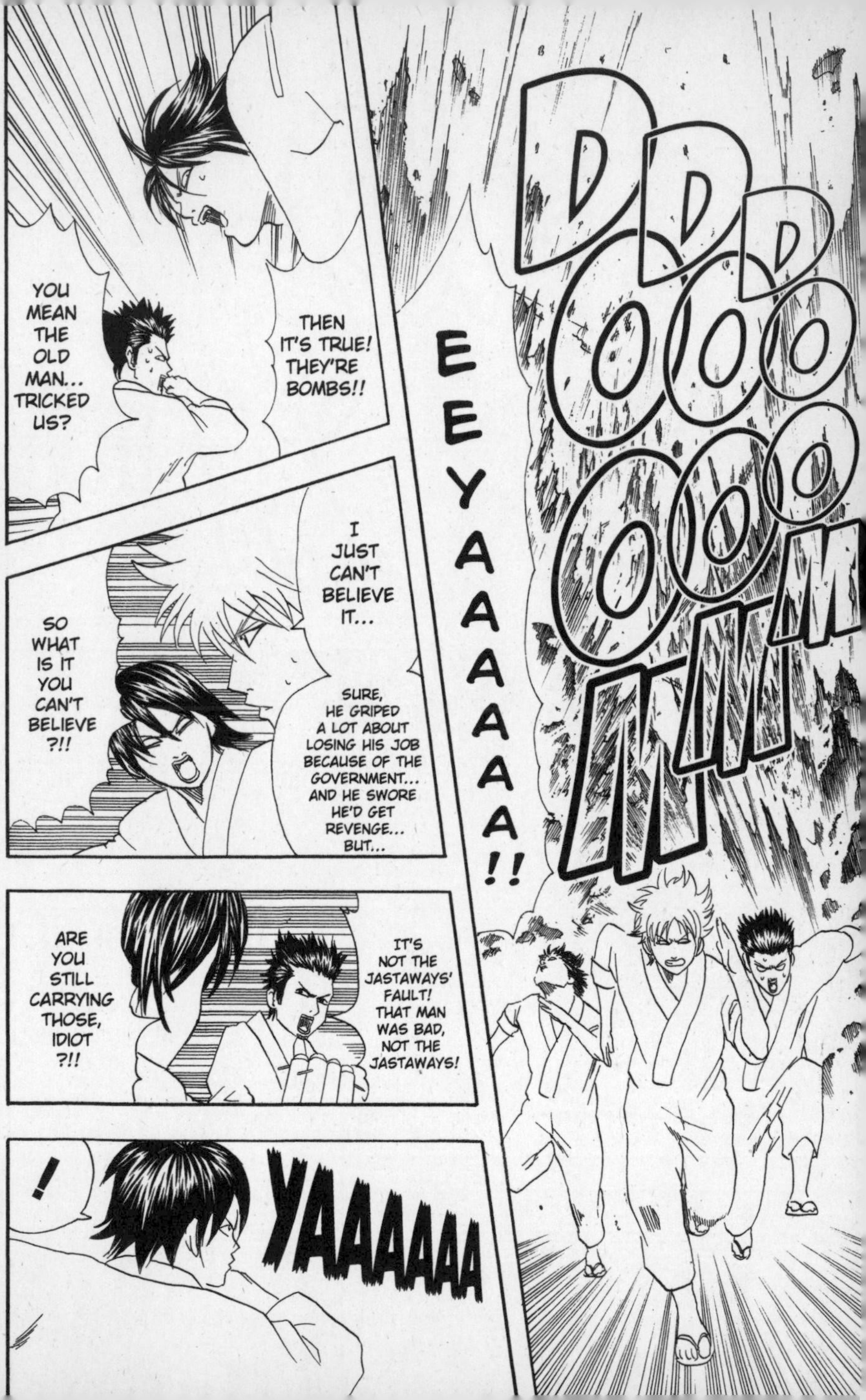
DOOOM
EEYAAAAAAA!!
THEN IT'S TRUE! THEY'RE BOMBS!!
YOU MEAN THE OLD MAN... TRICKED US?
I JUST CAN'T BELIEVE IT...
SURE, HE GRIPED A LOT ABOUT LOSING HIS JOB BECAUSE OF THE GOVERNMENT... AND HE SWORE HE'D GET REVENGE... BUT...
SO WHAT IS IT YOU CAN'T BELIEVE ?!!
IT'S NOT THE JASTAWAYS' FAULT! THAT MAN WAS BAD, NOT THE JASTAWAYS!
ARE YOU STILL CARRYING THOSE, IDIOT ?!!
YAAAAAA
!

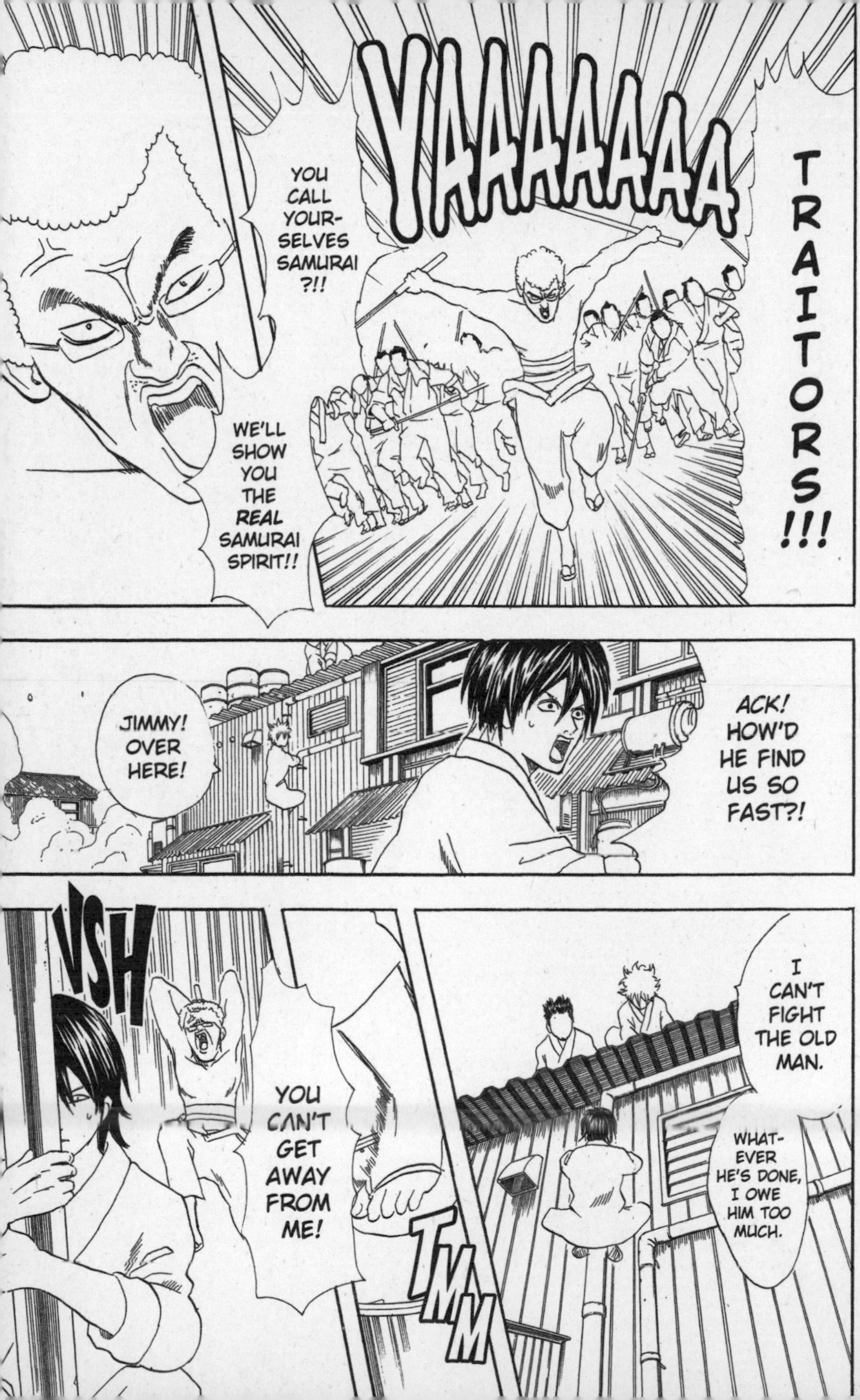
TRAITORS!!!
YAAAAAAA
YOU CALL YOURSELVES SAMURAI?!!
WE'LL SHOW YOU THE REAL SAMURAI SPIRIT!!
ACK! HOW'D HE FIND US SO FAST?!
JIMMY! OVER HERE!
I CAN'T FIGHT THE OLD MAN.
WHATEVER HE'S DONE, I OWE HIM TOO MUCH.
VSH
YOU CAN'T GET AWAY FROM ME!
TMM

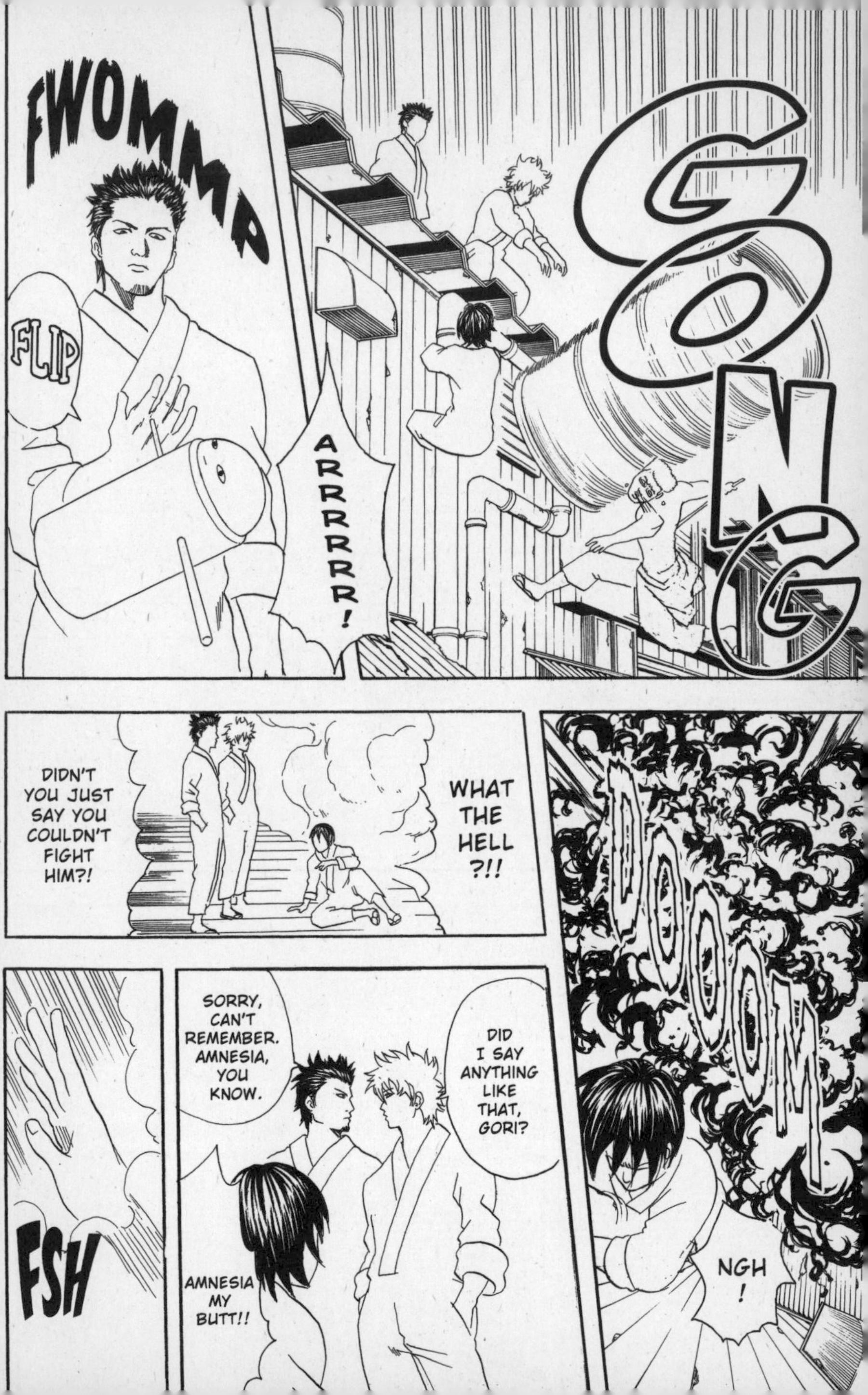
GONG
ARRRRRR!
FWOMMP
FLIP
DOOOOM
NGH!
WHAT THE HELL?!!
DIDN'T YOU JUST SAY YOU COULDN'T FIGHT HIM?!
DID I SAY ANYTHING LIKE THAT, GORI?
SORRY, CAN'T REMEMBER. AMNESIA, YOU KNOW.
AMNESIA MY BUTT!!
FSH

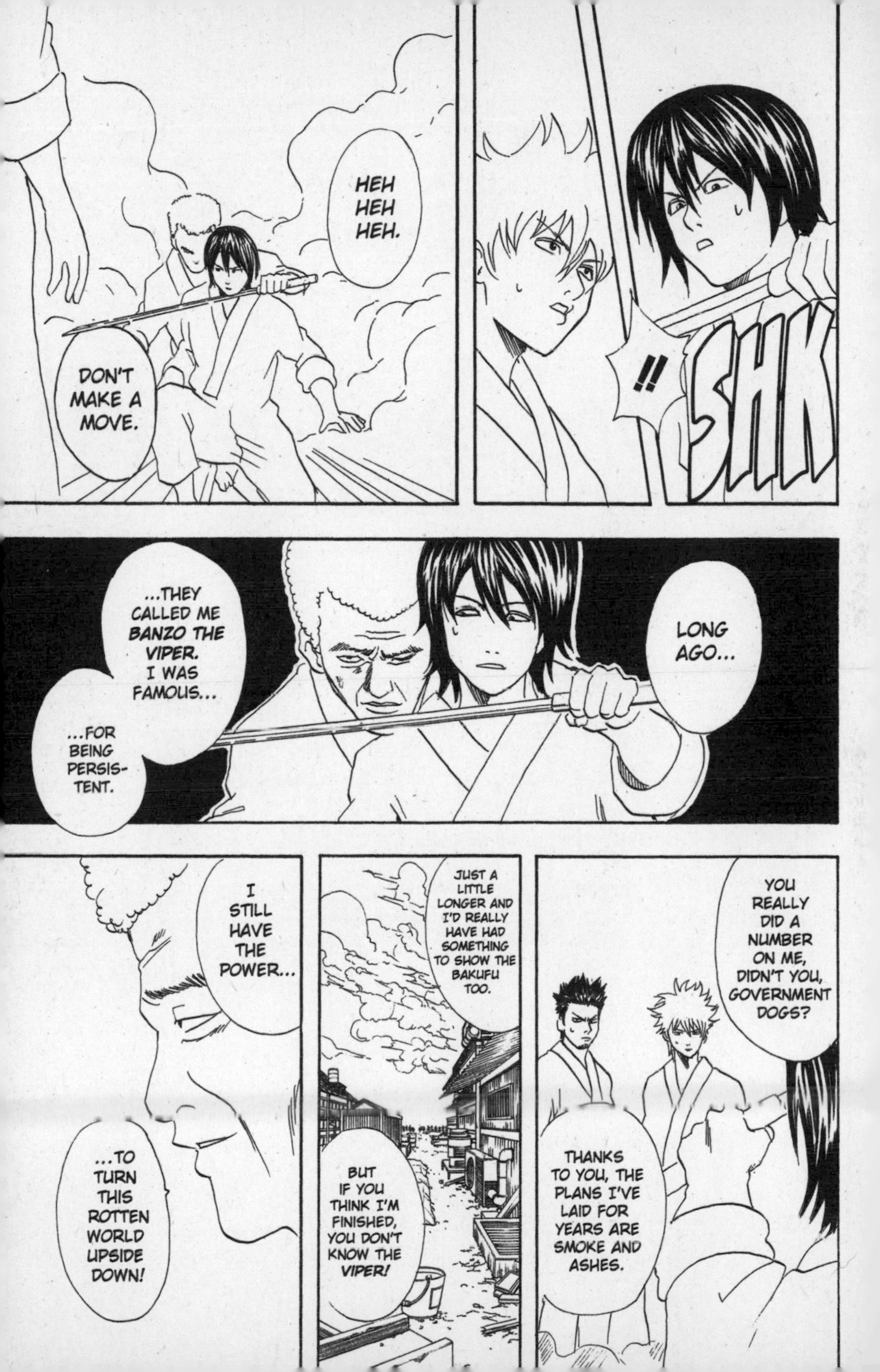
SHK
!!
HEH HEH HEH.
DON'T MAKE A MOVE.
LONG AGO...
...THEY CALLED ME BANZO THE VIPER. I WAS FAMOUS...
...FOR BEING PERSISTENT.
YOU REALLY DID A NUMBER ON ME, DIDN'T YOU, GOVERNMENT DOGS?
THANKS TO YOU, THE PLANS I'VE LAID FOR YEARS ARE SMOKE AND ASHES.
JUST A LITTLE LONGER AND I'D REALLY HAVE HAD SOMETHING TO SHOW THE BAKUFU TOO.
BUT IF YOU THINK I'M FINISHED, YOU DON'T KNOW THE VIPER!
I STILL HAVE THE POWER...
...TO TURN THIS ROTTEN WORLD UPSIDE DOWN!

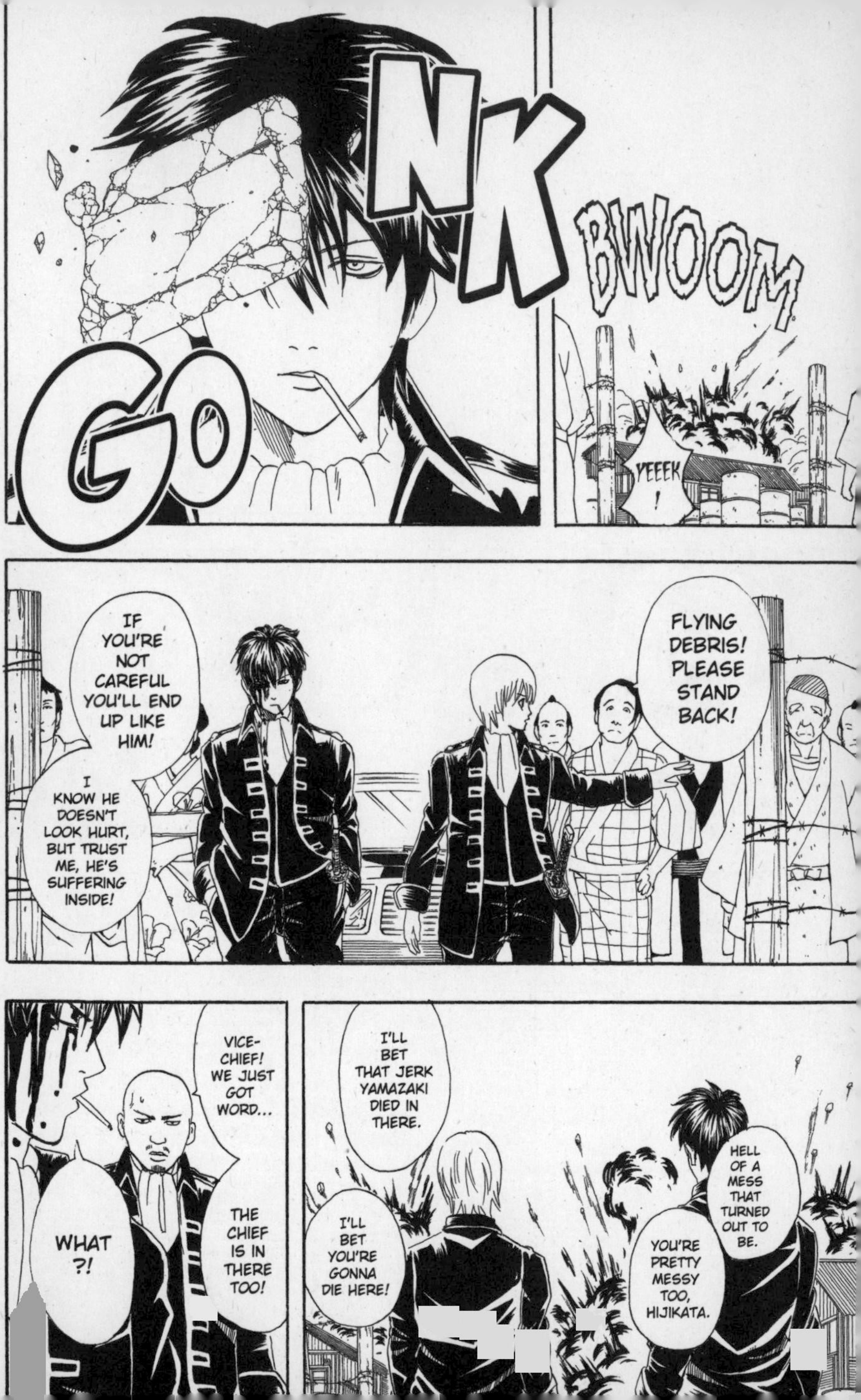
BWOOM
YEEEK!
GO
NK
FLYING DEBRIS! PLEASE STAND BACK!
IF YOU'RE NOT CAREFUL YOU'LL END UP LIKE HIM!
I KNOW HE DOESN'T LOOK HURT, BUT TRUST ME, HE'S SUFFERING INSIDE!
HELL OF A MESS THAT TURNED OUT TO BE.
I'LL BET THAT JERK YAMAZAKI DIED IN THERE.
YOU'RE PRETTY MESSY TOO, HIJIKATA.
I'LL BET YOU'RE GONNA DIE HERE!
VICE-CHIEF! WE JUST GOT WORD...
THE CHIEF IS IN THERE TOO!
WHAT?!

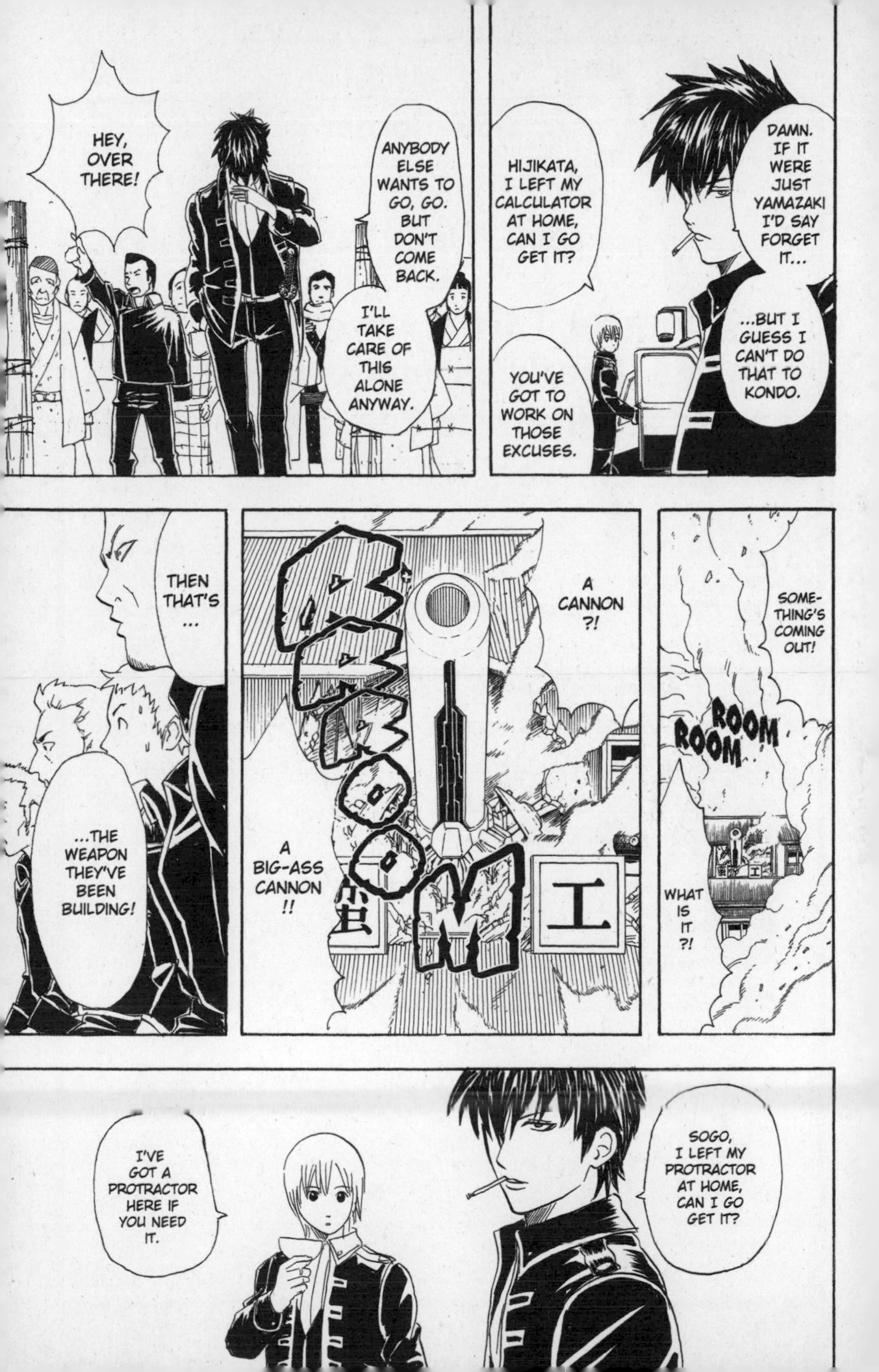
DAMN. IF IT WERE JUST YAMAZAKI I'D SAY FORGET IT...
...BUT I GUESS I CAN'T DO THAT TO KONDO.
HIJIKATA, I LEFT MY CALCULATOR AT HOME, CAN I GO GET IT?
YOU'VE GOT TO WORK ON THOSE EXCUSES.
ANYBODY ELSE WANTS TO GO, GO. BUT DON'T COME BACK.
I'LL TAKE CARE OF THIS ALONE ANYWAY.
HEY, OVER THERE!
SOME-THING'S COMING OUT!
ROOM ROOM
WHAT IS IT ?!
A CANNON ?!
A BIG-ASS CANNON !!
THEN THAT'S ...
...THE WEAPON THEY'VE BEEN BUILDING!
SOGO, I LEFT MY PROTRACTOR AT HOME, CAN I GO GET IT?
I'VE GOT A PROTRACTOR HERE IF YOU NEED IT.

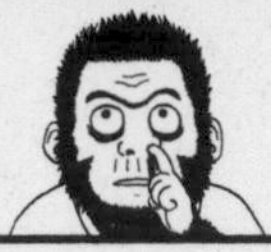

Sorachi's Q&A Corner #10

<Question from “Coffee-junkie,” Tottori Prefecture>

Hey, Sorachi. I always wanted to ask you this. Nearly all your characters' names are from old Edo...but where'd you get “Gin-san” from?

From Kintoki Sakata, also known as Kintaro, from a famous folk tale set in the Heian Period. One story says he's the child of a mountain witch, and he had such Herculean strength that he sumo-wrestled with bears.

Later, he became one of the “Four Braves” of the samurai Yorimitsu Minamoto, and is said to have driven the demon Shuten-doji off Mt. Oe.

It's not like Gin-san's supposed to be Kintaro's grandson or anything, I just stole a little from the story.

(Q&A #11 is on page 70)

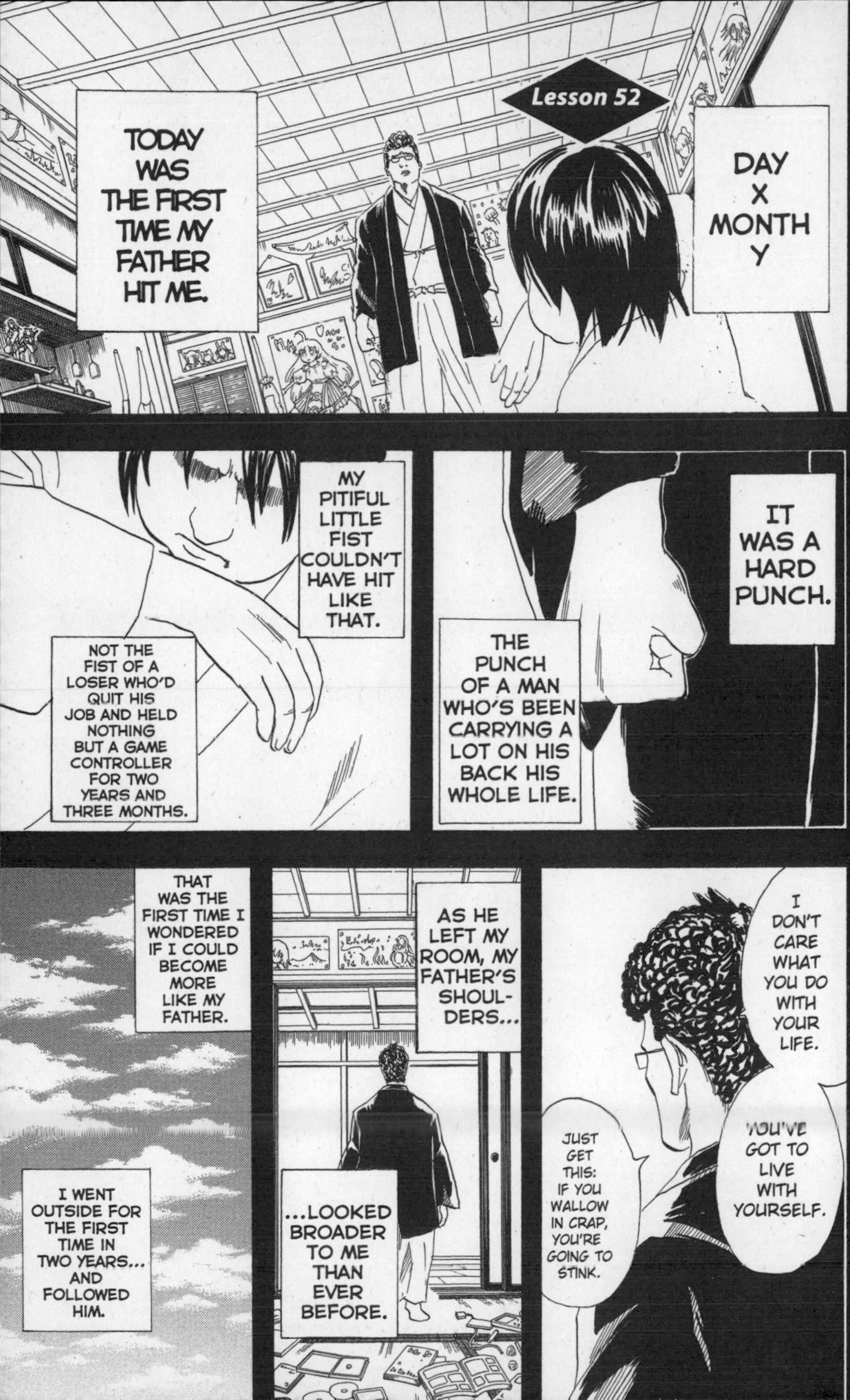
Lesson 52
DAY X MONTH Y
TODAY WAS THE FIRST TIME MY FATHER HIT ME.
IT WAS A HARD PUNCH.
THE PUNCH OF A MAN WHO'S BEEN CARRYING A LOT ON HIS BACK HIS WHOLE LIFE.
MY PITIFUL LITTLE FIST COULDN'T HAVE HIT LIKE THAT.
NOT THE FIST OF A LOSER WHO'D QUIT HIS JOB AND HELD NOTHING BUT A GAME CONTROLLER FOR TWO YEARS AND THREE MONTHS.
I DON'T CARE WHAT YOU DO WITH YOUR LIFE.
YOU'VE GOT TO LIVE WITH YOURSELF.
JUST GET THIS: IF YOU WALLOW IN CRAP, YOU'RE GOING TO STINK.
AS HE LEFT MY ROOM, MY FATHER'S SHOUL-DERS...
...LOOKED BROADER TO ME THAN EVER BEFORE.
THAT WAS THE FIRST TIME I WONDERED IF I COULD BECOME MORE LIKE MY FATHER.
I WENT OUTSIDE FOR THE FIRST TIME IN TWO YEARS... AND FOLLOWED HIM.

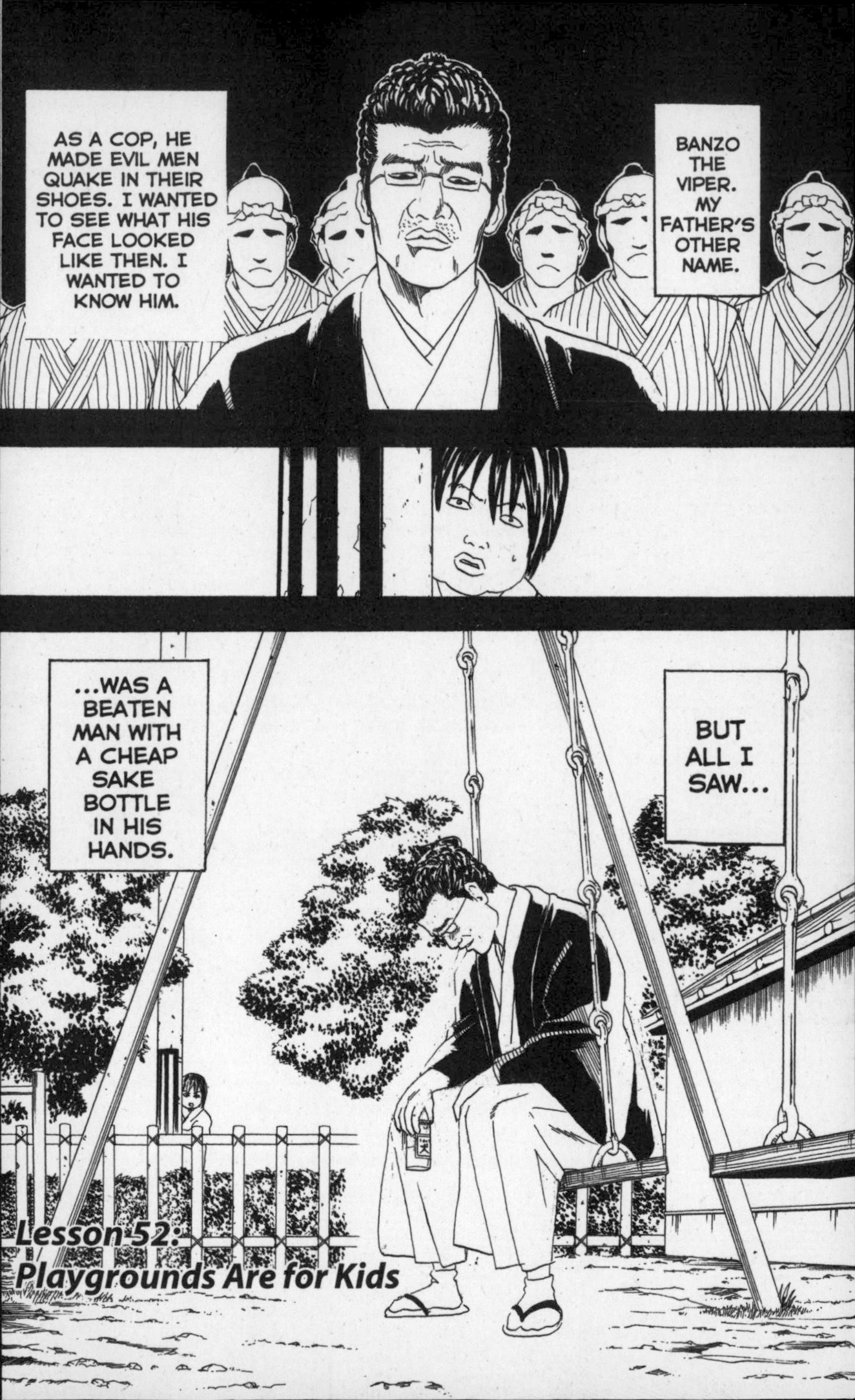
BANZO THE VIPER. MY FATHER'S OTHER NAME.
AS A COP, HE MADE EVIL MEN QUAKE IN THEIR SHOES. I WANTED TO SEE WHAT HIS FACE LOOKED LIKE THEN. I WANTED TO KNOW HIM.
BUT ALL I SAW...
...WAS A BEATEN MAN WITH A CHEAP SAKE BOTTLE IN HIS HANDS.
Lesson 52:
Playgrounds Are for Kids

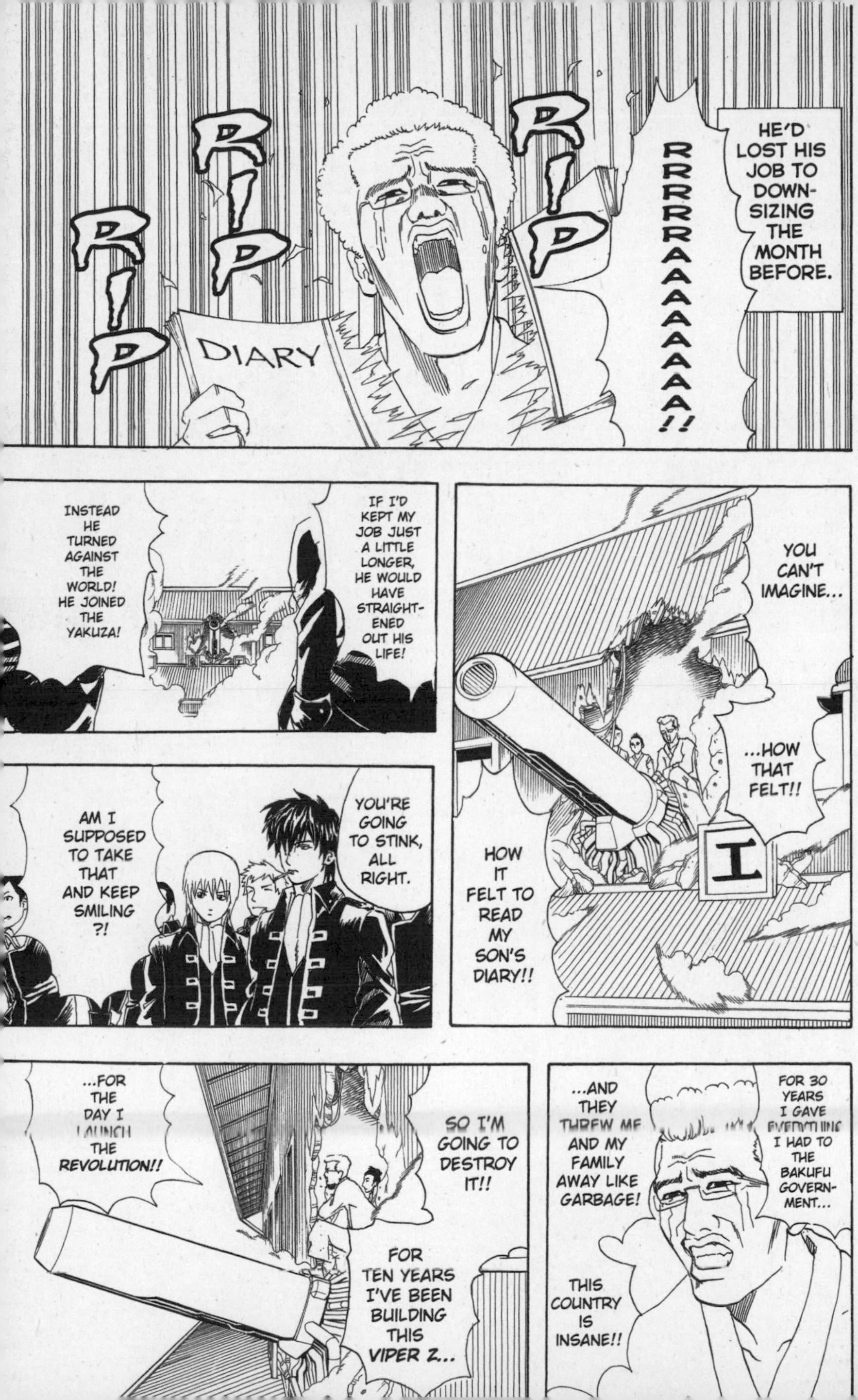
HE'D LOST HIS JOB TO DOWN-SIZING THE MONTH BEFORE.
RRRRAAAAAAAAA!!
RIP
RIP
RIP
DIARY
YOU CAN'T IMAGINE...
...HOW THAT FELT!!
HOW IT FELT TO READ MY SON'S DIARY!!
IF I'D KEPT MY JOB JUST A LITTLE LONGER, HE WOULD HAVE STRAIGHT-ENED OUT HIS LIFE!
INSTEAD HE TURNED AGAINST THE WORLD! HE JOINED THE YAKUZA!
YOU'RE GOING TO STINK, ALL RIGHT.
AM I SUPPOSED TO TAKE THAT AND KEEP SMILING ?!
FOR 30 YEARS I GAVE EVERYTHING I HAD TO THE BAKUFU GOVERN-MENT...
...AND THEY THREW ME AND MY FAMILY AWAY LIKE GARBAGE!
THIS COUNTRY IS INSANE!!
SO I'M GOING TO DESTROY IT!!
FOR TEN YEARS I'VE BEEN BUILDING THIS VIPER Z...
...FOR THE DAY I LAUNCH THE REVOLUTION!!

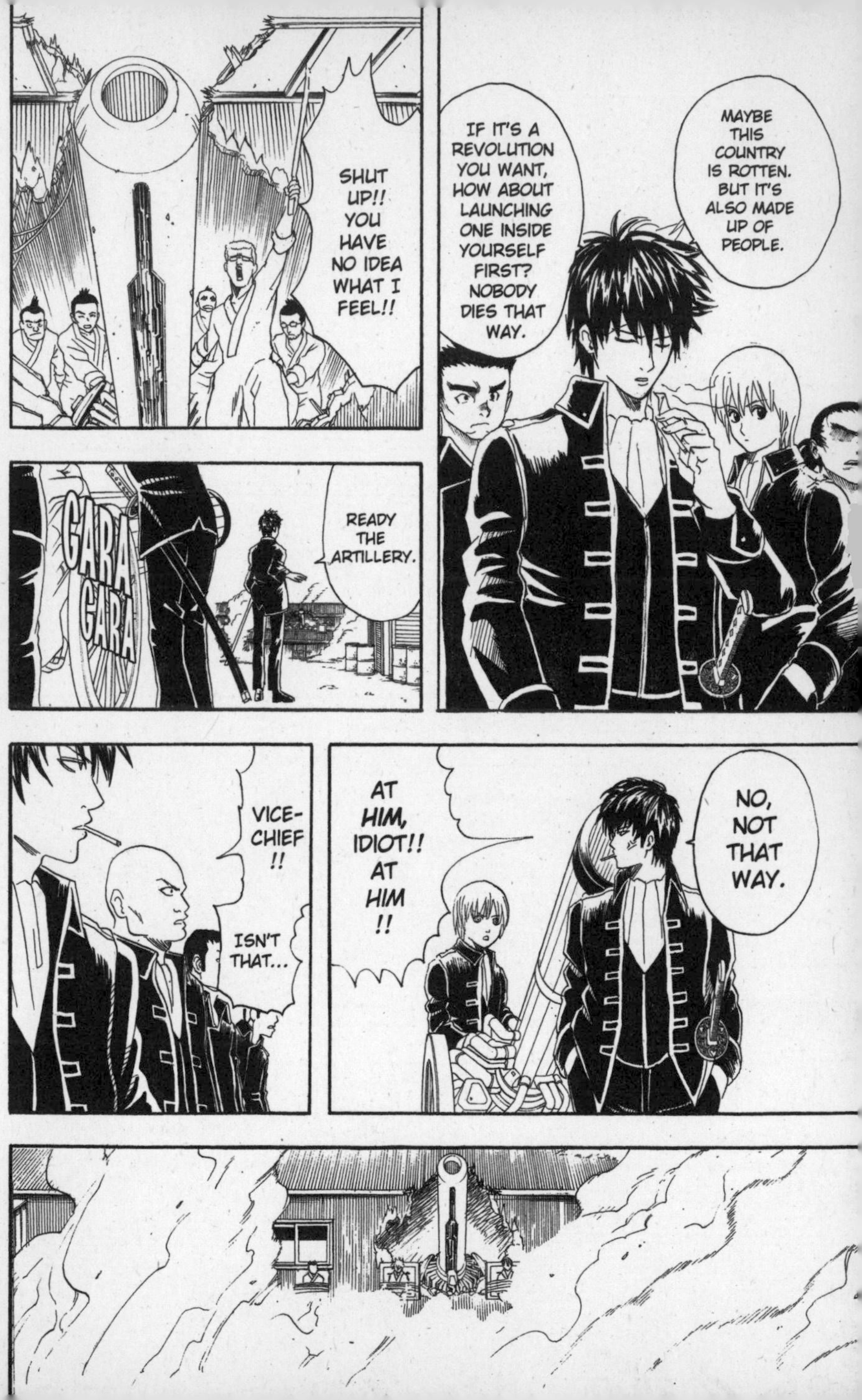
MAYBE THIS COUNTRY IS ROTTEN. BUT IT'S ALSO MADE UP OF PEOPLE.
IF IT'S A REVOLUTION YOU WANT, HOW ABOUT LAUNCHING ONE INSIDE YOURSELF FIRST? NOBODY DIES THAT WAY.
SHUT UP!! YOU HAVE NO IDEA WHAT I FEEL!!
READY THE ARTILLERY.
GARA GARA
NO, NOT THAT WAY.
AT HIM, IDIOT!! AT HIM!!
VICE-CHIEF!!
ISN'T THAT...

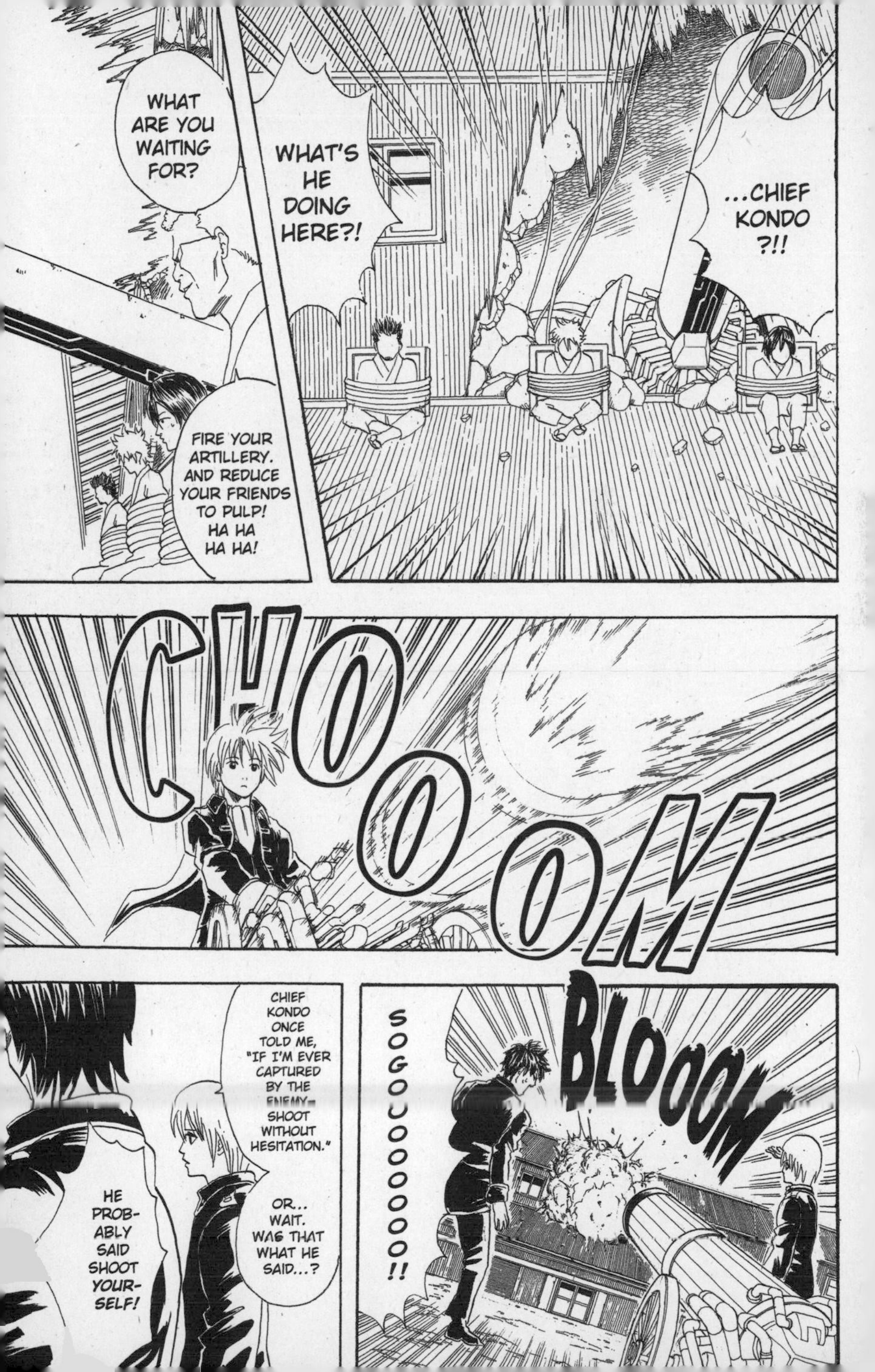
...CHIEF KONDO ?!!
WHAT'S HE DOING HERE?!
WHAT ARE YOU WAITING FOR?
FIRE YOUR ARTILLERY. AND REDUCE YOUR FRIENDS TO PULP! HA HA HA HA!
CHOOOOM
BLOOOM
SOGOOOOOOOOO!!
CHIEF KONDO ONCE TOLD ME, "IF I'M EVER CAPTURED BY THE ENEMY, SHOOT WITHOUT HESITATION."
OR.. WAIT. WAS THAT WHAT HE SAID...?
HE PROBABLY SAID SHOOT YOURSELF!

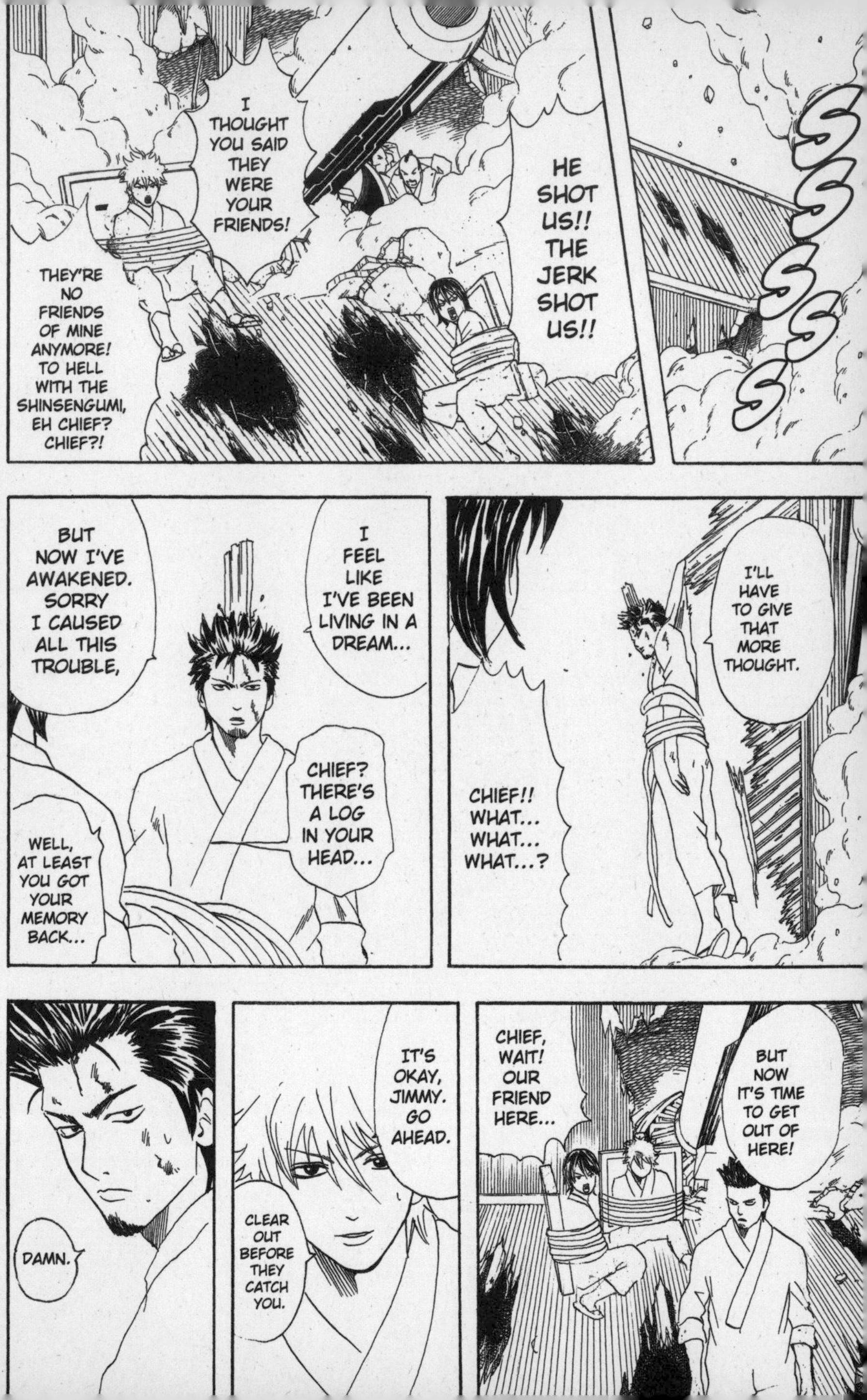
SSSSS
HE SHOT US!! THE JERK SHOT US!!
I THOUGHT YOU SAID THEY WERE YOUR FRIENDS!
THEY'RE NO FRIENDS OF MINE ANYMORE! TO HELL WITH THE SHINSENGUMI, EH CHIEF? CHIEF?!
I'LL HAVE TO GIVE THAT MORE THOUGHT.
CHIEF!! WHAT... WHAT... WHAT...?
I FEEL LIKE I'VE BEEN LIVING IN A DREAM...
BUT NOW I'VE AWAKENED. SORRY I CAUSED ALL THIS TROUBLE,
CHIEF? THERE'S A LOG IN YOUR HEAD...
WELL, AT LEAST YOU GOT YOUR MEMORY BACK...
BUT NOW IT'S TIME TO GET OUT OF HERE!
CHIEF, WAIT! OUR FRIEND HERE...
IT'S OKAY, JIMMY. GO AHEAD.
CLEAR OUT BEFORE THEY CATCH YOU.
DAMN.

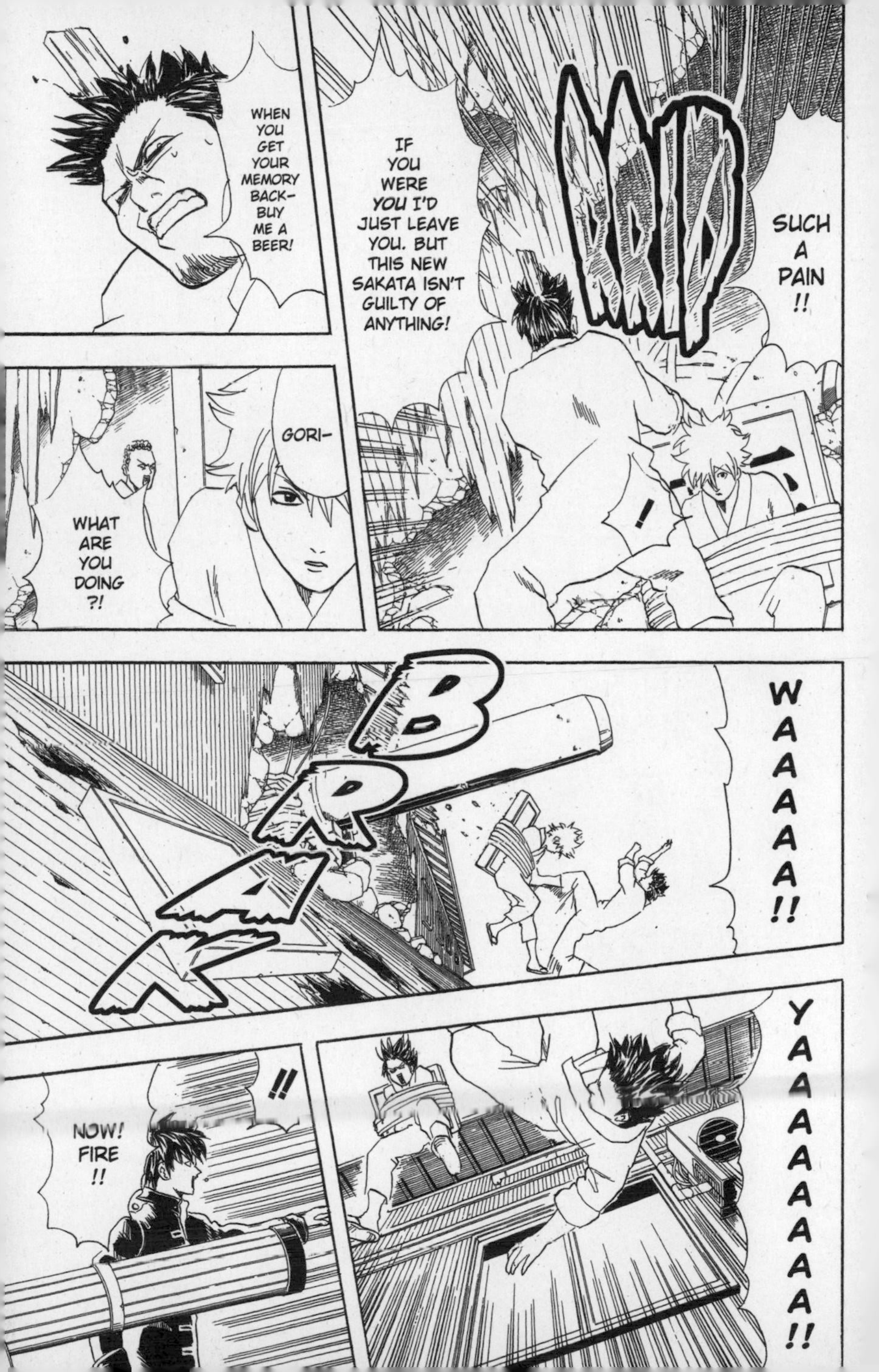
SUCH A PAIN!!
IF YOU WERE *YOU* I'D JUST LEAVE YOU. BUT THIS NEW SAKATA ISN'T GUILTY OF ANYTHING!
WHEN YOU GET YOUR MEMORY BACK- BUY ME A BEER!
GORI-
WHAT ARE YOU DOING?!
!
WAAAAAA!!
BRAAK
YAAAAAAAAA!!
!!
NOW! FIRE!!

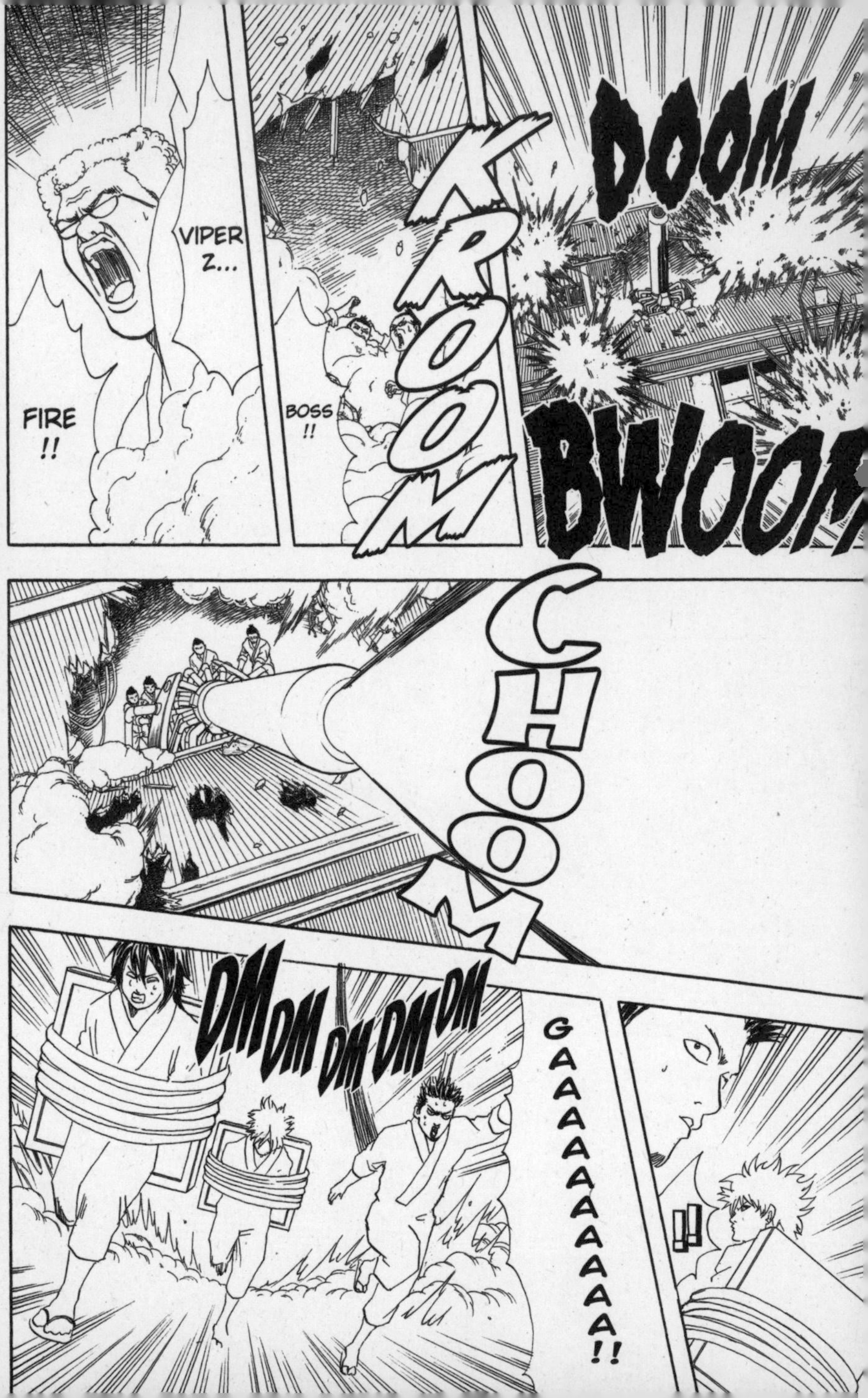
DOOM
BWOOM
KROOOM
BOSS!!
VIPER Z...
FIRE!!
CHOOOM
!!
GAAAAAAAAAAA!!
DM DM DM DM DM

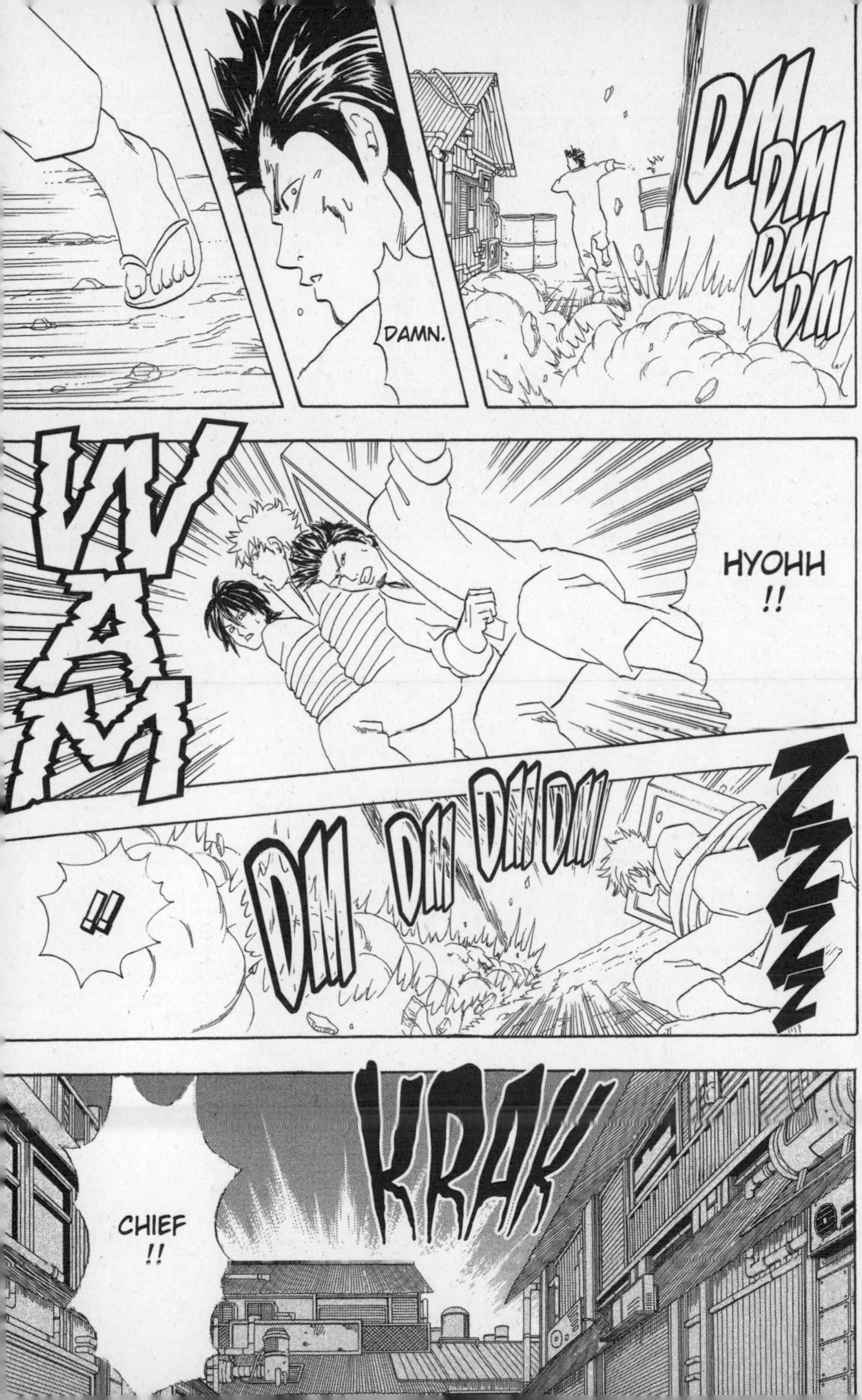
DM
DM
DM
DM
DM
DAMN.
HYOHH !!
WAM
DMDM
DM
DM
!!
KRAK
CHIEF !!

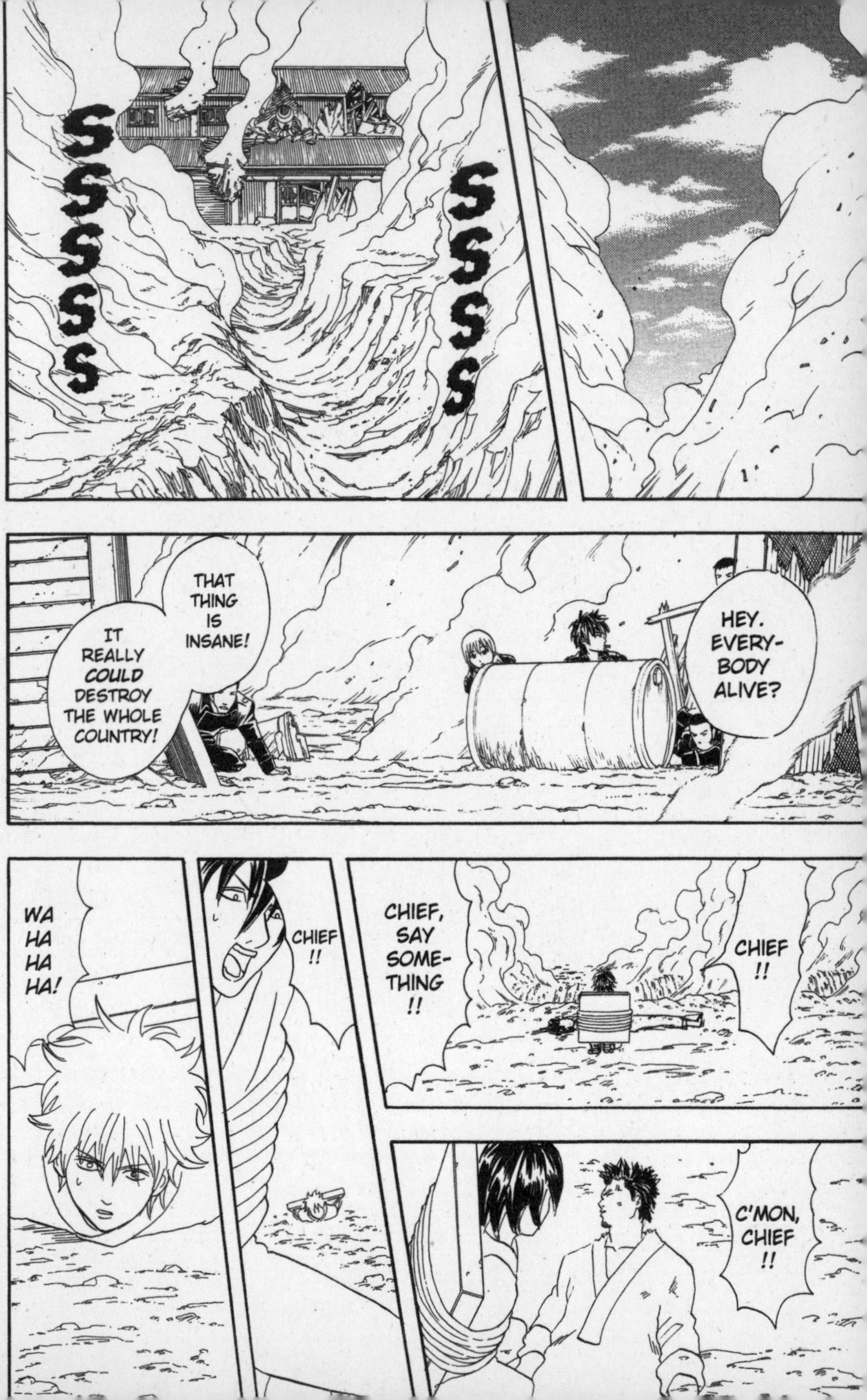
SSSS
SSSS
HEY. EVERY-BODY ALIVE?
THAT THING IS INSANE!
IT REALLY COULD DESTROY THE WHOLE COUNTRY!
CHIEF !!
CHIEF, SAY SOME-THING !!
C'MON, CHIEF !!
CHIEF !!
WA HA HA HA!

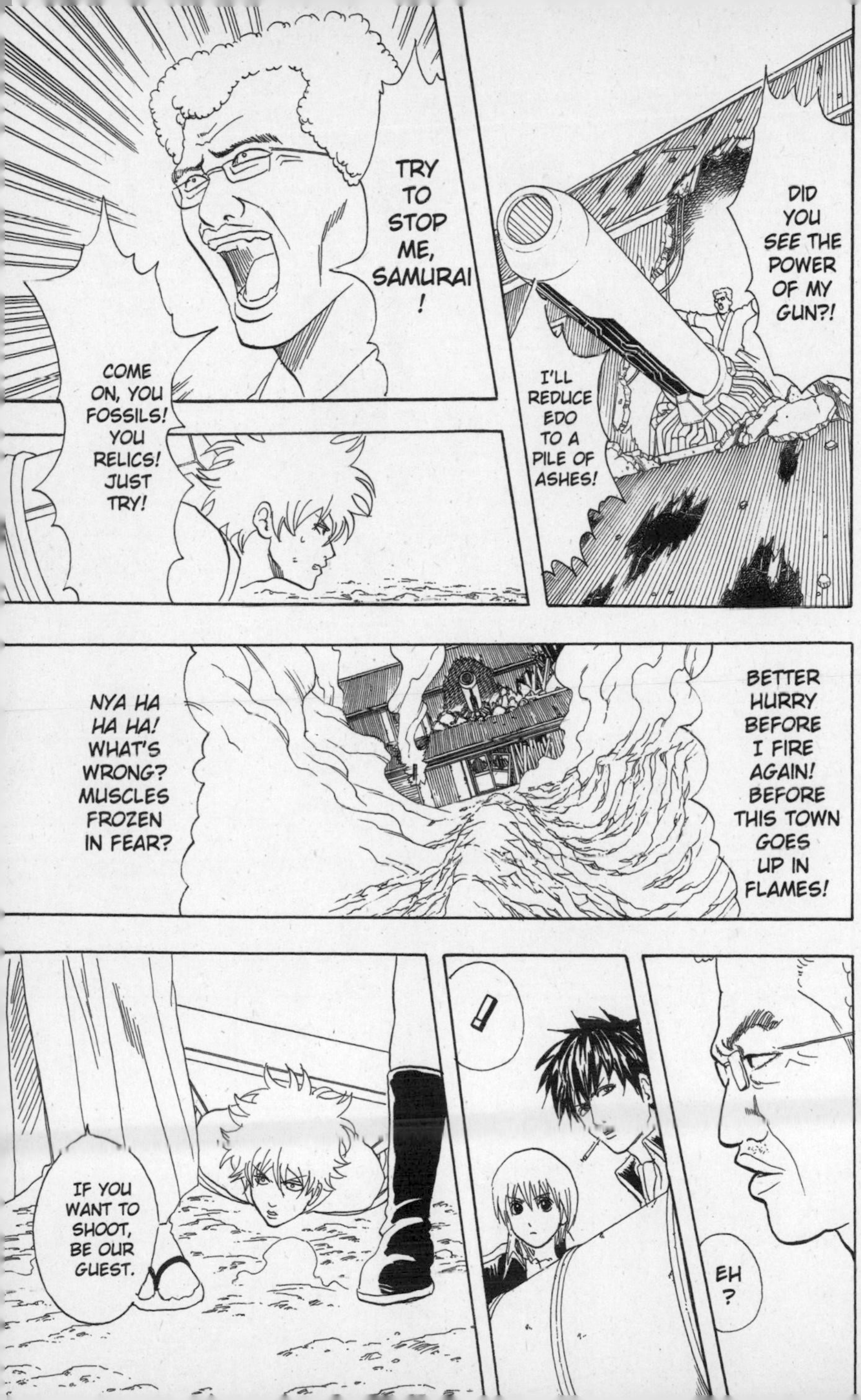
DID YOU SEE THE POWER OF MY GUN?!
I'LL REDUCE EDO TO A PILE OF ASHES!
TRY TO STOP ME, SAMURAI!
COME ON, YOU FOSSILS! YOU RELICS! JUST TRY!
BETTER HURRY BEFORE I FIRE AGAIN! BEFORE THIS TOWN GOES UP IN FLAMES!
NYA HA HA HA! WHAT'S WRONG? MUSCLES FROZEN IN FEAR?
EH?
!
IF YOU WANT TO SHOOT, BE OUR GUEST.

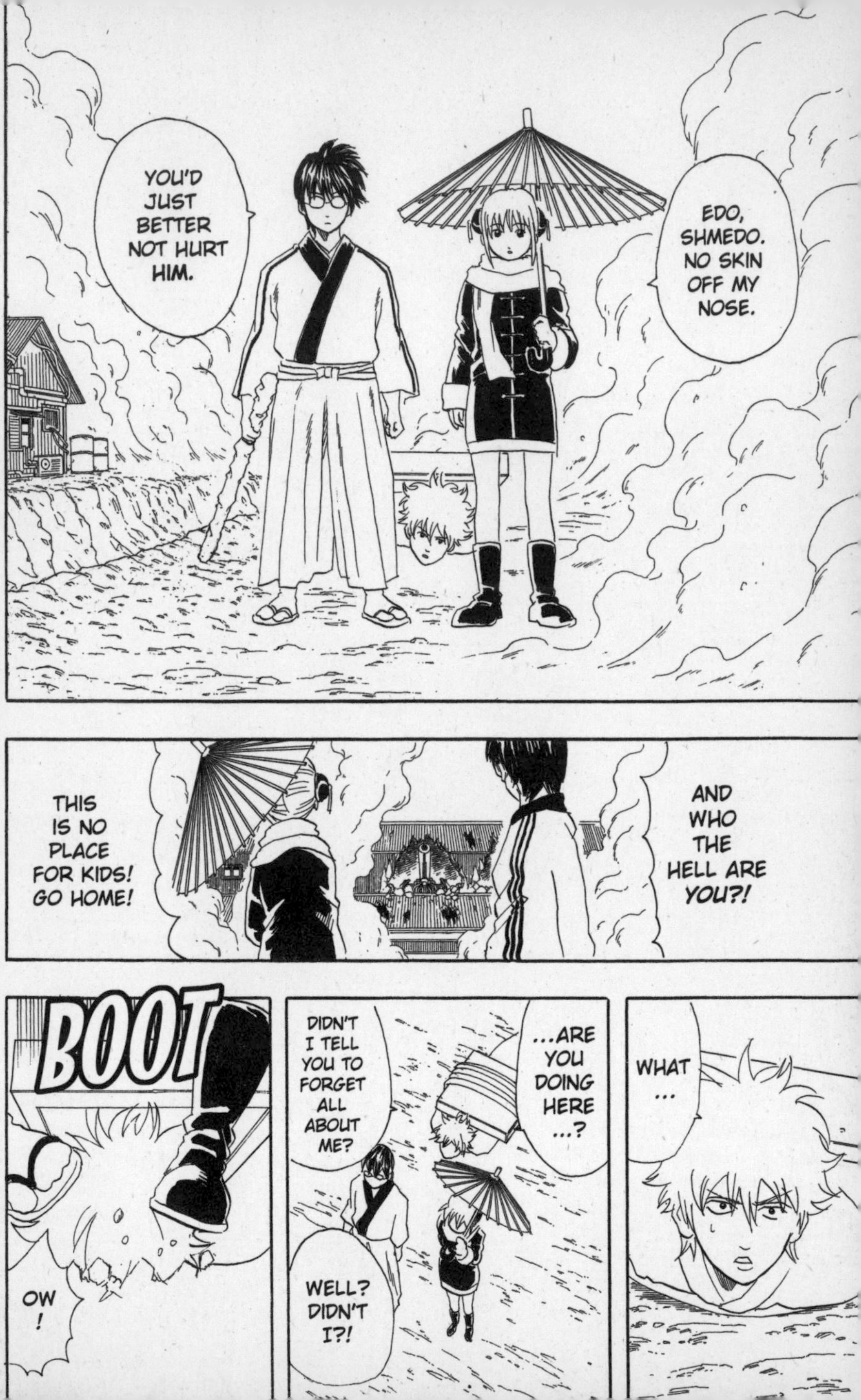
EDO, SHMEDO. NO SKIN OFF MY NOSE.
YOU'D JUST BETTER NOT HURT HIM.
AND WHO THE HELL ARE *YOU?!*
THIS IS NO PLACE FOR KIDS! GO HOME!
WHAT ...
...ARE YOU DOING HERE ...?
DIDN'T I TELL YOU TO FORGET ALL ABOUT ME?
WELL? DIDN'T I?!
BOOT
OW !

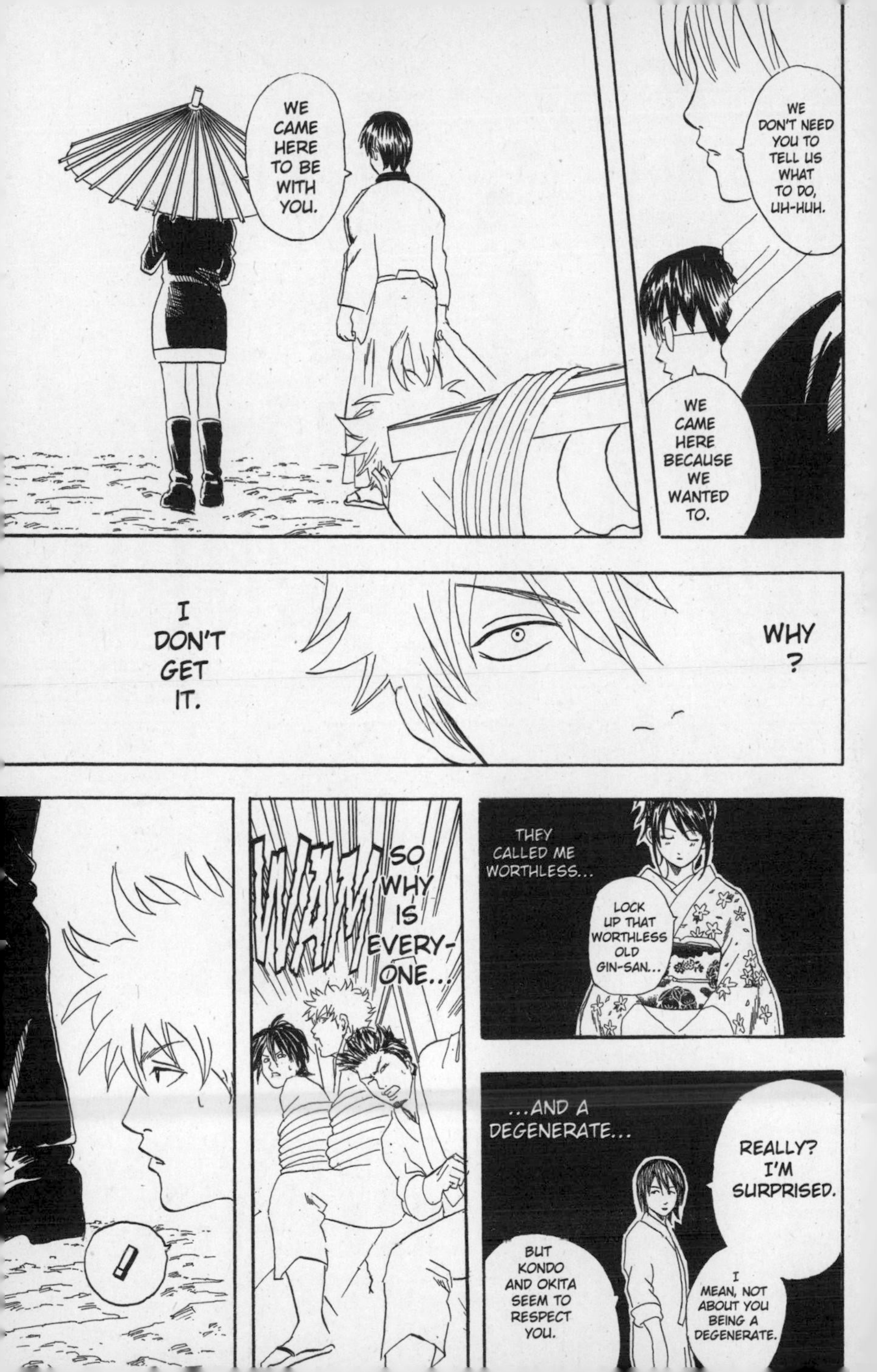
WE DON'T NEED YOU TO TELL US WHAT TO DO, UH-HUH.
WE CAME HERE BECAUSE WE WANTED TO.
WE CAME HERE TO BE WITH YOU.
WHY?
I DON'T GET IT.
THEY CALLED ME WORTHLESS...
LOCK UP THAT WORTHLESS OLD GIN-SAN...
...AND A DEGENERATE...
REALLY? I'M SURPRISED.
I MEAN, NOT ABOUT YOU BEING A DEGENERATE.
BUT KONDO AND OKITA SEEM TO RESPECT YOU.
SO WHY IS EVERY-ONE...
!

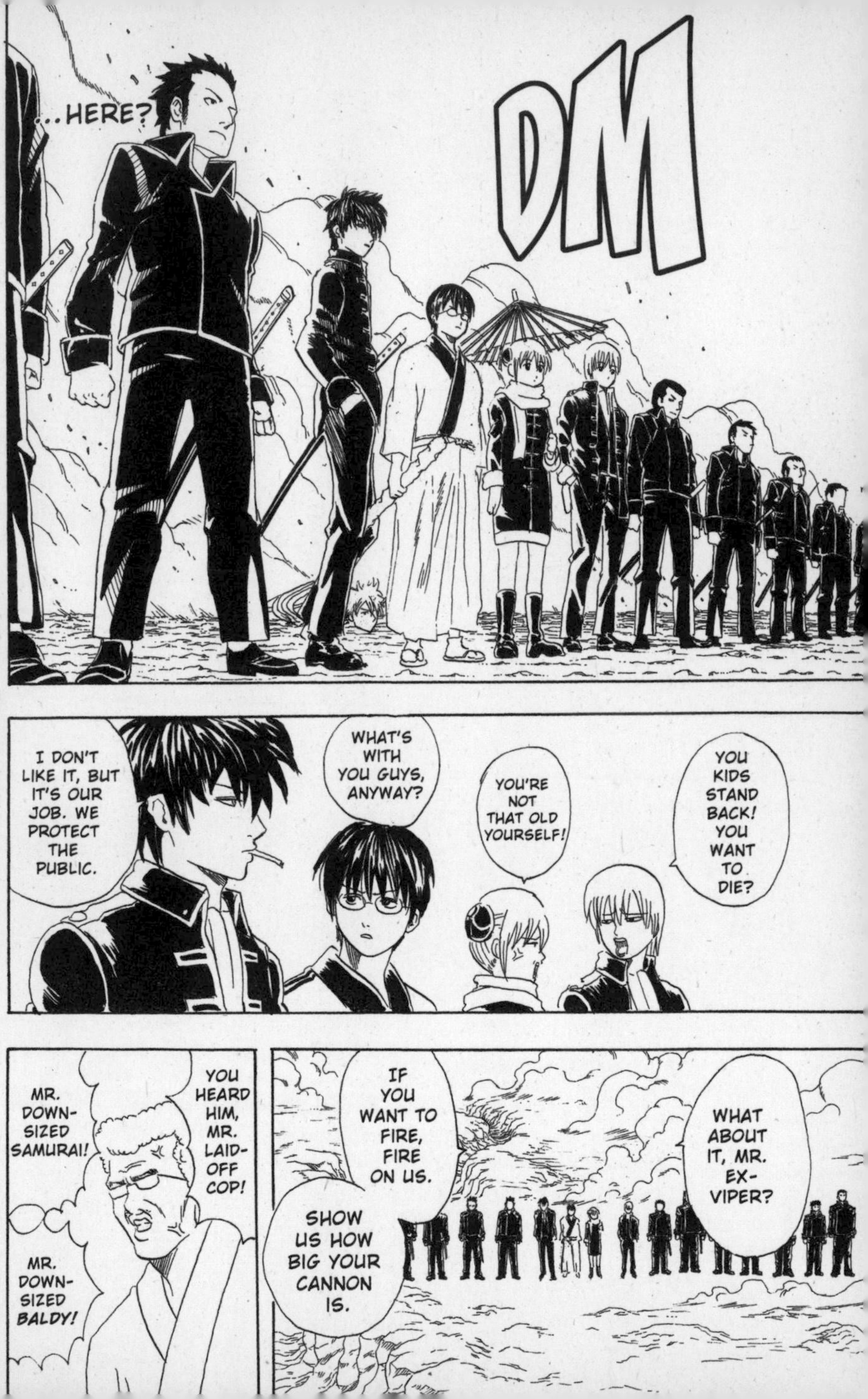
DM
...HERE?
YOU KIDS STAND BACK! YOU WANT TO DIE?
YOU'RE NOT THAT OLD YOURSELF!
WHAT'S WITH YOU GUYS, ANYWAY?
I DON'T LIKE IT, BUT IT'S OUR JOB. WE PROTECT THE PUBLIC.
WHAT ABOUT IT, MR. EX-VIPER?
IF YOU WANT TO FIRE, FIRE ON US.
SHOW US HOW BIG YOUR CANNON IS.
YOU HEARD HIM, MR. LAID-OFF COP!
MR. DOWNSIZED SAMURAI!
MR. DOWNSIZED BALDY!

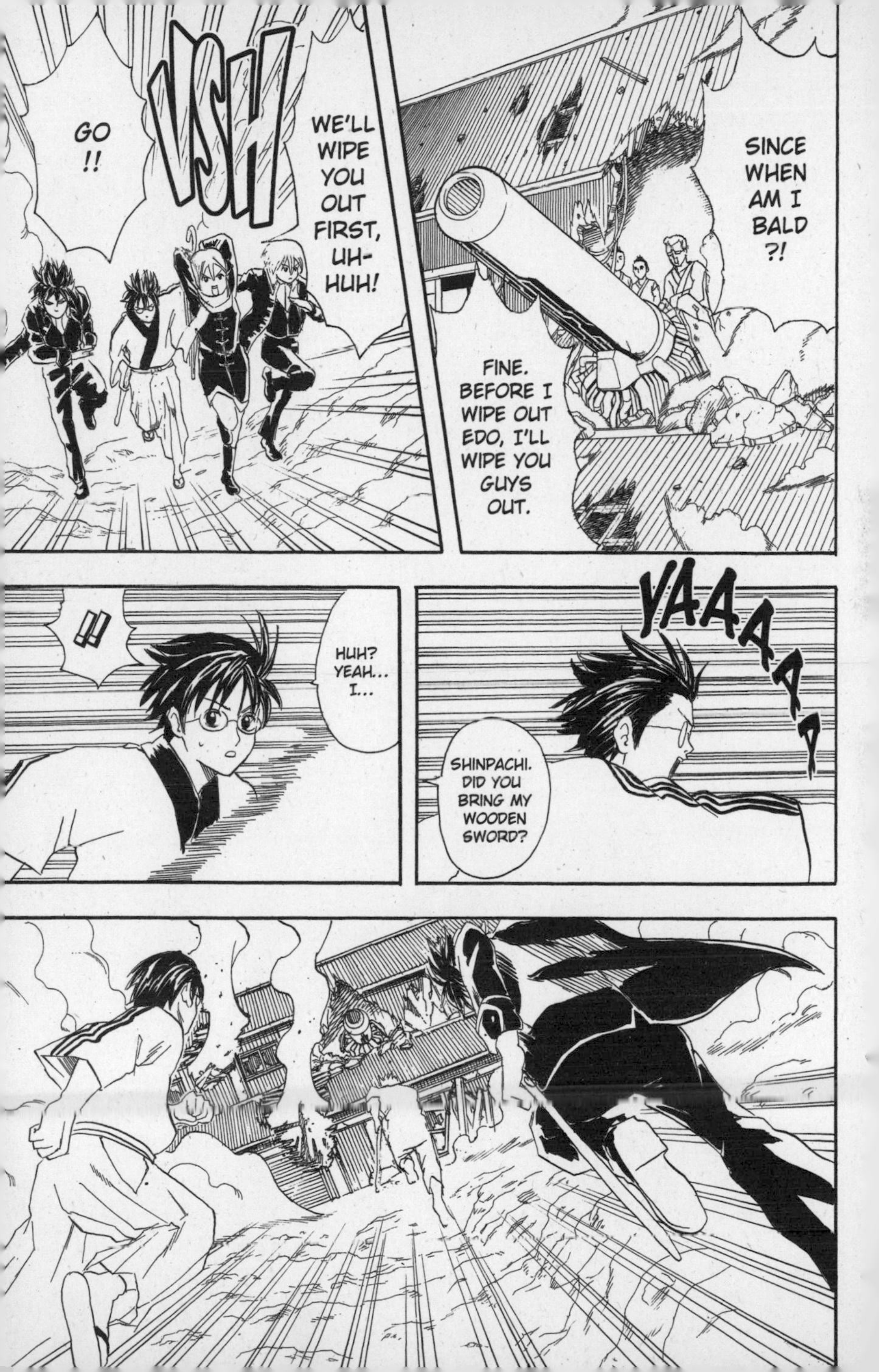

SINCE WHEN AM I BALD ?!
FINE. BEFORE I WIPE OUT EDO, I'LL WIPE YOU GUYS OUT.
WE'LL WIPE YOU OUT FIRST, UH-HUH!
VSH
GO !!
YAAAAAA
SHINPACHI. DID YOU BRING MY WOODEN SWORD?
HUH? YEAH... I...
!!

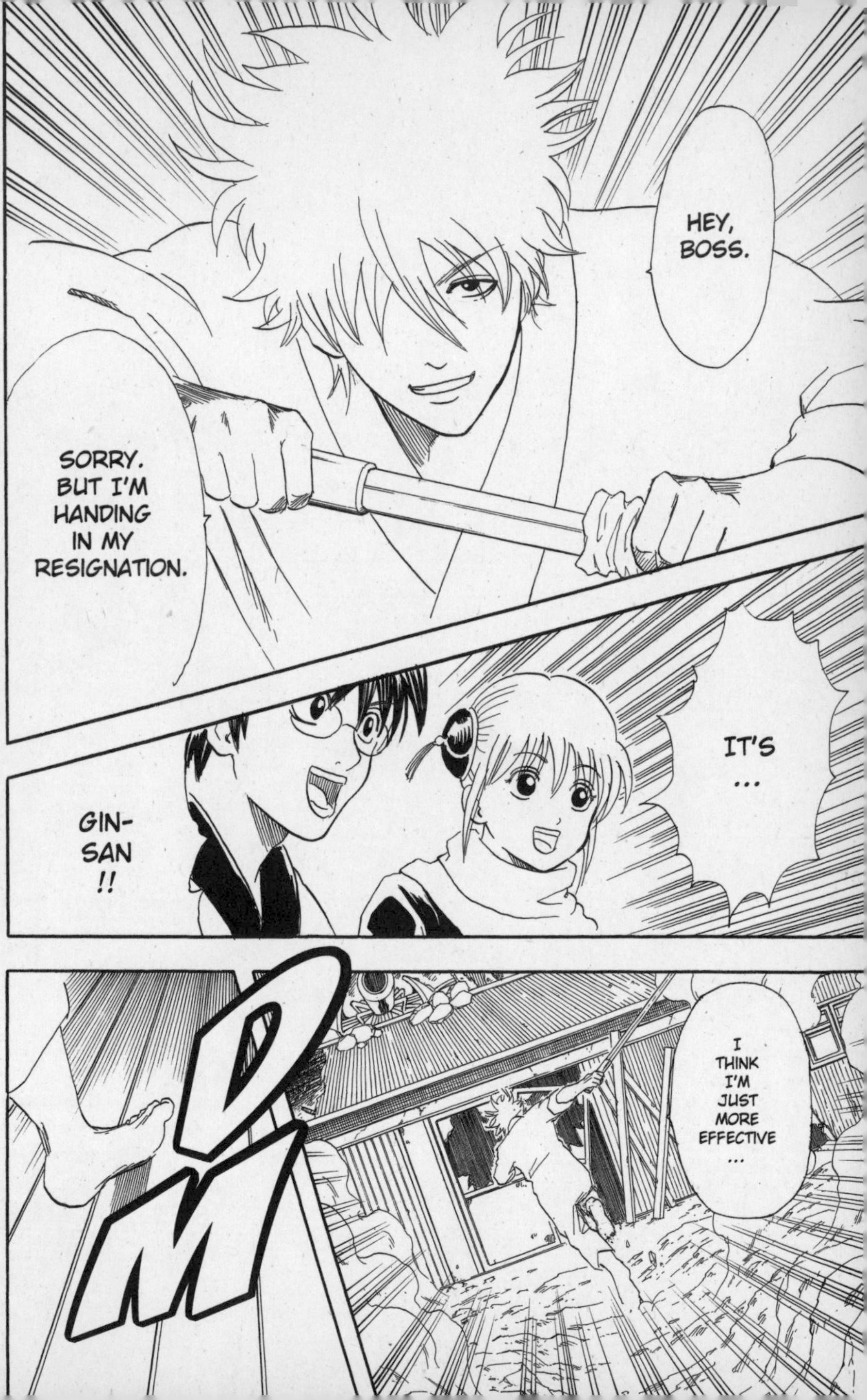
HEY, BOSS.
SORRY. BUT I'M HANDING IN MY RESIGNATION.
IT'S ...
GIN-SAN !!
I THINK I'M JUST MORE EFFECTIVE ...
DM

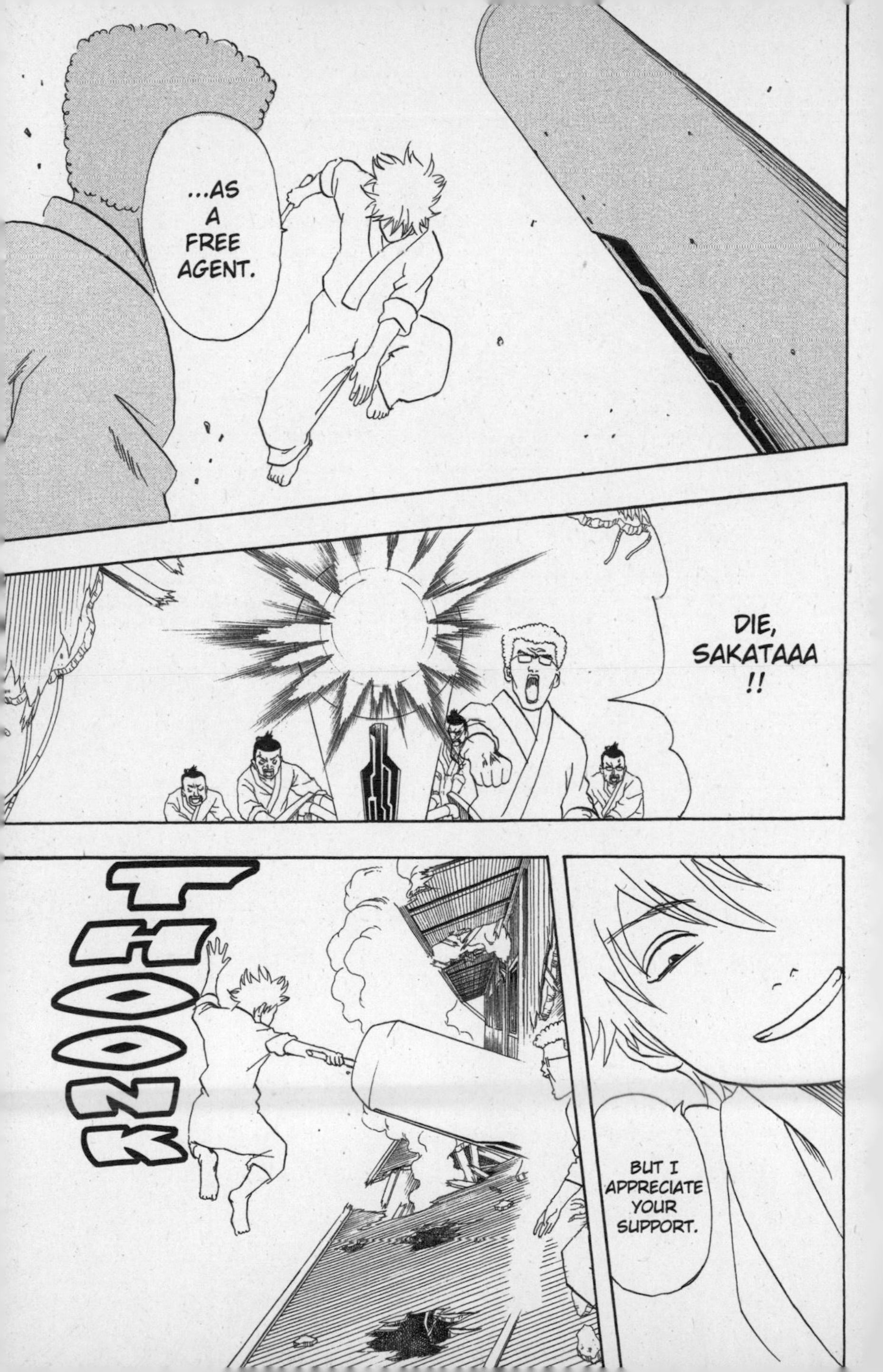
...AS A FREE AGENT.
DIE, SAKATAAA!!
BUT I APPRECIATE YOUR SUPPORT.

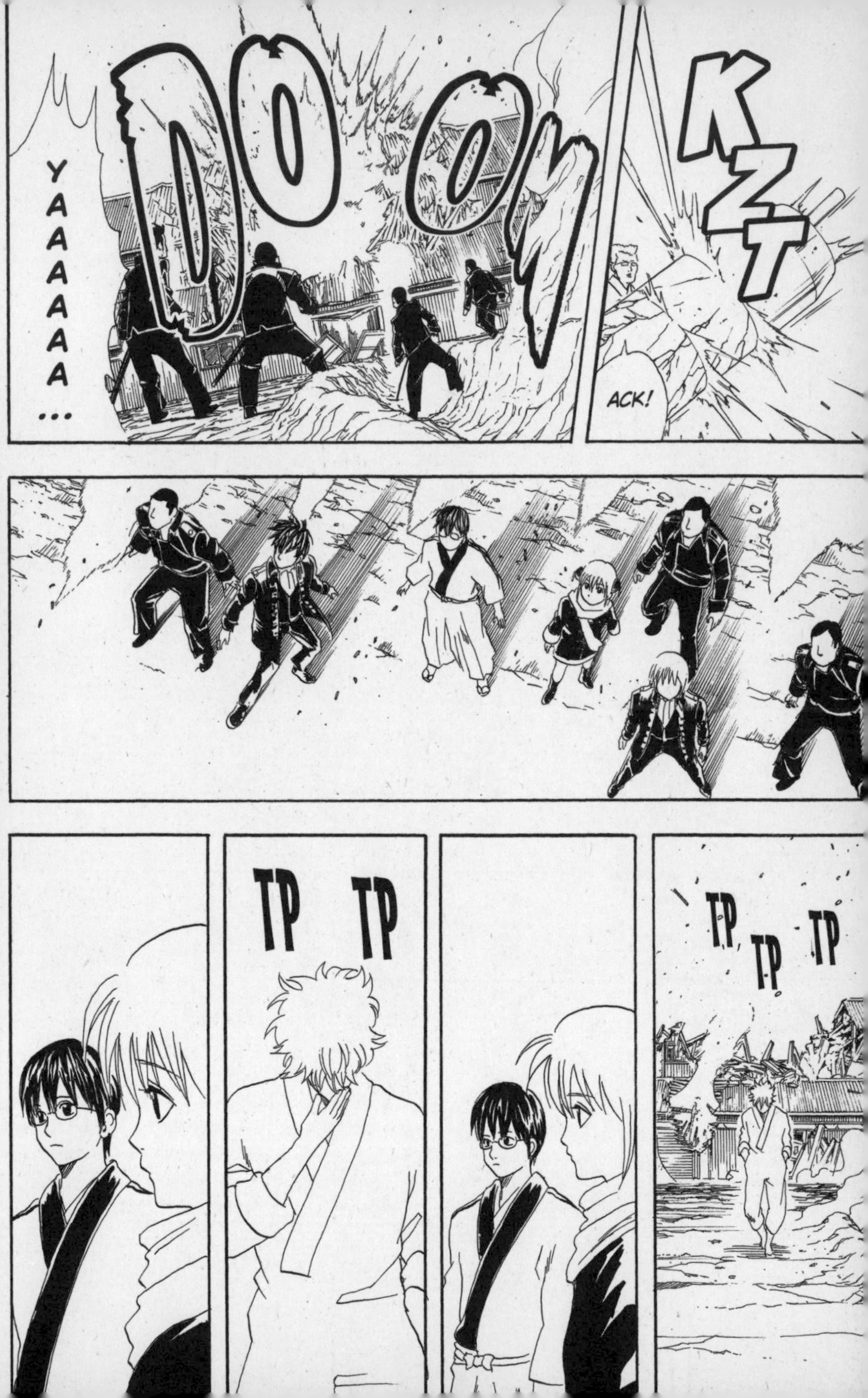
KZT
ACK!
DOOM
YAAAAAAA...
TP TP TP
TP TP

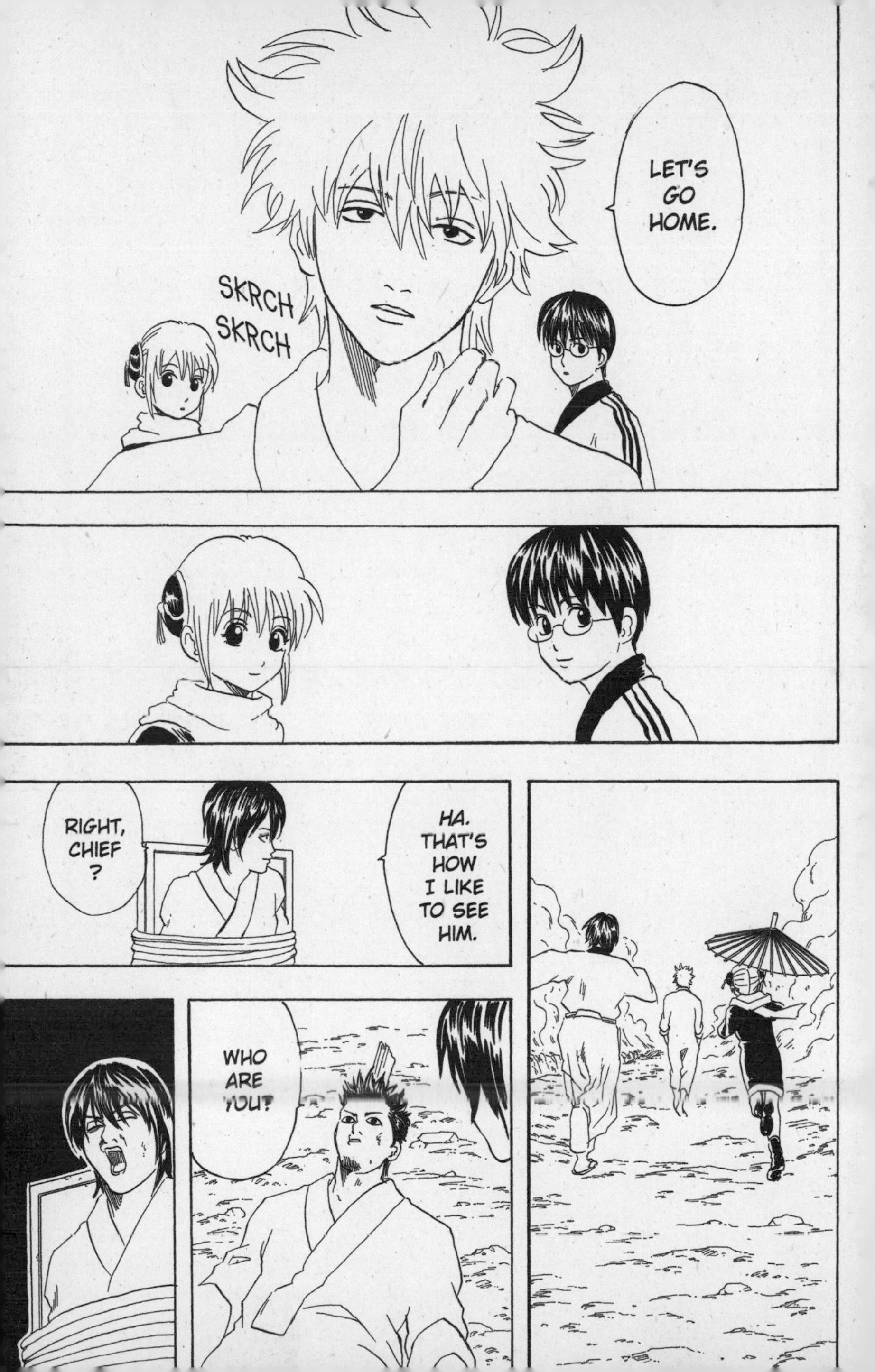
LET'S GO HOME.
SKRCH SKRCH
HA. THAT'S HOW I LIKE TO SEE HIM.
RIGHT, CHIEF?
WHO ARE YOU?

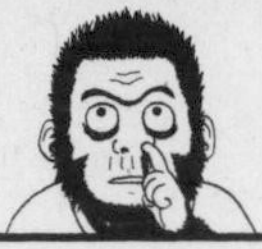

Sorachi's Q&A Corner #11

<Question from Sugiyama-san of Shizuoka Prefecture>

The *Gin Tama* chapter titles are always so different from other manga's. How do you keep thinking up titles like that?

I think about it after finishing writing the story. Sometimes it may seem like I just pull the titles out of a hat, but there's always a connection with the story somewhere. Look for them!

I have to admit, sometimes when I'm rushed the editor picks a title. Whenever you hit one that's not so good, please assume it's his fault.

(Q&A #12 is on page 90)

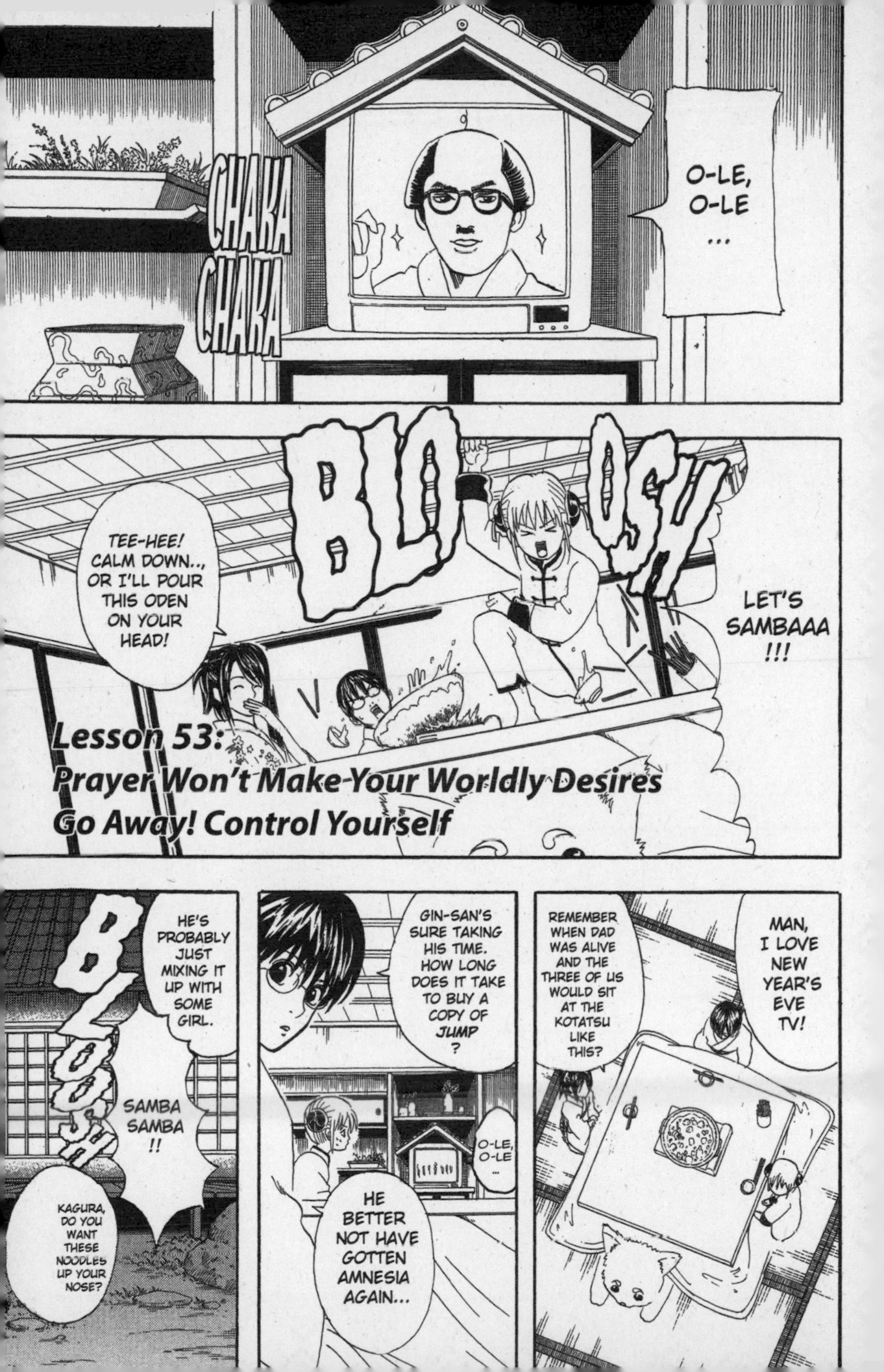
O-LE, O-LE ...
CHAKA CHAKA
LET'S SAMBAAA !!!
BLO-OSH
TEE-HEE! CALM DOWN.., OR I'LL POUR THIS ODEN ON YOUR HEAD!
Lesson 53: Prayer Won't Make Your Worldly Desires Go Away! Control Yourself
MAN, I LOVE NEW YEAR'S EVE TV!
REMEMBER WHEN DAD WAS ALIVE AND THE THREE OF US WOULD SIT AT THE KOTATSU LIKE THIS?
GIN-SAN'S SURE TAKING HIS TIME. HOW LONG DOES IT TAKE TO BUY A COPY OF JUMP ?
O-LE, O-LE ...
HE BETTER NOT HAVE GOTTEN AMNESIA AGAIN...
HE'S PROBABLY JUST MIXING IT UP WITH SOME GIRL.
BLOOSH
SAMBA SAMBA !!
KAGURA, DO YOU WANT THESE NOODLES UP YOUR NOSE?

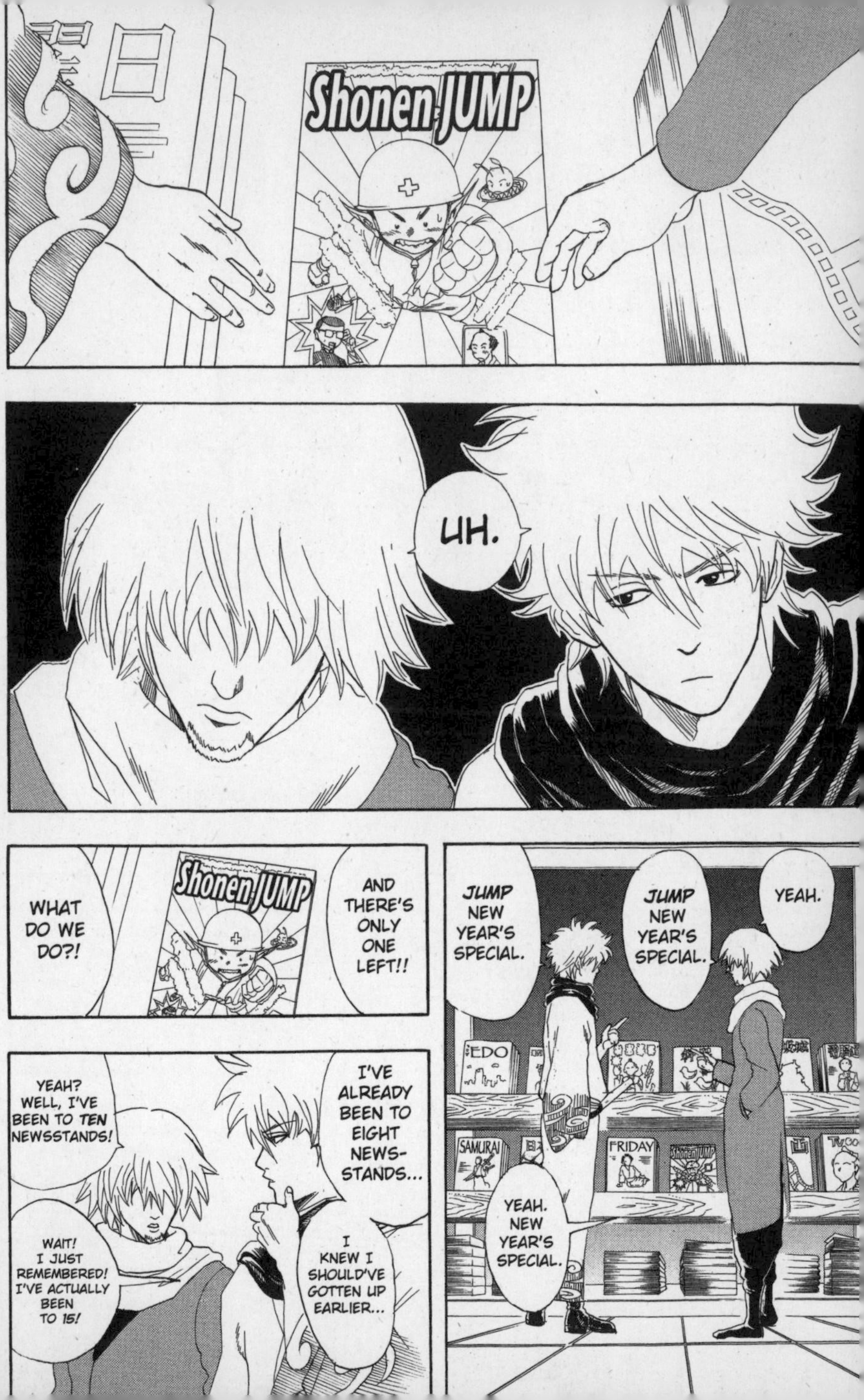
Shonen JUMP
UH.
YEAH.
JUMP NEW YEAR'S SPECIAL.
JUMP NEW YEAR'S SPECIAL.
YEAH. NEW YEAR'S SPECIAL.
AND THERE'S ONLY ONE LEFT!!
WHAT DO WE DO?!
I'VE ALREADY BEEN TO EIGHT NEWS-STANDS...
YEAH? WELL, I'VE BEEN TO *TEN* NEWSSTANDS!
I KNEW I SHOULD'VE GOTTEN UP EARLIER...
WAIT! I JUST REMEMBERED! I'VE ACTUALLY BEEN TO 15!

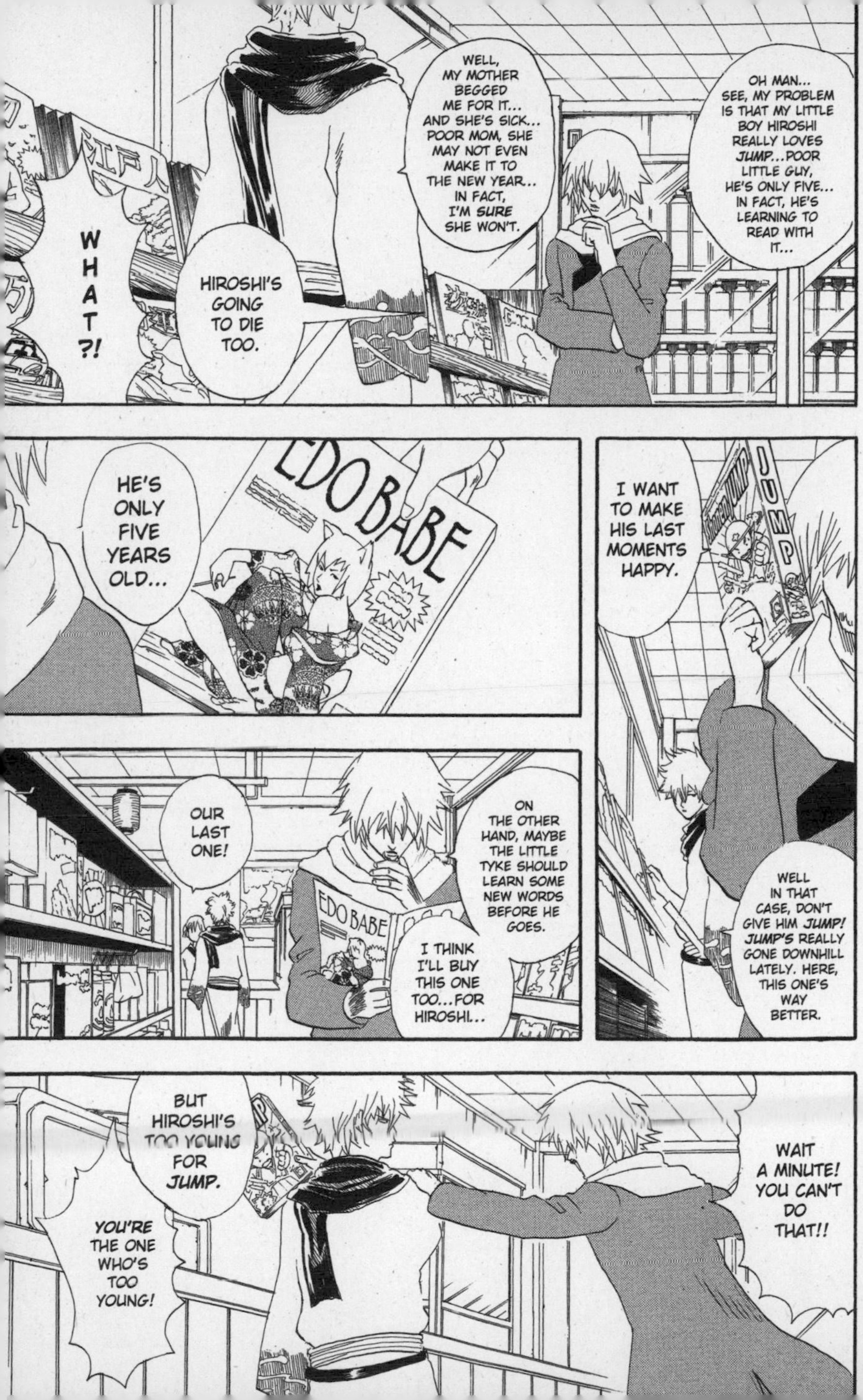
OH MAN... SEE, MY PROBLEM IS THAT MY LITTLE BOY HIROSHI REALLY LOVES *JUMP*...POOR LITTLE GUY, HE'S ONLY FIVE... IN FACT, HE'S LEARNING TO READ WITH IT...
WELL, MY MOTHER BEGGED ME FOR IT... AND SHE'S SICK... POOR MOM, SHE MAY NOT EVEN MAKE IT TO THE NEW YEAR... IN FACT, I'M *SURE* SHE WON'T.
HIROSHI'S GOING TO DIE TOO.
WHAT?!
JUMP
I WANT TO MAKE HIS LAST MOMENTS HAPPY.
WELL IN THAT CASE, DON'T GIVE HIM *JUMP*! *JUMP'S* REALLY GONE DOWNHILL LATELY. HERE, THIS ONE'S WAY BETTER.
EDO BABE
HE'S ONLY FIVE YEARS OLD...
ON THE OTHER HAND, MAYBE THE LITTLE TYKE SHOULD LEARN SOME NEW WORDS BEFORE HE GOES.
OUR LAST ONE!
EDO BABE
I THINK I'LL BUY THIS ONE TOO...FOR HIROSHI...
WAIT A MINUTE! YOU CAN'T DO THAT!!
BUT HIROSHI'S TOO YOUNG FOR *JUMP*.
YOU'RE THE ONE WHO'S TOO YOUNG!

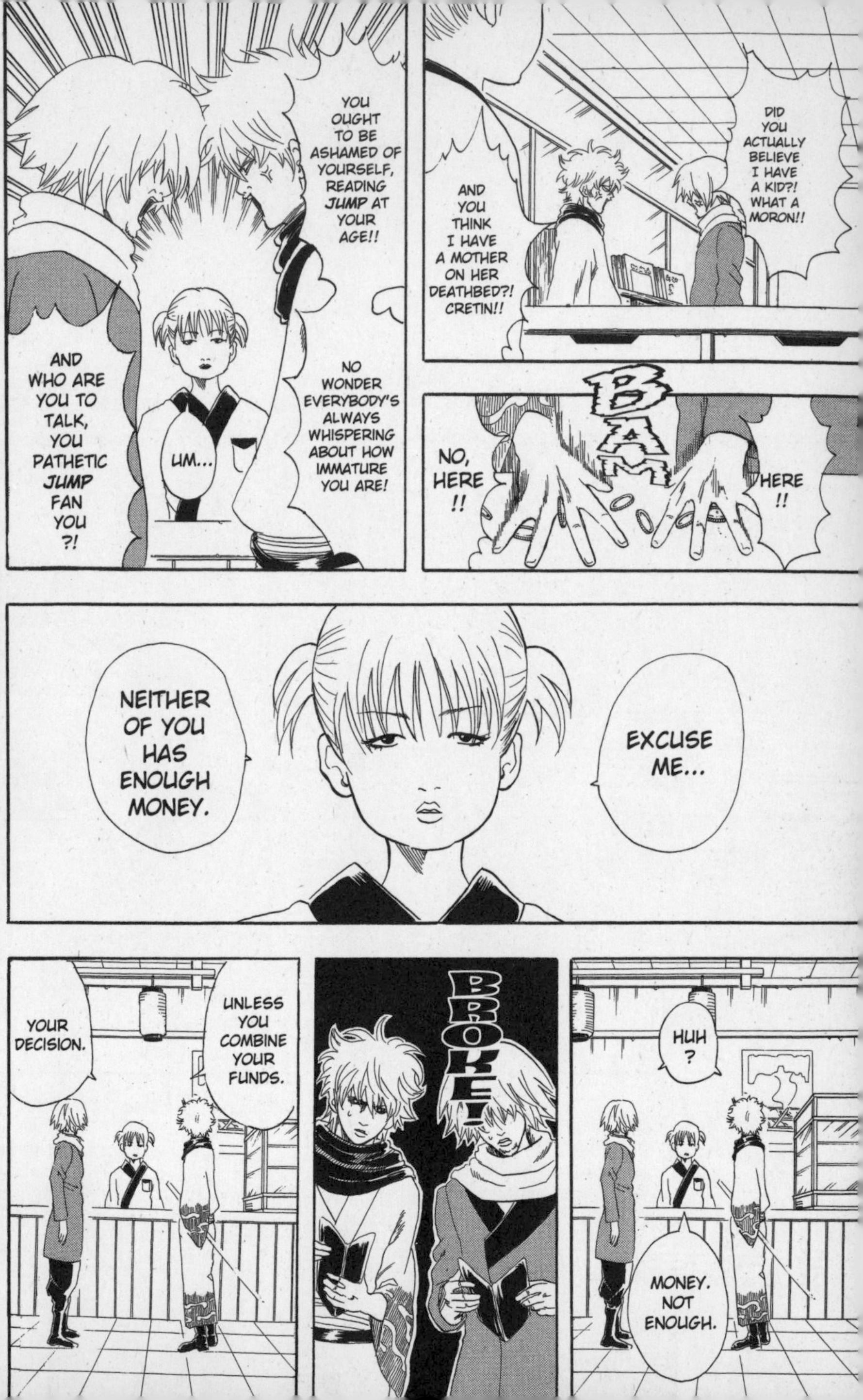
DID YOU ACTUALLY BELIEVE I HAVE A KID?! WHAT A MORON!!
AND YOU THINK I HAVE A MOTHER ON HER DEATHBED?! CRETIN!!
BAM
HERE !!
NO, HERE !!
YOU OUGHT TO BE ASHAMED OF YOURSELF, READING JUMP AT YOUR AGE!!
NO WONDER EVERYBODY'S ALWAYS WHISPERING ABOUT HOW IMMATURE YOU ARE!
AND WHO ARE YOU TO TALK, YOU PATHETIC JUMP FAN YOU ?!
UM...
EXCUSE ME...
NEITHER OF YOU HAS ENOUGH MONEY.
HUH ?
MONEY. NOT ENOUGH.
BROKE!
UNLESS YOU COMBINE YOUR FUNDS.
YOUR DECISION.

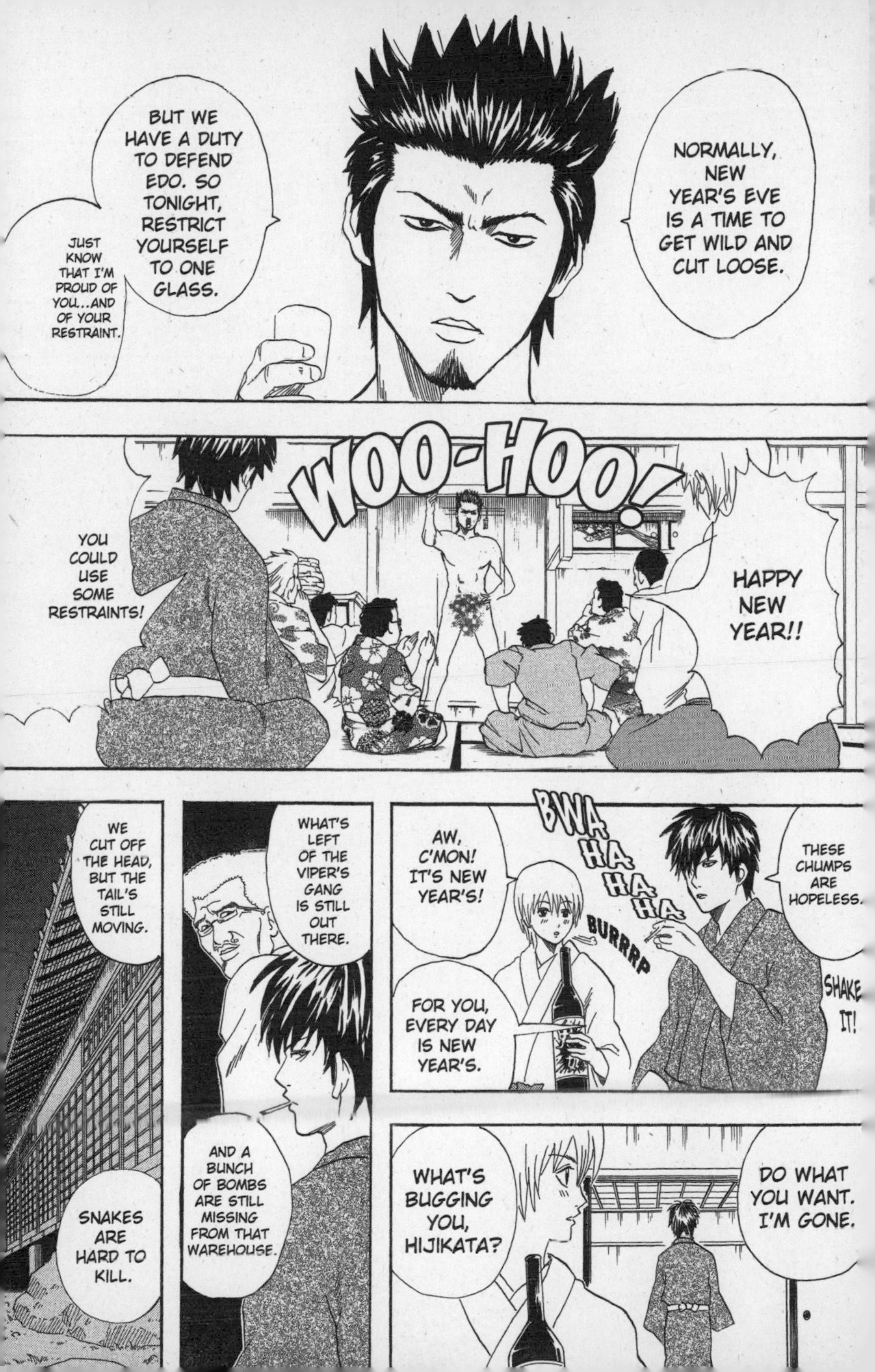
NORMALLY, NEW YEAR'S EVE IS A TIME TO GET WILD AND CUT LOOSE.
BUT WE HAVE A DUTY TO DEFEND EDO. SO TONIGHT, RESTRICT YOURSELF TO ONE GLASS.
JUST KNOW THAT I'M PROUD OF YOU...AND OF YOUR RESTRAINT.
WOO-HOO!
HAPPY NEW YEAR!!
YOU COULD USE SOME RESTRAINTS!
THESE CHUMPS ARE HOPELESS.
SHAKE IT!
BWA HA HA HA
AW, C'MON! IT'S NEW YEAR'S!
BURRRP
FOR YOU, EVERY DAY IS NEW YEAR'S.
DO WHAT YOU WANT. I'M GONE.
WHAT'S BUGGING YOU, HIJIKATA?
WHAT'S LEFT OF THE VIPER'S GANG IS STILL OUT THERE.
AND A BUNCH OF BOMBS ARE STILL MISSING FROM THAT WAREHOUSE.
WE CUT OFF THE HEAD, BUT THE TAIL'S STILL MOVING.
SNAKES ARE HARD TO KILL.

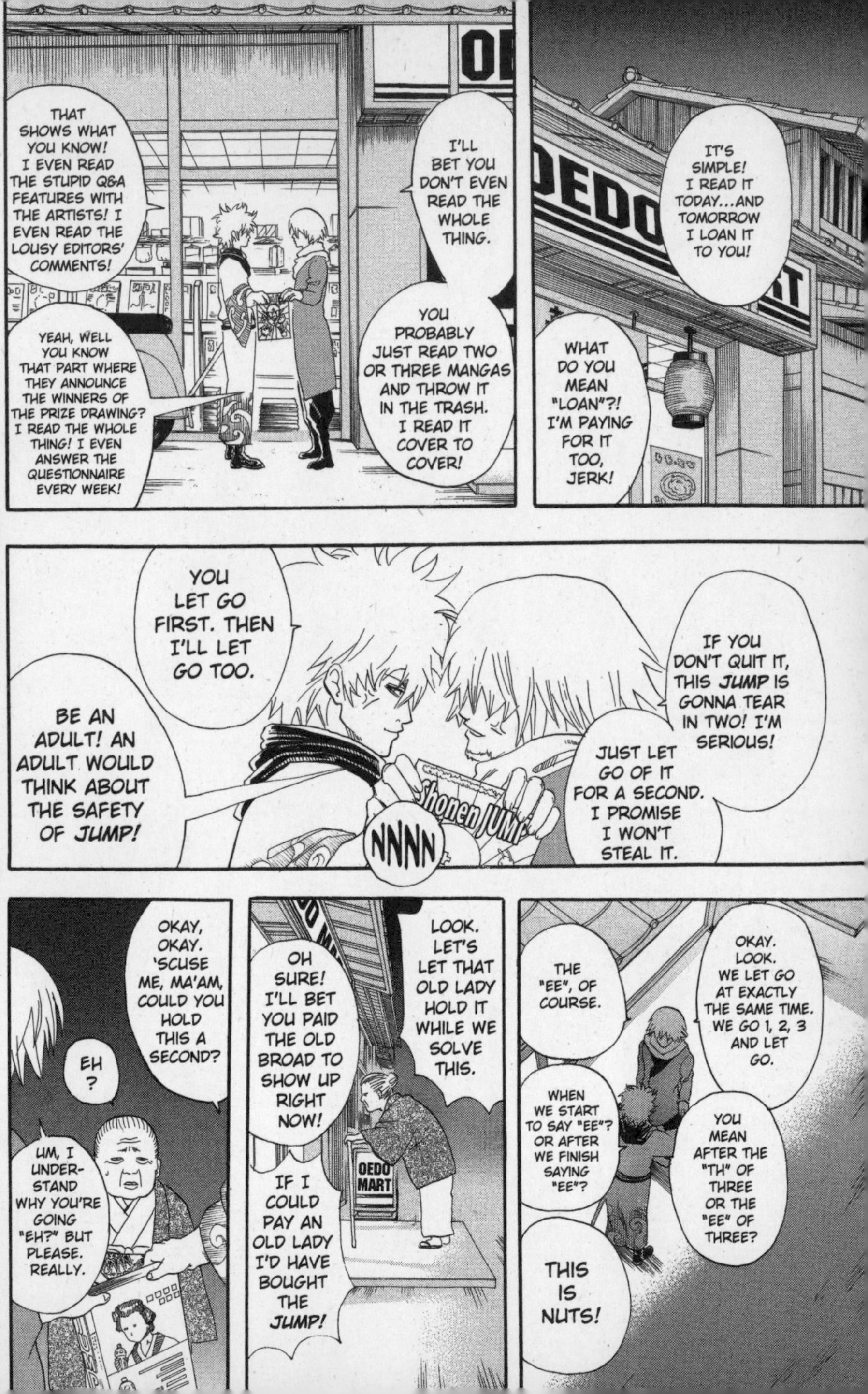
IT'S SIMPLE! I READ IT TODAY...AND TOMORROW I LOAN IT TO YOU!
WHAT DO YOU MEAN "LOAN"?! I'M PAYING FOR IT TOO, JERK!
I'LL BET YOU DON'T EVEN READ THE WHOLE THING.
YOU PROBABLY JUST READ TWO OR THREE MANGAS AND THROW IT IN THE TRASH. I READ IT COVER TO COVER!
THAT SHOWS WHAT YOU KNOW! I EVEN READ THE STUPID Q&A FEATURES WITH THE ARTISTS! I EVEN READ THE LOUSY EDITORS' COMMENTS!
YEAH, WELL YOU KNOW THAT PART WHERE THEY ANNOUNCE THE WINNERS OF THE PRIZE DRAWING? I READ THE WHOLE THING! I EVEN ANSWER THE QUESTIONNAIRE EVERY WEEK!
IF YOU DON'T QUIT IT, THIS *JUMP* IS GONNA TEAR IN TWO! I'M SERIOUS!
JUST LET GO OF IT FOR A SECOND. I PROMISE I WON'T STEAL IT.
YOU LET GO FIRST. THEN I'LL LET GO TOO.
BE AN ADULT! AN ADULT WOULD THINK ABOUT THE SAFETY OF *JUMP*!
Shonen JUMP
NNNN
OKAY. LOOK. WE LET GO AT EXACTLY THE SAME TIME. WE GO 1, 2, 3 AND LET GO.
YOU MEAN AFTER THE "TH" OF THREE OR THE "EE" OF THREE?
THE "EE", OF COURSE.
WHEN WE START TO SAY "EE"? OR AFTER WE FINISH SAYING "EE"?
THIS IS NUTS!
LOOK. LET'S LET THAT OLD LADY HOLD IT WHILE WE SOLVE THIS.
OH SURE! I'LL BET YOU PAID THE OLD BROAD TO SHOW UP RIGHT NOW!
OEDO MART
IF I COULD PAY AN OLD LADY I'D HAVE BOUGHT THE *JUMP*!
OKAY, OKAY. 'SCUSE ME, MA'AM, COULD YOU HOLD THIS A SECOND?
EH ?
UM, I UNDER-STAND WHY YOU'RE GOING "EH?" BUT PLEASE. REALLY.

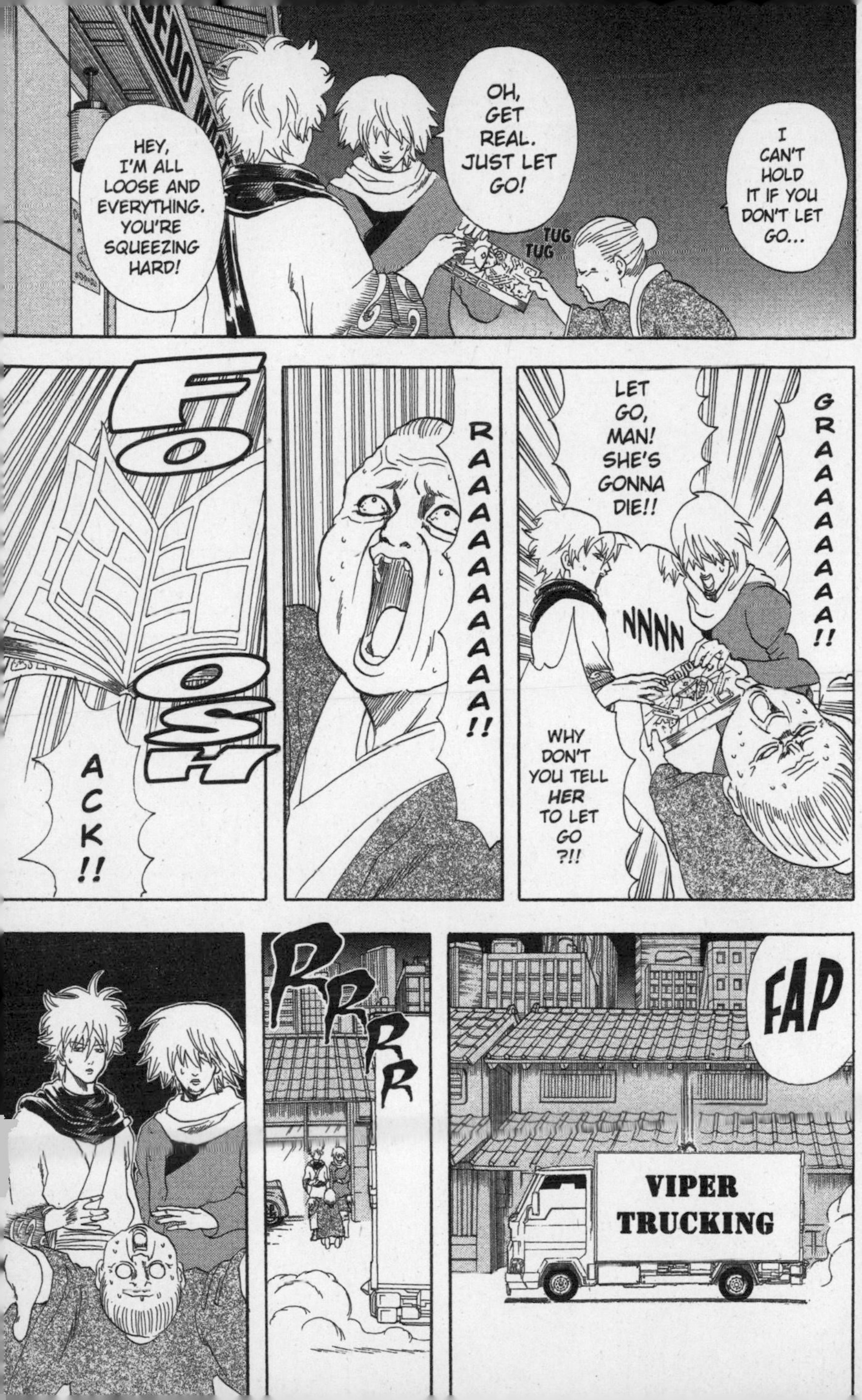

I CAN'T HOLD IT IF YOU DON'T LET GO...
OH, GET REAL. JUST LET GO!
TUG TUG
HEY, I'M ALL LOOSE AND EVERYTHING. YOU'RE SQUEEZING HARD!
GRAAAAAAAAA!!
LET GO, MAN! SHE'S GONNA DIE!!
NNNN
WHY DON'T YOU TELL HER TO LET GO?!!
RAAAAAAAAAAAA!!
FOOSH
ACK!!
FAP
VIPER TRUCKING
RRRR

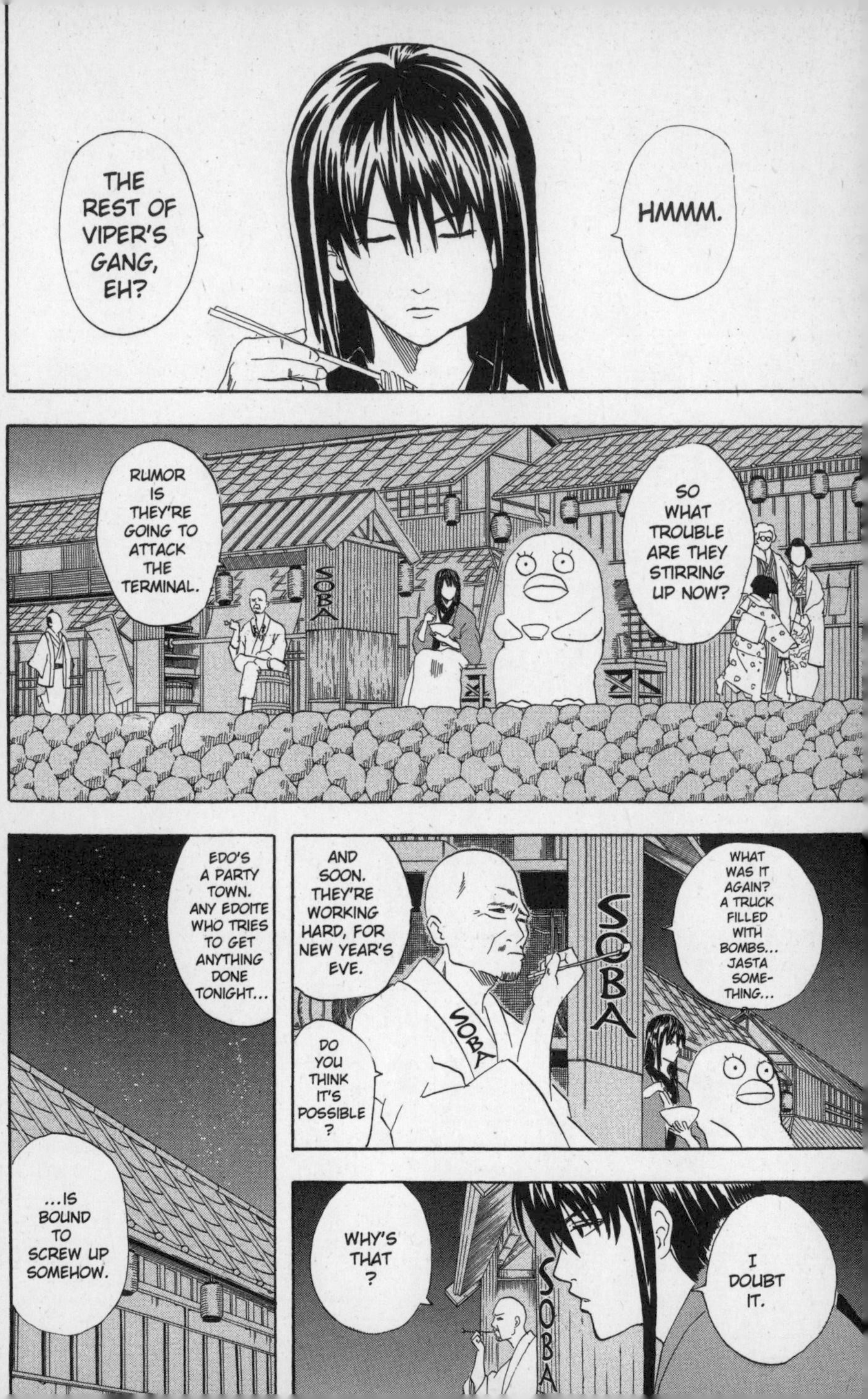
HMMM.
THE REST OF VIPER'S GANG, EH?
SO WHAT TROUBLE ARE THEY STIRRING UP NOW?
SOBA
RUMOR IS THEY'RE GOING TO ATTACK THE TERMINAL.
WHAT WAS IT AGAIN? A TRUCK FILLED WITH BOMBS... JASTA SOME-THING...
SOBA
AND SOON. THEY'RE WORKING HARD, FOR NEW YEAR'S EVE.
SOBA
DO YOU THINK IT'S POSSIBLE?
I DOUBT IT.
SOBA
WHY'S THAT?
EDO'S A PARTY TOWN. ANY EDOITE WHO TRIES TO GET ANYTHING DONE TONIGHT...
...IS BOUND TO SCREW UP SOMEHOW.

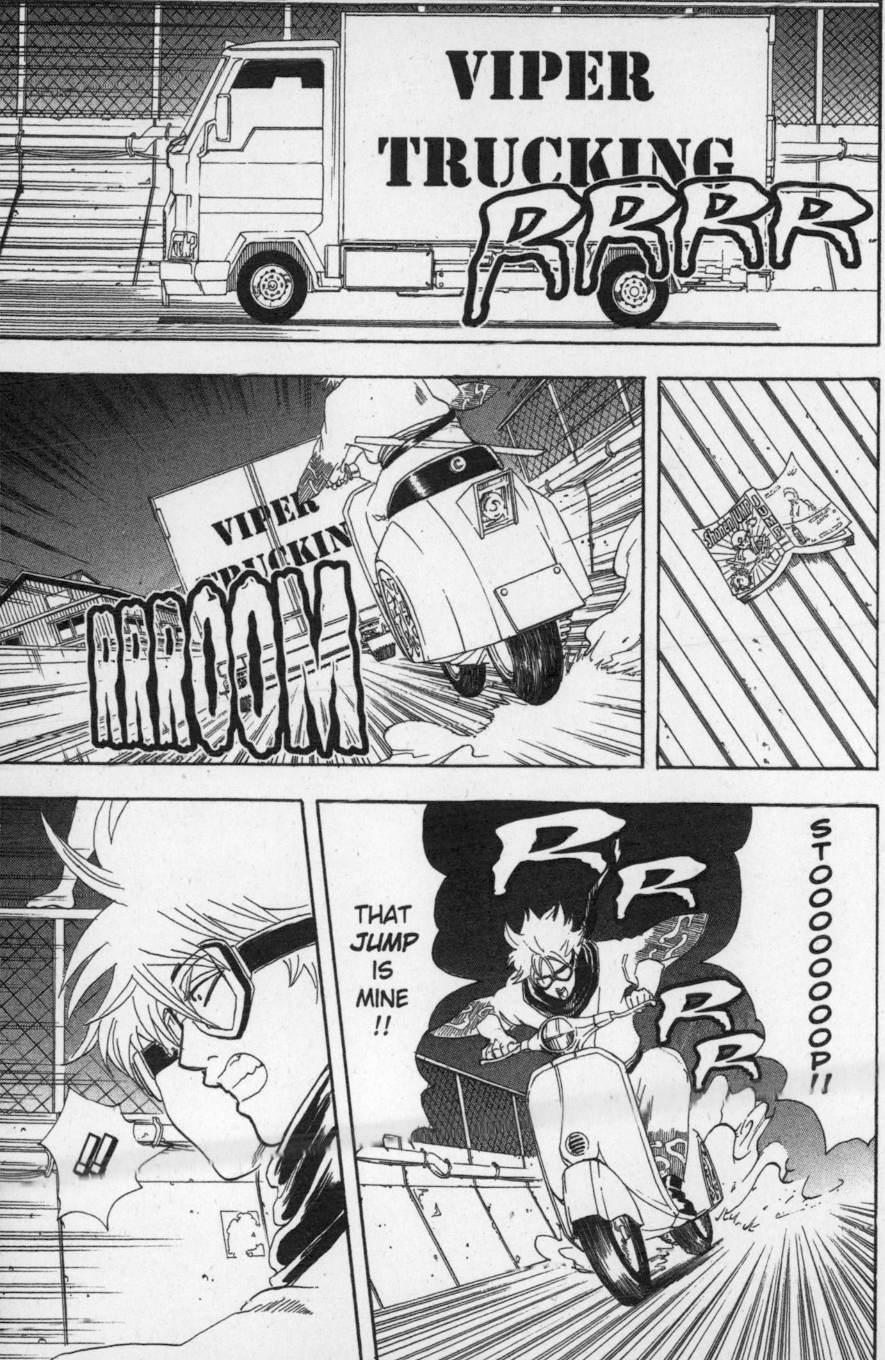
VIPER
TRUCKING
RRRR
VIPER
TRUCKIN
ARROOM
STOOOOOOOOP!!
THAT JUMP IS MINE!!
RRRR
!!

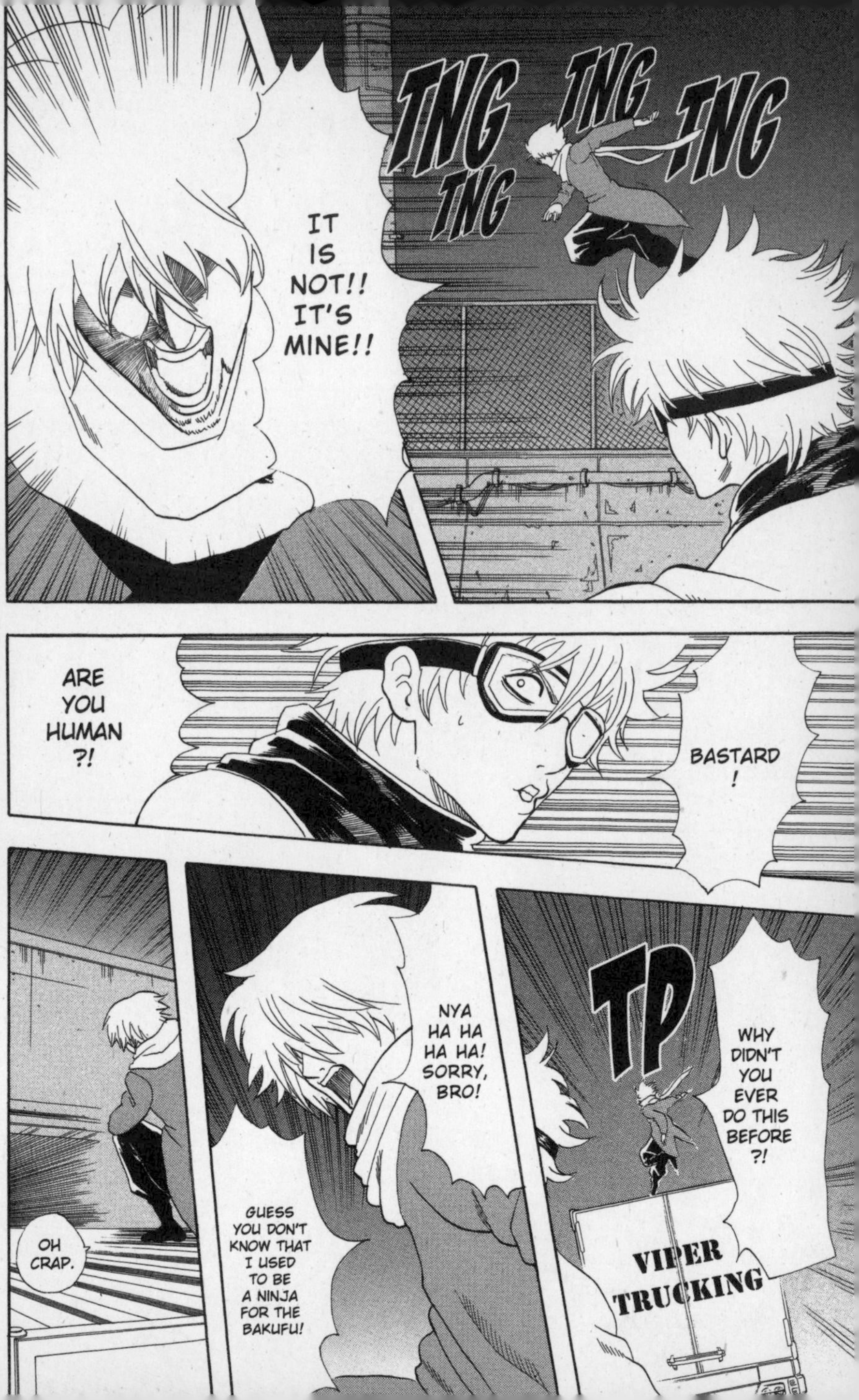
TNG TNG TNG TNG
IT IS NOT!! IT'S MINE!!
BASTARD!
ARE YOU HUMAN?!
TP
WHY DIDN'T YOU EVER DO THIS BEFORE?!
VIPER TRUCKING
NYA HA HA HA HA! SORRY, BRO!
GUESS YOU DON'T KNOW THAT I USED TO BE A NINJA FOR THE BAKUFU!
OH CRAP.

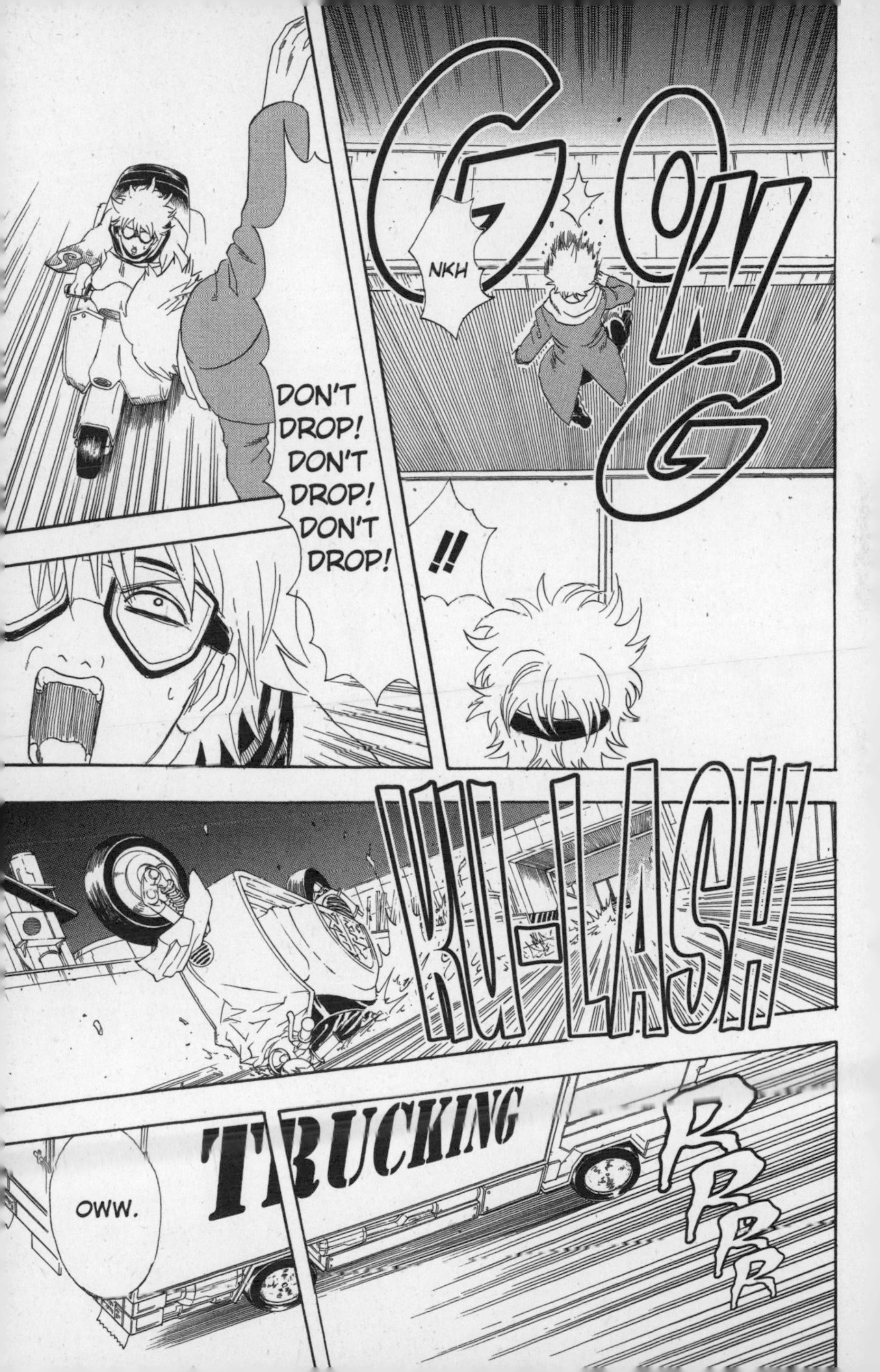
GOWNG
NKH
DON'T DROP! DON'T DROP! DON'T DROP!
!!
KU-LASH
TRUCKING
BRRR
OWW.

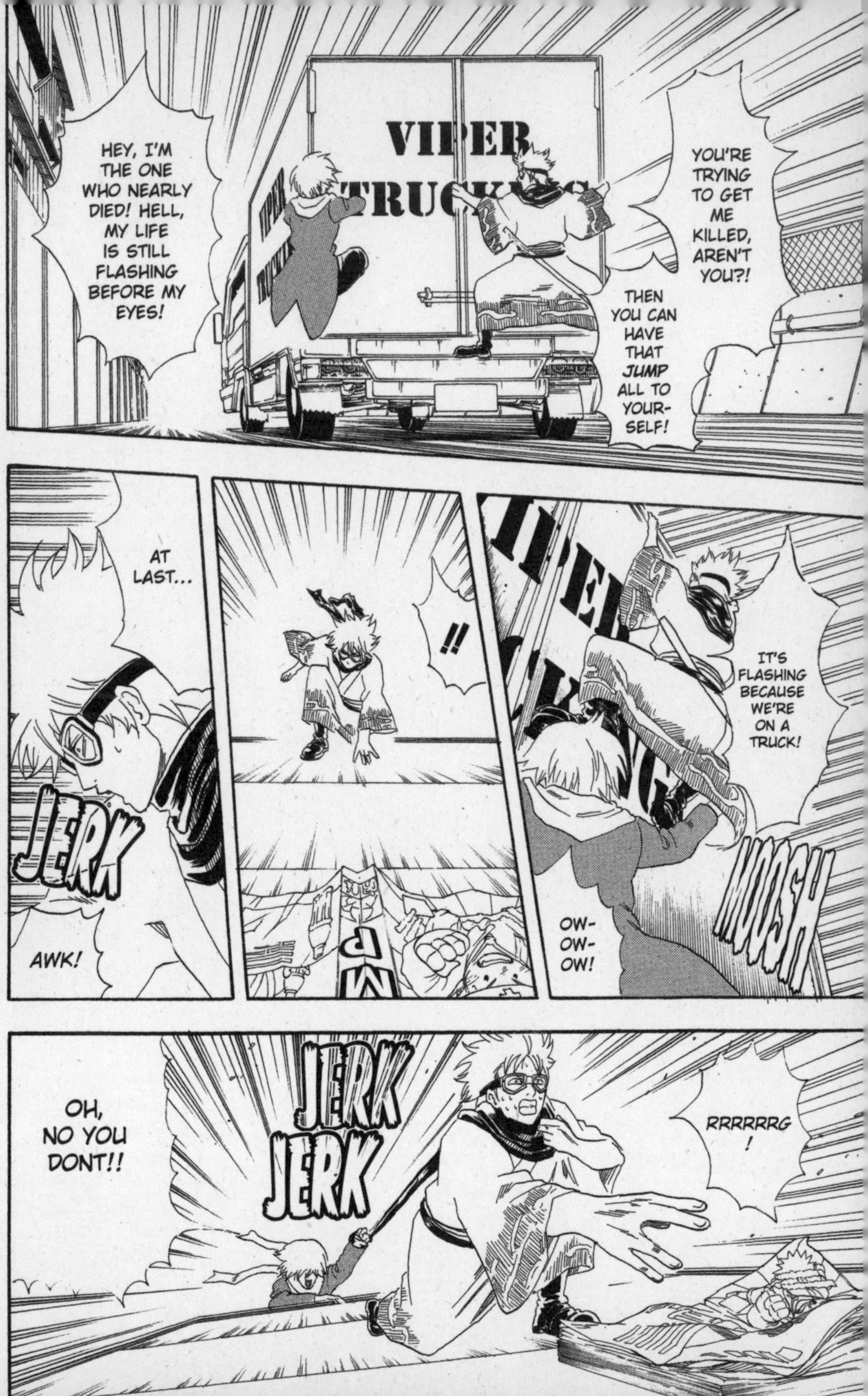
YOU'RE TRYING TO GET ME KILLED, AREN'T YOU?!
THEN YOU CAN HAVE THAT JUMP ALL TO YOURSELF!
HEY, I'M THE ONE WHO NEARLY DIED! HELL, MY LIFE IS STILL FLASHING BEFORE MY EYES!
IT'S FLASHING BECAUSE WE'RE ON A TRUCK!
WOOSH
OW-OW-OW!
!!
AT LAST...
JERK
AWK!
RRRRRRG!
JERK JERK
OH, NO YOU DONT!!

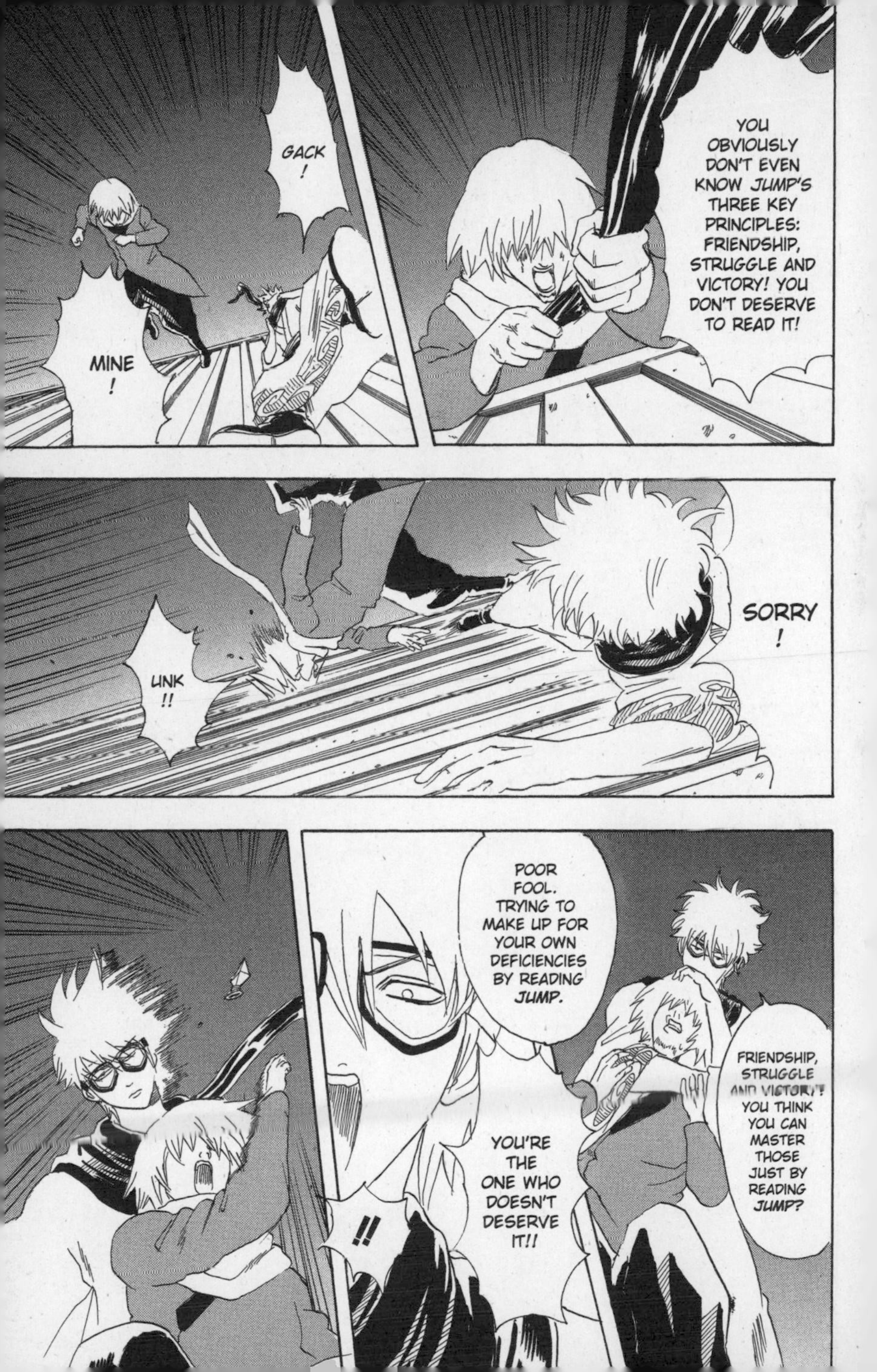
YOU OBVIOUSLY DON'T EVEN KNOW JUMP'S THREE KEY PRINCIPLES: FRIENDSHIP, STRUGGLE AND VICTORY! YOU DON'T DESERVE TO READ IT!
GACK!
MINE!
SORRY!
UNK!!
POOR FOOL. TRYING TO MAKE UP FOR YOUR OWN DEFICIENCIES BY READING JUMP.
FRIENDSHIP, STRUGGLE AND VICTORY!? YOU THINK YOU CAN MASTER THOSE JUST BY READING JUMP?
YOU'RE THE ONE WHO DOESN'T DESERVE IT!!
!!

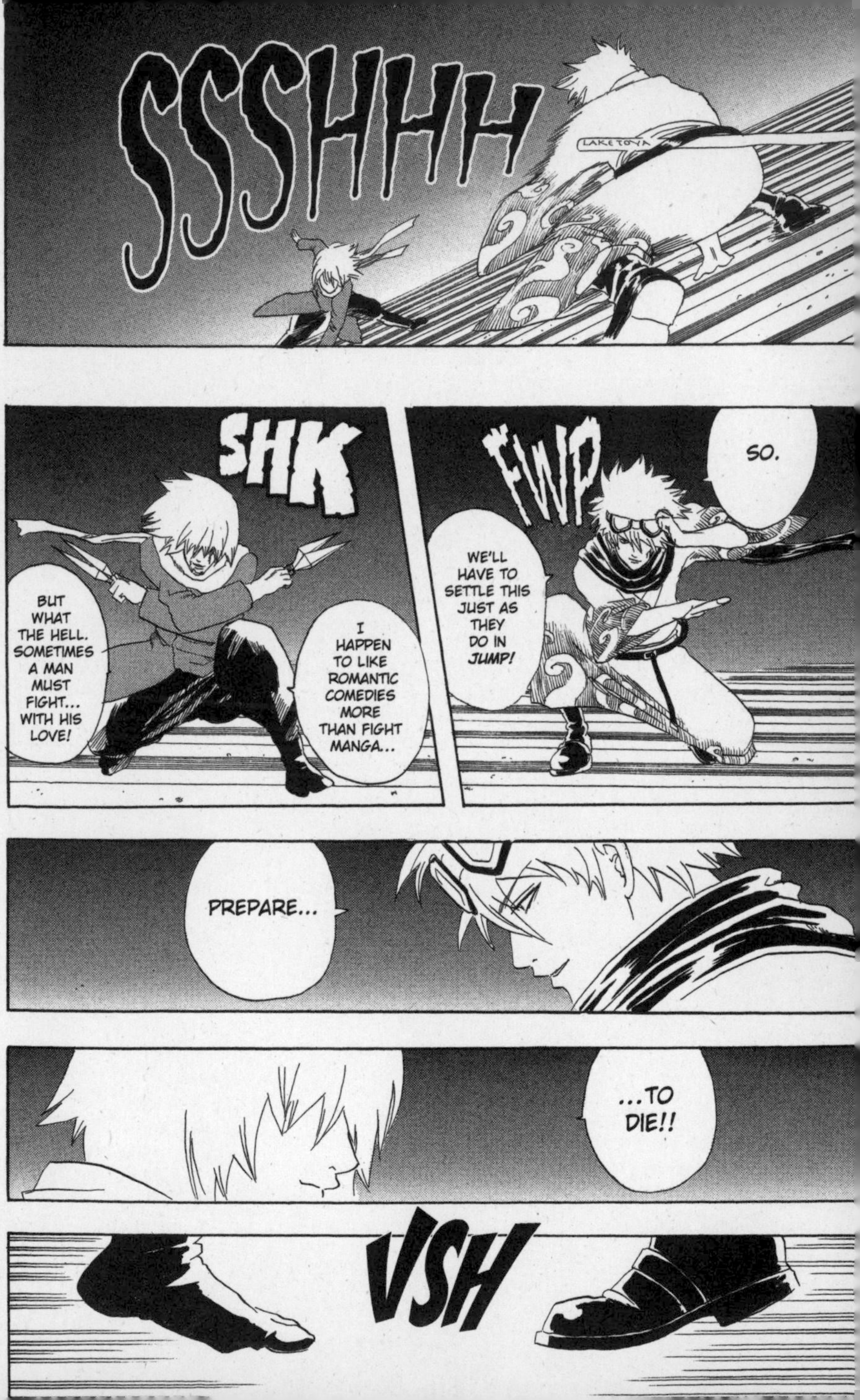
SSSHHH
LAKETOYA
SO.
FWP
WE'LL HAVE TO SETTLE THIS JUST AS THEY DO IN JUMP!
SHK
I HAPPEN TO LIKE ROMANTIC COMEDIES MORE THAN FIGHT MANGA...
BUT WHAT THE HELL. SOMETIMES A MAN MUST FIGHT... WITH HIS LOVE!
PREPARE...
...TO DIE!!
VSH

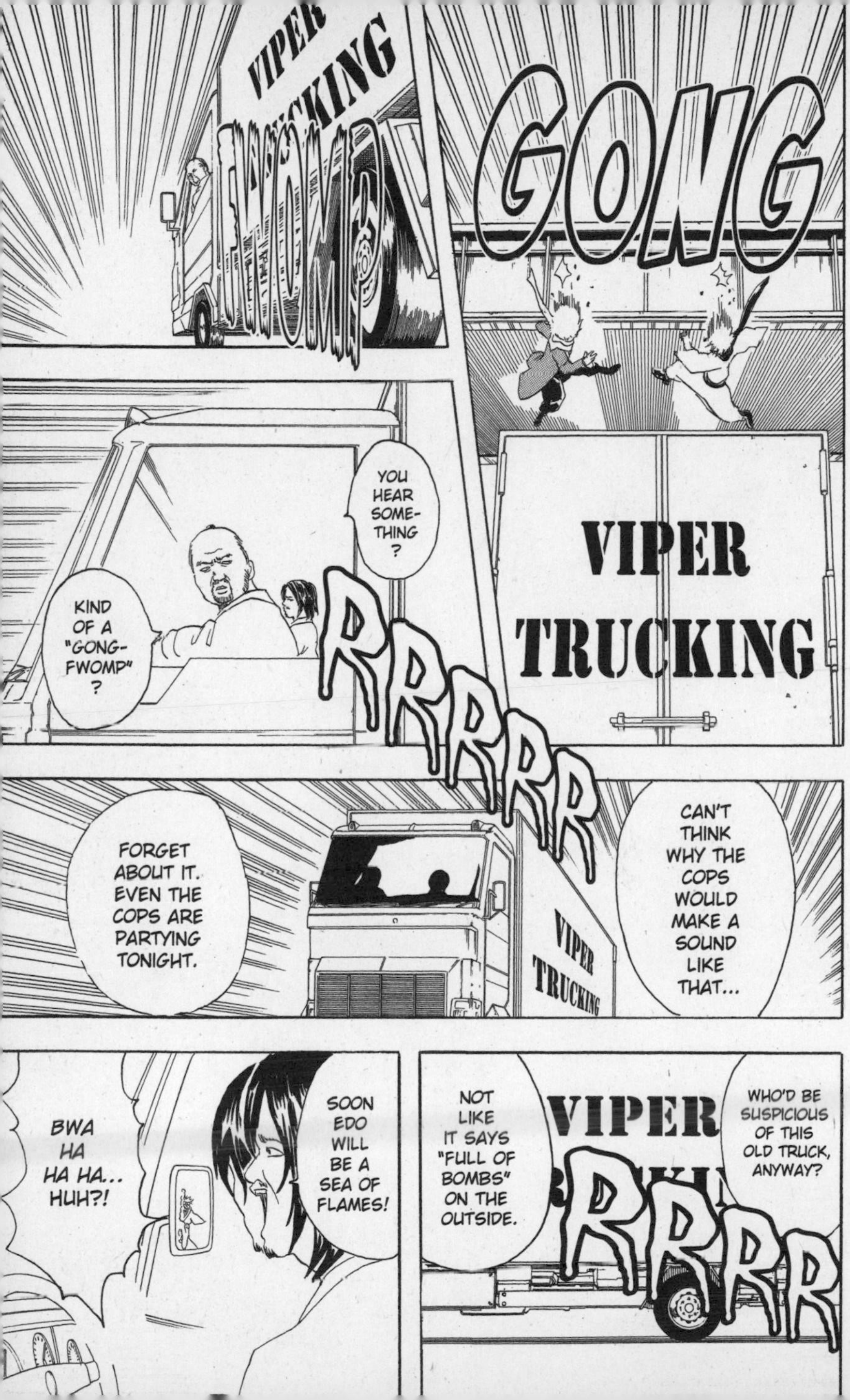
GONG
VIPER TRUCKING
VIPER TRUCKING
FWOMP
YOU HEAR SOMETHING?
KIND OF A "GONG-FWOMP"?
RRRRR
CAN'T THINK WHY THE COPS WOULD MAKE A SOUND LIKE THAT...
FORGET ABOUT IT. EVEN THE COPS ARE PARTYING TONIGHT.
VIPER TRUCKING
WHO'D BE SUSPICIOUS OF THIS OLD TRUCK, ANYWAY?
NOT LIKE IT SAYS "FULL OF BOMBS" ON THE OUTSIDE.
VIPER
RRRR
SOON EDO WILL BE A SEA OF FLAMES!
BWA HA HA HA... HUH?!

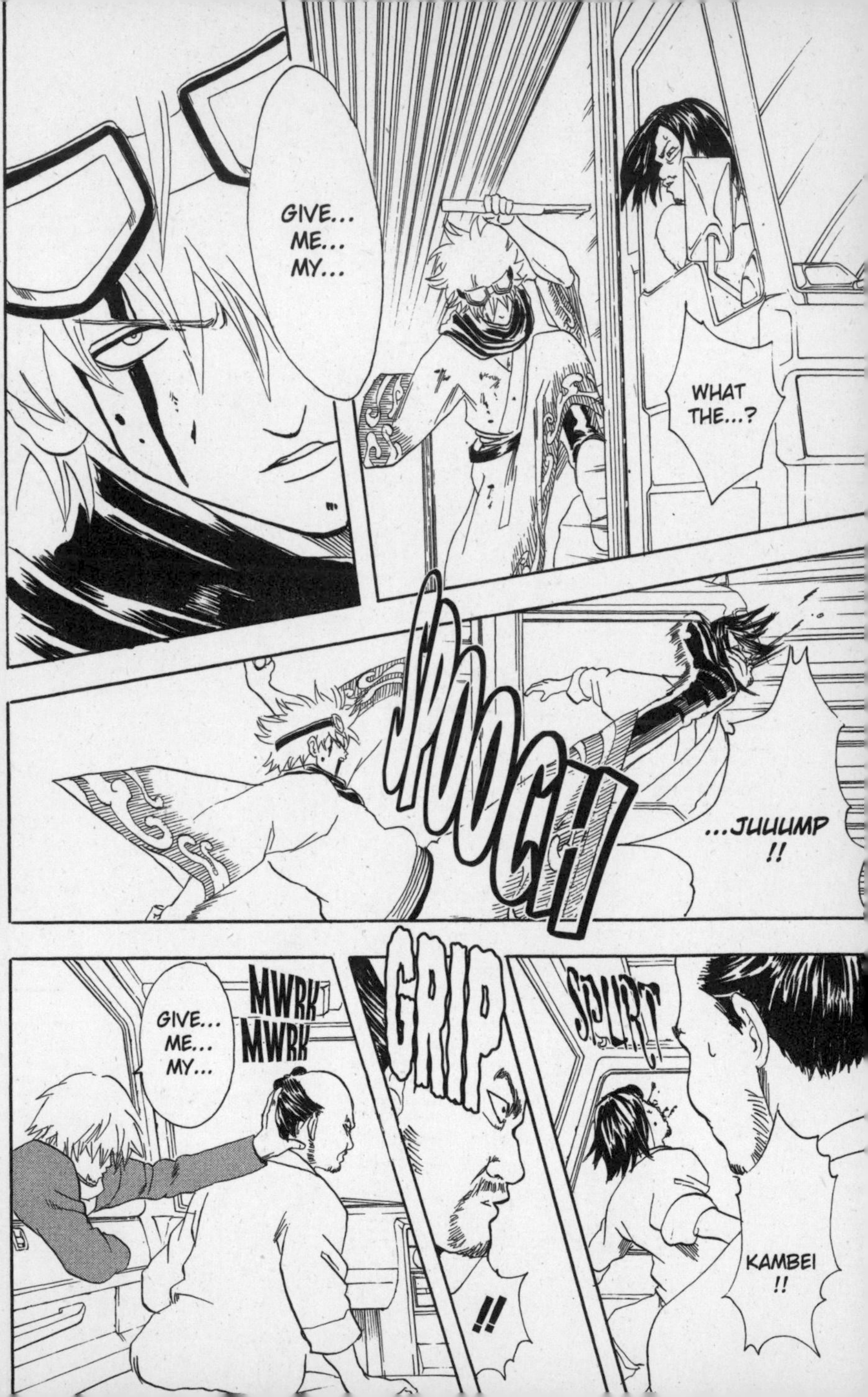
WHAT THE...?
GIVE... ME... MY...
SPLOOCH
...JUUUMP !!
SPLURT
KAMBEI !!
GRIP
!!
GIVE... ME... MY...
MWRK MWRK

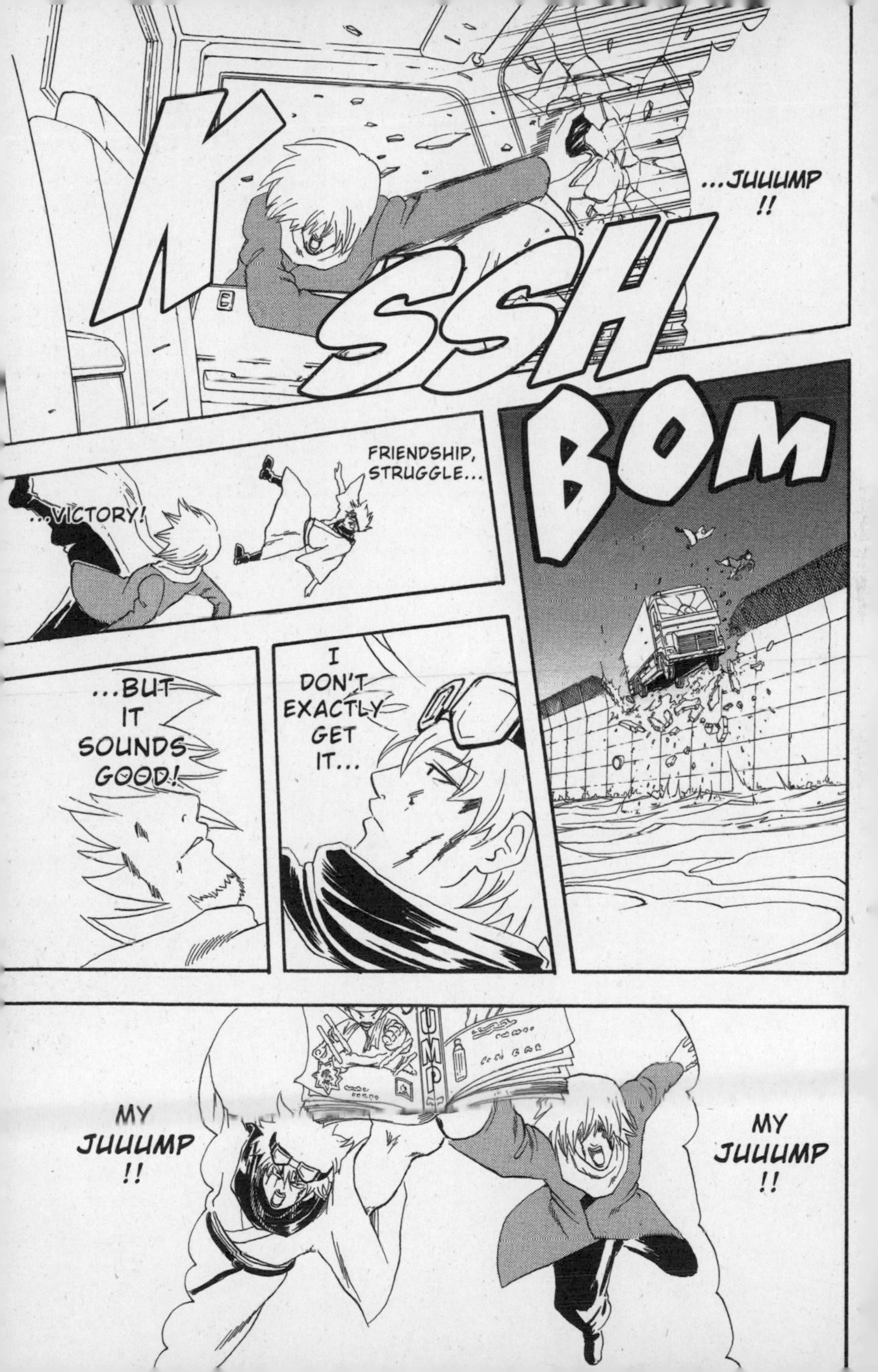

...JUUUMP !!
KSSH
BOM
FRIENDSHIP, STRUGGLE...
...VICTORY!
I DON'T EXACTLY GET IT...
...BUT IT SOUNDS GOOD!
JUMP
MY JUUUMP !!
MY JUUUMP !!

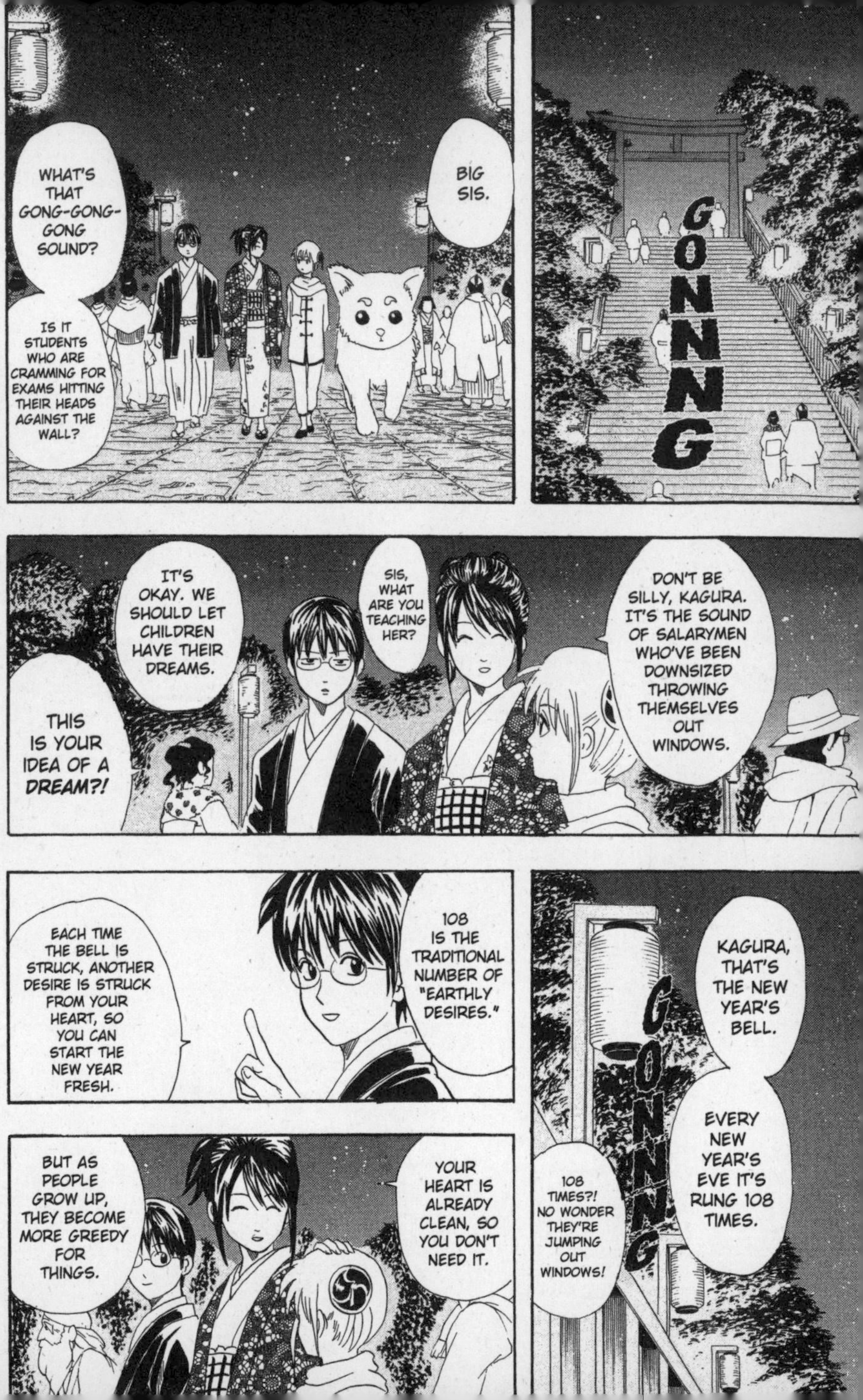
GONNG
BIG SIS.
WHAT'S THAT GONG-GONG-GONG SOUND?
IS IT STUDENTS WHO ARE CRAMMING FOR EXAMS HITTING THEIR HEADS AGAINST THE WALL?
DON'T BE SILLY, KAGURA. IT'S THE SOUND OF SALARYMEN WHO'VE BEEN DOWNSIZED THROWING THEMSELVES OUT WINDOWS.
SIS, WHAT ARE YOU TEACHING HER?
IT'S OKAY. WE SHOULD LET CHILDREN HAVE THEIR DREAMS.
THIS IS YOUR IDEA OF A DREAM?!
KAGURA, THAT'S THE NEW YEAR'S BELL.
GONNG
EVERY NEW YEAR'S EVE IT'S RUNG 108 TIMES.
108 TIMES?! NO WONDER THEY'RE JUMPING OUT WINDOWS!
108 IS THE TRADITIONAL NUMBER OF "EARTHLY DESIRES."
EACH TIME THE BELL IS STRUCK, ANOTHER DESIRE IS STRUCK FROM YOUR HEART, SO YOU CAN START THE NEW YEAR FRESH.
YOUR HEART IS ALREADY CLEAN, SO YOU DON'T NEED IT.
BUT AS PEOPLE GROW UP, THEY BECOME MORE GREEDY FOR THINGS.

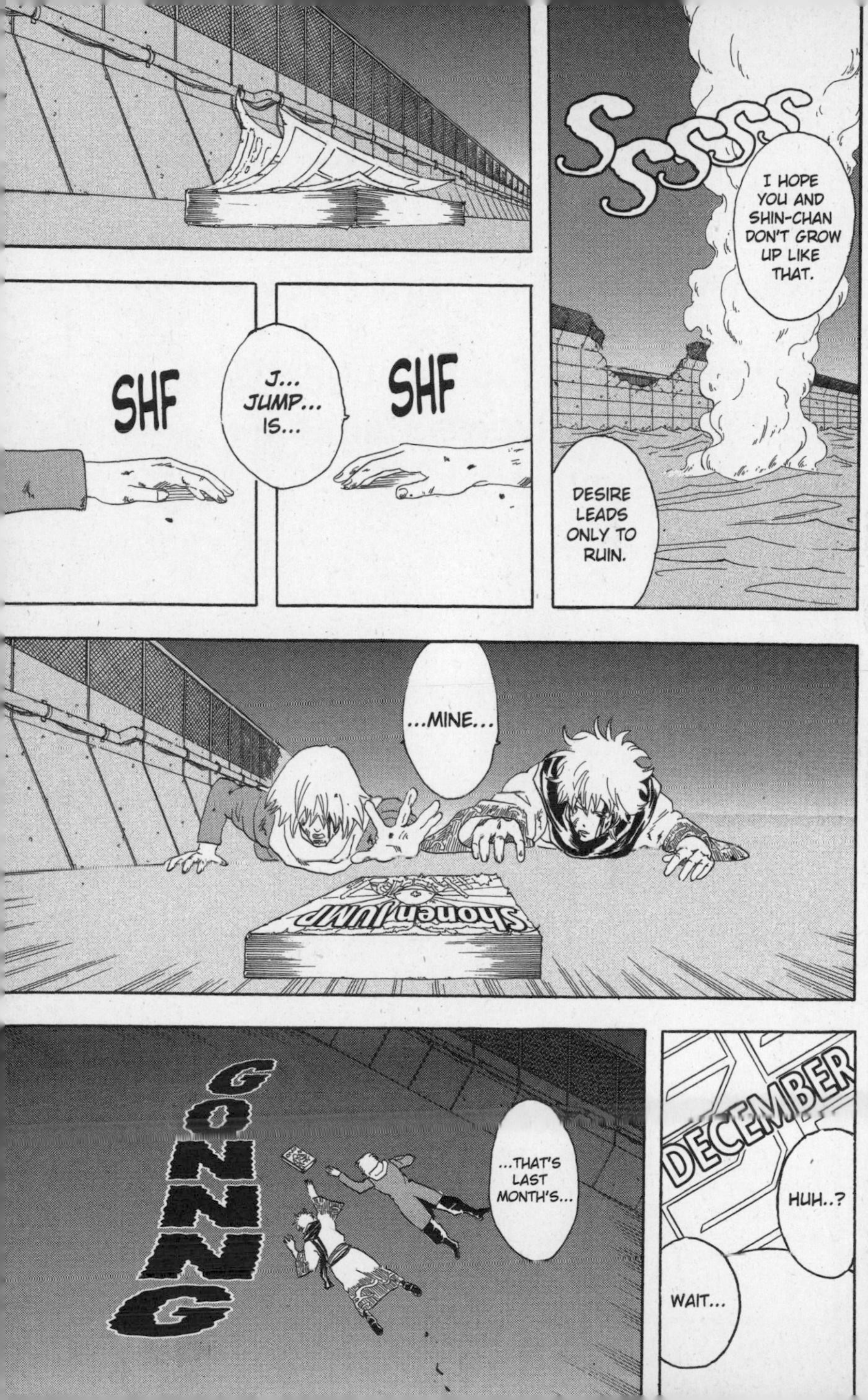
SSSSS
I HOPE YOU AND SHIN-CHAN DON'T GROW UP LIKE THAT.
DESIRE LEADS ONLY TO RUIN.
SHF
J... JUMP... IS...
SHF
...MINE...
Shonen JUMP
DECEMBER
HUH..?
WAIT...
...THAT'S LAST MONTH'S...
GONNG

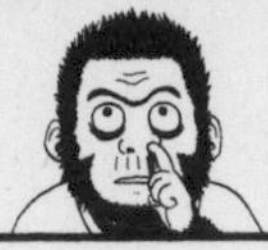

Sorachi's Q&A Corner #12

<Question from Choco-san of Aichi Prefecture>

Whenever I flip through *JUMP*, *Gin Tama* always stands out. What's your trick?

Well... First, I don't use screen-tone much, so the art is a lot whiter.

Also, I work hard at not making the drawings very good. Since everybody else draws so well, mine always stands out...

Hey! I wasn't supposed to reveal that!

(Q&A #13 is on page 110)

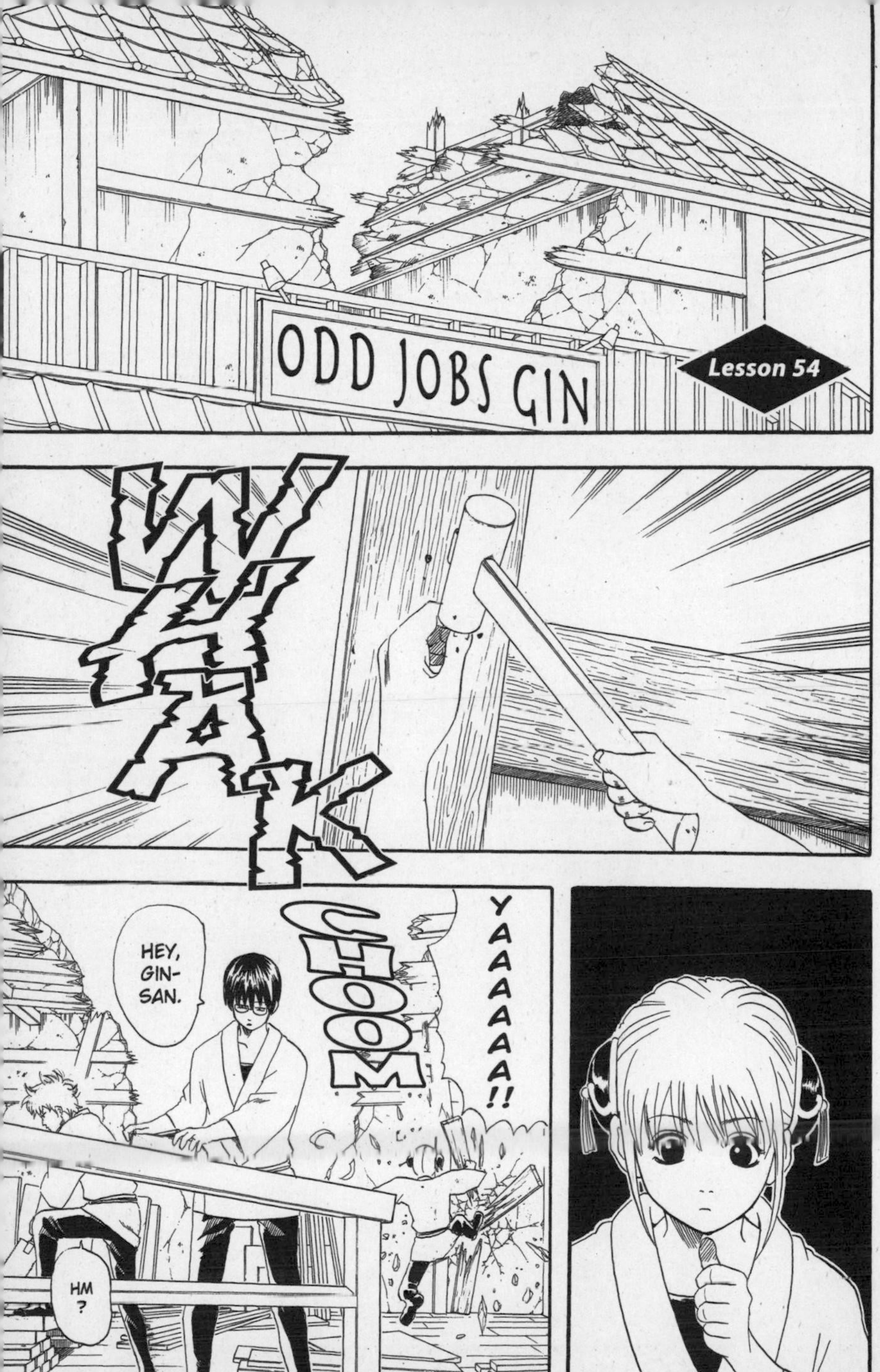
ODD JOBS GIN
Lesson 54
WHAK
YAAAAAAA!!
CHOOM
HEY, GIN-SAN.
HM?

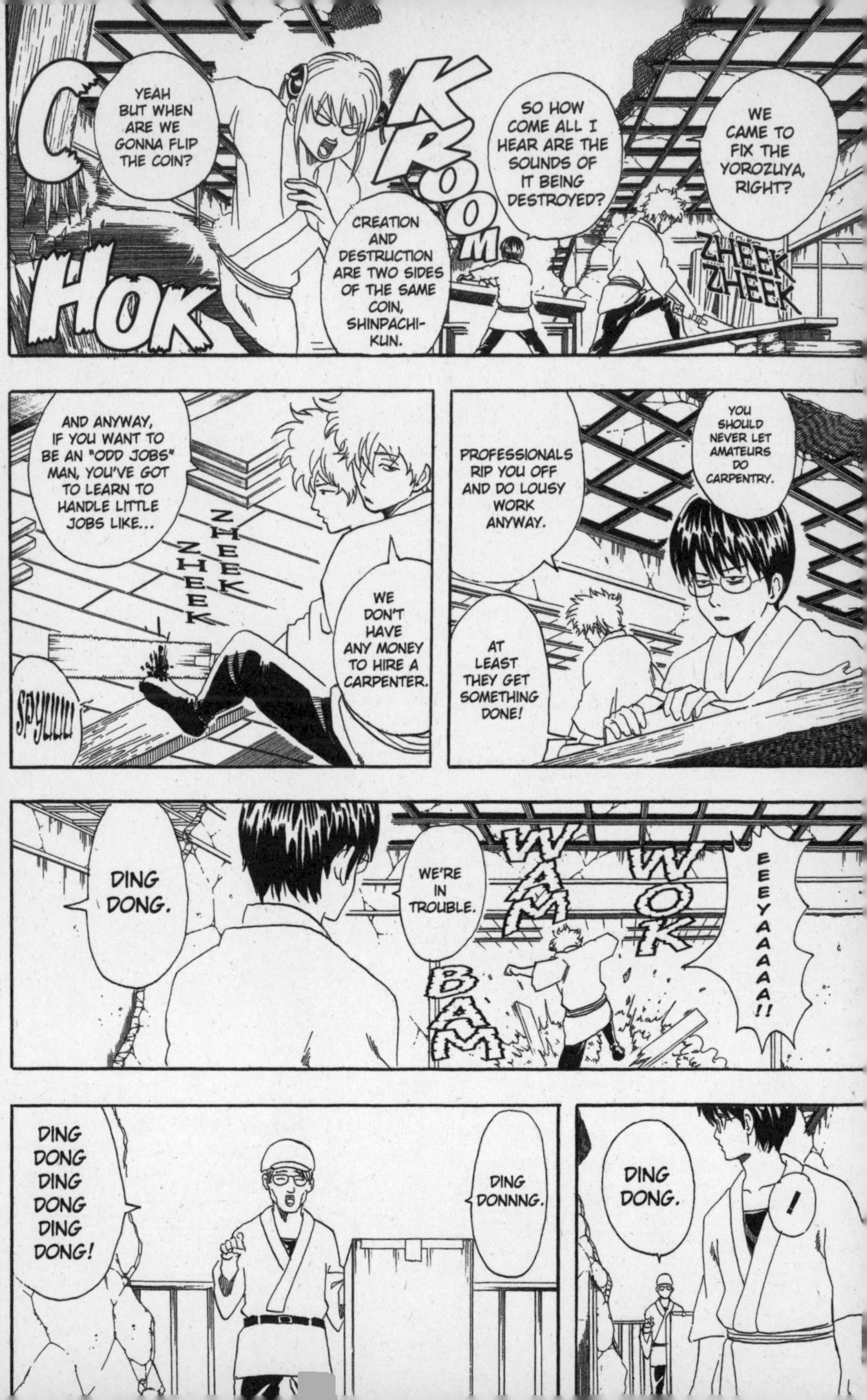
WE CAME TO FIX THE YOROZUYA, RIGHT?
ZHEEK ZHEEK
SO HOW COME ALL I HEAR ARE THE SOUNDS OF IT BEING DESTROYED?
KROOOM
CREATION AND DESTRUCTION ARE TWO SIDES OF THE SAME COIN, SHINPACHI-KUN.
YEAH BUT WHEN ARE WE GONNA FLIP THE COIN?
CHOK
YOU SHOULD NEVER LET AMATEURS DO CARPENTRY.
PROFESSIONALS RIP YOU OFF AND DO LOUSY WORK ANYWAY.
AT LEAST THEY GET SOMETHING DONE!
AND ANYWAY, IF YOU WANT TO BE AN "ODD JOBS" MAN, YOU'VE GOT TO LEARN TO HANDLE LITTLE JOBS LIKE...
WE DON'T HAVE ANY MONEY TO HIRE A CARPENTER.
ZHEEK ZHEEK
EEEYAAAAAA!!
WOK
WAM
BAM
WE'RE IN TROUBLE.
DING DONG.
!
DING DONG.
DING DONNNG.
DING DONG DING DONG DING DONG!

Lesson 54: Mistaking Someone's Name Is Rude!

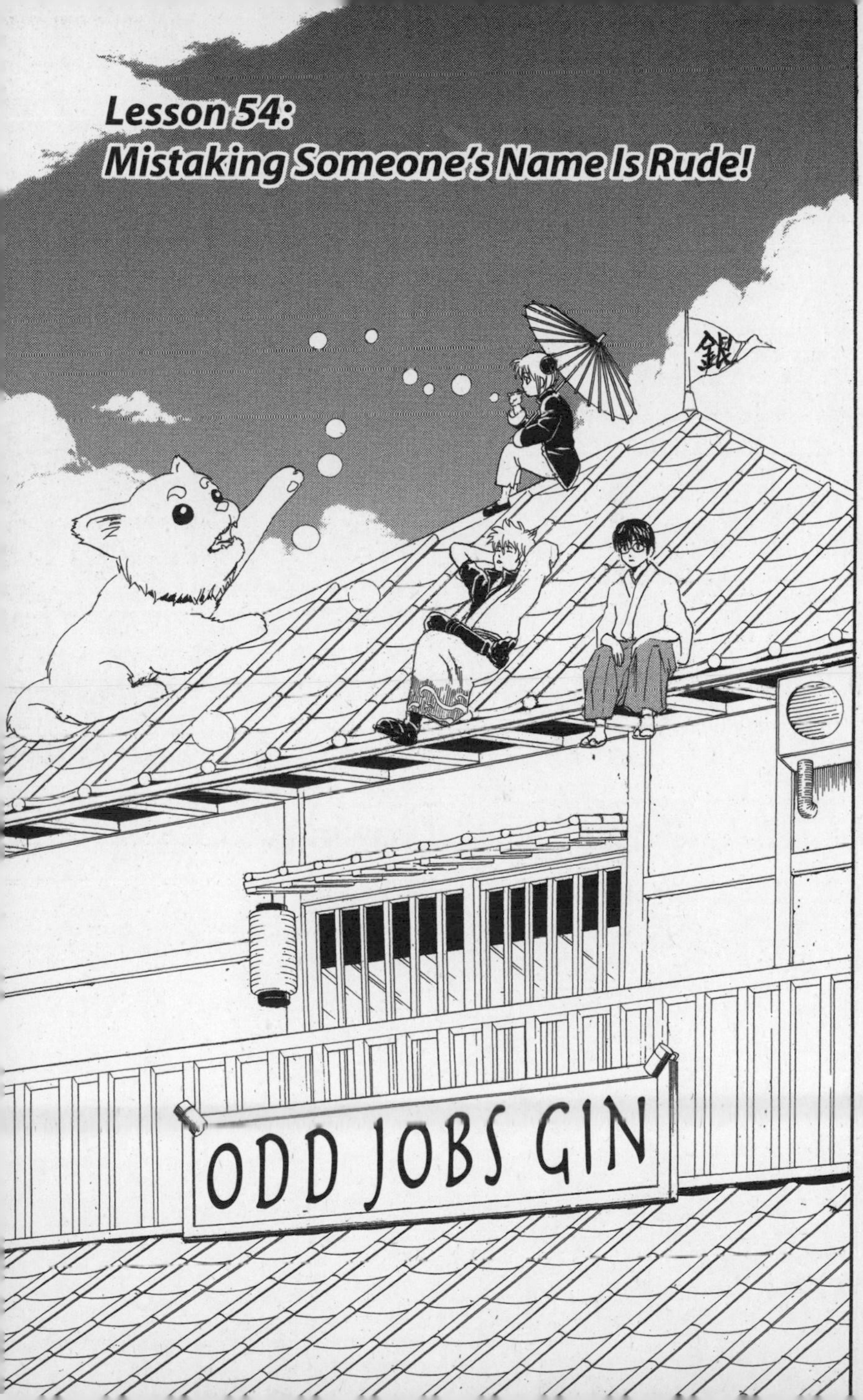

銀
ODD JOBS GIN

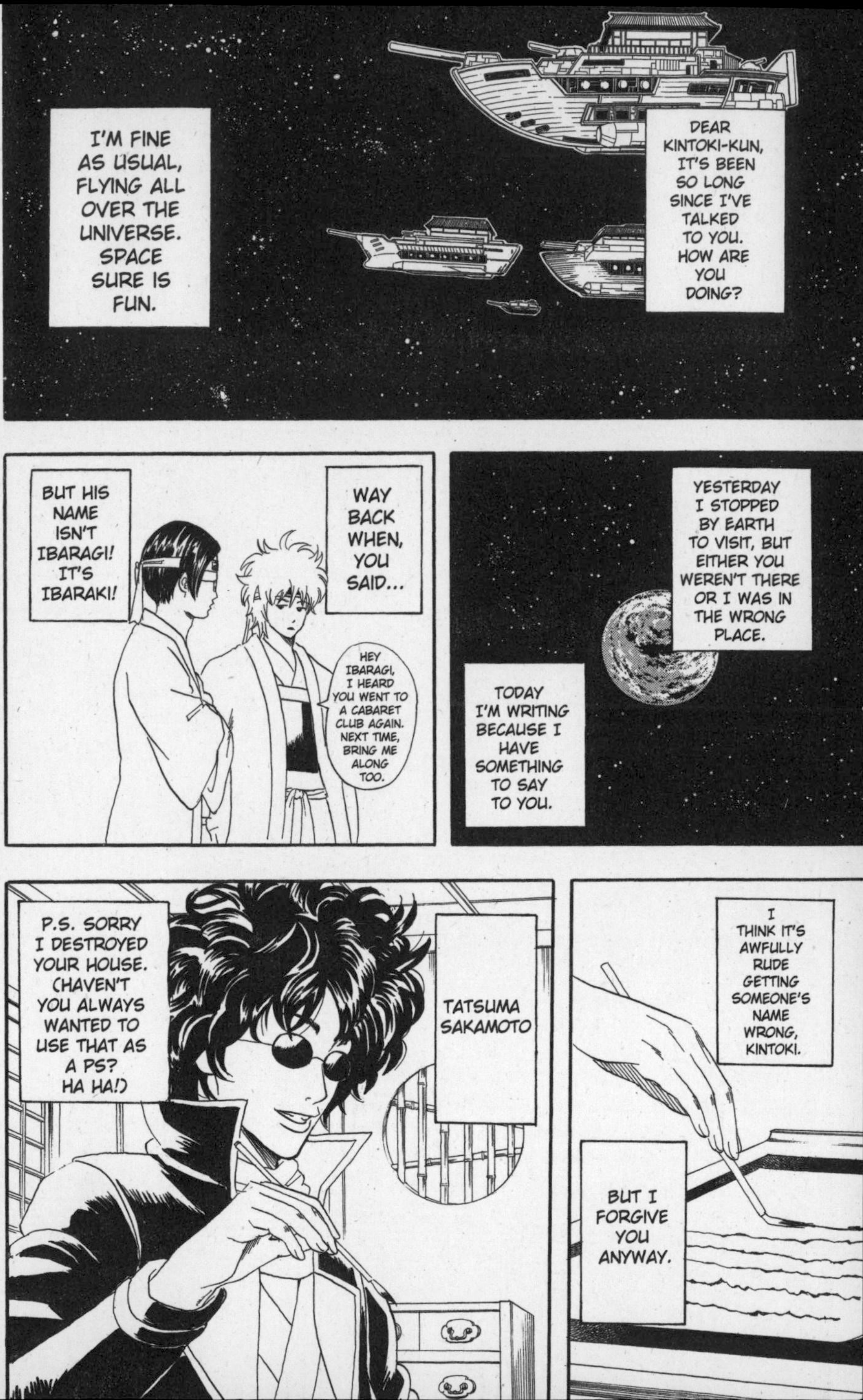
DEAR KINTOKI-KUN, IT'S BEEN SO LONG SINCE I'VE TALKED TO YOU. HOW ARE YOU DOING?
I'M FINE AS USUAL, FLYING ALL OVER THE UNIVERSE. SPACE SURE IS FUN.
YESTERDAY I STOPPED BY EARTH TO VISIT, BUT EITHER YOU WEREN'T THERE OR I WAS IN THE WRONG PLACE.
TODAY I'M WRITING BECAUSE I HAVE SOMETHING TO SAY TO YOU.
WAY BACK WHEN, YOU SAID...
HEY IBARAGI, I HEARD YOU WENT TO A CABARET CLUB AGAIN. NEXT TIME, BRING ME ALONG TOO.
BUT HIS NAME ISN'T IBARAGI! IT'S IBARAKI!
I THINK IT'S AWFULLY RUDE GETTING SOMEONE'S NAME WRONG, KINTOKI.
BUT I FORGIVE YOU ANYWAY.
TATSUMA SAKAMOTO
P.S. SORRY I DESTROYED YOUR HOUSE. (HAVEN'T YOU ALWAYS WANTED TO USE THAT AS A PS? HA HA!)

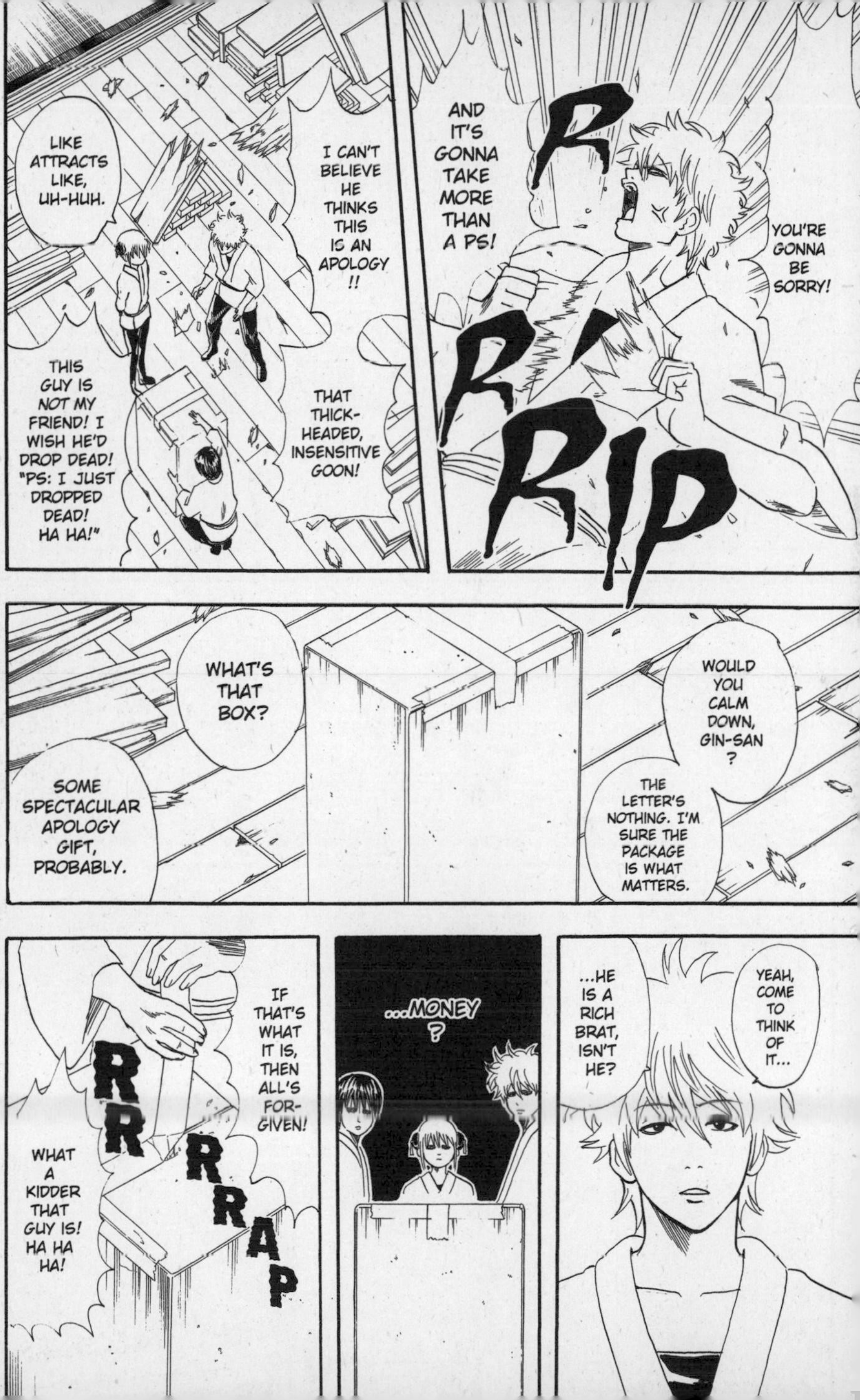
AND IT'S GONNA TAKE MORE THAN A PS!
YOU'RE GONNA BE SORRY!
R R RIP
I CAN'T BELIEVE HE THINKS THIS IS AN APOLOGY!!
LIKE ATTRACTS LIKE, UH-HUH.
THAT THICK-HEADED, INSENSITIVE GOON!
THIS GUY IS NOT MY FRIEND! I WISH HE'D DROP DEAD! "PS: I JUST DROPPED DEAD! HA HA!"
WOULD YOU CALM DOWN, GIN-SAN?
THE LETTER'S NOTHING. I'M SURE THE PACKAGE IS WHAT MATTERS.
WHAT'S THAT BOX?
SOME SPECTACULAR APOLOGY GIFT, PROBABLY.
YEAH, COME TO THINK OF IT...
...HE IS A RICH BRAT, ISN'T HE?
...MONEY?
IF THAT'S WHAT IT IS, THEN ALL'S FOR-GIVEN!
RRRRAP
WHAT A KIDDER THAT GUY IS! HA HA HA!

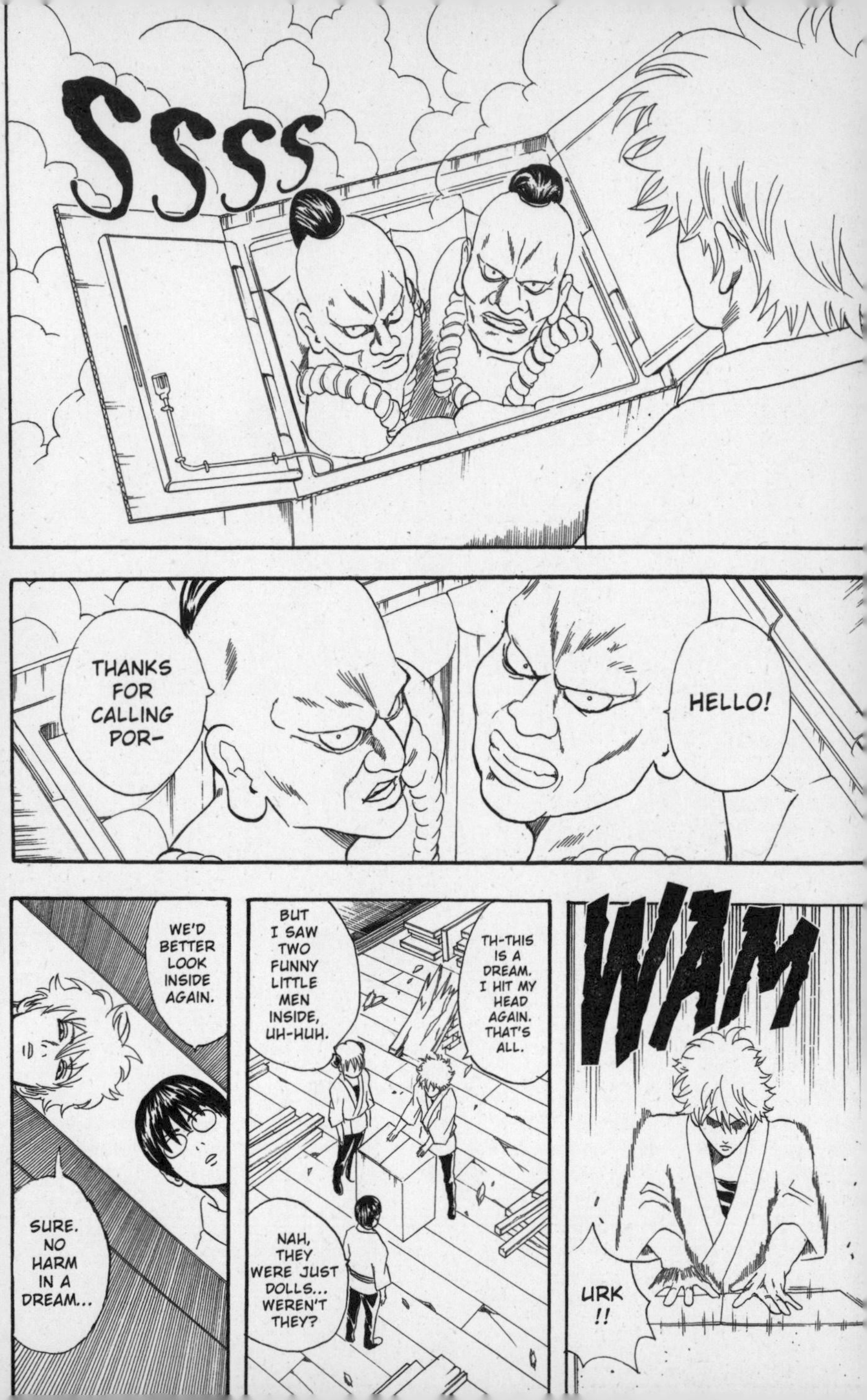
SSSS
HELLO!
THANKS FOR CALLING POR-
WAM
URK !!
TH-THIS IS A DREAM. I HIT MY HEAD AGAIN. THAT'S ALL.
BUT I SAW TWO FUNNY LITTLE MEN INSIDE, UH-HUH.
NAH, THEY WERE JUST DOLLS... WEREN'T THEY?
WE'D BETTER LOOK INSIDE AGAIN.
SURE. NO HARM IN A DREAM...

READ THIS WAY

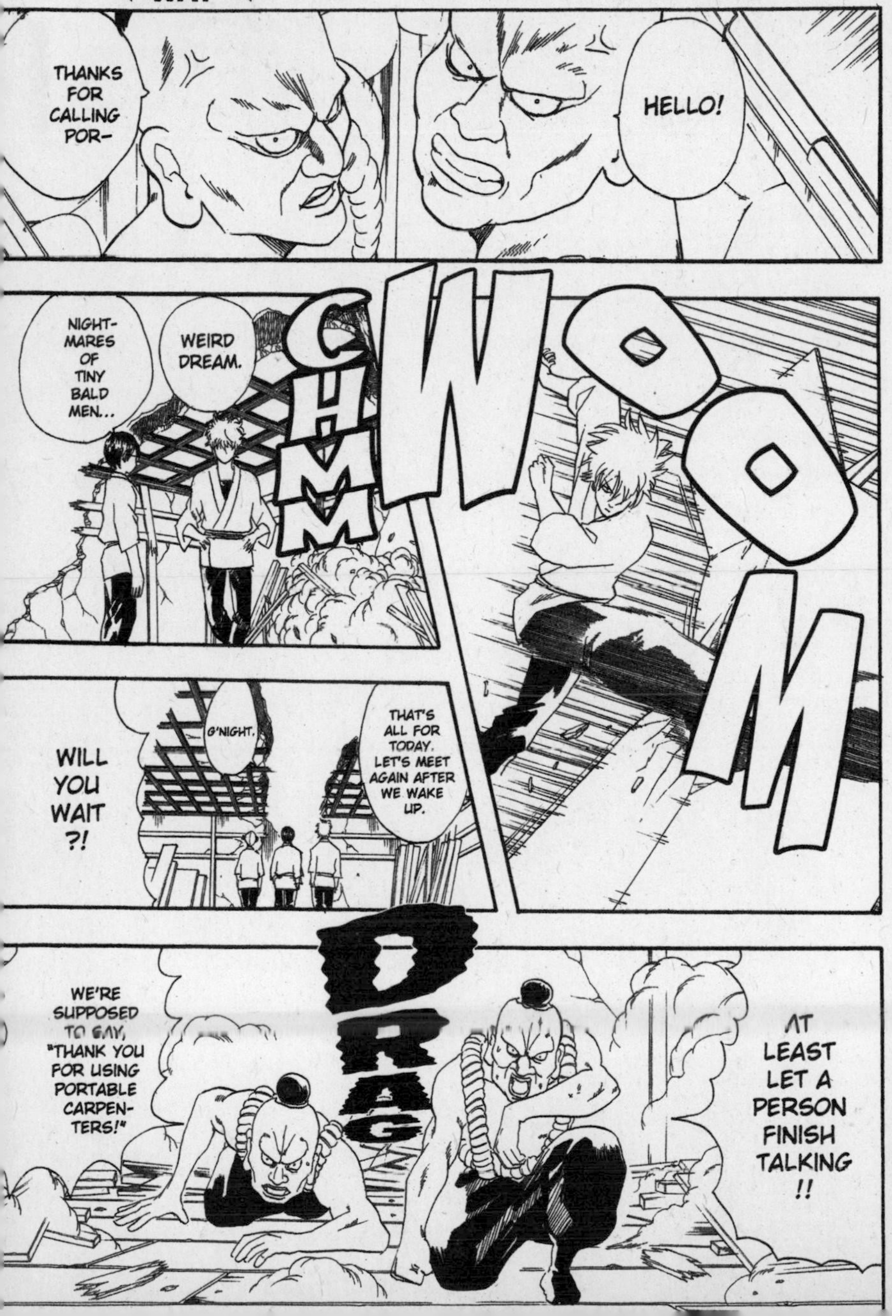
HELLO!
THANKS FOR CALLING POR-
WOOOM
CHMMM
WEIRD DREAM.
NIGHT-MARES OF TINY BALD MEN...
THAT'S ALL FOR TODAY. LET'S MEET AGAIN AFTER WE WAKE UP.
G'NIGHT.
WILL YOU WAIT ?!
DRAG
AT LEAST LET A PERSON FINISH TALKING !!
WE'RE SUPPOSED TO SAY, "THANK YOU FOR USING PORTABLE CARPEN-TERS!"

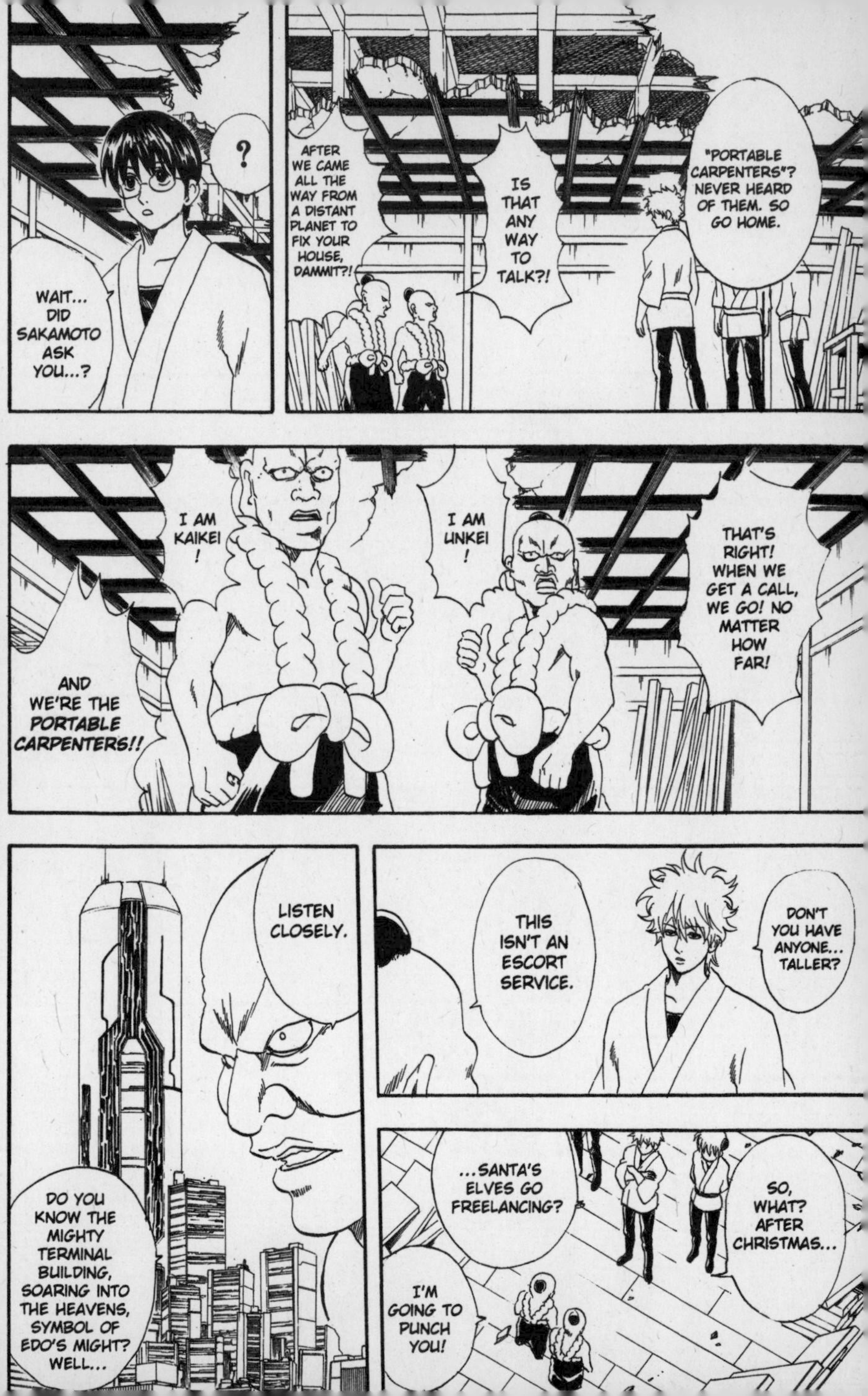
"PORTABLE CARPENTERS"? NEVER HEARD OF THEM. SO GO HOME.
IS THAT ANY WAY TO TALK?!
AFTER WE CAME ALL THE WAY FROM A DISTANT PLANET TO FIX YOUR HOUSE, DAMMIT?!
?
WAIT... DID SAKAMOTO ASK YOU...?
THAT'S RIGHT! WHEN WE GET A CALL, WE GO! NO MATTER HOW FAR!
I AM UNKEI!
I AM KAIKEI!
AND WE'RE THE PORTABLE CARPENTERS!!
DON'T YOU HAVE ANYONE... TALLER?
THIS ISN'T AN ESCORT SERVICE.
SO, WHAT? AFTER CHRISTMAS...
...SANTA'S ELVES GO FREELANCING?
I'M GOING TO PUNCH YOU!
LISTEN CLOSELY.
DO YOU KNOW THE MIGHTY TERMINAL BUILDING, SOARING INTO THE HEAVENS, SYMBOL OF EDO'S MIGHT? WELL...

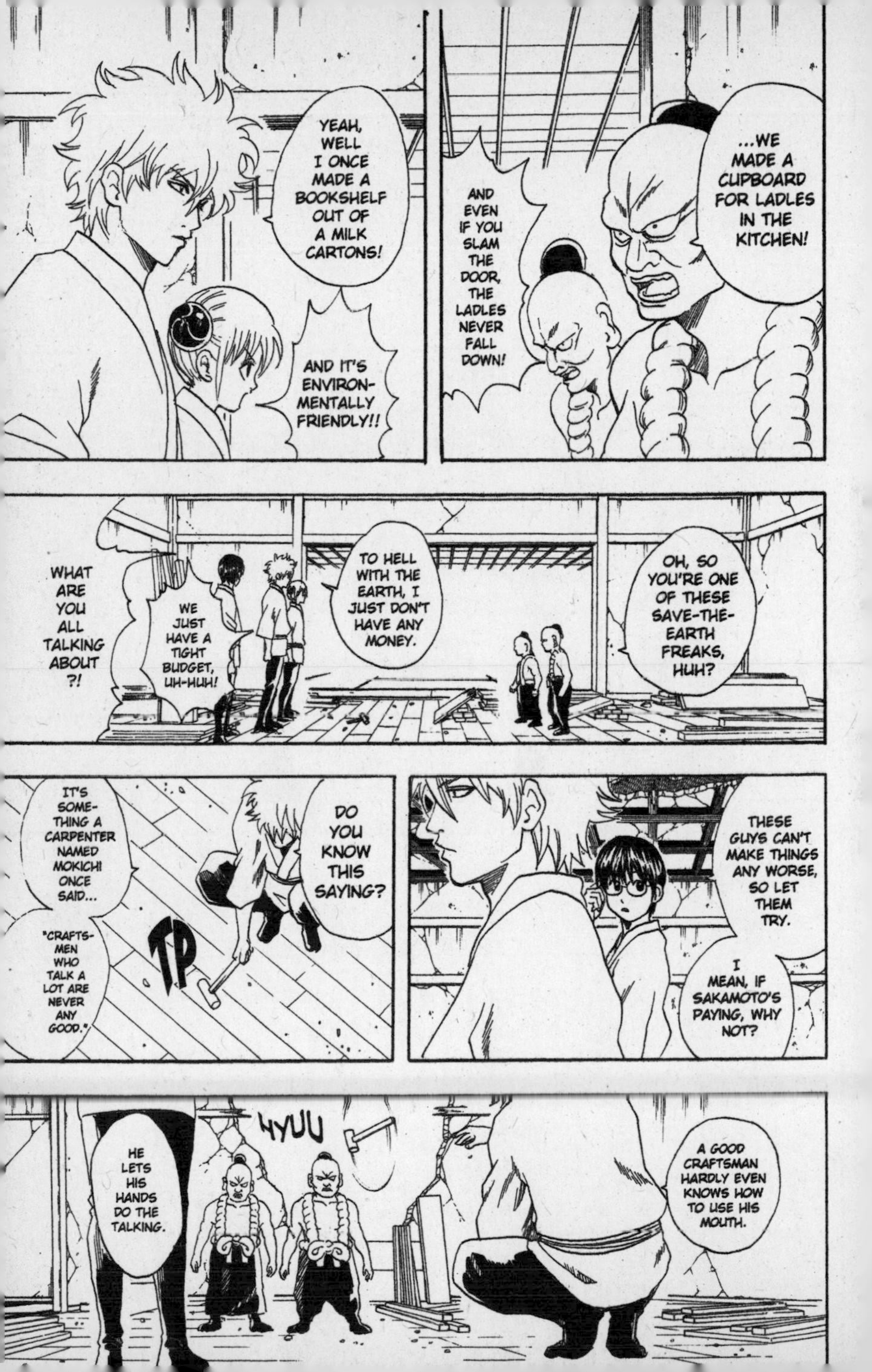
...WE MADE A CUPBOARD FOR LADLES IN THE KITCHEN!
AND EVEN IF YOU SLAM THE DOOR, THE LADLES NEVER FALL DOWN!
YEAH, WELL I ONCE MADE A BOOKSHELF OUT OF A MILK CARTONS!
AND IT'S ENVIRON-MENTALLY FRIENDLY!!
OH, SO YOU'RE ONE OF THESE SAVE-THE-EARTH FREAKS, HUH?
TO HELL WITH THE EARTH, I JUST DON'T HAVE ANY MONEY.
WE JUST HAVE A TIGHT BUDGET, UH-HUH!
WHAT ARE YOU ALL TALKING ABOUT?!
THESE GUYS CAN'T MAKE THINGS ANY WORSE, SO LET THEM TRY.
I MEAN, IF SAKAMOTO'S PAYING, WHY NOT?
DO YOU KNOW THIS SAYING?
IT'S SOME-THING A CARPENTER NAMED MOKICHI ONCE SAID...
TP
"CRAFTS-MEN WHO TALK A LOT ARE NEVER ANY GOOD."
A GOOD CRAFTSMAN HARDLY EVEN KNOWS HOW TO USE HIS MOUTH.
HYUU
HE LETS HIS HANDS DO THE TALKING.

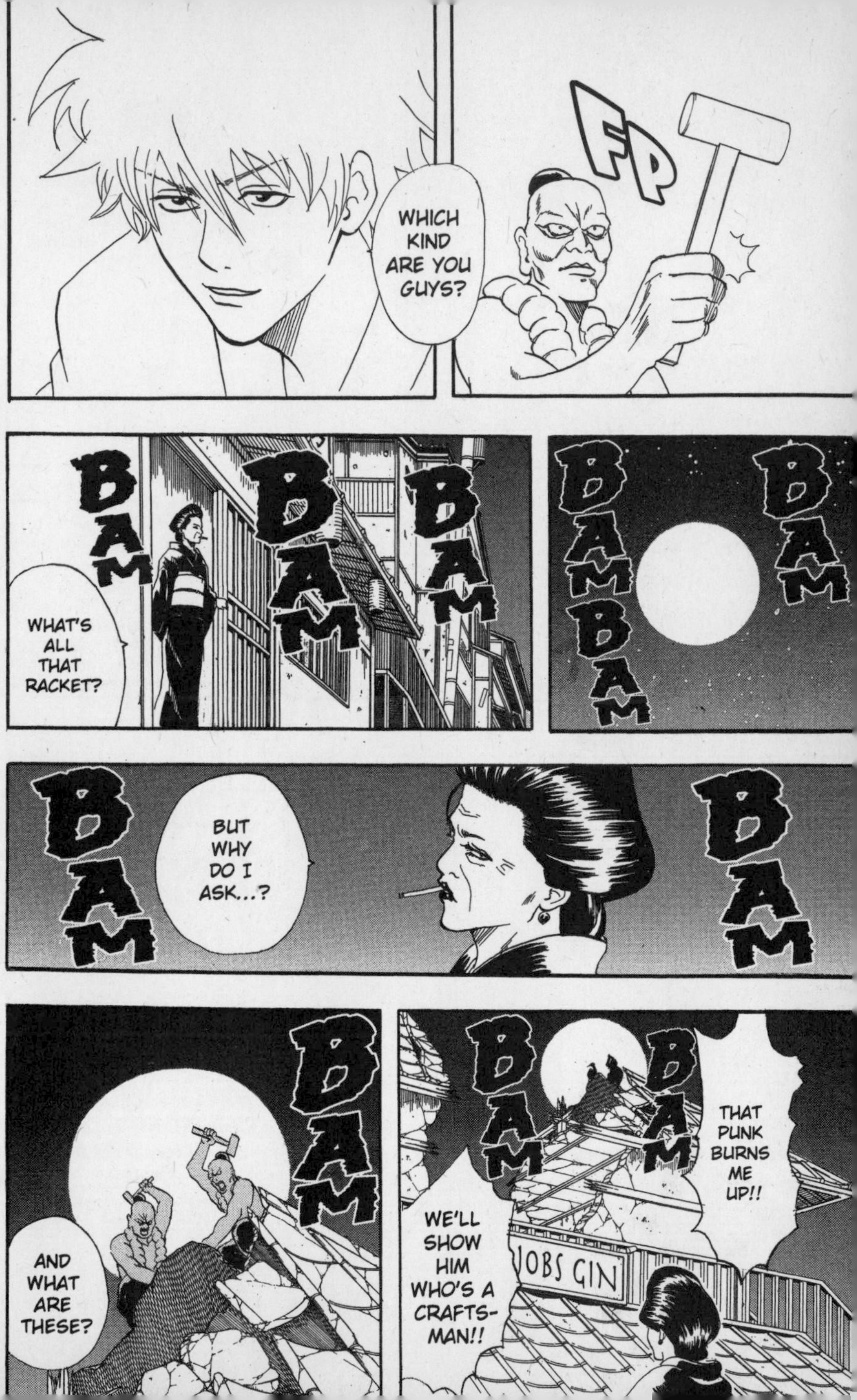

FP
WHICH KIND ARE YOU GUYS?
BAM BAM
BAM
BAM
BAM
BAM
WHAT'S ALL THAT RACKET?
BAM
BUT WHY DO I ASK...?
BAM
THAT PUNK BURNS ME UP!!
BAM
BAM
WE'LL SHOW HIM WHO'S A CRAFTS-MAN!!
JOBS GIN
BAM
AND WHAT ARE THESE?

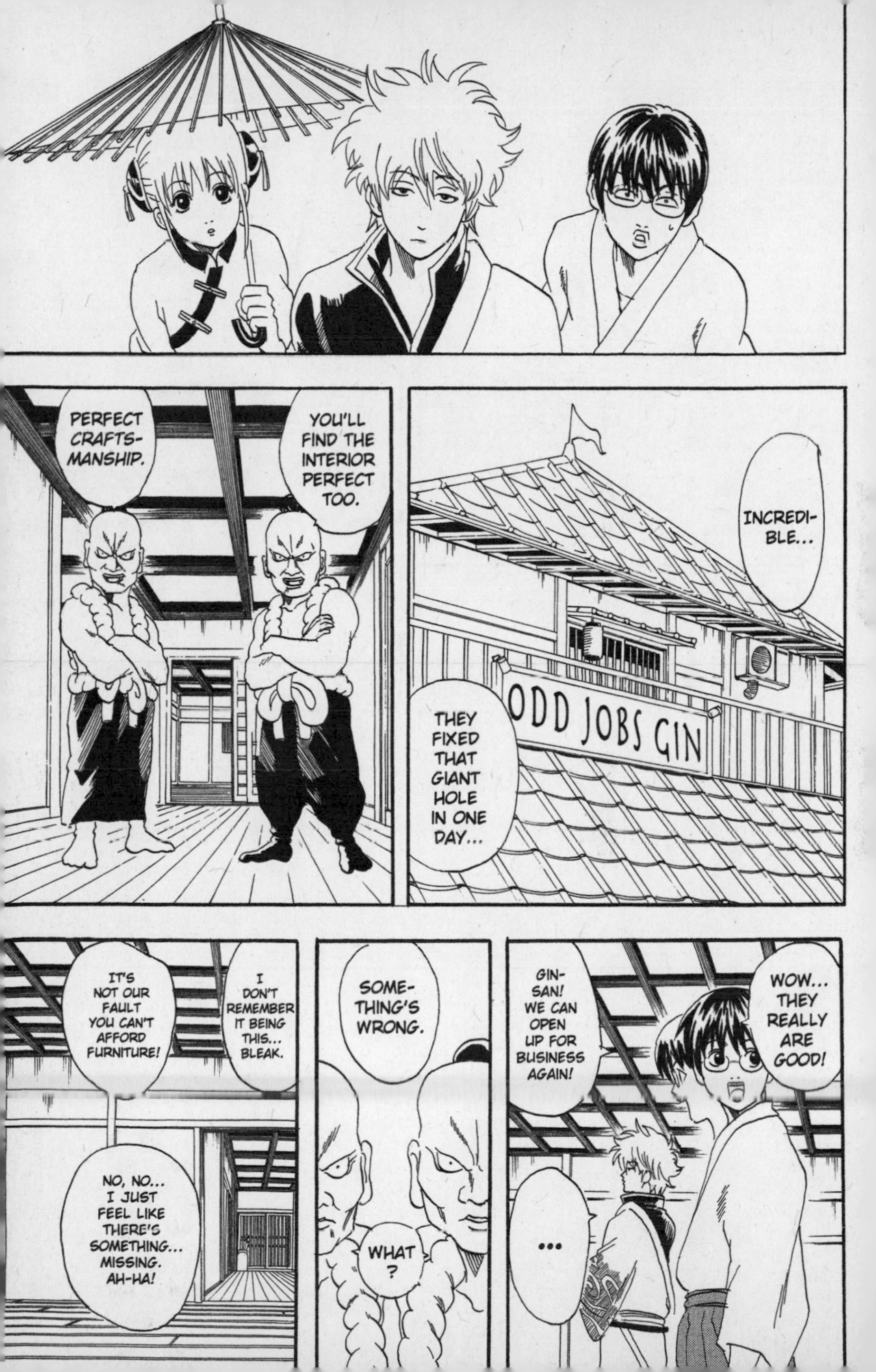
INCREDIBLE...
THEY FIXED THAT GIANT HOLE IN ONE DAY...
ODD JOBS GIN
YOU'LL FIND THE INTERIOR PERFECT TOO.
PERFECT CRAFTSMANSHIP.
WOW... THEY REALLY ARE GOOD!
GIN-SAN! WE CAN OPEN UP FOR BUSINESS AGAIN!
...
SOMETHING'S WRONG.
WHAT?
I DON'T REMEMBER IT BEING THIS... BLEAK.
IT'S NOT OUR FAULT YOU CAN'T AFFORD FURNITURE!
NO, NO... I JUST FEEL LIKE THERE'S SOMETHING... MISSING. AH-HA!

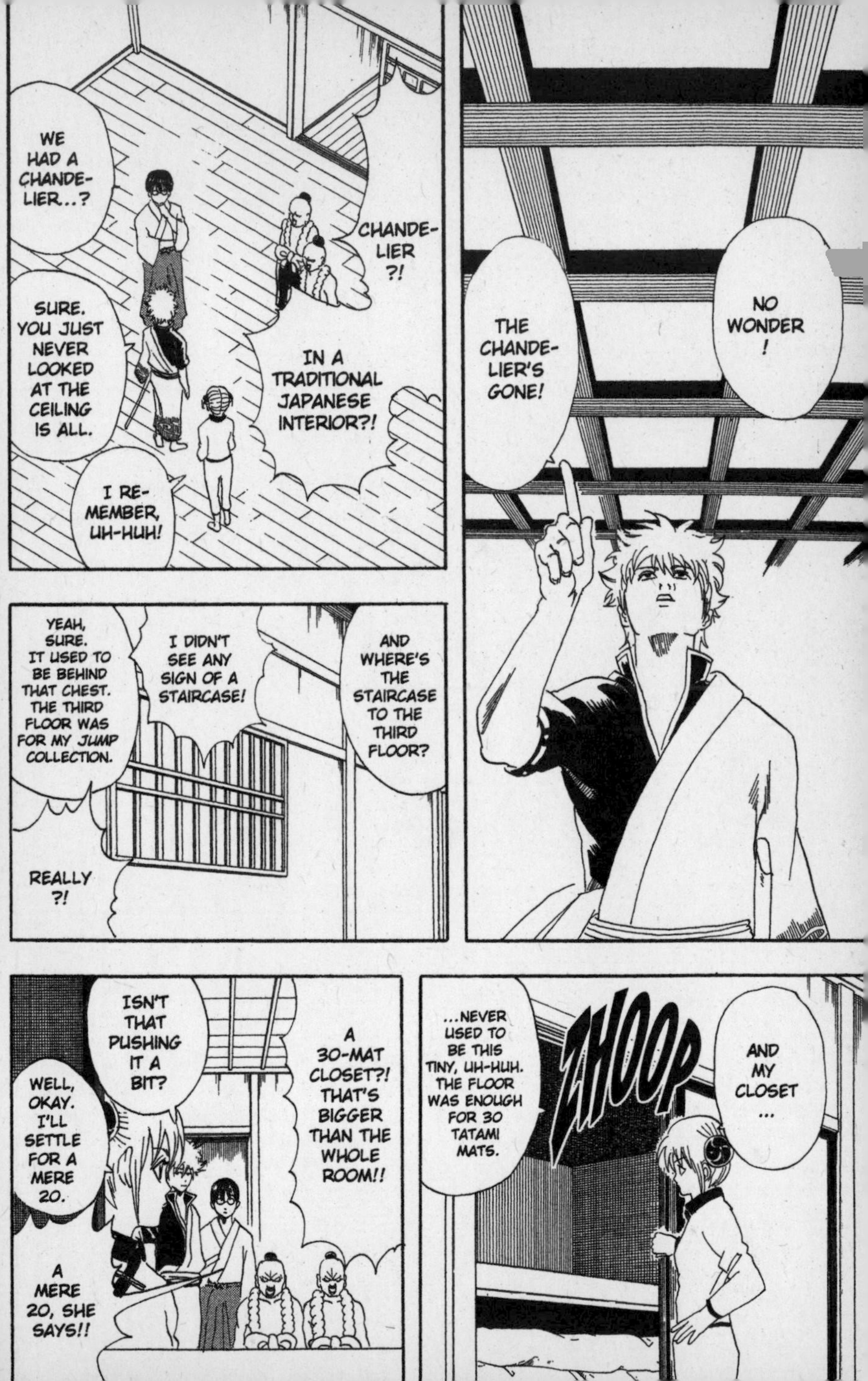

NO WONDER!
THE CHANDELIER'S GONE!
CHANDELIER?!
WE HAD A CHANDELIER...?
IN A TRADITIONAL JAPANESE INTERIOR?!
SURE. YOU JUST NEVER LOOKED AT THE CEILING IS ALL.
I REMEMBER, UH-HUH!
AND WHERE'S THE STAIRCASE TO THE THIRD FLOOR?
I DIDN'T SEE ANY SIGN OF A STAIRCASE!
YEAH, SURE. IT USED TO BE BEHIND THAT CHEST. THE THIRD FLOOR WAS FOR MY JUMP COLLECTION.
REALLY?!
AND MY CLOSET...
ZHOOP
...NEVER USED TO BE THIS TINY, UH-HUH. THE FLOOR WAS ENOUGH FOR 30 TATAMI MATS.
A 30-MAT CLOSET?! THAT'S BIGGER THAN THE WHOLE ROOM!!
ISN'T THAT PUSHING IT A BIT?
WELL, OKAY. I'LL SETTLE FOR A MERE 20.
A MERE 20, SHE SAYS!!

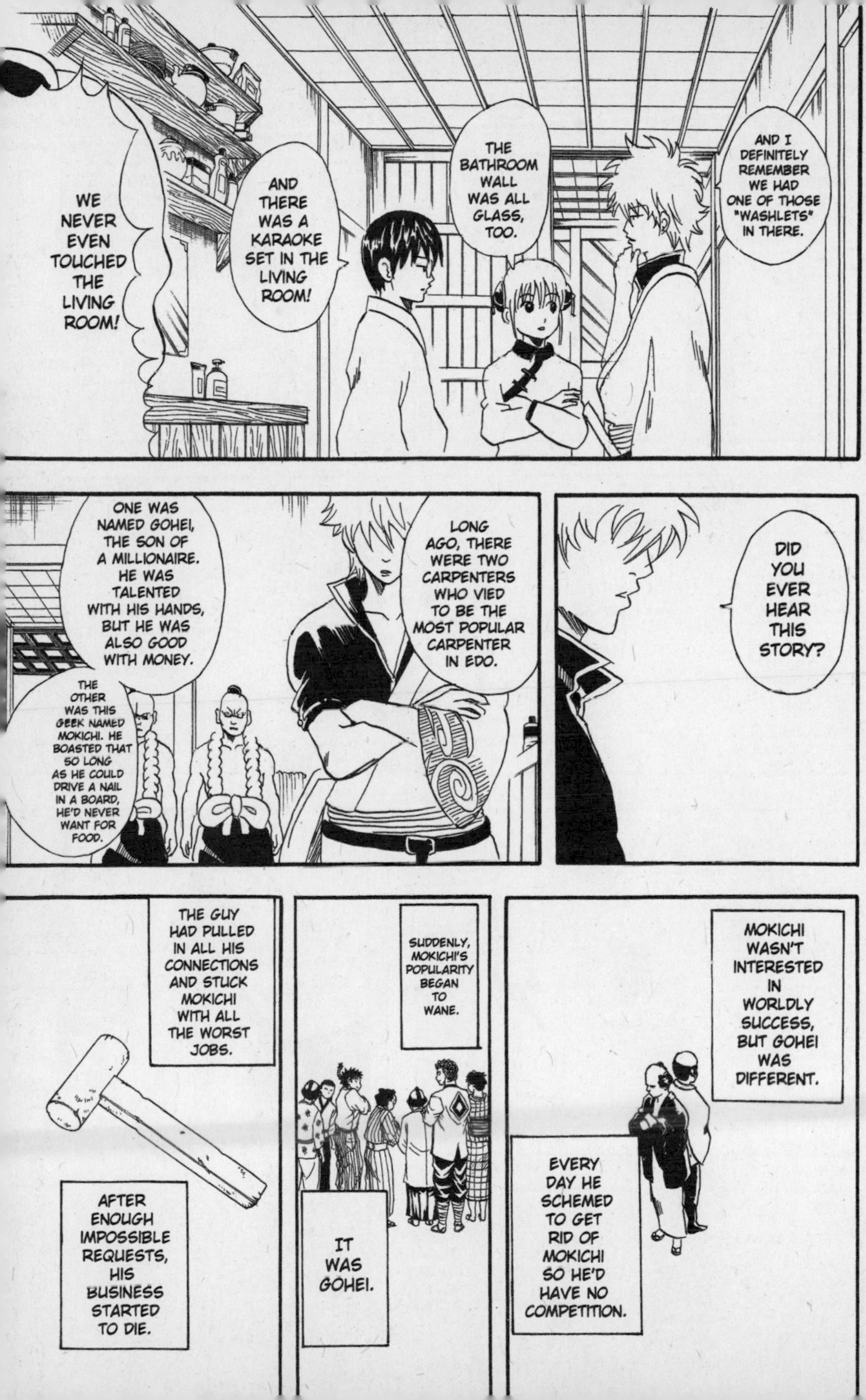
AND I DEFINITELY REMEMBER WE HAD ONE OF THOSE "WASHLETS" IN THERE.
THE BATHROOM WALL WAS ALL GLASS, TOO.
AND THERE WAS A KARAOKE SET IN THE LIVING ROOM!
WE NEVER EVEN TOUCHED THE LIVING ROOM!
DID YOU EVER HEAR THIS STORY?
LONG AGO, THERE WERE TWO CARPENTERS WHO VIED TO BE THE MOST POPULAR CARPENTER IN EDO.
ONE WAS NAMED GOHEI, THE SON OF A MILLIONAIRE. HE WAS TALENTED WITH HIS HANDS, BUT HE WAS ALSO GOOD WITH MONEY.
THE OTHER WAS THIS GEEK NAMED MOKICHI. HE BOASTED THAT SO LONG AS HE COULD DRIVE A NAIL IN A BOARD, HE'D NEVER WANT FOR FOOD.
MOKICHI WASN'T INTERESTED IN WORLDLY SUCCESS, BUT GOHEI WAS DIFFERENT.
EVERY DAY HE SCHEMED TO GET RID OF MOKICHI SO HE'D HAVE NO COMPETITION.
SUDDENLY, MOKICHI'S POPULARITY BEGAN TO WANE.
IT WAS GOHEI.
THE GUY HAD PULLED IN ALL HIS CONNECTIONS AND STUCK MOKICHI WITH ALL THE WORST JOBS.
AFTER ENOUGH IMPOSSIBLE REQUESTS, HIS BUSINESS STARTED TO DIE.

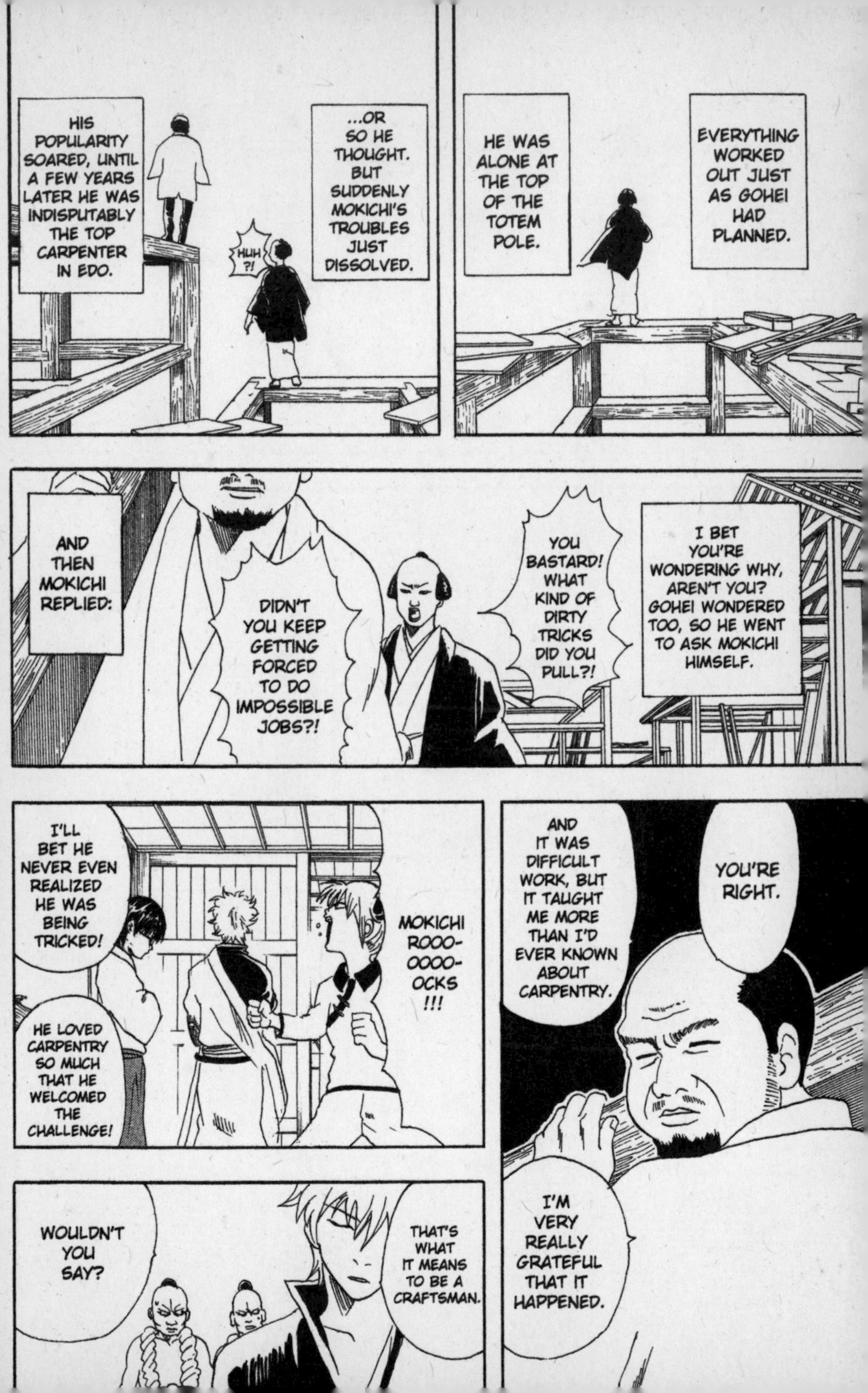
EVERYTHING WORKED OUT JUST AS GOHEI HAD PLANNED.
HE WAS ALONE AT THE TOP OF THE TOTEM POLE.
...OR SO HE THOUGHT. BUT SUDDENLY MOKICHI'S TROUBLES JUST DISSOLVED.
HUH ?!
HIS POPULARITY SOARED, UNTIL A FEW YEARS LATER HE WAS INDISPUTABLY THE TOP CARPENTER IN EDO.
I BET YOU'RE WONDERING WHY, AREN'T YOU? GOHEI WONDERED TOO, SO HE WENT TO ASK MOKICHI HIMSELF.
YOU BASTARD! WHAT KIND OF DIRTY TRICKS DID YOU PULL?!
DIDN'T YOU KEEP GETTING FORCED TO DO IMPOSSIBLE JOBS?!
AND THEN MOKICHI REPLIED:
YOU'RE RIGHT.
AND IT WAS DIFFICULT WORK, BUT IT TAUGHT ME MORE THAN I'D EVER KNOWN ABOUT CARPENTRY.
I'M VERY REALLY GRATEFUL THAT IT HAPPENED.
MOKICHI ROOO-OOOO-OCKS !!!
I'LL BET HE NEVER EVEN REALIZED HE WAS BEING TRICKED!
HE LOVED CARPENTRY SO MUCH THAT HE WELCOMED THE CHALLENGE!
THAT'S WHAT IT MEANS TO BE A CRAFTSMAN.
WOULDN'T YOU SAY?

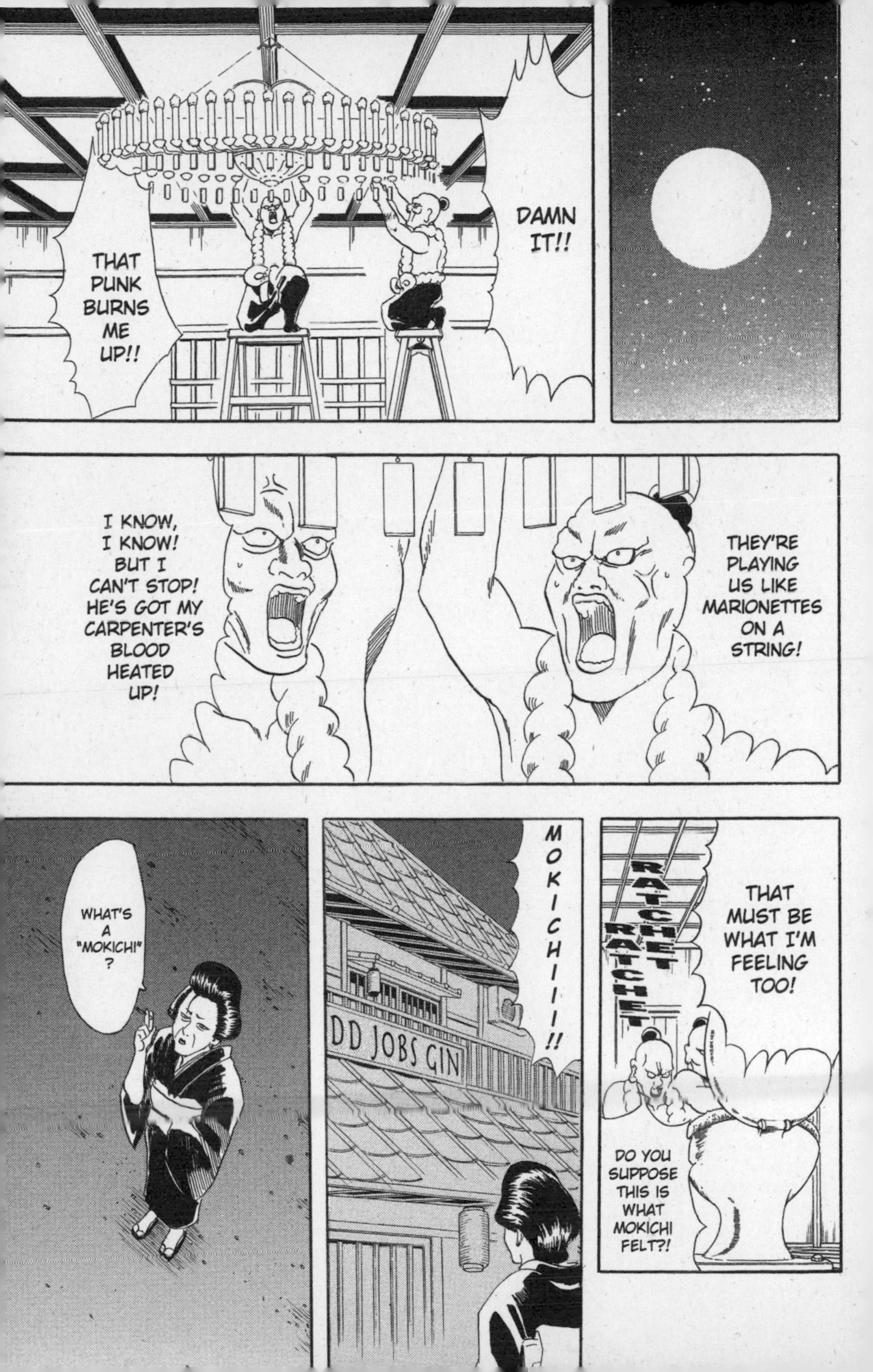
DAMN IT!!
THAT PUNK BURNS ME UP!!
THEY'RE PLAYING US LIKE MARIONETTES ON A STRING!
I KNOW, I KNOW! BUT I CAN'T STOP! HE'S GOT MY CARPENTER'S BLOOD HEATED UP!
RATCHET RATCHET
THAT MUST BE WHAT I'M FEELING TOO!
DO YOU SUPPOSE THIS IS WHAT MOKICHI FELT?!
MOKICHIIIII!!
DD JOBS GIN
WHAT'S A "MOKICHI"?

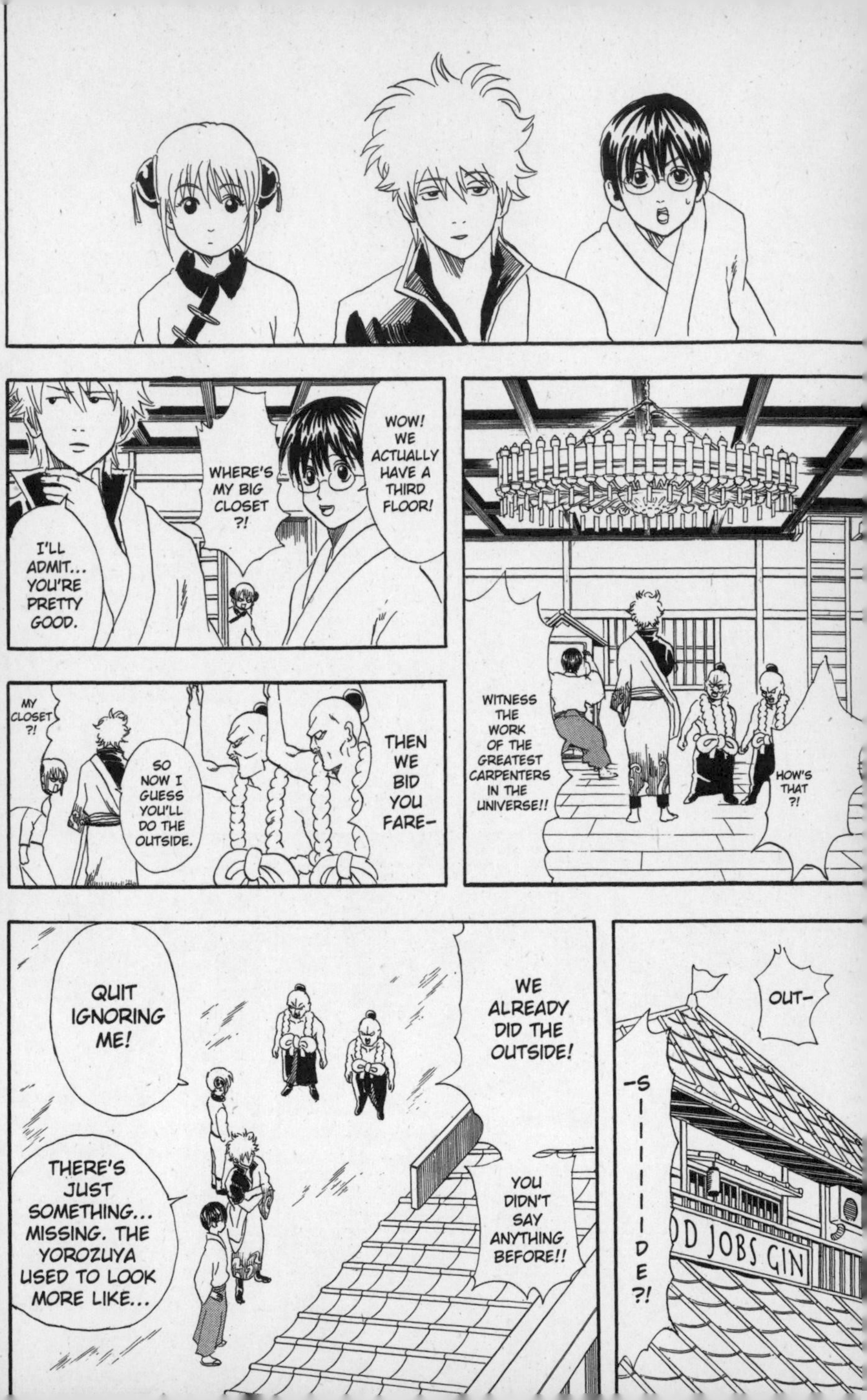
WITNESS THE WORK OF THE GREATEST CARPENTERS IN THE UNIVERSE!!
HOW'S THAT ?!
WOW! WE ACTUALLY HAVE A THIRD FLOOR!
WHERE'S MY BIG CLOSET ?!
I'LL ADMIT... YOU'RE PRETTY GOOD.
THEN WE BID YOU FARE-
SO NOW I GUESS YOU'LL DO THE OUTSIDE.
MY CLOSET ?!
OUT-
-S-I-I-I-I-I-DE ?!
D JOBS GIN
WE ALREADY DID THE OUTSIDE!
QUIT IGNORING ME!
YOU DIDN'T SAY ANYTHING BEFORE!!
THERE'S JUST SOMETHING... MISSING. THE YOROZUYA USED TO LOOK MORE LIKE...

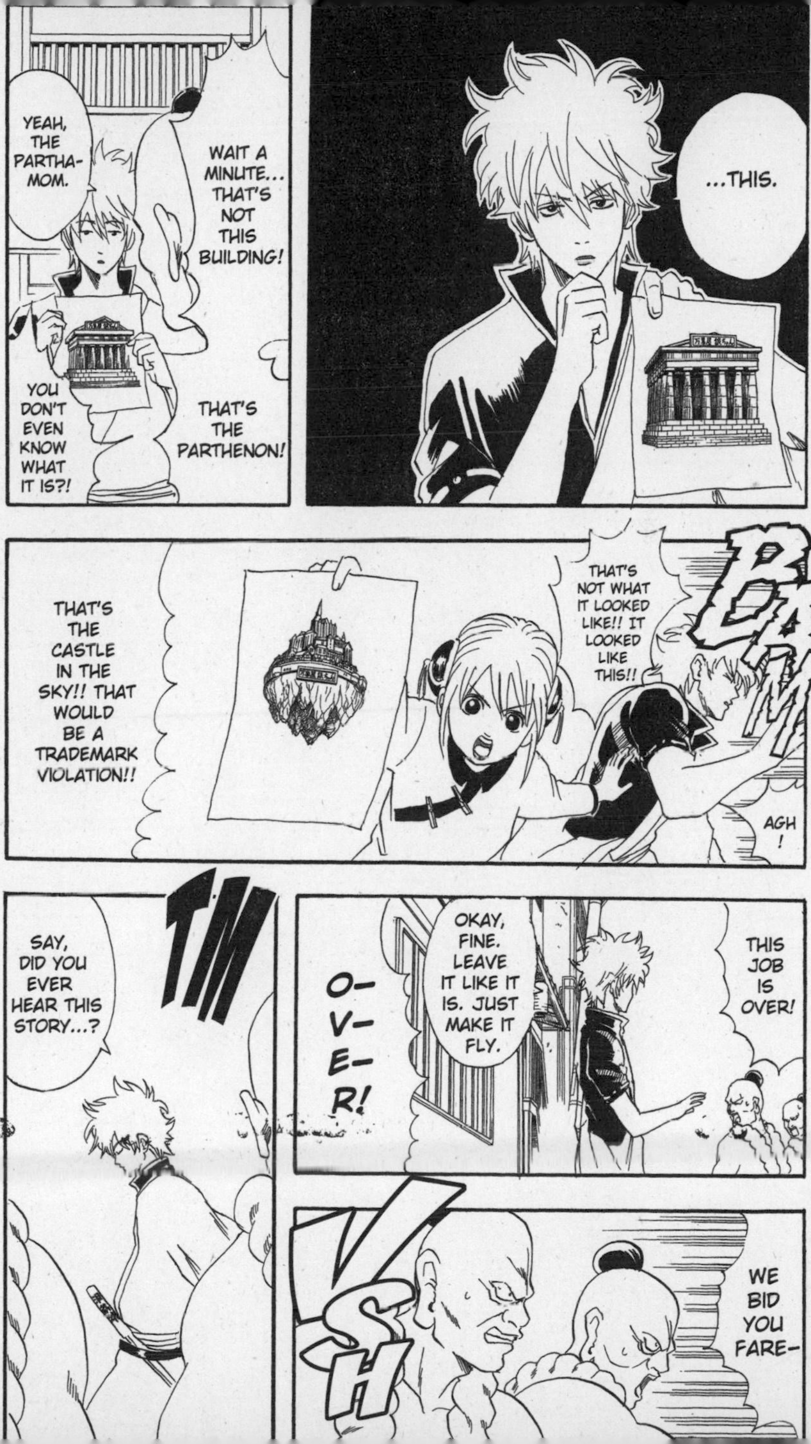
...THIS.
YEAH, THE PARTHA-MOM.
WAIT A MINUTE... THAT'S NOT THIS BUILDING!
THAT'S THE PARTHENON!
YOU DON'T EVEN KNOW WHAT IT IS?!
BAM
THAT'S NOT WHAT IT LOOKED LIKE!! IT LOOKED LIKE THIS!!
AGH!
THAT'S THE CASTLE IN THE SKY!! THAT WOULD BE A TRADEMARK VIOLATION!!
THIS JOB IS OVER!
OKAY, FINE. LEAVE IT LIKE IT IS. JUST MAKE IT FLY.
O-V-E-R!
WE BID YOU FARE-
VSH
TM
SAY, DID YOU EVER HEAR THIS STORY...?

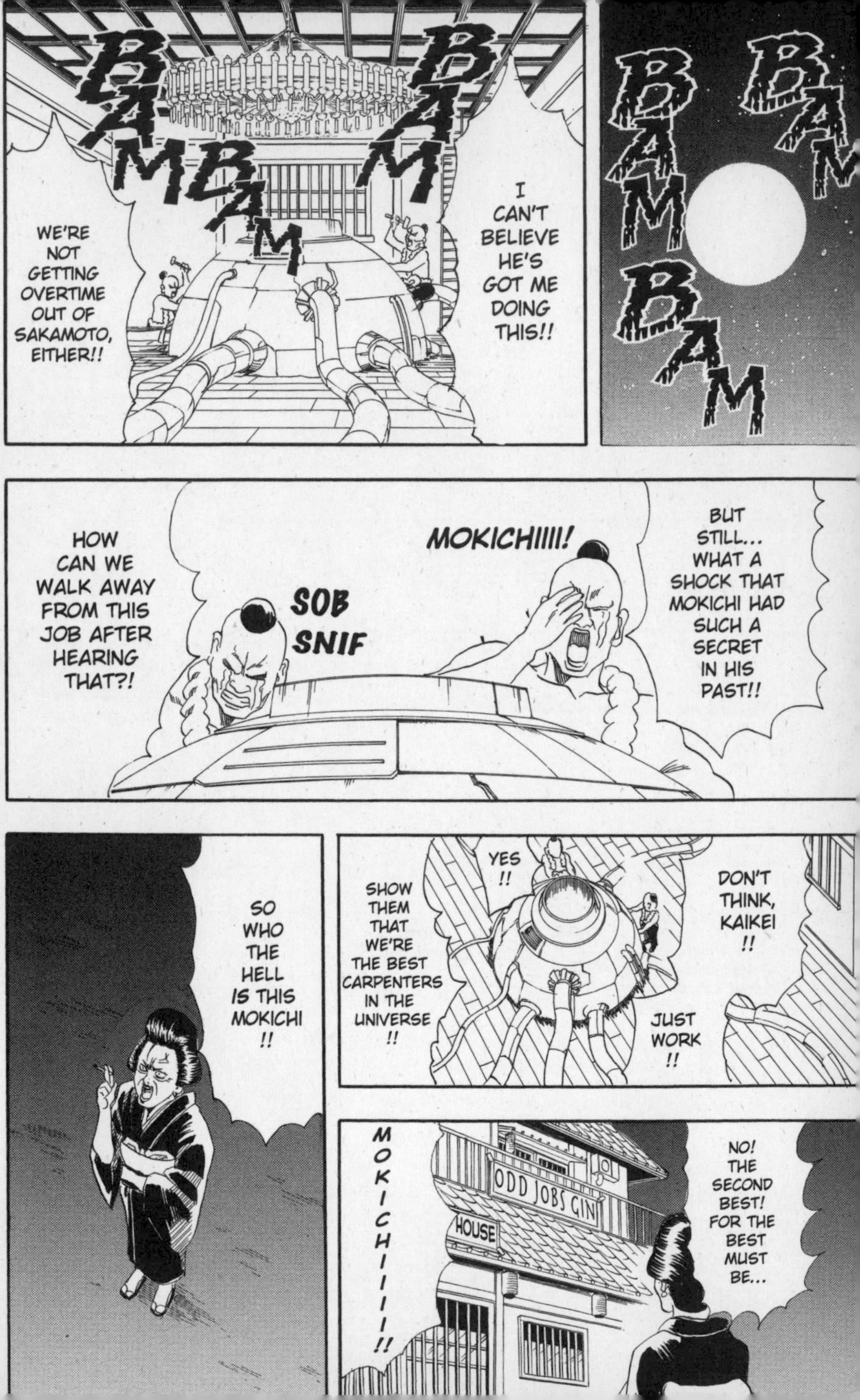
BAM BAM
BAM BAM
BAM BAM BAM
I CAN'T BELIEVE HE'S GOT ME DOING THIS!!
WE'RE NOT GETTING OVERTIME OUT OF SAKAMOTO, EITHER!!
BUT STILL... WHAT A SHOCK THAT MOKICHI HAD SUCH A SECRET IN HIS PAST!!
MOKICHIIIII!
SOB SNIF
HOW CAN WE WALK AWAY FROM THIS JOB AFTER HEARING THAT?!
DON'T THINK, KAIKEI!!
JUST WORK!!
YES!!
SHOW THEM THAT WE'RE THE BEST CARPENTERS IN THE UNIVERSE!!
NO! THE SECOND BEST! FOR THE BEST MUST BE...
ODD JOBS GIN
HOUSE
MOKICHIIIIII!!
SO WHO THE HELL IS THIS MOKICHI!!

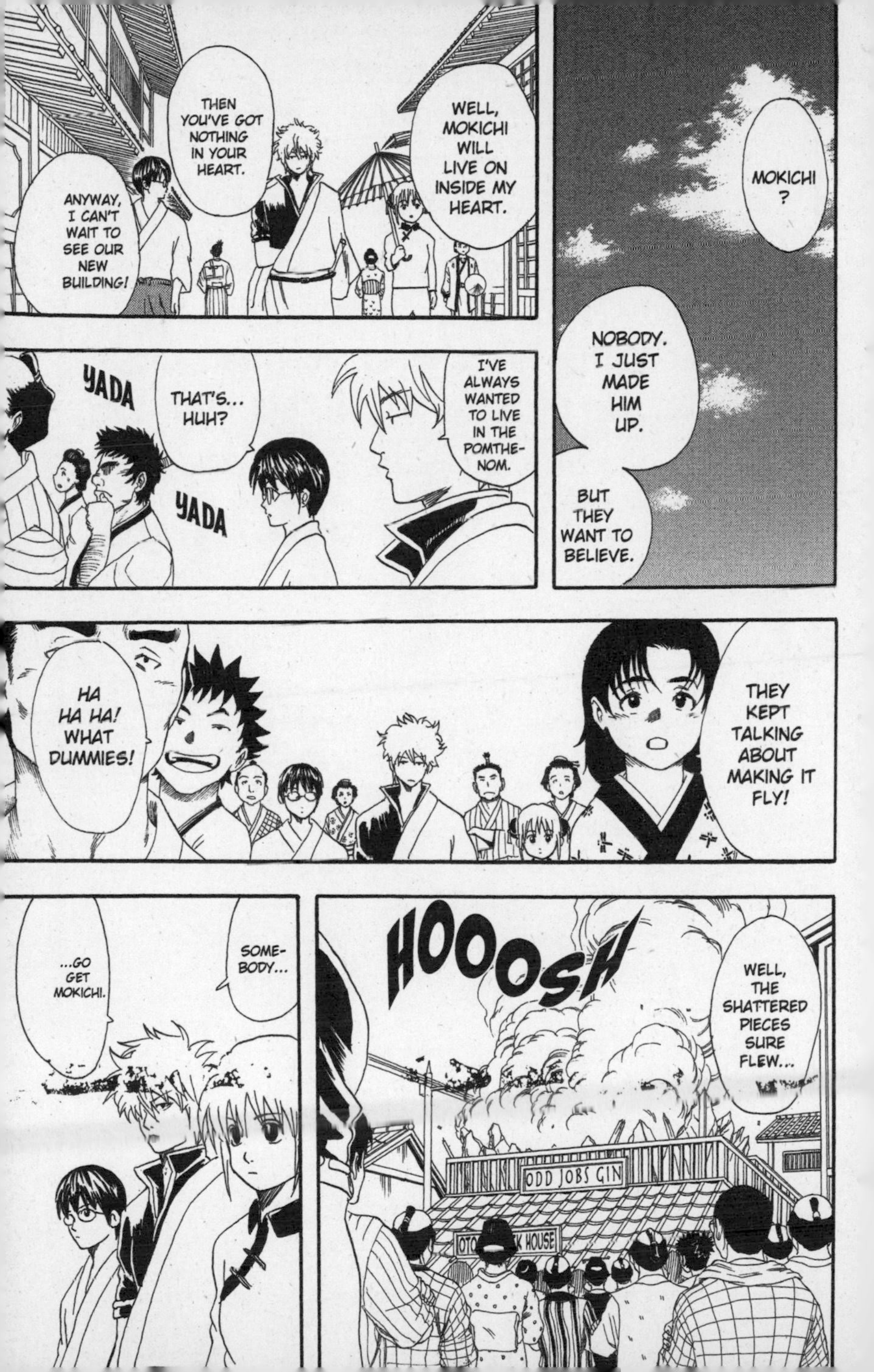
MOKICHI ?
NOBODY. I JUST MADE HIM UP.
BUT THEY WANT TO BELIEVE.
WELL, MOKICHI WILL LIVE ON INSIDE MY HEART.
THEN YOU'VE GOT NOTHING IN YOUR HEART.
ANYWAY, I CAN'T WAIT TO SEE OUR NEW BUILDING!
I'VE ALWAYS WANTED TO LIVE IN THE POMTHE-NOM.
THAT'S... HUH?
YADA
YADA
THEY KEPT TALKING ABOUT MAKING IT FLY!
HA HA HA! WHAT DUMMIES!
HOOOSH
WELL, THE SHATTERED PIECES SURE FLEW...
ODD JOBS GIN
SOME-BODY...
...GO GET MOKICHI.

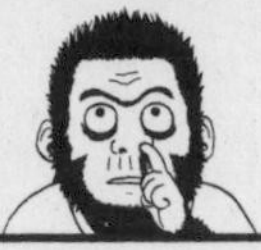

Sorachi's Q&A Corner #13

<Question from Corowan-san of Tokyo>

Please ask my big sister out! She's 19 and really pretty and she loves pickled seaweed. This is a secret, so when you call her, don't tell her about this letter!

This letter was in very cute handwriting, with a photo-booth sticker showing a girl in 3rd or 4th grade with her beautiful older sister. And a cell-phone number.

But sorry! I'm not falling for it! Just because I'm a hick from the country doesn't mean I'm going to fall for an obvious stunt like this! Her big sister sure is cute, though...

Nope! I'm not falling for this, no sir! The phone number will turn out to be something weird or embarrassing! No Tokyo smart-ass is going to make a fool out of me! Her big sister sure is cute, though...

Ha ha ha! I'm just playing! Obviously this little kid is just trying to mess with me! If it's really a little kid at all! Her big sister sure is cute, though...

No, no, no, no, no................
But she sure is cute...

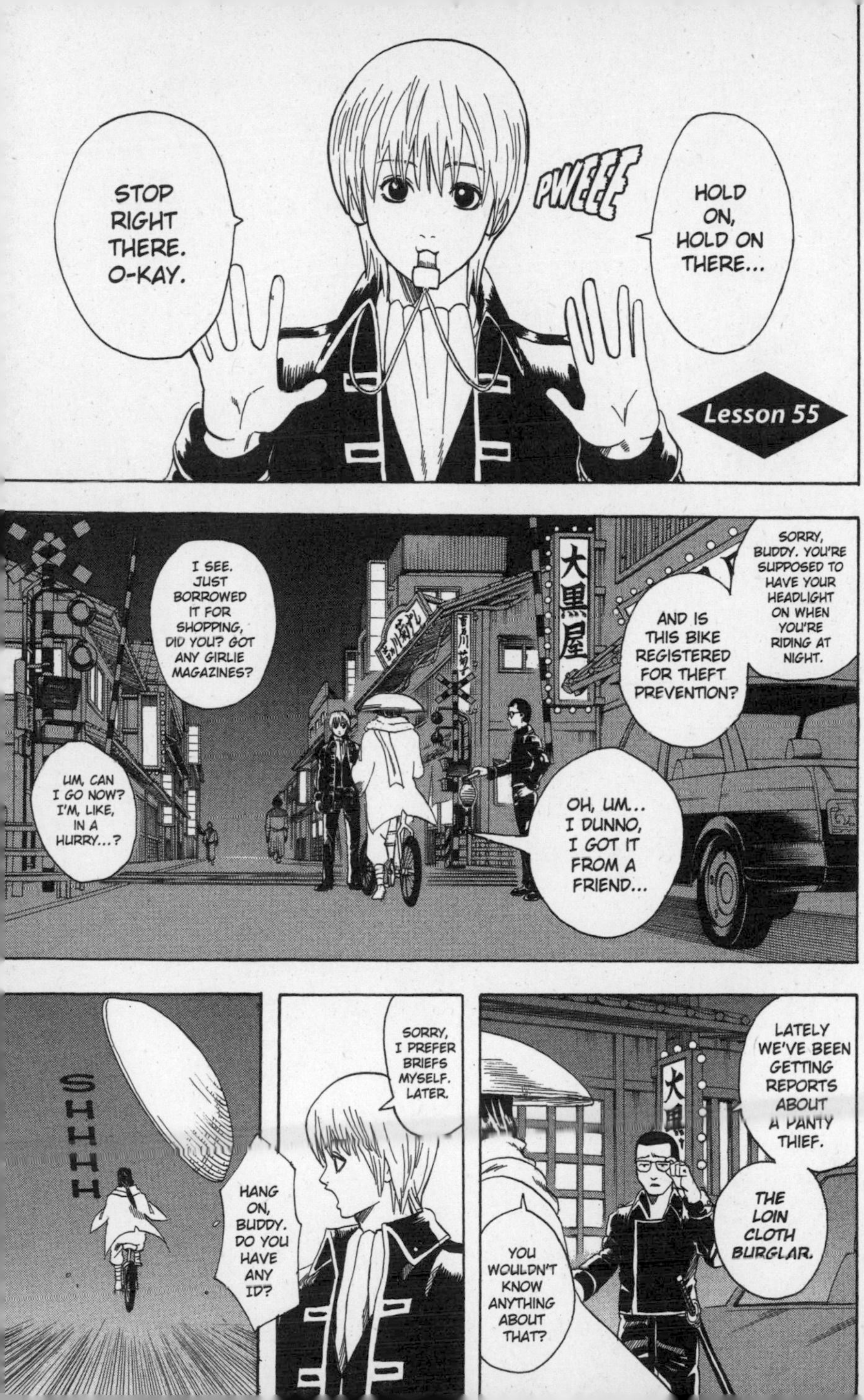
HOLD ON, HOLD ON THERE...
PWEEE
STOP RIGHT THERE. O-KAY.
Lesson 55
SORRY, BUDDY. YOU'RE SUPPOSED TO HAVE YOUR HEADLIGHT ON WHEN YOU'RE RIDING AT NIGHT.
AND IS THIS BIKE REGISTERED FOR THEFT PREVENTION?
OH, UM... I DUNNO, I GOT IT FROM A FRIEND...
I SEE. JUST BORROWED IT FOR SHOPPING, DID YOU? GOT ANY GIRLIE MAGAZINES?
UM, CAN I GO NOW? I'M, LIKE, IN A HURRY...?
LATELY WE'VE BEEN GETTING REPORTS ABOUT A PANTY THIEF.
THE LOIN CLOTH BURGLAR.
YOU WOULDN'T KNOW ANYTHING ABOUT THAT?
SORRY, I PREFER BRIEFS MYSELF. LATER.
HANG ON, BUDDY. DO YOU HAVE ANY ID?
SHHHH

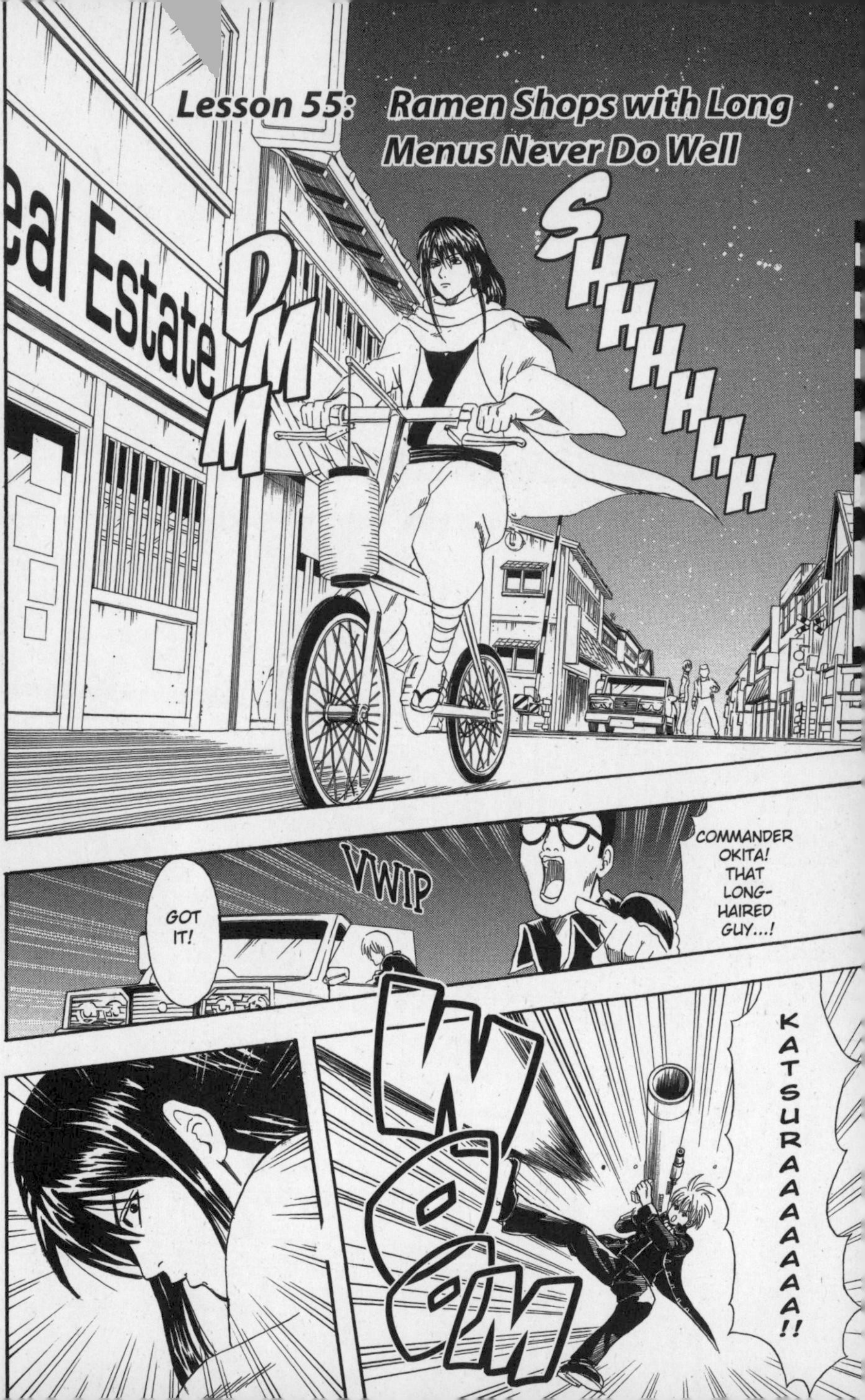
Lesson 55: Ramen Shops with Long Menus Never Do Well
SHHHHHHH
DMM
eal Estate
COMMANDER OKITA! THAT LONG-HAIRED GUY...!
VWIP
GOT IT!
KATSURAAAAAAAAAA!!
WOOOM

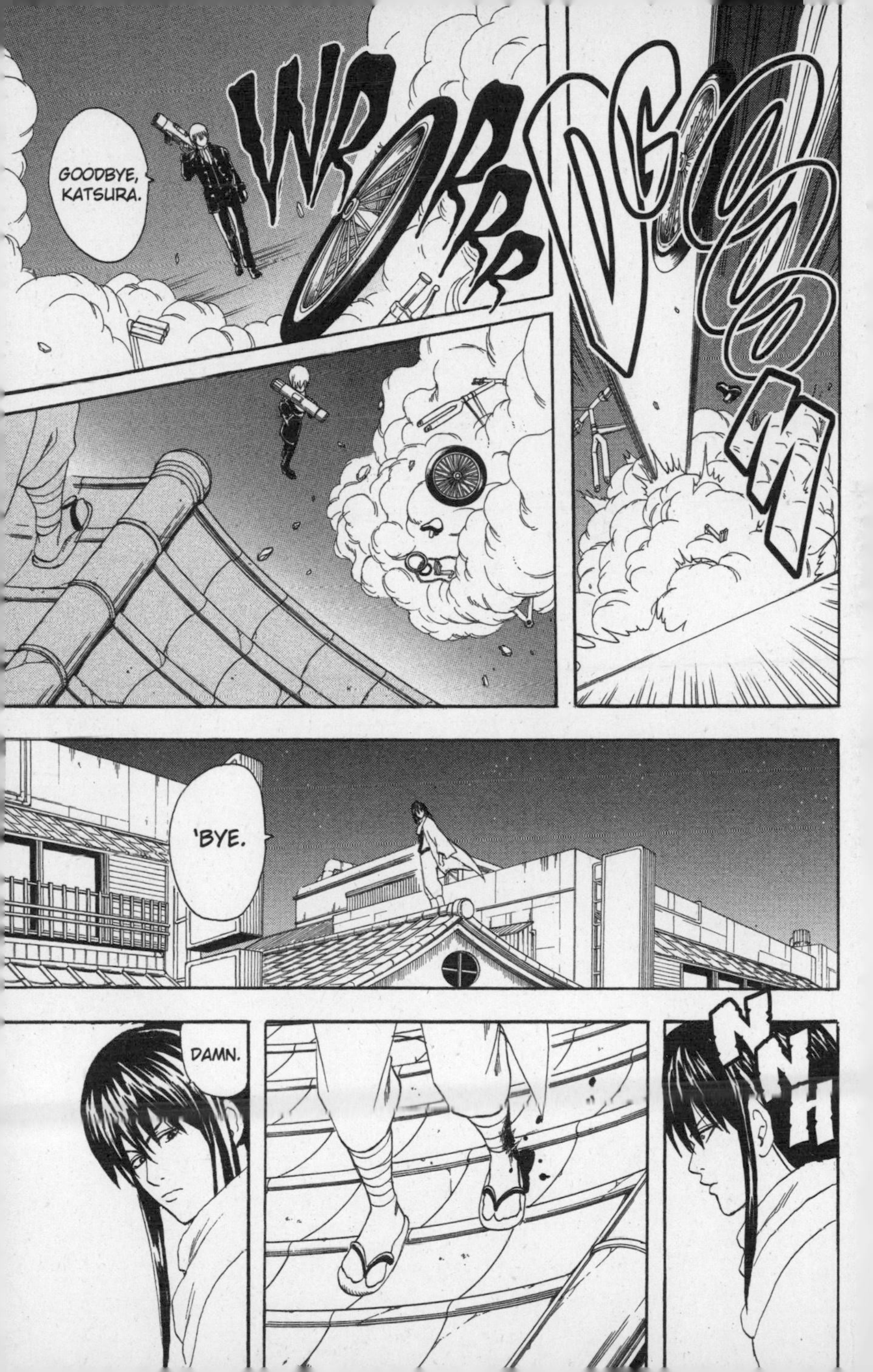
VGOOOM
GOODBYE, KATSURA.
'BYE.
NNH
DAMN.

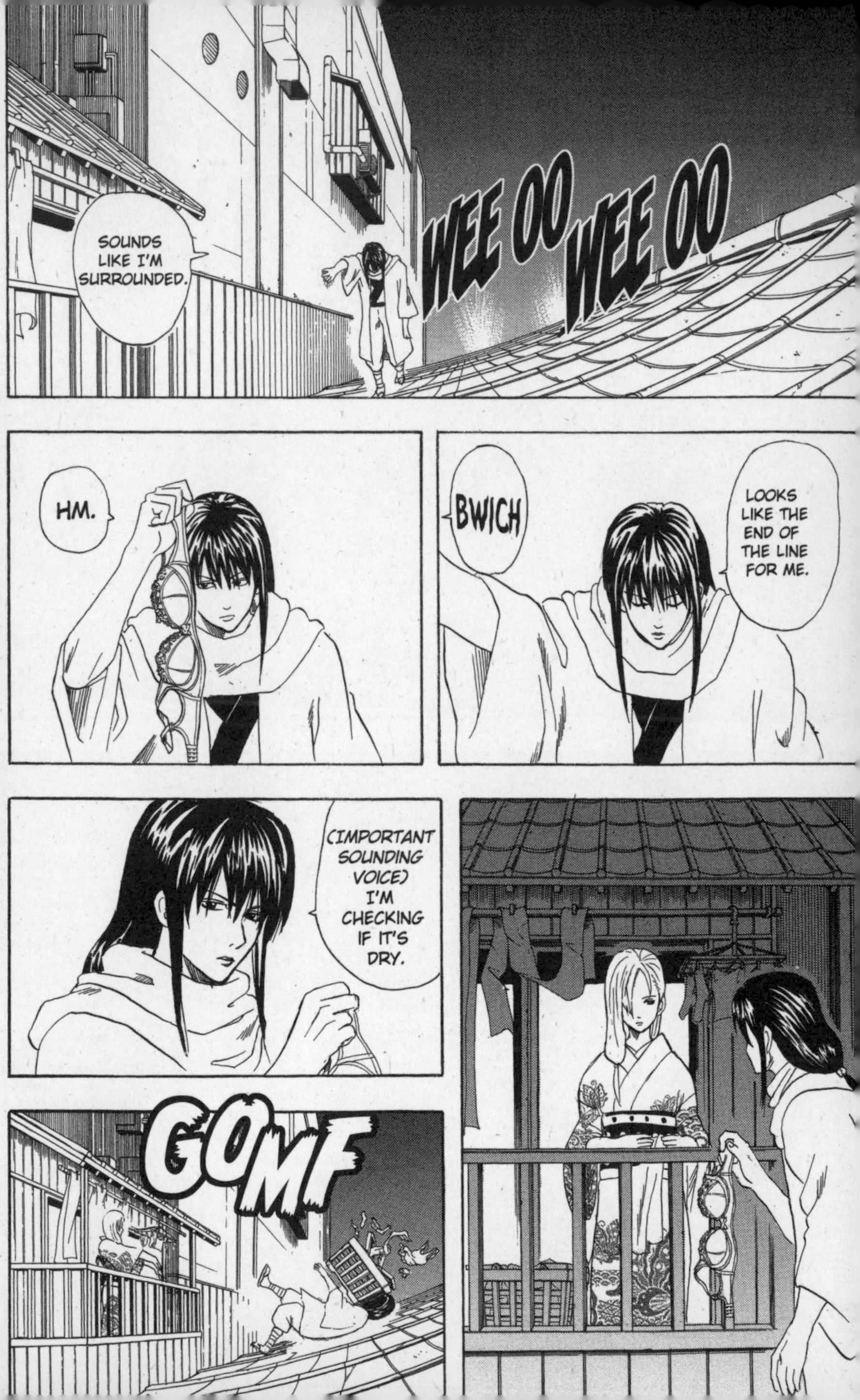
WEE OO WEE OO
SOUNDS LIKE I'M SURROUNDED.
LOOKS LIKE THE END OF THE LINE FOR ME.
BWICH
HM.
(IMPORTANT SOUNDING VOICE) I'M CHECKING IF IT'S DRY.
GOMF

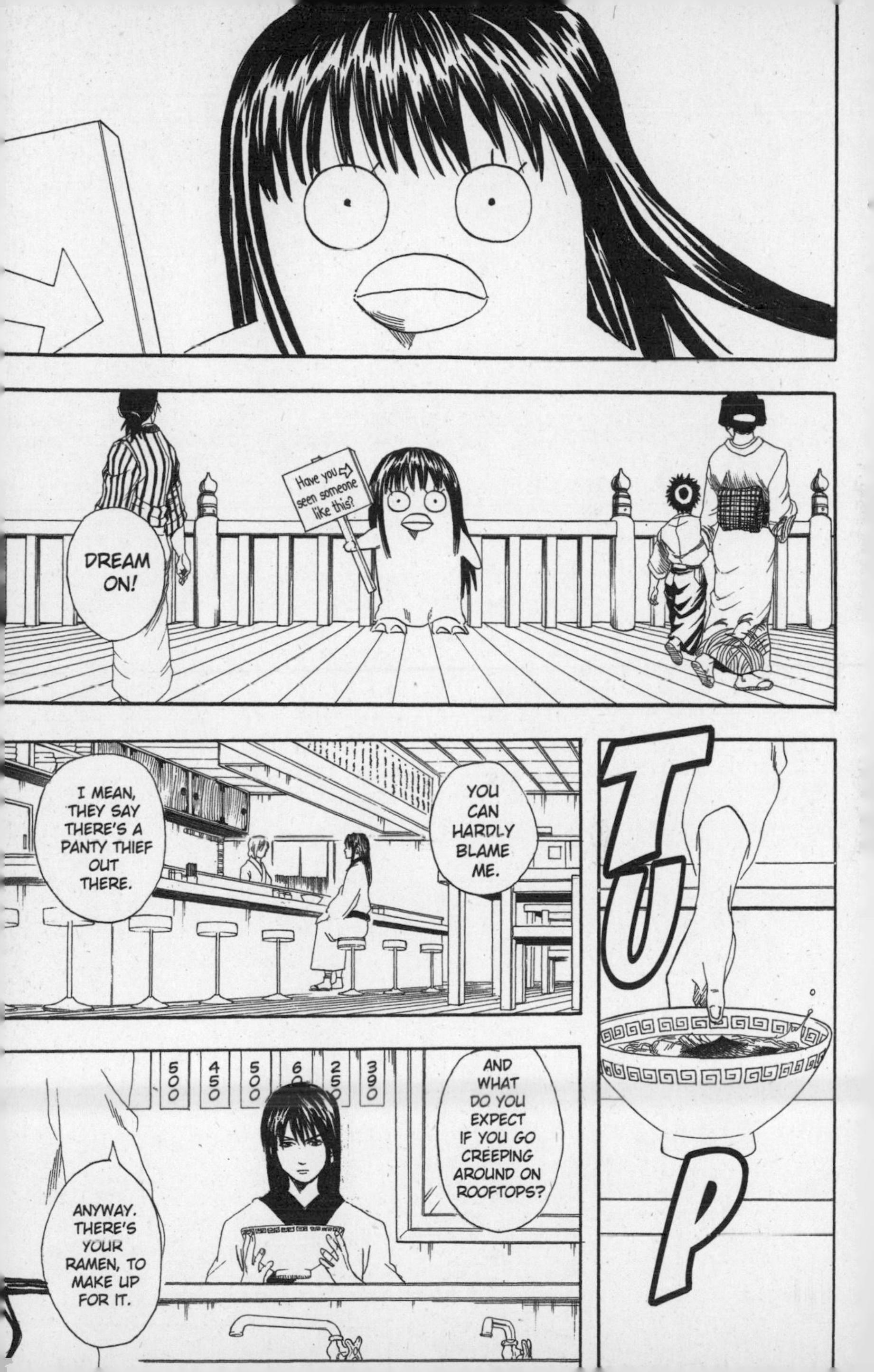
Have you seen someone like this?
DREAM ON!
TUP
YOU CAN HARDLY BLAME ME.
I MEAN, THEY SAY THERE'S A PANTY THIEF OUT THERE.
390
250
500
450
500
AND WHAT DO YOU EXPECT IF YOU GO CREEPING AROUND ON ROOFTOPS?
ANYWAY. THERE'S YOUR RAMEN, TO MAKE UP FOR IT.

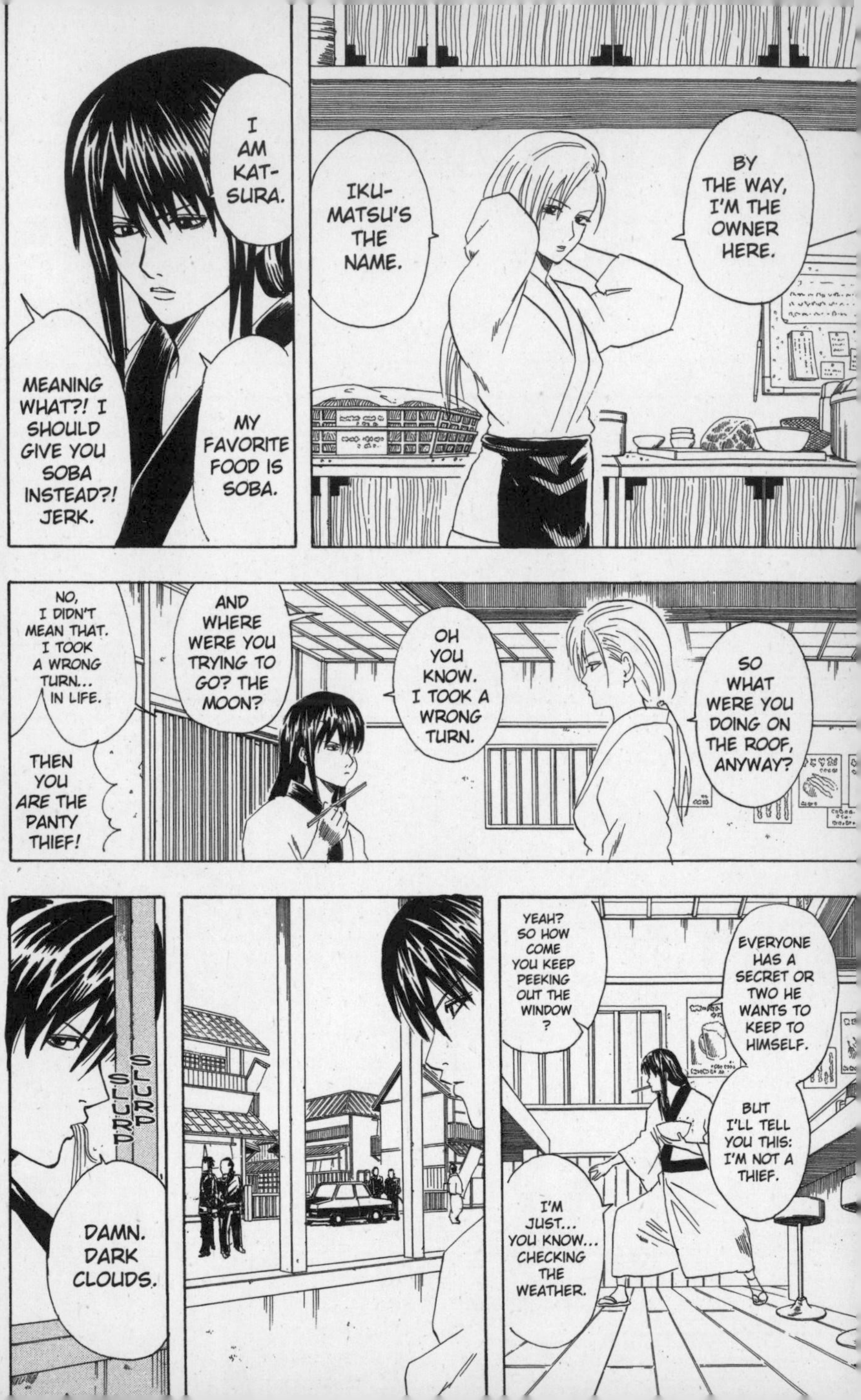
BY THE WAY, I'M THE OWNER HERE.
IKU-MATSU'S THE NAME.
I AM KAT-SURA.
MY FAVORITE FOOD IS SOBA.
MEANING WHAT?! I SHOULD GIVE YOU SOBA INSTEAD?! JERK.
SO WHAT WERE YOU DOING ON THE ROOF, ANYWAY?
OH YOU KNOW. I TOOK A WRONG TURN.
AND WHERE WERE YOU TRYING TO GO? THE MOON?
NO, I DIDN'T MEAN THAT. I TOOK A WRONG TURN... IN LIFE.
THEN YOU ARE THE PANTY THIEF!
EVERYONE HAS A SECRET OR TWO HE WANTS TO KEEP TO HIMSELF.
BUT I'LL TELL YOU THIS: I'M NOT A THIEF.
YEAH? SO HOW COME YOU KEEP PEEKING OUT THE WINDOW?
I'M JUST... YOU KNOW... CHECKING THE WEATHER.
SLURP
SLURP
DAMN. DARK CLOUDS.

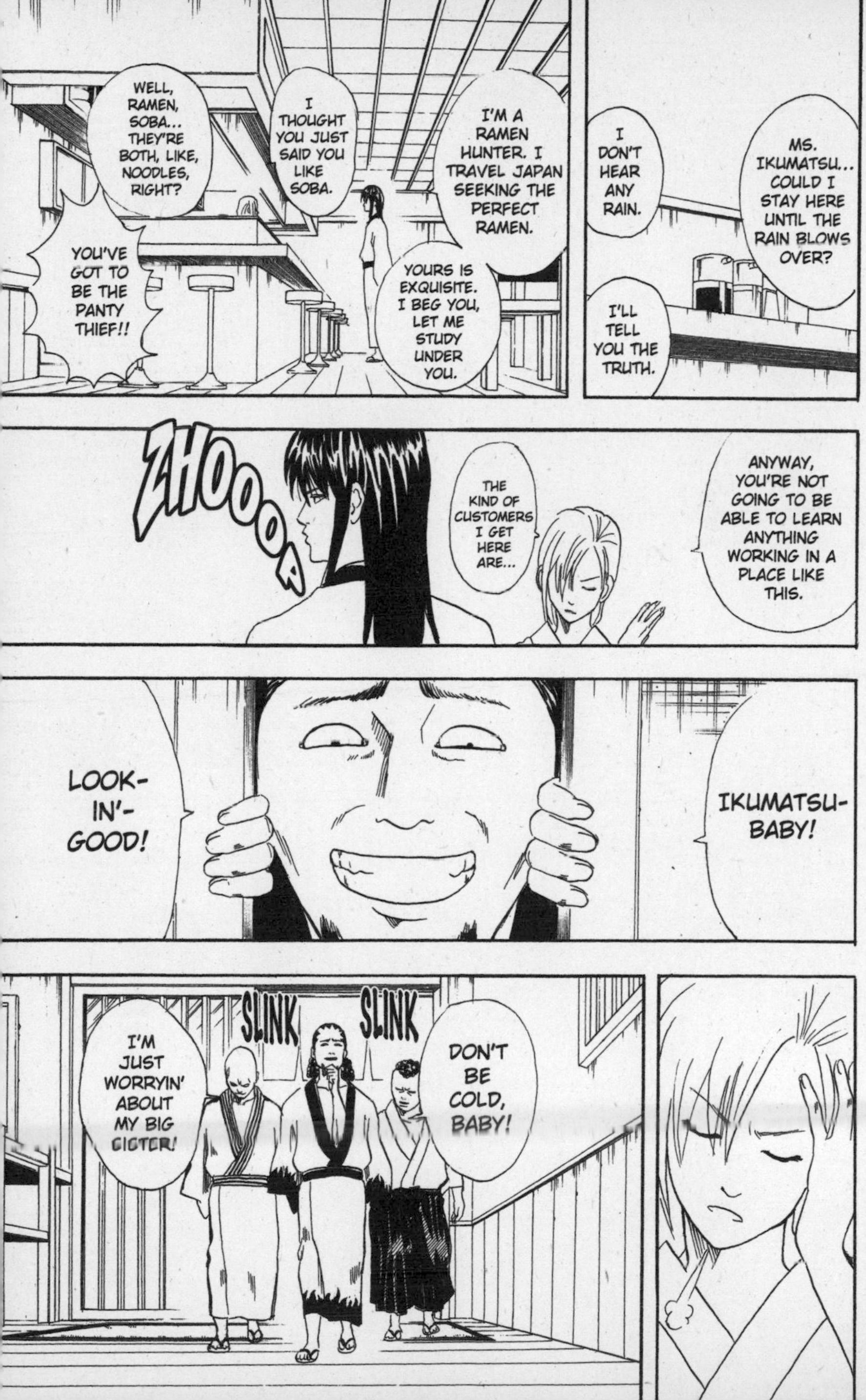
MS. IKUMATSU... COULD I STAY HERE UNTIL THE RAIN BLOWS OVER?
I DON'T HEAR ANY RAIN.
I'LL TELL YOU THE TRUTH.
I'M A RAMEN HUNTER. I TRAVEL JAPAN SEEKING THE PERFECT RAMEN.
YOURS IS EXQUISITE. I BEG YOU, LET ME STUDY UNDER YOU.
I THOUGHT YOU JUST SAID YOU LIKE SOBA.
WELL, RAMEN, SOBA... THEY'RE BOTH, LIKE, NOODLES, RIGHT?
YOU'VE GOT TO BE THE PANTY THIEF!!
ANYWAY, YOU'RE NOT GOING TO BE ABLE TO LEARN ANYTHING WORKING IN A PLACE LIKE THIS.
THE KIND OF CUSTOMERS I GET HERE ARE...
ZHOOOOP
IKUMATSU-BABY!
LOOK-IN'-GOOD!
DON'T BE COLD, BABY!
SLINK
SLINK
I'M JUST WORRYIN' ABOUT MY BIG SISTER!

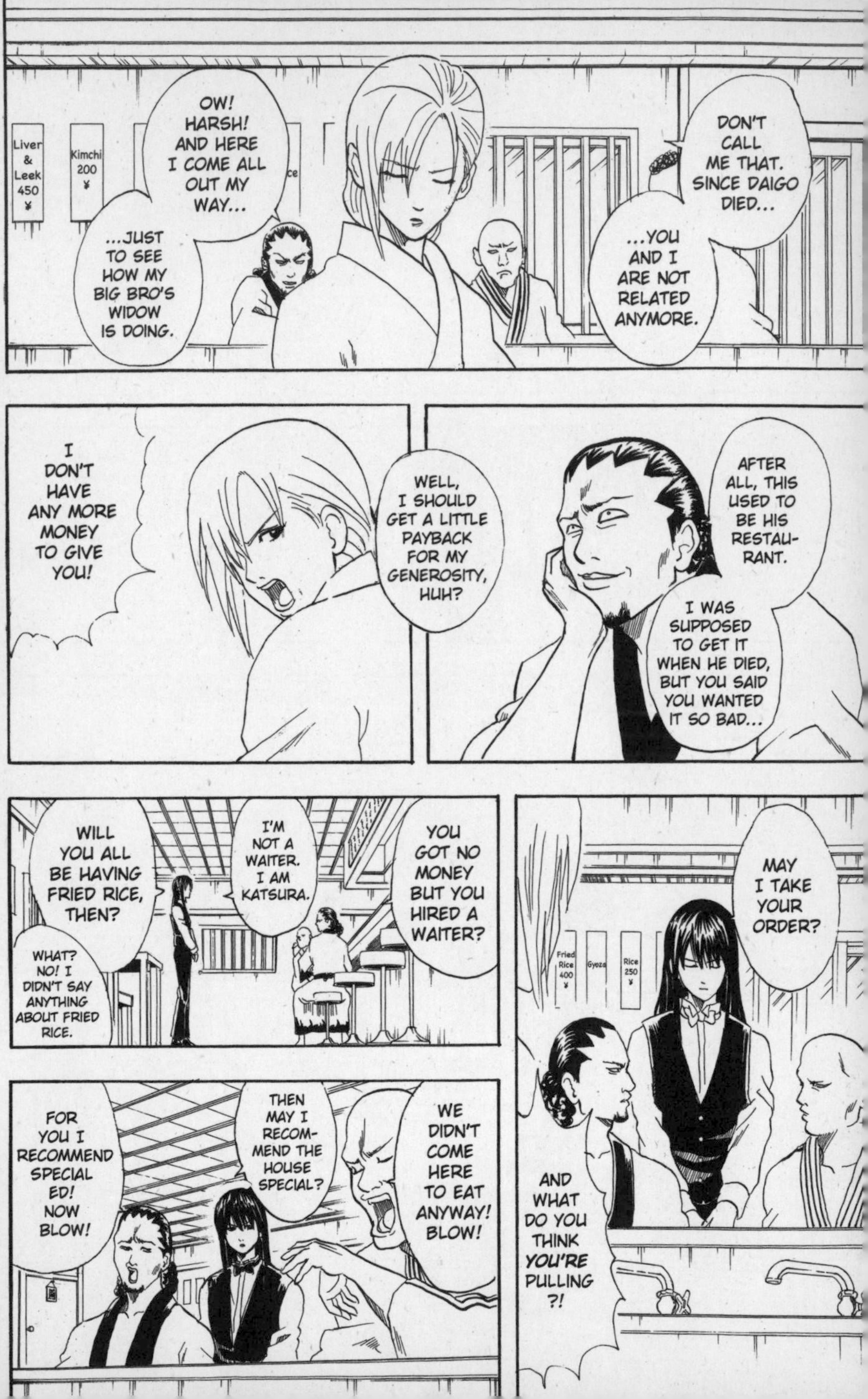
Liver & Leek 450 ¥
Kimchi 200 ¥
DON'T CALL ME THAT. SINCE DAIGO DIED...
...YOU AND I ARE NOT RELATED ANYMORE.
OW! HARSH! AND HERE I COME ALL OUT MY WAY...
...JUST TO SEE HOW MY BIG BRO'S WIDOW IS DOING.
AFTER ALL, THIS USED TO BE HIS RESTAURANT.
I WAS SUPPOSED TO GET IT WHEN HE DIED, BUT YOU SAID YOU WANTED IT SO BAD...
WELL, I SHOULD GET A LITTLE PAYBACK FOR MY GENEROSITY, HUH?
I DON'T HAVE ANY MORE MONEY TO GIVE YOU!
MAY I TAKE YOUR ORDER?
Fried Rice 400 ¥
Gyoza
Rice 250 ¥
AND WHAT DO YOU THINK *YOU'RE* PULLING ?!
YOU GOT NO MONEY BUT YOU HIRED A WAITER?
I'M NOT A WAITER. I AM KATSURA.
WILL YOU ALL BE HAVING FRIED RICE, THEN?
WHAT? NO! I DIDN'T SAY ANYTHING ABOUT FRIED RICE.
WE DIDN'T COME HERE TO EAT ANYWAY! BLOW!
THEN MAY I RECOMMEND THE HOUSE SPECIAL?
FOR YOU I RECOMMEND SPECIAL ED! NOW BLOW!

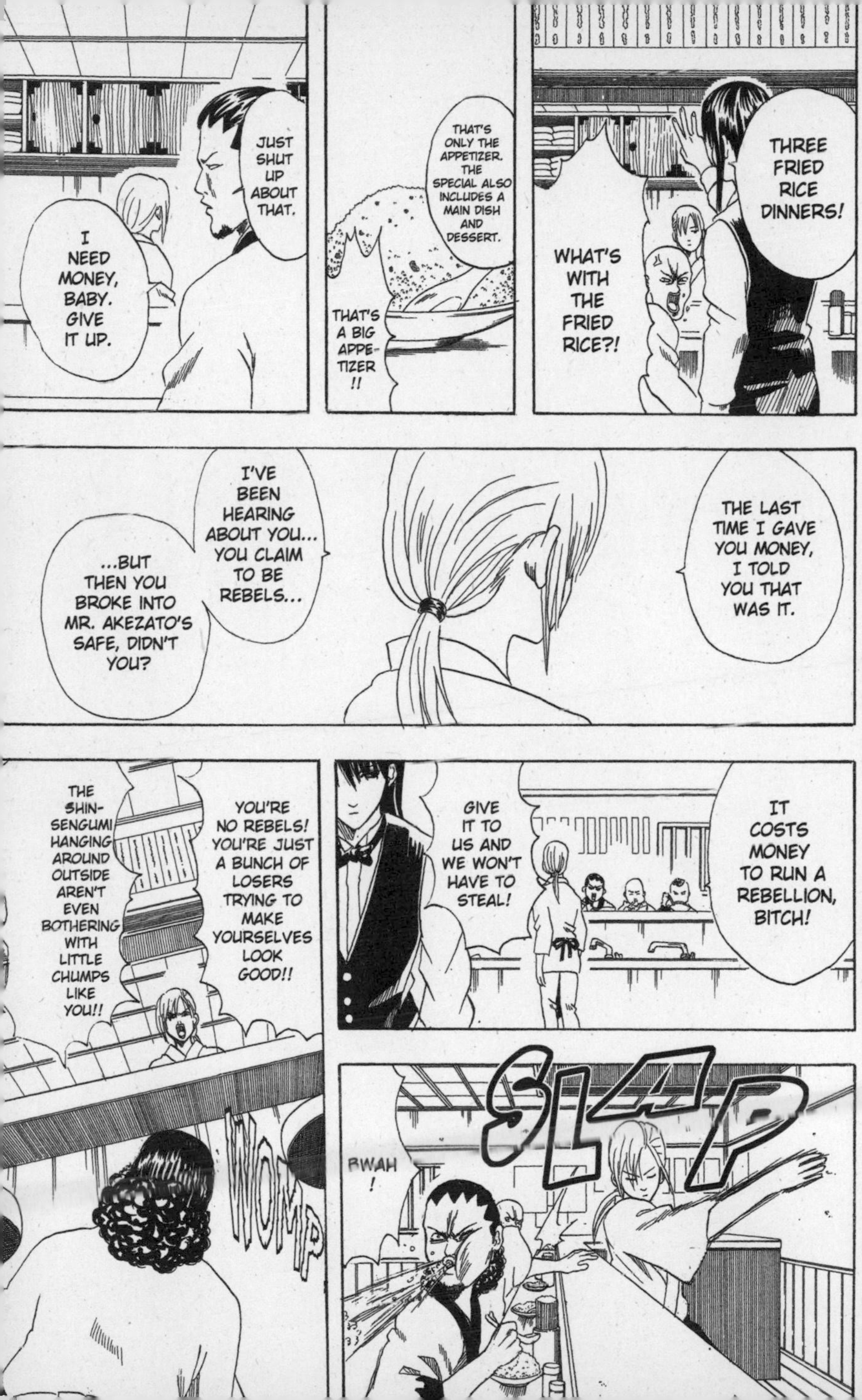
THREE FRIED RICE DINNERS!
WHAT'S WITH THE FRIED RICE?!
THAT'S ONLY THE APPETIZER. THE SPECIAL ALSO INCLUDES A MAIN DISH AND DESSERT.
THAT'S A BIG APPETIZER!!
JUST SHUT UP ABOUT THAT.
I NEED MONEY, BABY. GIVE IT UP.
THE LAST TIME I GAVE YOU MONEY, I TOLD YOU THAT WAS IT.
I'VE BEEN HEARING ABOUT YOU... YOU CLAIM TO BE REBELS...
...BUT THEN YOU BROKE INTO MR. AKEZATO'S SAFE, DIDN'T YOU?
IT COSTS MONEY TO RUN A REBELLION, BITCH!
GIVE IT TO US AND WE WON'T HAVE TO STEAL!
SLAP
BWAH!
YOU'RE NO REBELS! YOU'RE JUST A BUNCH OF LOSERS TRYING TO MAKE YOURSELVES LOOK GOOD!!
THE SHIN-SENGUMI HANGING AROUND OUTSIDE AREN'T EVEN BOTHERING WITH LITTLE CHUMPS LIKE YOU!!
WOMP

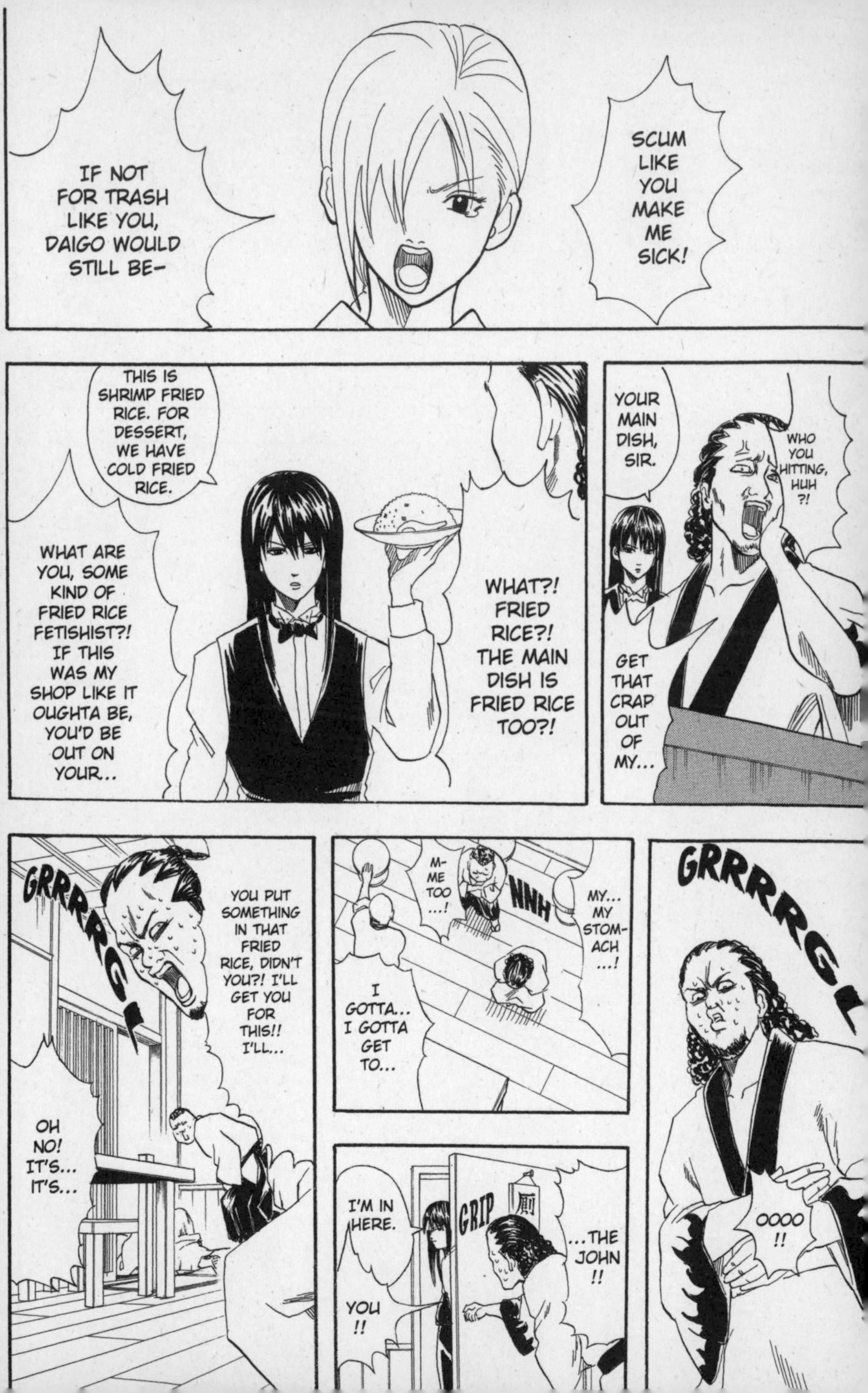
SCUM LIKE YOU MAKE ME SICK!
IF NOT FOR TRASH LIKE YOU, DAIGO WOULD STILL BE-
WHO YOU HITTING, HUH?!
YOUR MAIN DISH, SIR.
GET THAT CRAP OUT OF MY...
THIS IS SHRIMP FRIED RICE. FOR DESSERT, WE HAVE COLD FRIED RICE.
WHAT?! FRIED RICE?! THE MAIN DISH IS FRIED RICE TOO?!
WHAT ARE YOU, SOME KIND OF FRIED RICE FETISHIST?! IF THIS WAS MY SHOP LIKE IT OUGHTA BE, YOU'D BE OUT ON YOUR...
GRRRRGL
OOOO!!
MY... MY STOMACH...!
NNH
M-ME TOO...!
I GOTTA... I GOTTA GET TO...
...THE JOHN!!
GRIP
厠
I'M IN HERE.
YOU!!
YOU PUT SOMETHING IN THAT FRIED RICE, DIDN'T YOU?! I'LL GET YOU FOR THIS!! I'LL...
GRRRRGL
OH NO! IT'S... IT'S...

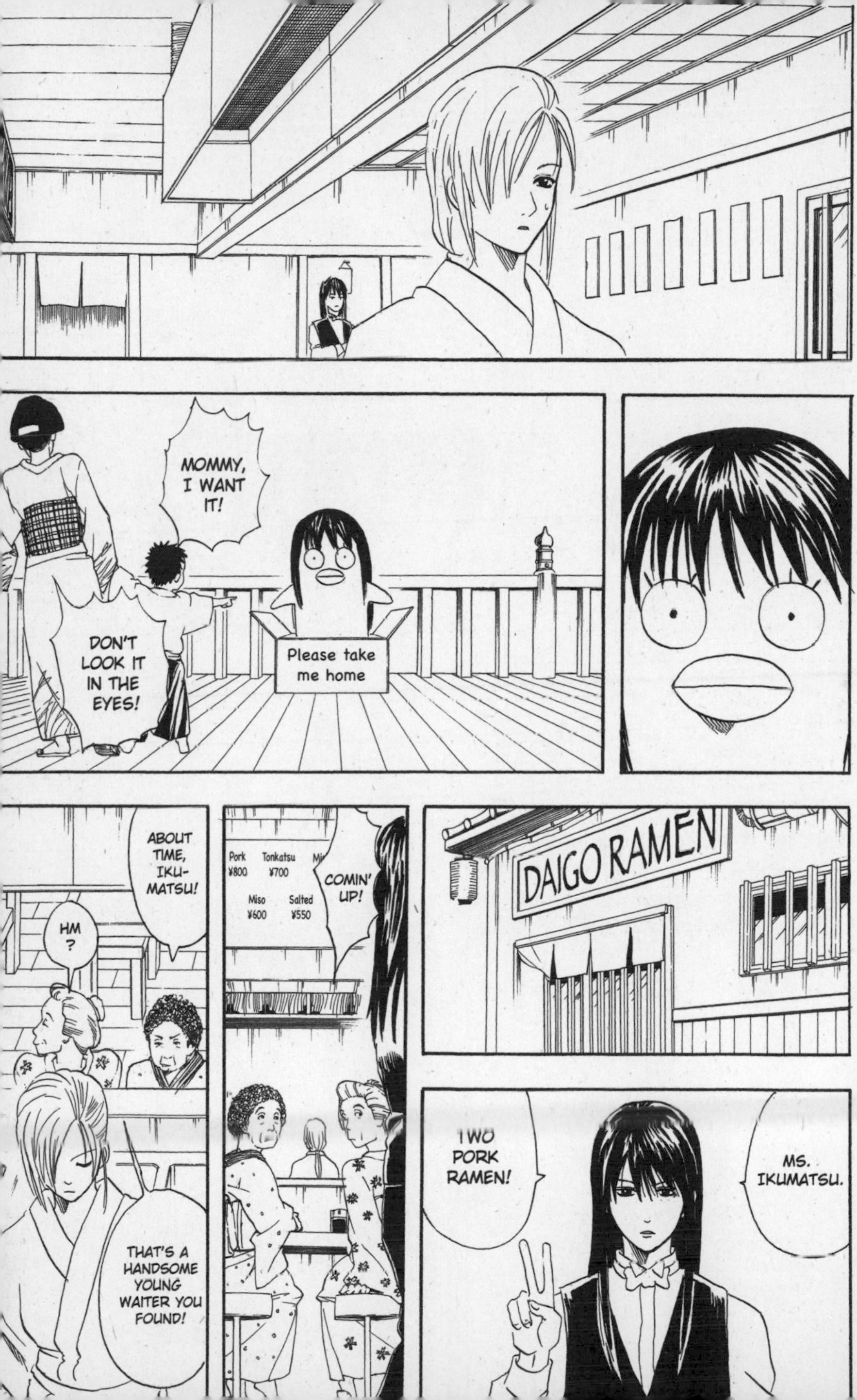
MOMMY, I WANT IT!
Please take me home
DON'T LOOK IT IN THE EYES!
DAIGO RAMEN
MS. IKUMATSU.
TWO PORK RAMEN!
COMIN' UP!
Pork ¥800
Tonkatsu ¥700
Miso ¥600
Salted ¥550
ABOUT TIME, IKUMATSU!
HM?
THAT'S A HANDSOME YOUNG WAITER YOU FOUND!

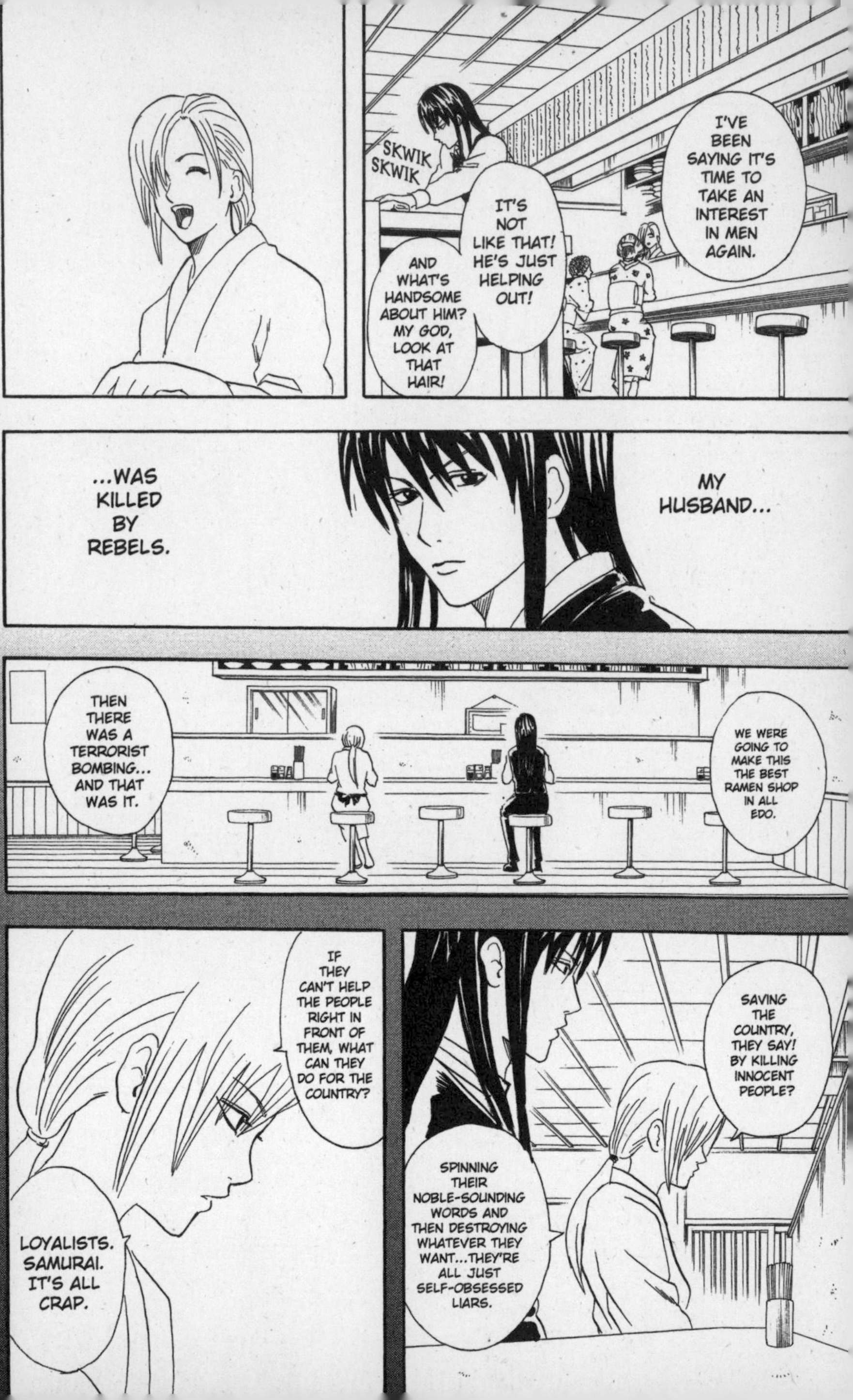
I'VE BEEN SAYING IT'S TIME TO TAKE AN INTEREST IN MEN AGAIN.
IT'S NOT LIKE THAT! HE'S JUST HELPING OUT!
AND WHAT'S HANDSOME ABOUT HIM? MY GOD, LOOK AT THAT HAIR!
SKWIK SKWIK
MY HUSBAND...
...WAS KILLED BY REBELS.
WE WERE GOING TO MAKE THIS THE BEST RAMEN SHOP IN ALL EDO.
THEN THERE WAS A TERRORIST BOMBING... AND THAT WAS IT.
SAVING THE COUNTRY, THEY SAY! BY KILLING INNOCENT PEOPLE?
SPINNING THEIR NOBLE-SOUNDING WORDS AND THEN DESTROYING WHATEVER THEY WANT...THEY'RE ALL JUST SELF-OBSESSED LIARS.
IF THEY CAN'T HELP THE PEOPLE RIGHT IN FRONT OF THEM, WHAT CAN THEY DO FOR THE COUNTRY?
LOYALISTS. SAMURAI. IT'S ALL CRAP.

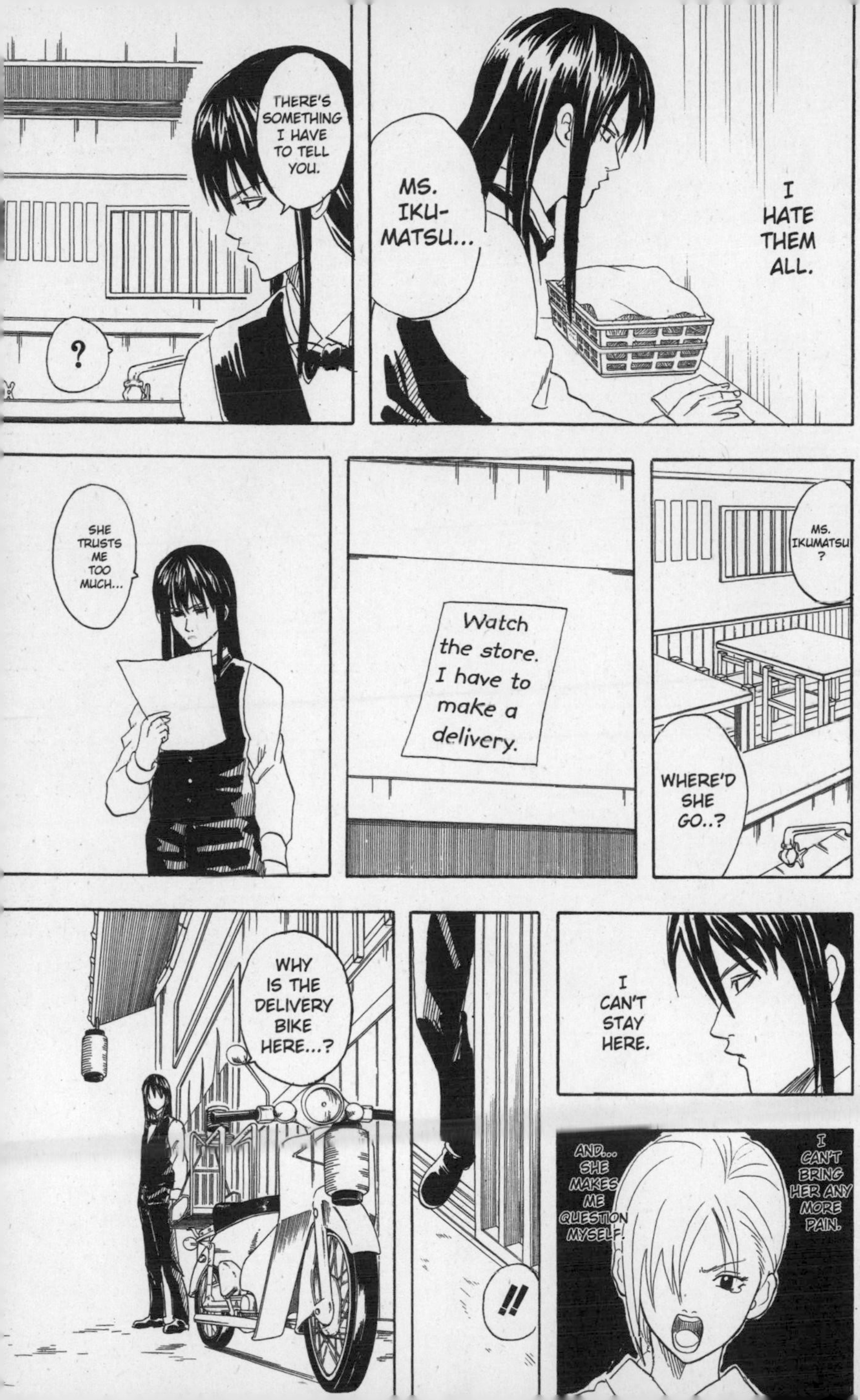
I HATE THEM ALL.
MS. IKU-MATSU...
THERE'S SOMETHING I HAVE TO TELL YOU.
?
MS. IKUMATSU?
WHERE'D SHE GO..?
Watch the store. I have to make a delivery.
SHE TRUSTS ME TOO MUCH...
I CAN'T STAY HERE.
I CAN'T BRING HER ANY MORE PAIN.
AND... SHE MAKES ME QUESTION MYSELF.
!!
WHY IS THE DELIVERY BIKE HERE...?

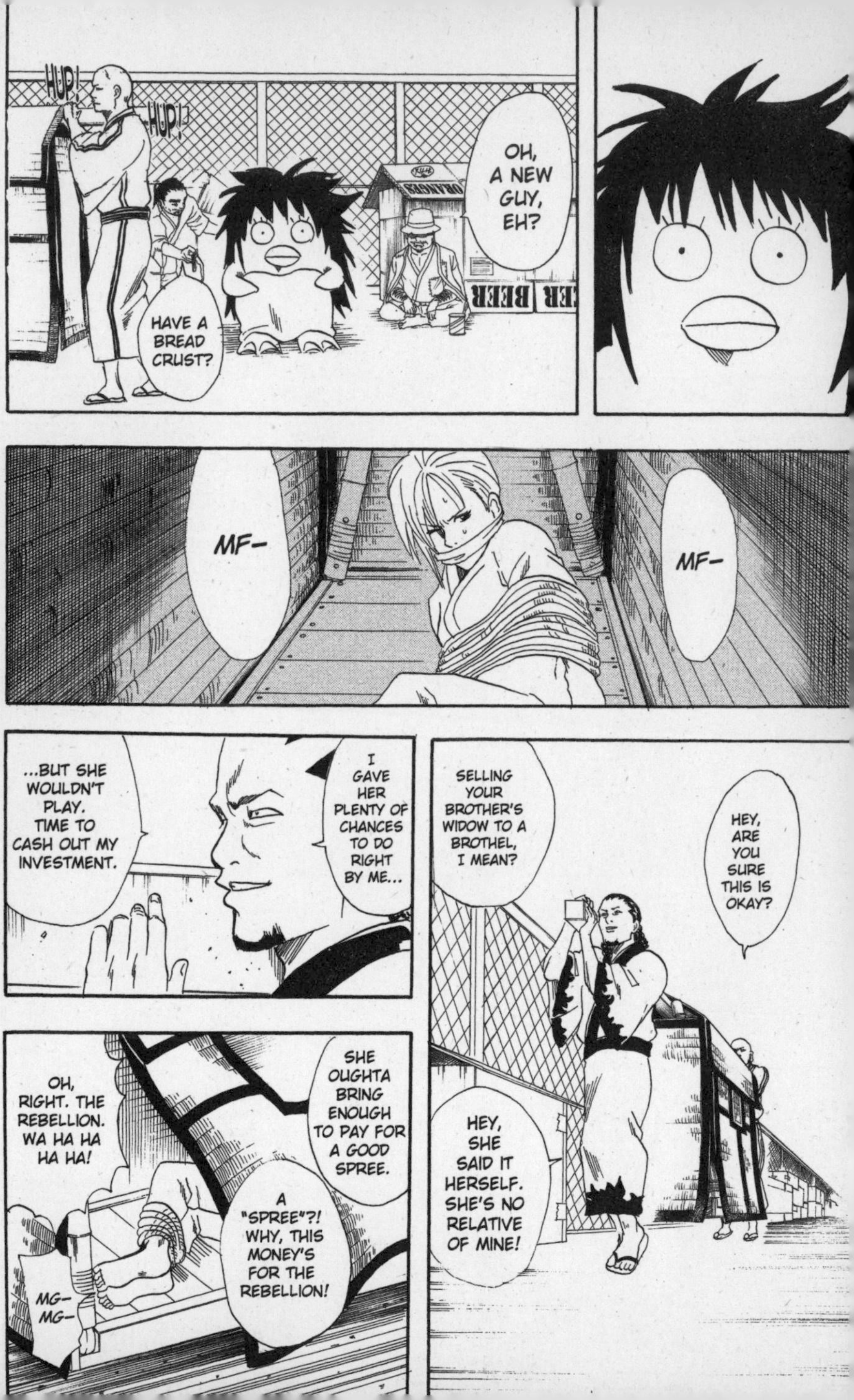
OH, A NEW GUY, EH?
HUP!
HUP!
HAVE A BREAD CRUST?
MF–
MF–
HEY, ARE YOU SURE THIS IS OKAY?
SELLING YOUR BROTHER'S WIDOW TO A BROTHEL, I MEAN?
HEY, SHE SAID IT HERSELF. SHE'S NO RELATIVE OF MINE!
I GAVE HER PLENTY OF CHANCES TO DO RIGHT BY ME...
...BUT SHE WOULDN'T PLAY. TIME TO CASH OUT MY INVESTMENT.
SHE OUGHTA BRING ENOUGH TO PAY FOR A GOOD SPREE.
A "SPREE"?! WHY, THIS MONEY'S FOR THE REBELLION!
OH, RIGHT. THE REBELLION. WA HA HA HA HA!
MG– MG–

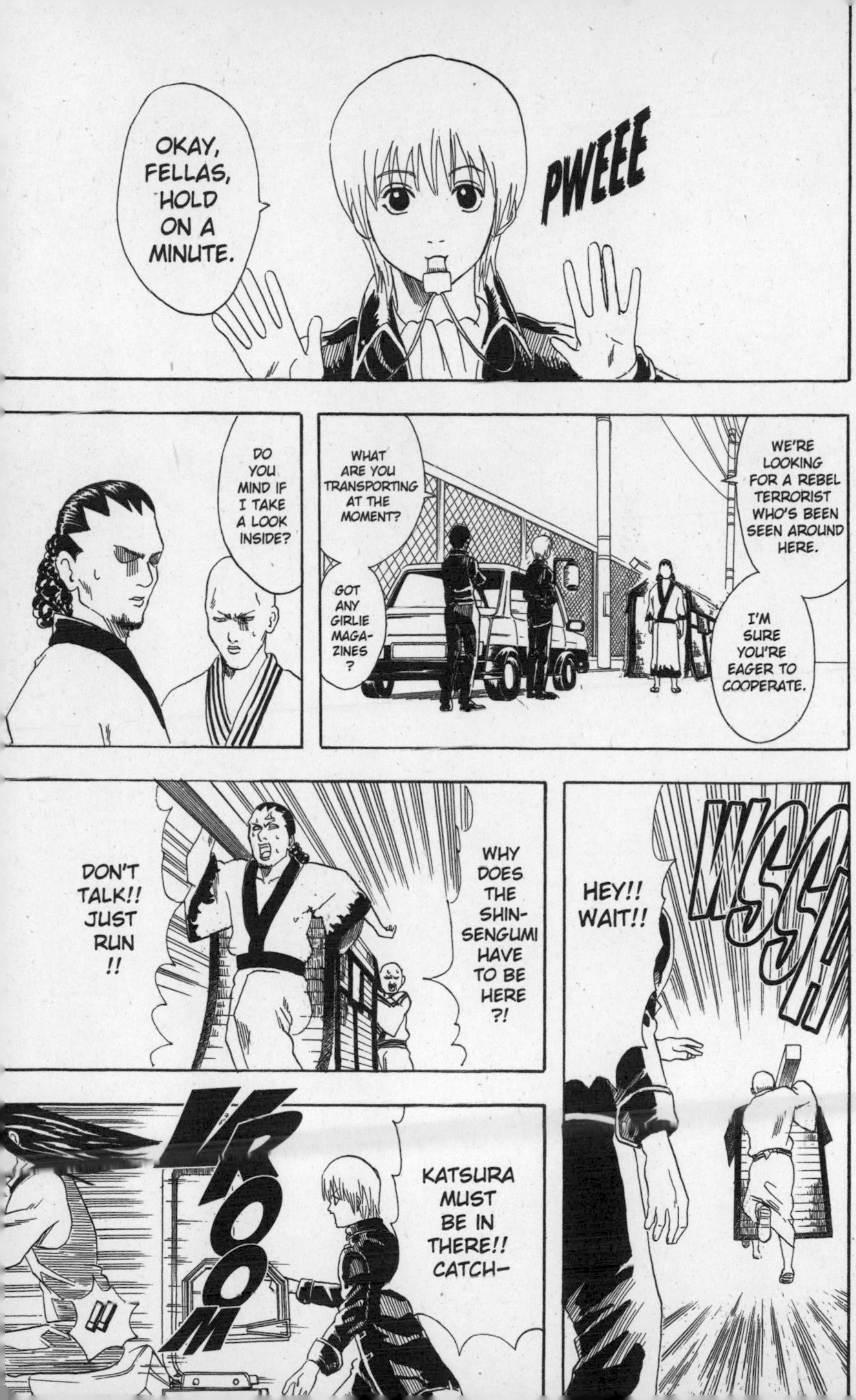
PWEEE
OKAY, FELLAS, HOLD ON A MINUTE.
WE'RE LOOKING FOR A REBEL TERRORIST WHO'S BEEN SEEN AROUND HERE.
I'M SURE YOU'RE EAGER TO COOPERATE.
WHAT ARE YOU TRANSPORTING AT THE MOMENT?
GOT ANY GIRLIE MAGA-ZINES?
DO YOU MIND IF I TAKE A LOOK INSIDE?
HEY!! WAIT!!
WHY DOES THE SHIN-SENGUMI HAVE TO BE HERE?!
DON'T TALK!! JUST RUN!!
KATSURA MUST BE IN THERE!! CATCH-
KROOM
!!

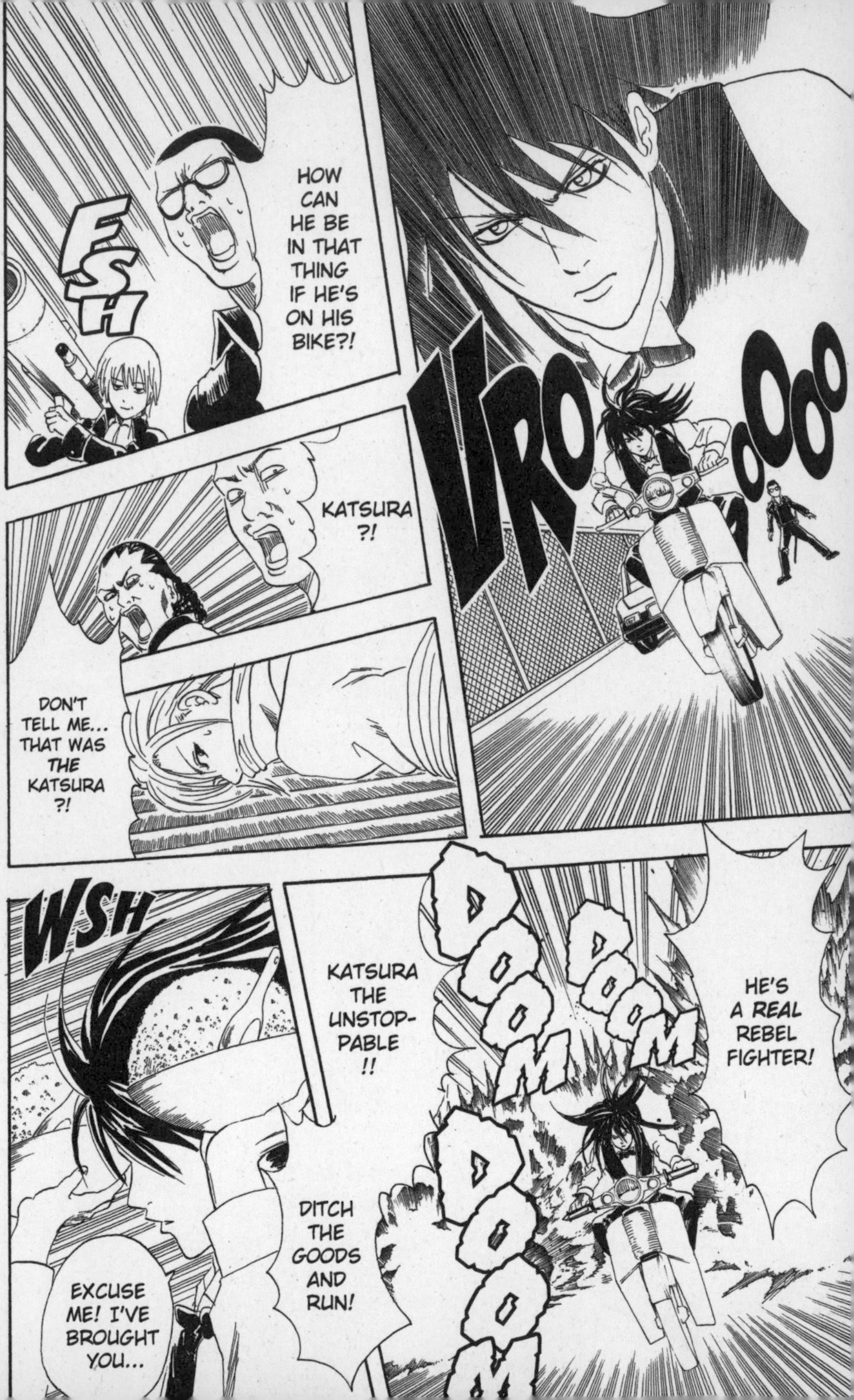
VROOOOOO
FSH
HOW CAN HE BE IN THAT THING IF HE'S ON HIS BIKE?!
KATSURA ?!
DON'T TELL ME... THAT WAS THE KATSURA ?!
HE'S A REAL REBEL FIGHTER!
KATSURA THE UNSTOP-PABLE !!
DOOM DOOM
DITCH THE GOODS AND RUN!
DOOOOOM
WSH
EXCUSE ME! I'VE BROUGHT YOU...

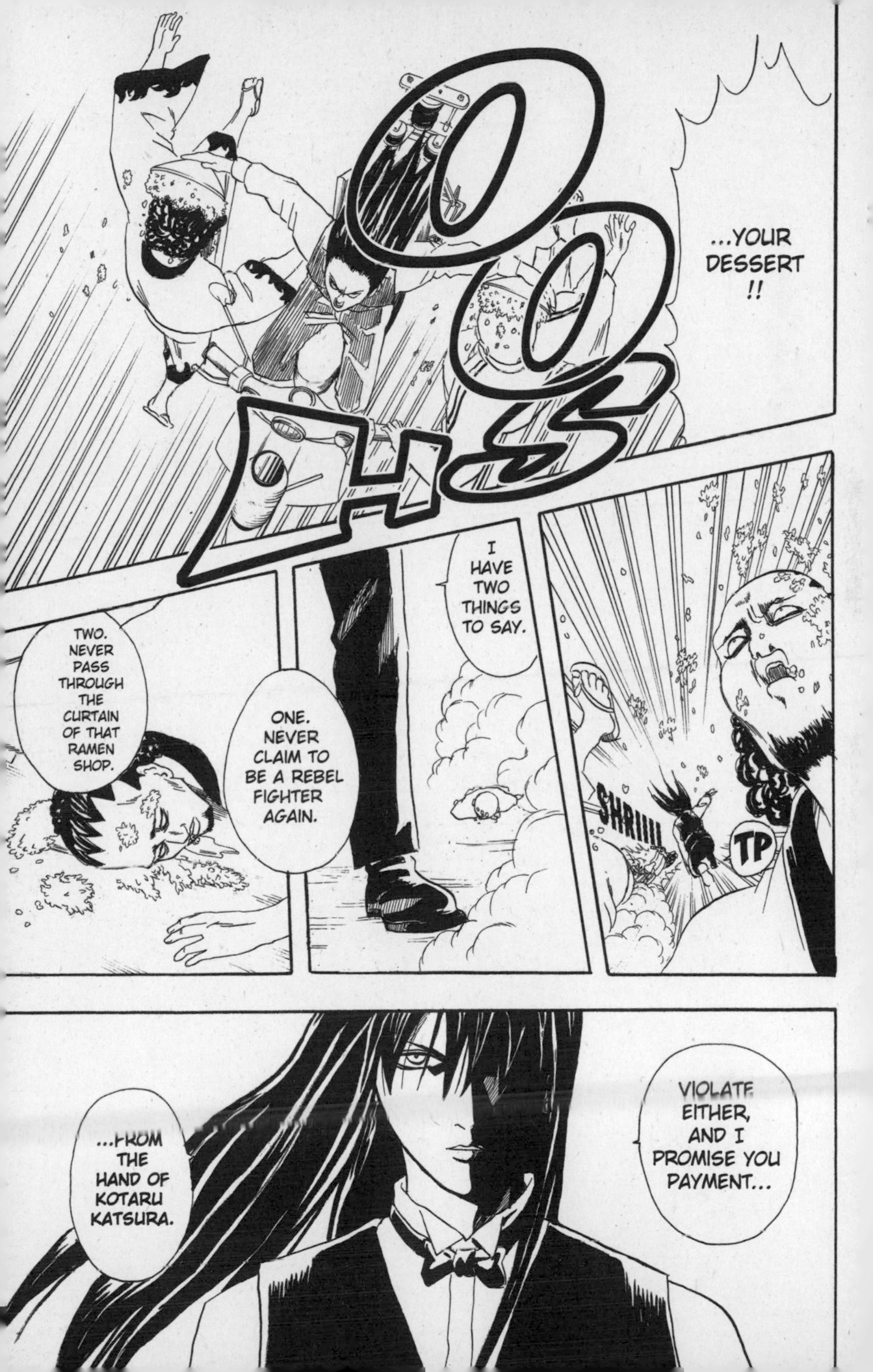
...YOUR DESSERT !!
SHRIIII
TP
I HAVE TWO THINGS TO SAY.
ONE. NEVER CLAIM TO BE A REBEL FIGHTER AGAIN.
TWO. NEVER PASS THROUGH THE CURTAIN OF THAT RAMEN SHOP.
VIOLATE EITHER, AND I PROMISE YOU PAYMENT...
...FROM THE HAND OF KOTARU KATSURA.

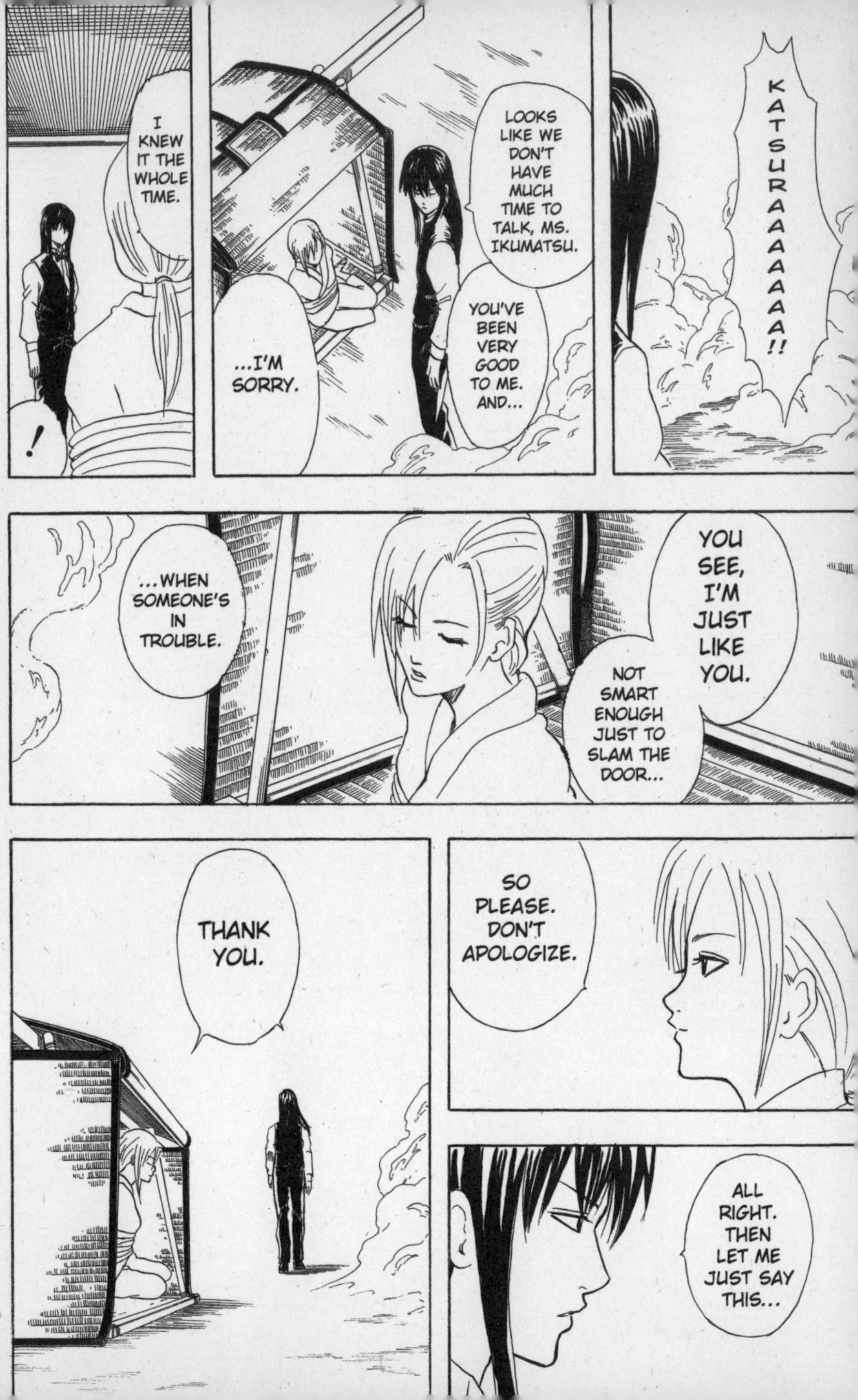
KATSURAAAAAAA!!
LOOKS LIKE WE DON'T HAVE MUCH TIME TO TALK, MS. IKUMATSU.
YOU'VE BEEN VERY GOOD TO ME. AND...
...I'M SORRY.
I KNEW IT THE WHOLE TIME.
!
YOU SEE, I'M JUST LIKE YOU.
NOT SMART ENOUGH JUST TO SLAM THE DOOR...
...WHEN SOMEONE'S IN TROUBLE.
SO PLEASE. DON'T APOLOGIZE.
ALL RIGHT. THEN LET ME JUST SAY THIS...
THANK YOU.

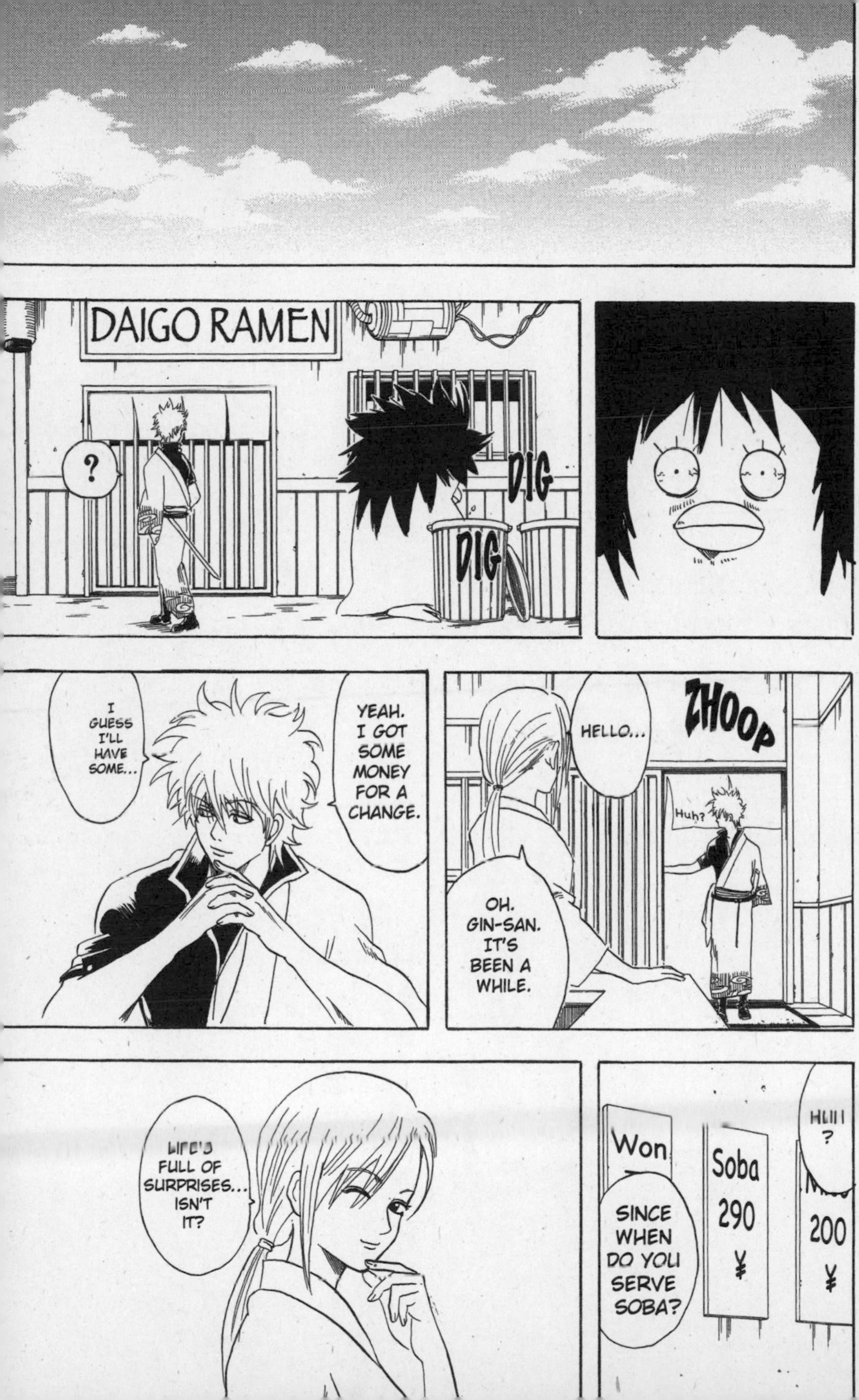
DIG
DIG
DAIGO RAMEN
?
ZHOOP
HELLO...
Huh?
OH. GIN-SAN. IT'S BEEN A WHILE.
YEAH. I GOT SOME MONEY FOR A CHANGE.
I GUESS I'LL HAVE SOME...
HUH?
200 ¥
Soba 290 ¥
Won
SINCE WHEN DO YOU SERVE SOBA?
LIFE'S FULL OF SURPRISES... ISN'T IT?

Sachan's Song

Sachan's real name, see...

...is Ayame Sarutobi. Like the famous ninja Sarutobi, meaning "flying monkey." Seriously.

But since everyone was calling her "Monkey" ("Hey, Monkey!") we told her, "We'd better come up with a better nickname for you." So we started calling her Sachan.

Aren't we nice to our characters?

You didn't have to name me "flying monkey" in the first place, jerk!

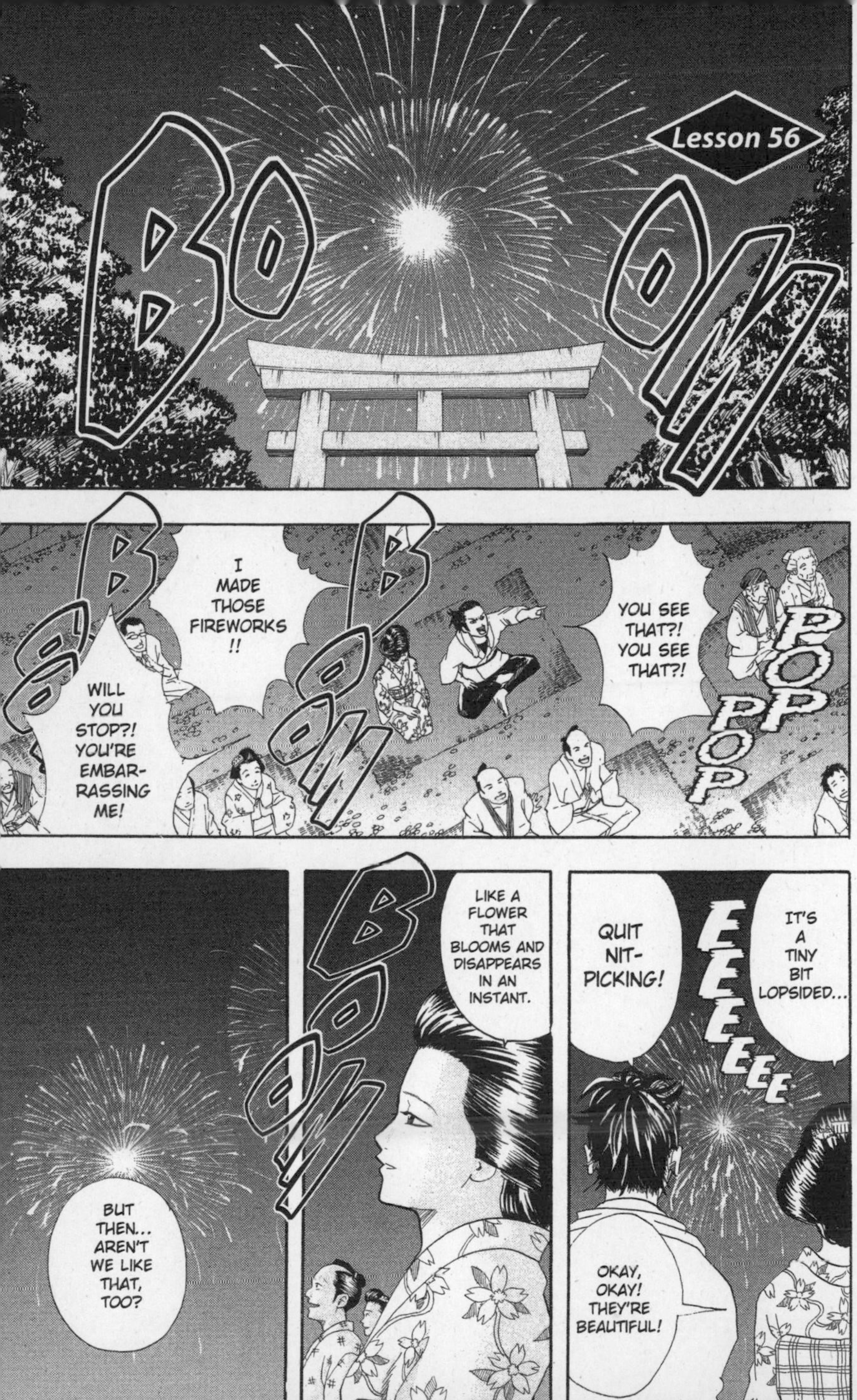
Lesson 56
BOOM
POP
POP
POP
POP
YOU SEE THAT?! YOU SEE THAT?!
BOOM
I MADE THOSE FIREWORKS !!
WILL YOU STOP?! YOU'RE EMBARRASSING ME!
IT'S A TINY BIT LOPSIDED...
EEEEEEEE
QUIT NIT-PICKING!
OKAY, OKAY! THEY'RE BEAUTIFUL!
LIKE A FLOWER THAT BLOOMS AND DISAPPEARS IN AN INSTANT.
BOOM
BUT THEN... AREN'T WE LIKE THAT, TOO?

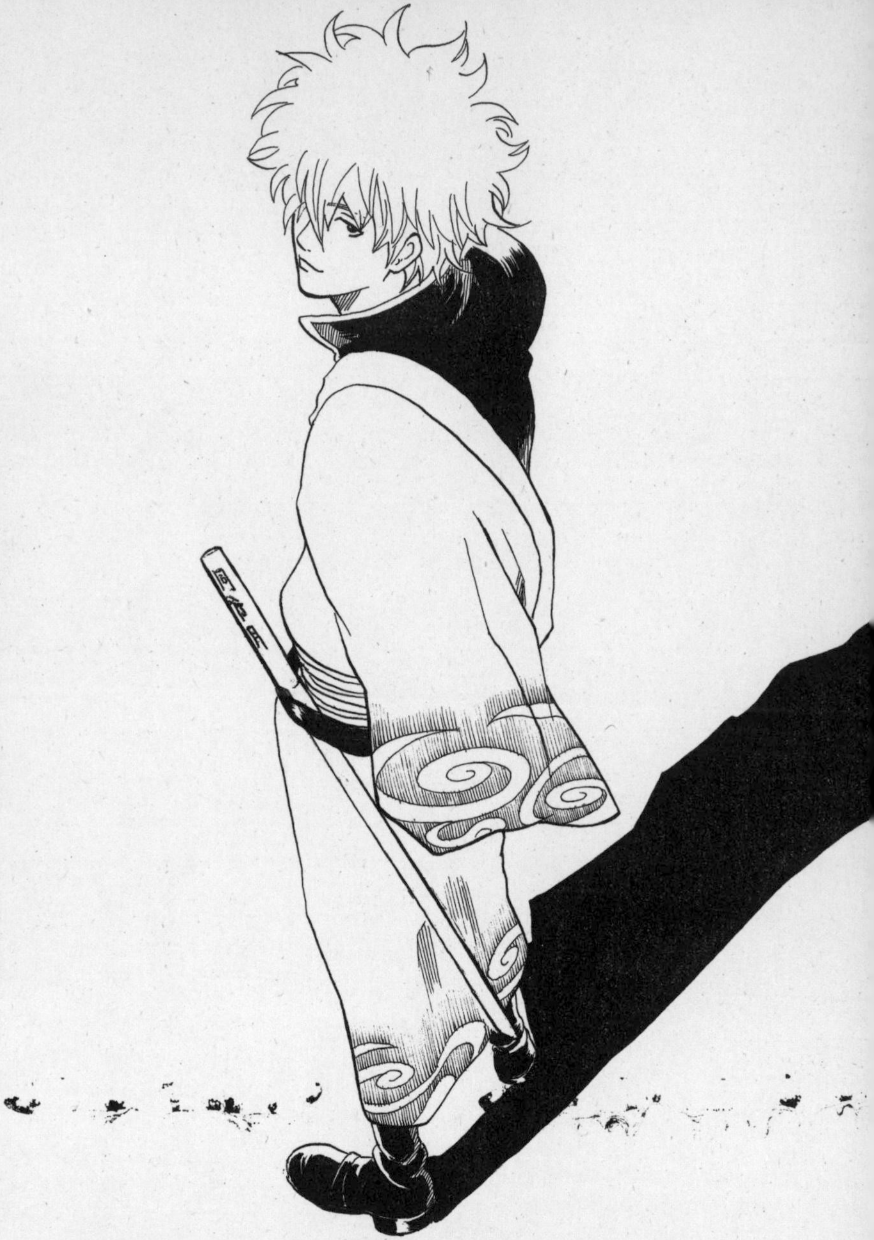

Lesson 56:
Eating Ice Cream in Winter Is Awesome

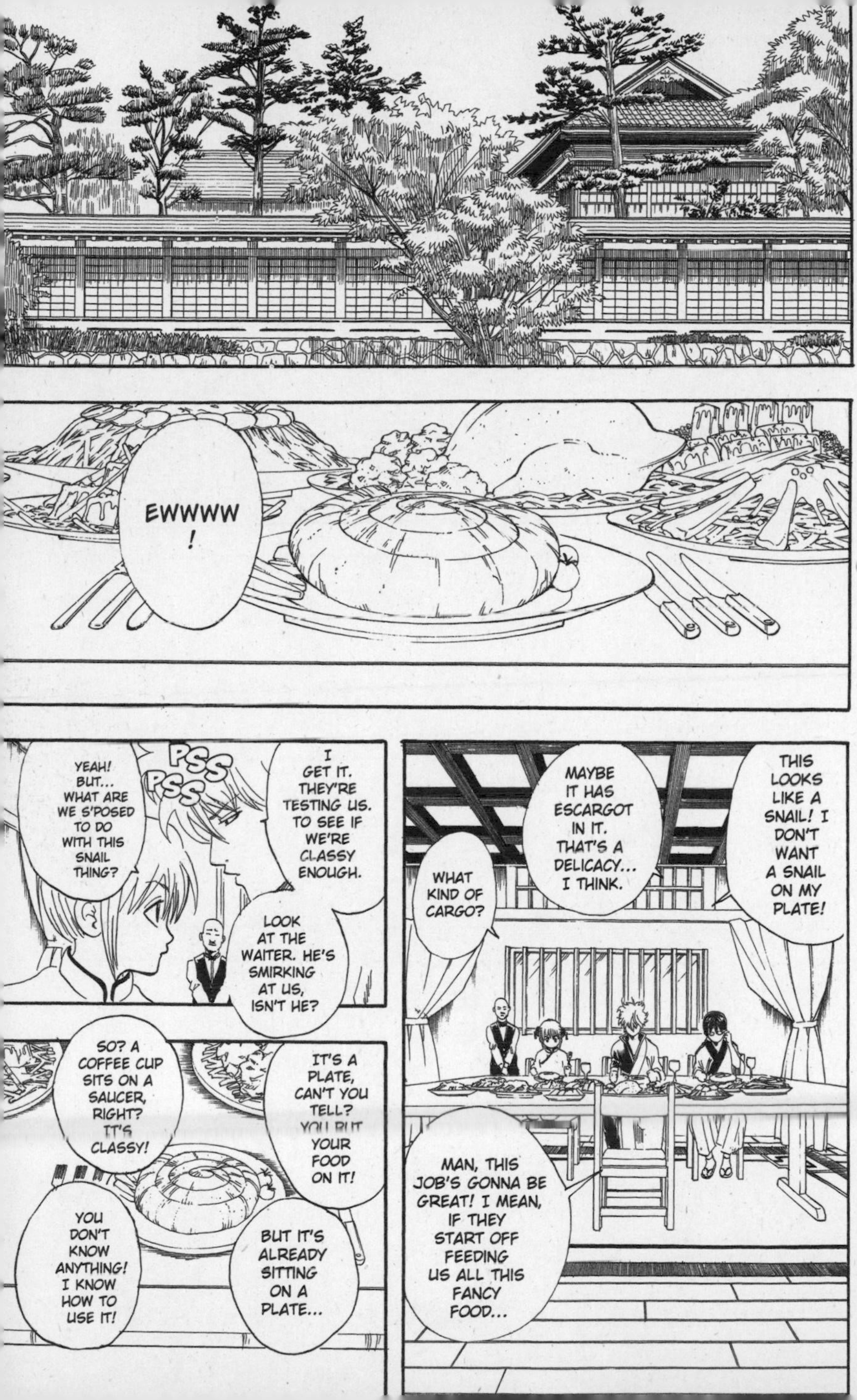
EWWWW!
THIS LOOKS LIKE A SNAIL! I DON'T WANT A SNAIL ON MY PLATE!
MAYBE IT HAS ESCARGOT IN IT. THAT'S A DELICACY... I THINK.
WHAT KIND OF CARGO?
MAN, THIS JOB'S GONNA BE GREAT! I MEAN, IF THEY START OFF FEEDING US ALL THIS FANCY FOOD...
I GET IT. THEY'RE TESTING US. TO SEE IF WE'RE CLASSY ENOUGH.
PSS PSS
YEAH! BUT... WHAT ARE WE S'POSED TO DO WITH THIS SNAIL THING?
LOOK AT THE WAITER. HE'S SMIRKING AT US, ISN'T HE?
IT'S A PLATE, CAN'T YOU TELL? YOU PUT YOUR FOOD ON IT!
SO? A COFFEE CUP SITS ON A SAUCER, RIGHT? IT'S CLASSY!
BUT IT'S ALREADY SITTING ON A PLATE...
YOU DON'T KNOW ANYTHING! I KNOW HOW TO USE IT!

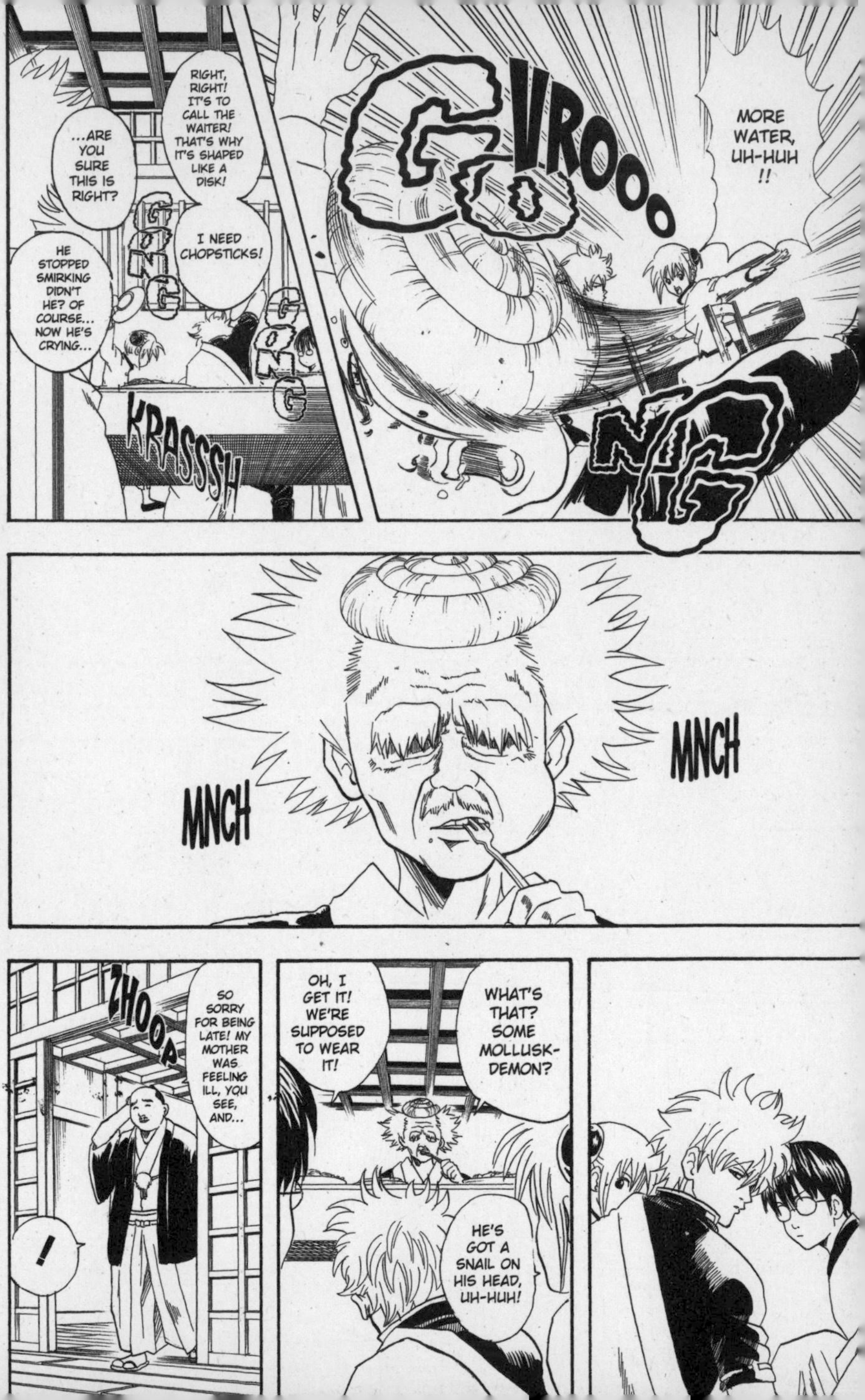
MORE WATER, UH-HUH !!
VROOO
RIGHT, RIGHT! IT'S TO CALL THE WAITER! THAT'S WHY IT'S SHAPED LIKE A DISK!
...ARE YOU SURE THIS IS RIGHT?
I NEED CHOPSTICKS!
GONG
GONG
HE STOPPED SMIRKING DIDN'T HE? OF COURSE... NOW HE'S CRYING...
KRASSSH
MNCH
MNCH
WHAT'S THAT? SOME MOLLUSK-DEMON?
OH, I GET IT! WE'RE SUPPOSED TO WEAR IT!
HE'S GOT A SNAIL ON HIS HEAD, UH-HUH!
ZHOOP
SO SORRY FOR BEING LATE! MY MOTHER WAS FEELING ILL, YOU SEE, AND...
!

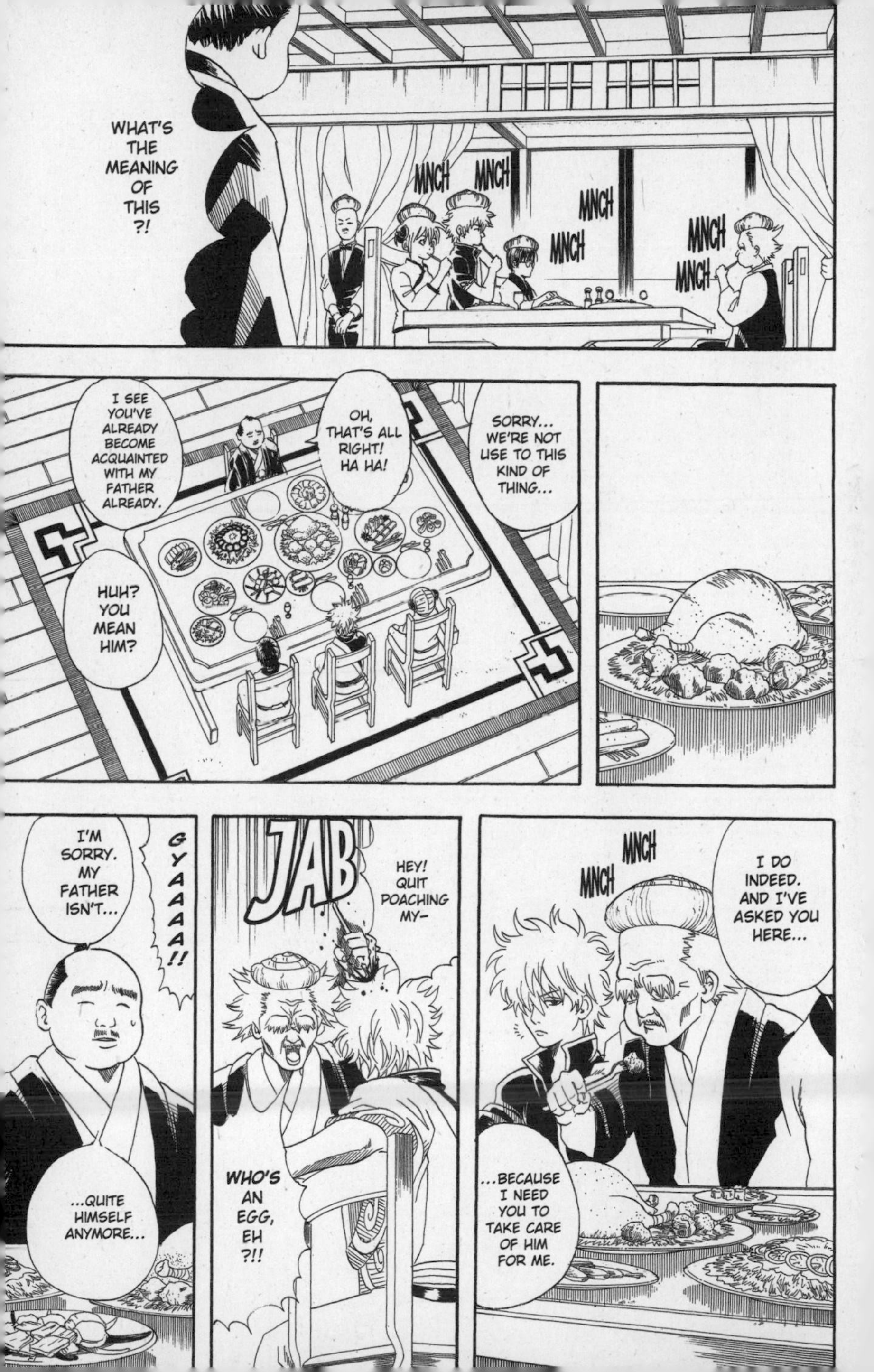
WHAT'S THE MEANING OF THIS ?!
MNCH
MNCH
MNCH
MNCH
MNCH
MNCH
SORRY... WE'RE NOT USE TO THIS KIND OF THING...
OH, THAT'S ALL RIGHT! HA HA!
I SEE YOU'VE ALREADY BECOME ACQUAINTED WITH MY FATHER ALREADY.
HUH? YOU MEAN HIM?
MNCH
MNCH
I DO INDEED. AND I'VE ASKED YOU HERE...
...BECAUSE I NEED YOU TO TAKE CARE OF HIM FOR ME.
JAB
HEY! QUIT POACHING MY-
WHO'S AN EGG, EH ?!!
GYAAAAA!!
I'M SORRY. MY FATHER ISN'T...
...QUITE HIMSELF ANYMORE...

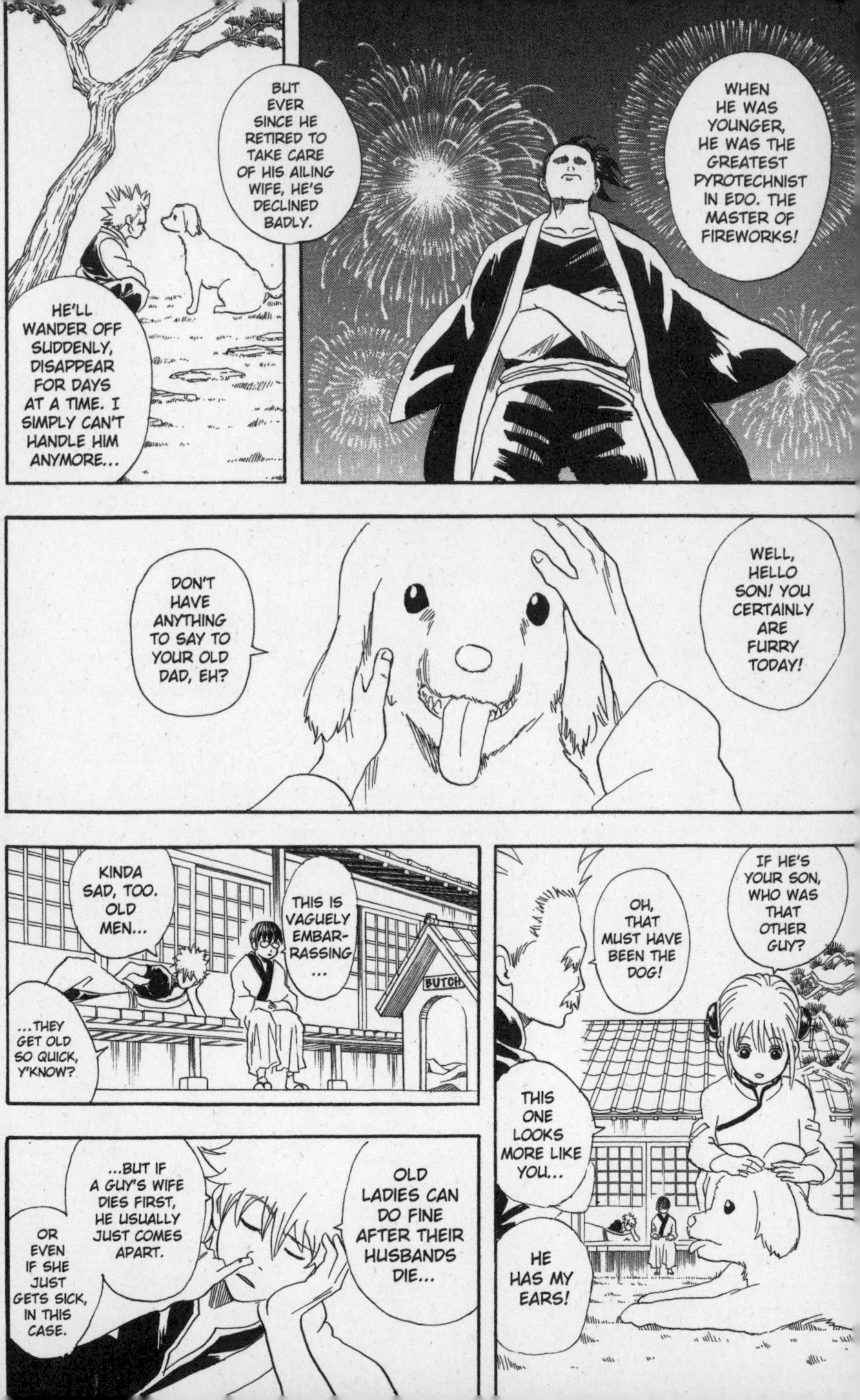
WHEN HE WAS YOUNGER, HE WAS THE GREATEST PYROTECHNIST IN EDO. THE MASTER OF FIREWORKS!
BUT EVER SINCE HE RETIRED TO TAKE CARE OF HIS AILING WIFE, HE'S DECLINED BADLY.
HE'LL WANDER OFF SUDDENLY, DISAPPEAR FOR DAYS AT A TIME. I SIMPLY CAN'T HANDLE HIM ANYMORE...
WELL, HELLO SON! YOU CERTAINLY ARE FURRY TODAY!
DON'T HAVE ANYTHING TO SAY TO YOUR OLD DAD, EH?
IF HE'S YOUR SON, WHO WAS THAT OTHER GUY?
OH, THAT MUST HAVE BEEN THE DOG!
THIS ONE LOOKS MORE LIKE YOU...
HE HAS MY EARS!
THIS IS VAGUELY EMBARRASSING...
KINDA SAD, TOO. OLD MEN...
BUTCH
...THEY GET OLD SO QUICK, Y'KNOW?
OLD LADIES CAN DO FINE AFTER THEIR HUSBANDS DIE...
...BUT IF A GUY'S WIFE DIES FIRST, HE USUALLY JUST COMES APART.
OR EVEN IF SHE JUST GETS SICK, IN THIS CASE.

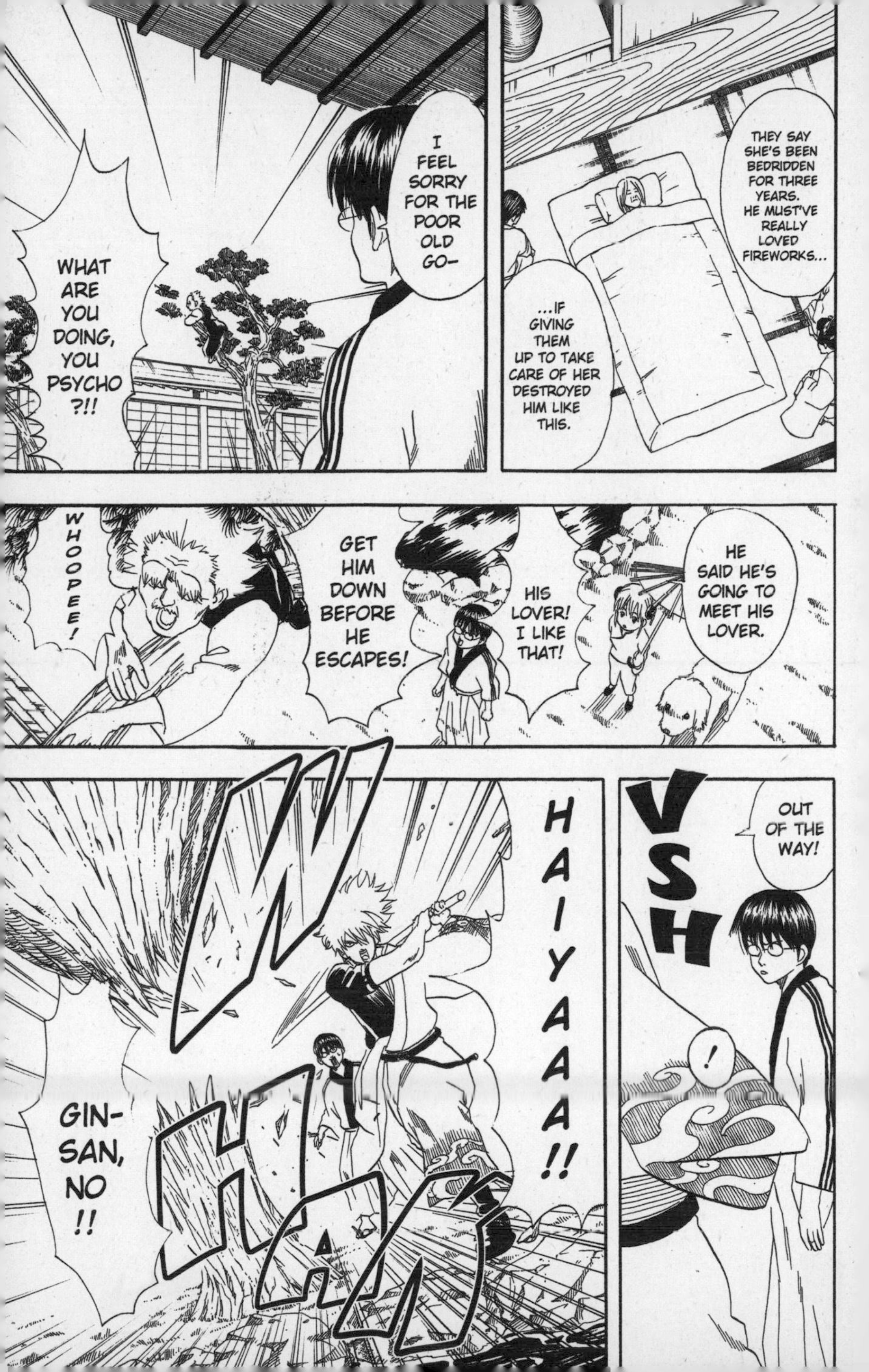
THEY SAY SHE'S BEEN BEDRIDDEN FOR THREE YEARS. HE MUST'VE REALLY LOVED FIREWORKS...
...IF GIVING THEM UP TO TAKE CARE OF HER DESTROYED HIM LIKE THIS.
I FEEL SORRY FOR THE POOR OLD GO–
WHAT ARE YOU DOING, YOU PSYCHO?!!
HE SAID HE'S GOING TO MEET HIS LOVER.
HIS LOVER! I LIKE THAT!
GET HIM DOWN BEFORE HE ESCAPES!
WHOOPEE!
OUT OF THE WAY!
VSH
!
HAIYAAAA!!
GIN-SAN, NO!!

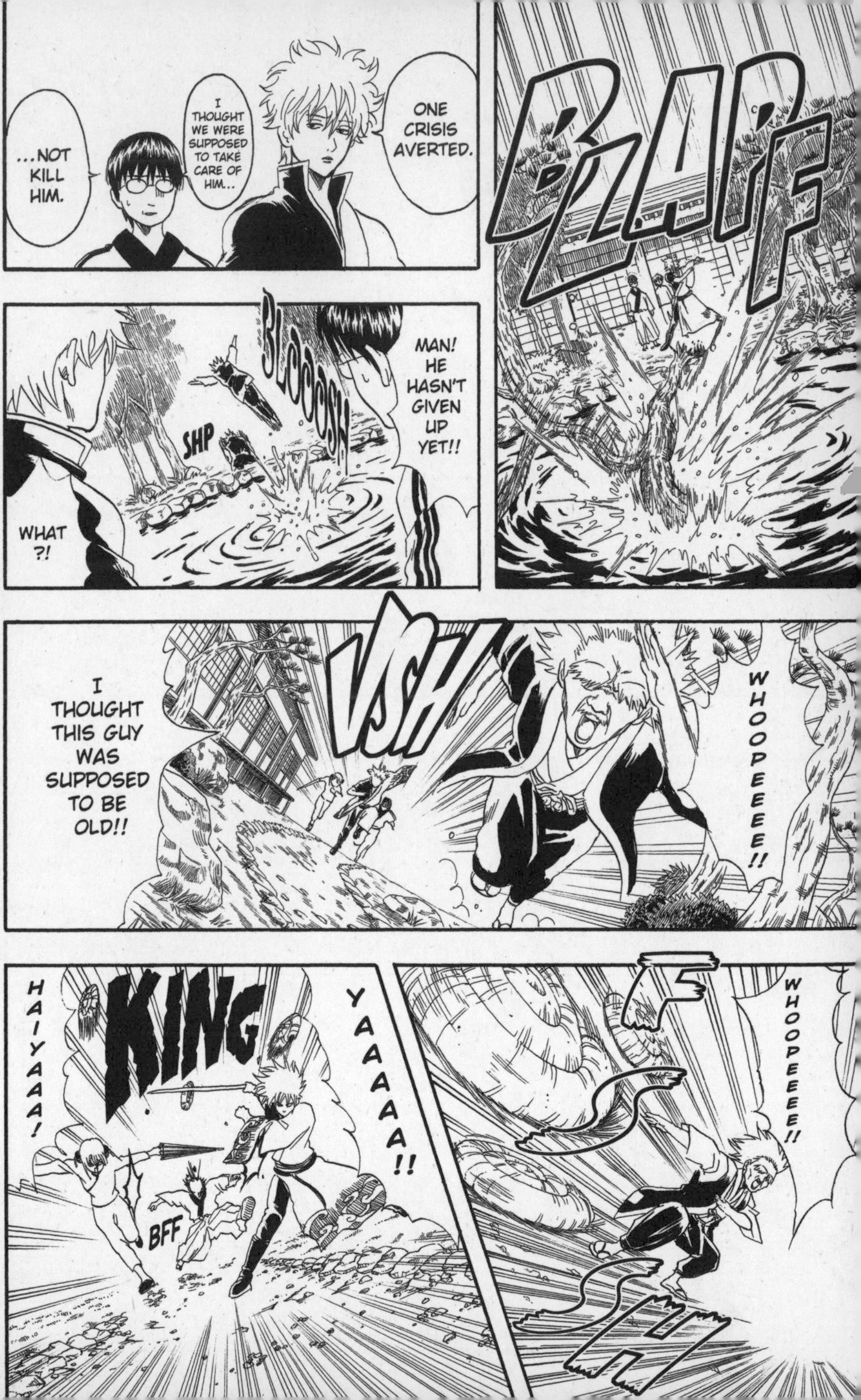
BZAPF
ONE CRISIS AVERTED.
I THOUGHT WE WERE SUPPOSED TO TAKE CARE OF HIM...
...NOT KILL HIM.
MAN! HE HASN'T GIVEN UP YET!!
BLOOOOSH
SHP
WHAT ?!
WHOOPEEEE!!
VSH
I THOUGHT THIS GUY WAS SUPPOSED TO BE OLD!!
WHOOPEEEE!!
YAAAAAA!!
KING
HAIYAAA!
BFF

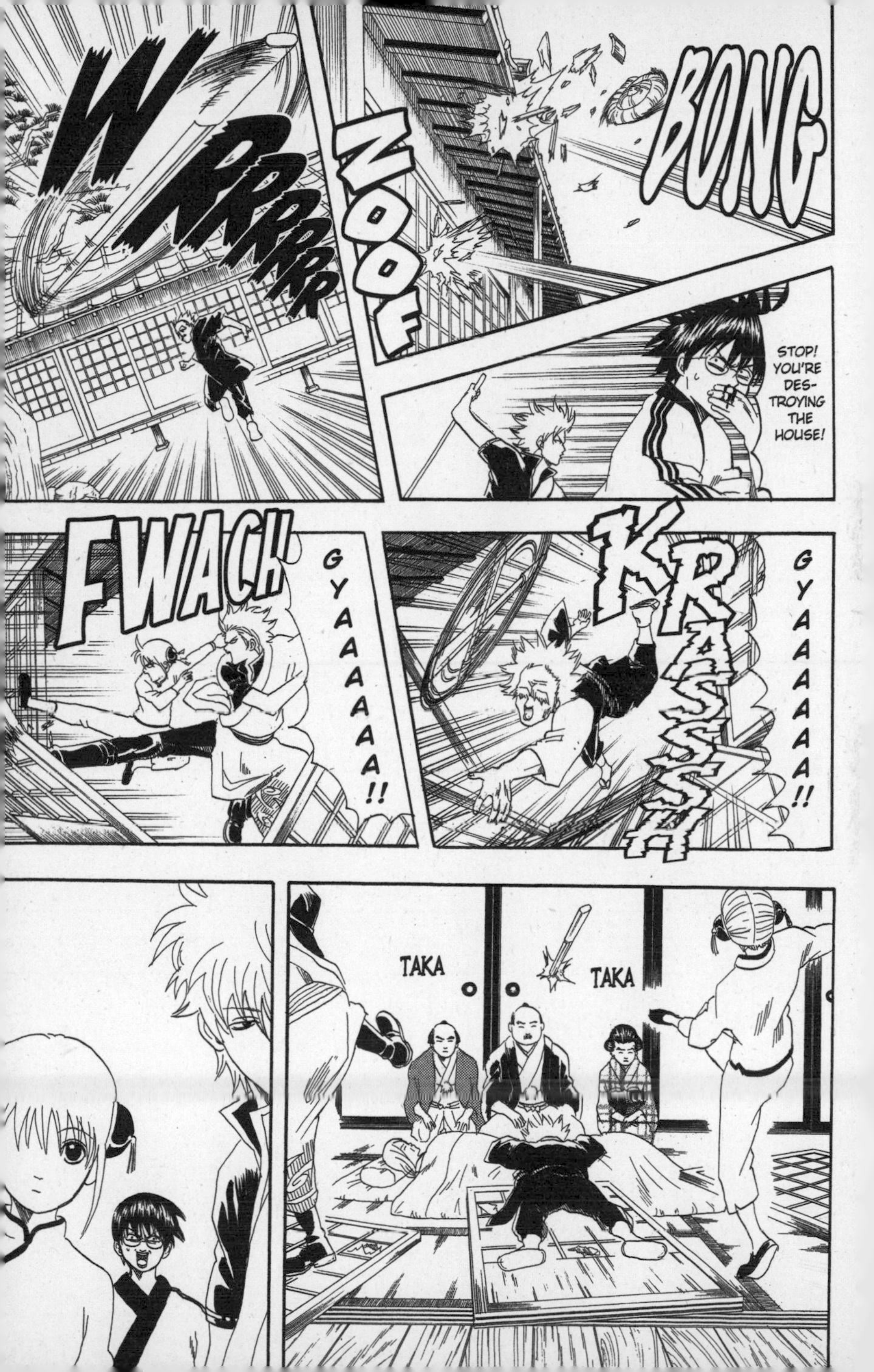
BONG
ZOOOF
STOP! YOU'RE DES-TROYING THE HOUSE!
WRRRRRR
KRASSHA
GYAAAAAAAA!!
FWACH!
GYAAAAAAA!!
TAKA
TAKA

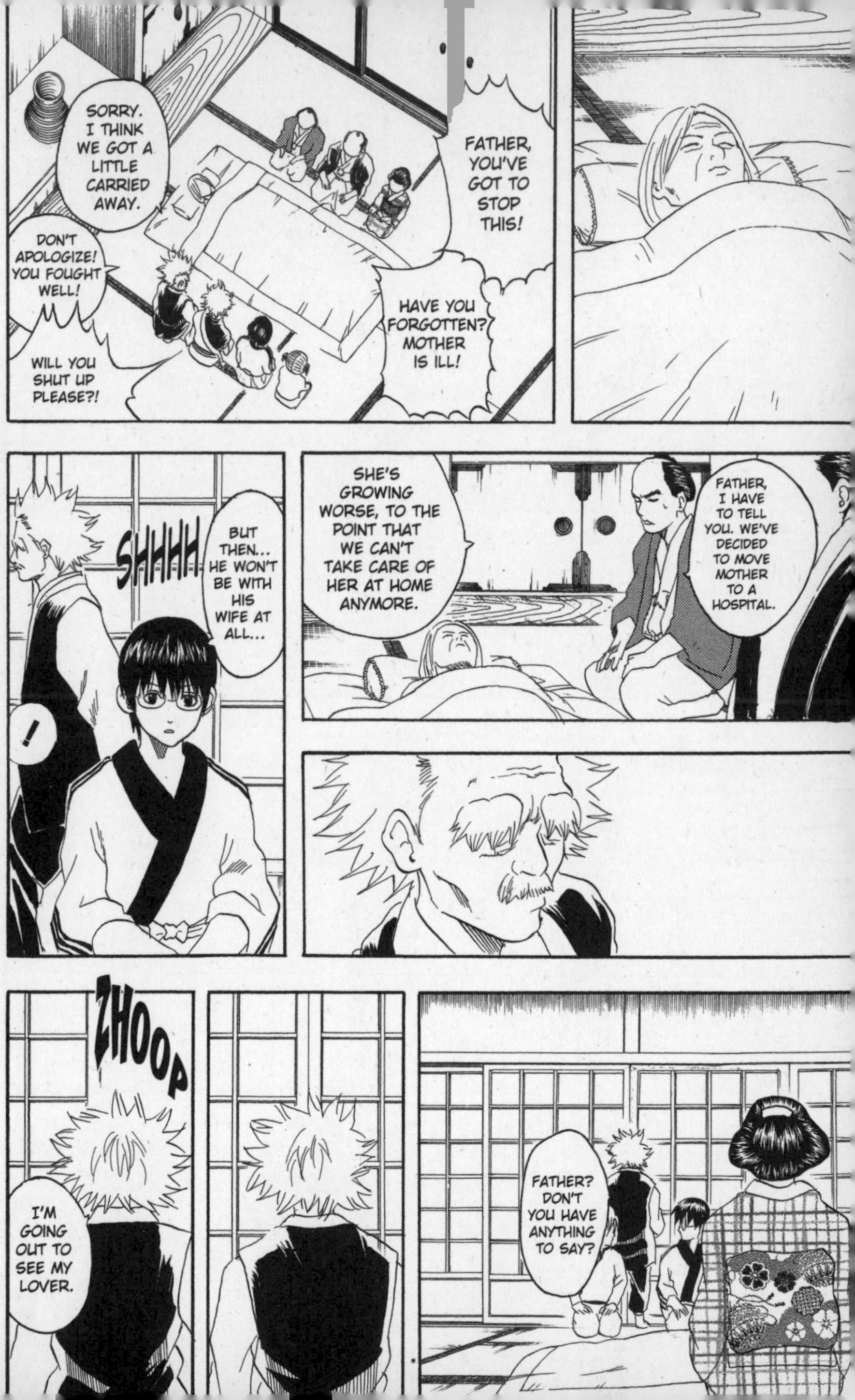
FATHER, YOU'VE GOT TO STOP THIS!
HAVE YOU FORGOTTEN? MOTHER IS ILL!
SORRY. I THINK WE GOT A LITTLE CARRIED AWAY.
DON'T APOLOGIZE! YOU FOUGHT WELL!
WILL YOU SHUT UP PLEASE?!
FATHER, I HAVE TO TELL YOU. WE'VE DECIDED TO MOVE MOTHER TO A HOSPITAL.
SHE'S GROWING WORSE, TO THE POINT THAT WE CAN'T TAKE CARE OF HER AT HOME ANYMORE.
SHHHH
BUT THEN... HE WON'T BE WITH HIS WIFE AT ALL...
!
FATHER? DON'T YOU HAVE ANYTHING TO SAY?
ZHOOP
I'M GOING OUT TO SEE MY LOVER.

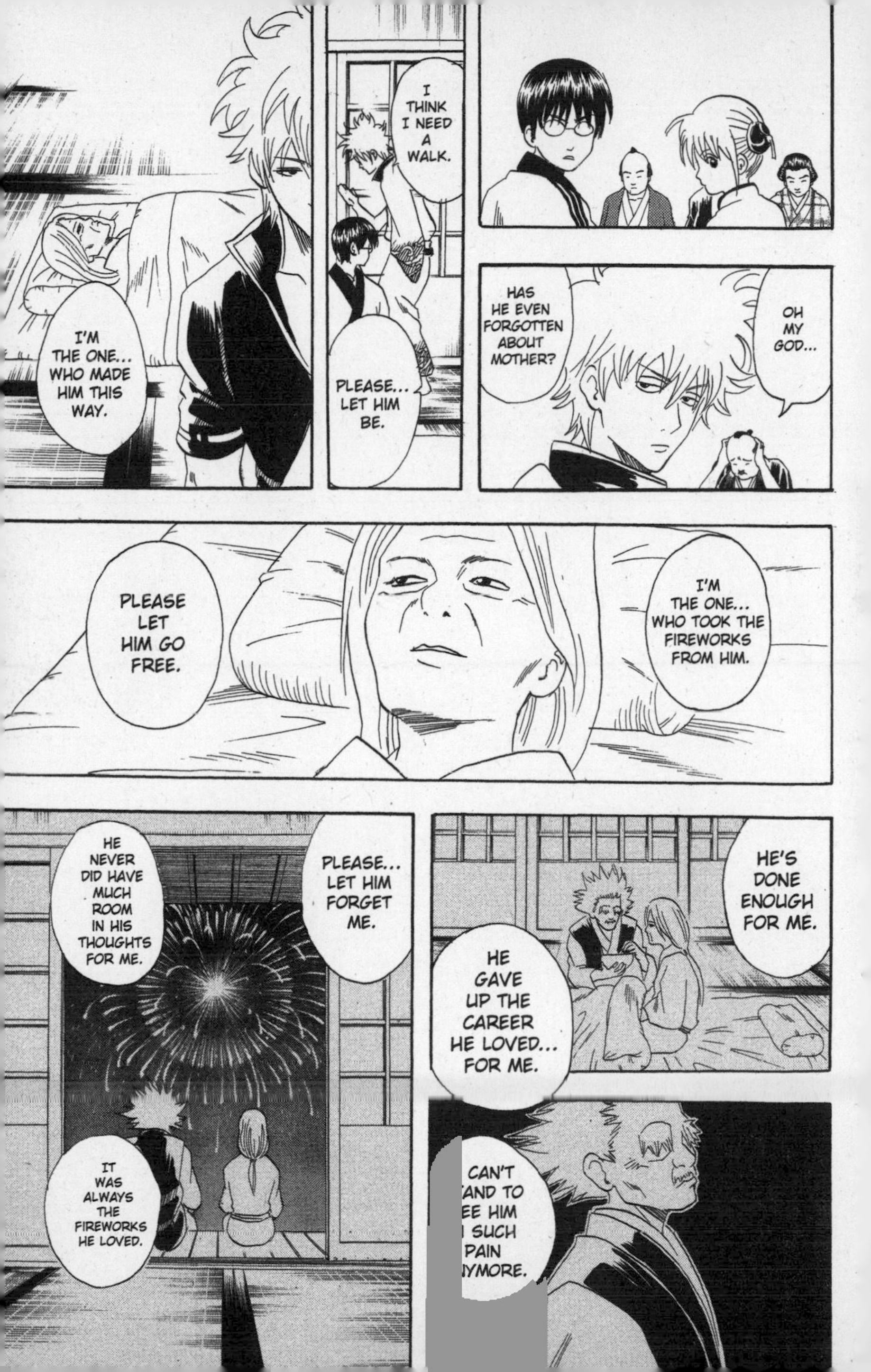
OH MY GOD...
HAS HE EVEN FORGOTTEN ABOUT MOTHER?
I THINK I NEED A WALK.
PLEASE... LET HIM BE.
I'M THE ONE... WHO MADE HIM THIS WAY.
I'M THE ONE... WHO TOOK THE FIREWORKS FROM HIM.
PLEASE LET HIM GO FREE.
HE'S DONE ENOUGH FOR ME.
HE GAVE UP THE CAREER HE LOVED... FOR ME.
CAN'T TAND TO EE HIM SUCH PAIN NYMORE.
PLEASE... LET HIM FORGET ME.
HE NEVER DID HAVE MUCH ROOM IN HIS THOUGHTS FOR ME.
IT WAS ALWAYS THE FIREWORKS HE LOVED.

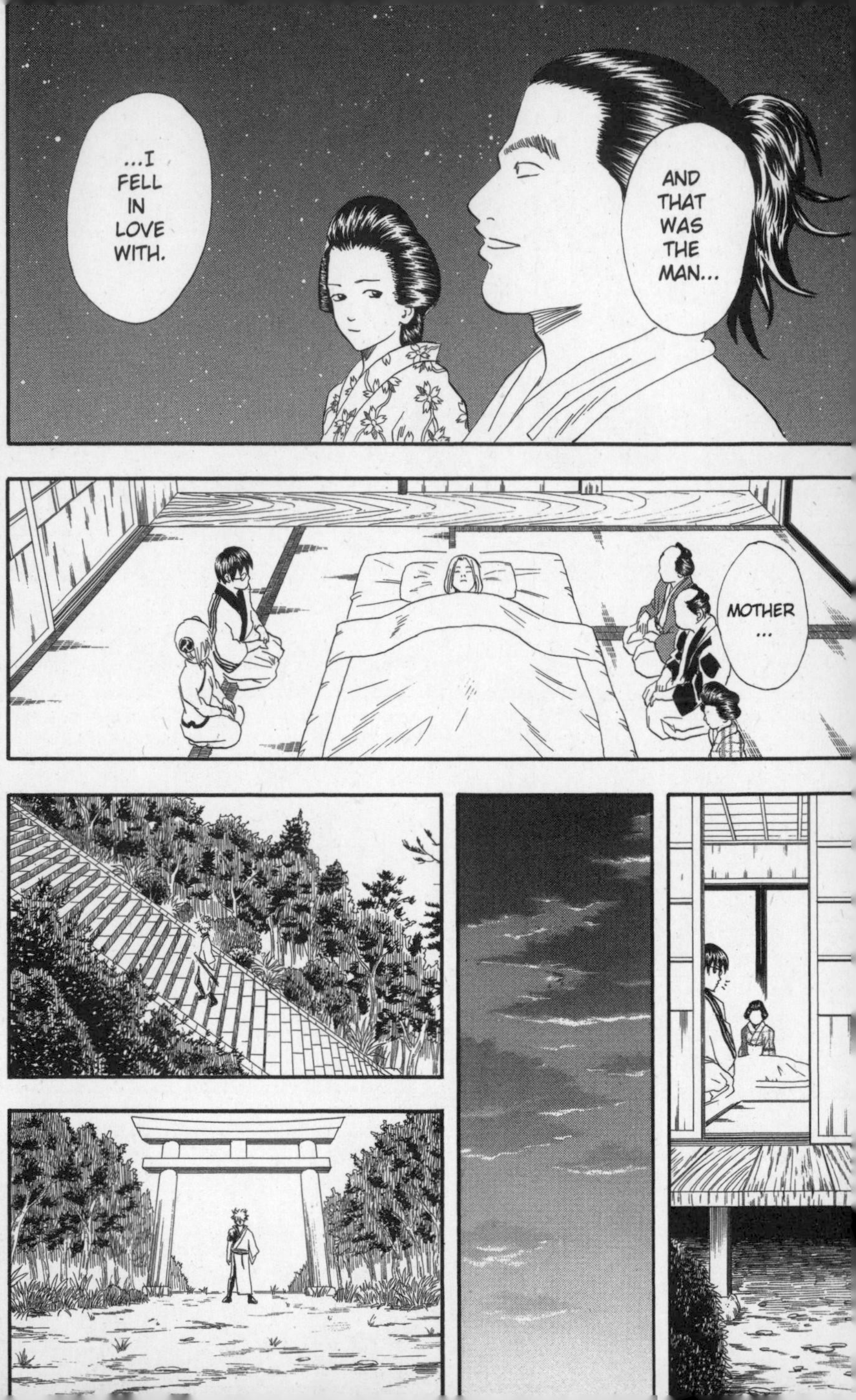
AND THAT WAS THE MAN...
...I FELL IN LOVE WITH.
MOTHER ...

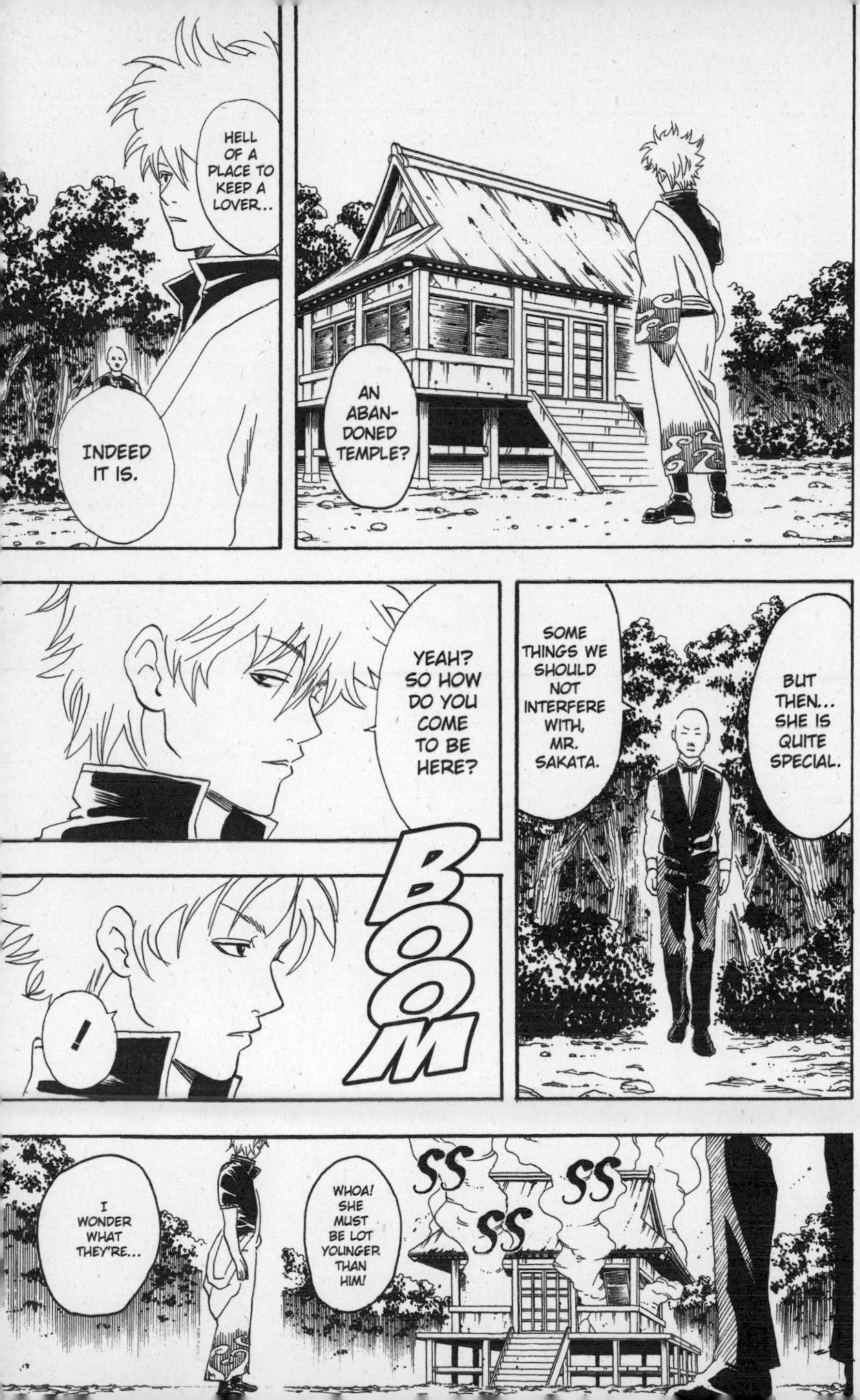
AN ABAN-DONED TEMPLE?
HELL OF A PLACE TO KEEP A LOVER...
INDEED IT IS.
BUT THEN... SHE IS QUITE SPECIAL.
SOME THINGS WE SHOULD NOT INTERFERE WITH, MR. SAKATA.
YEAH? SO HOW DO YOU COME TO BE HERE?
BOOM
!
SS
SS
SS
WHOA! SHE MUST BE LOT YOUNGER THAN HIM!
I WONDER WHAT THEY'RE...

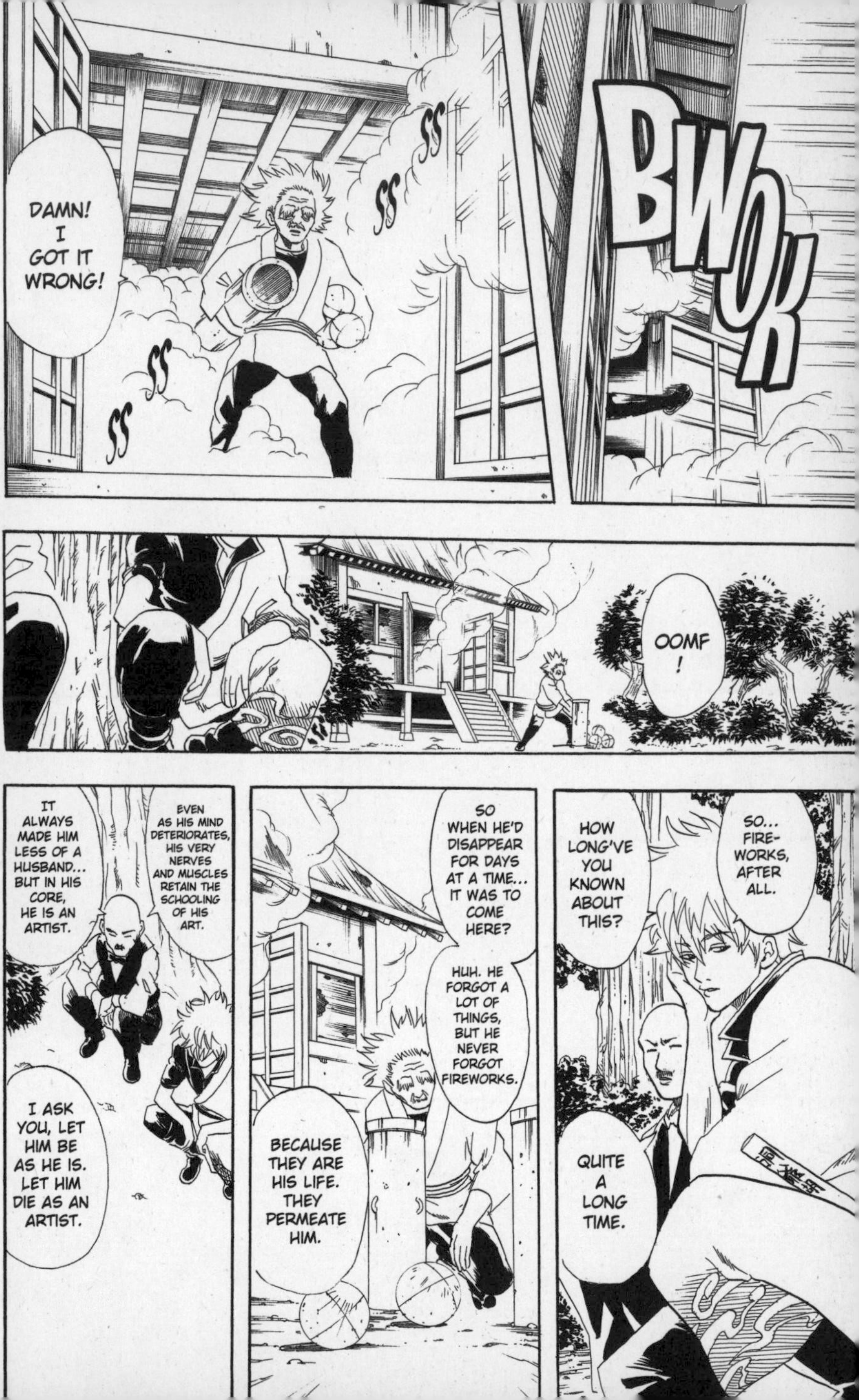
BWOOK
DAMN! I GOT IT WRONG!
OOMF!
SO... FIRE-WORKS, AFTER ALL.
HOW LONG'VE YOU KNOWN ABOUT THIS?
QUITE A LONG TIME.
SO WHEN HE'D DISAPPEAR FOR DAYS AT A TIME... IT WAS TO COME HERE?
HUH. HE FORGOT A LOT OF THINGS, BUT HE NEVER FORGOT FIREWORKS.
BECAUSE THEY ARE HIS LIFE. THEY PERMEATE HIM.
EVEN AS HIS MIND DETERIORATES, HIS VERY NERVES AND MUSCLES RETAIN THE SCHOOLING OF HIS ART.
IT ALWAYS MADE HIM LESS OF A HUSBAND... BUT IN HIS CORE, HE IS AN ARTIST.
I ASK YOU, LET HIM BE AS HE IS. LET HIM DIE AS AN ARTIST.

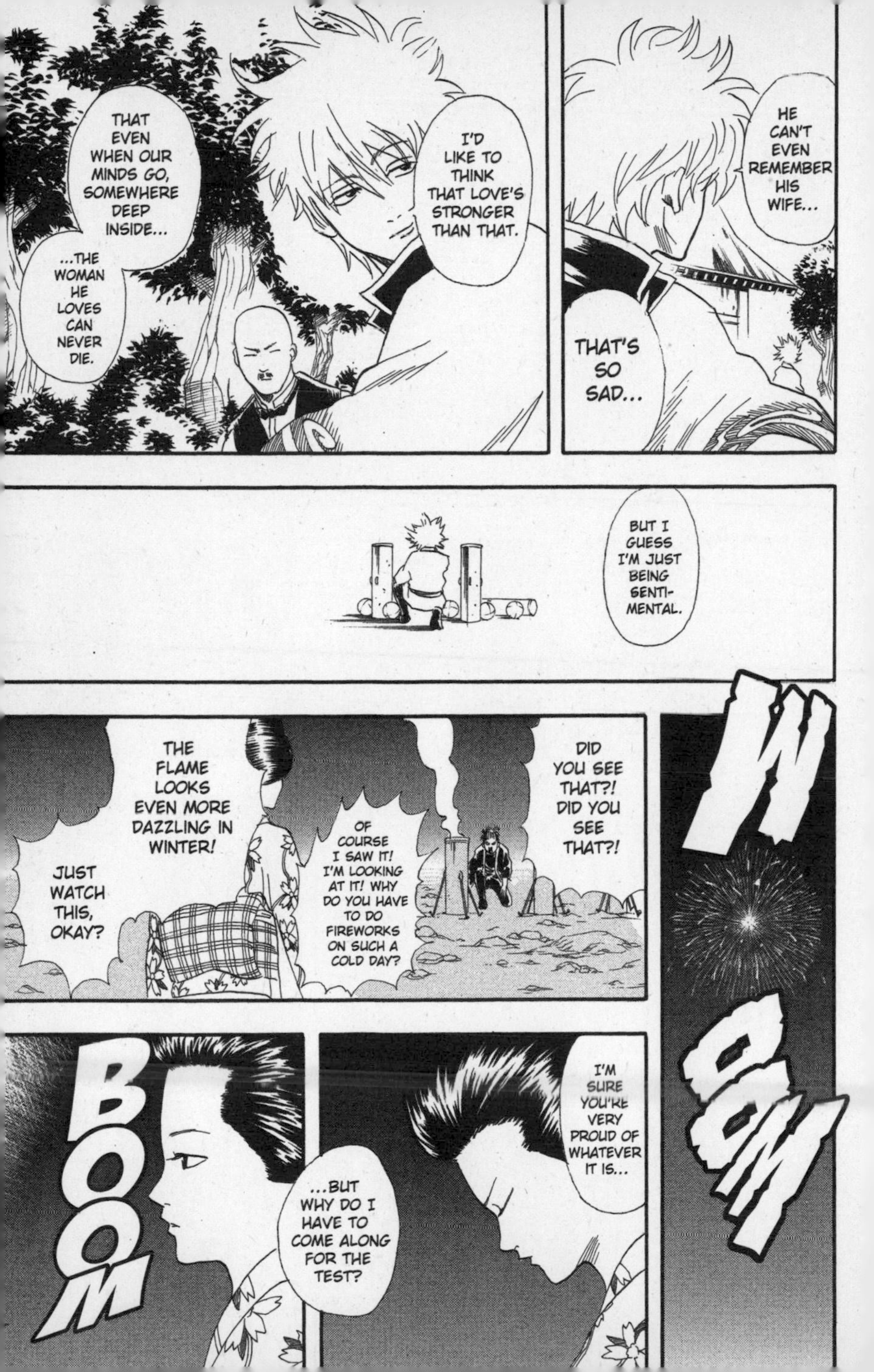
HE CAN'T EVEN REMEMBER HIS WIFE...
THAT'S SO SAD...
I'D LIKE TO THINK THAT LOVE'S STRONGER THAN THAT.
THAT EVEN WHEN OUR MINDS GO, SOMEWHERE DEEP INSIDE...
...THE WOMAN HE LOVES CAN NEVER DIE.
BUT I GUESS I'M JUST BEING SENTI-MENTAL.
WOOM
DID YOU SEE THAT?! DID YOU SEE THAT?!
OF COURSE I SAW IT! I'M LOOKING AT IT! WHY DO YOU HAVE TO DO FIREWORKS ON SUCH A COLD DAY?
THE FLAME LOOKS EVEN MORE DAZZLING IN WINTER!
JUST WATCH THIS, OKAY?
I'M SURE YOU'RE VERY PROUD OF WHATEVER IT IS...
BOOM
...BUT WHY DO I HAVE TO COME ALONG FOR THE TEST?

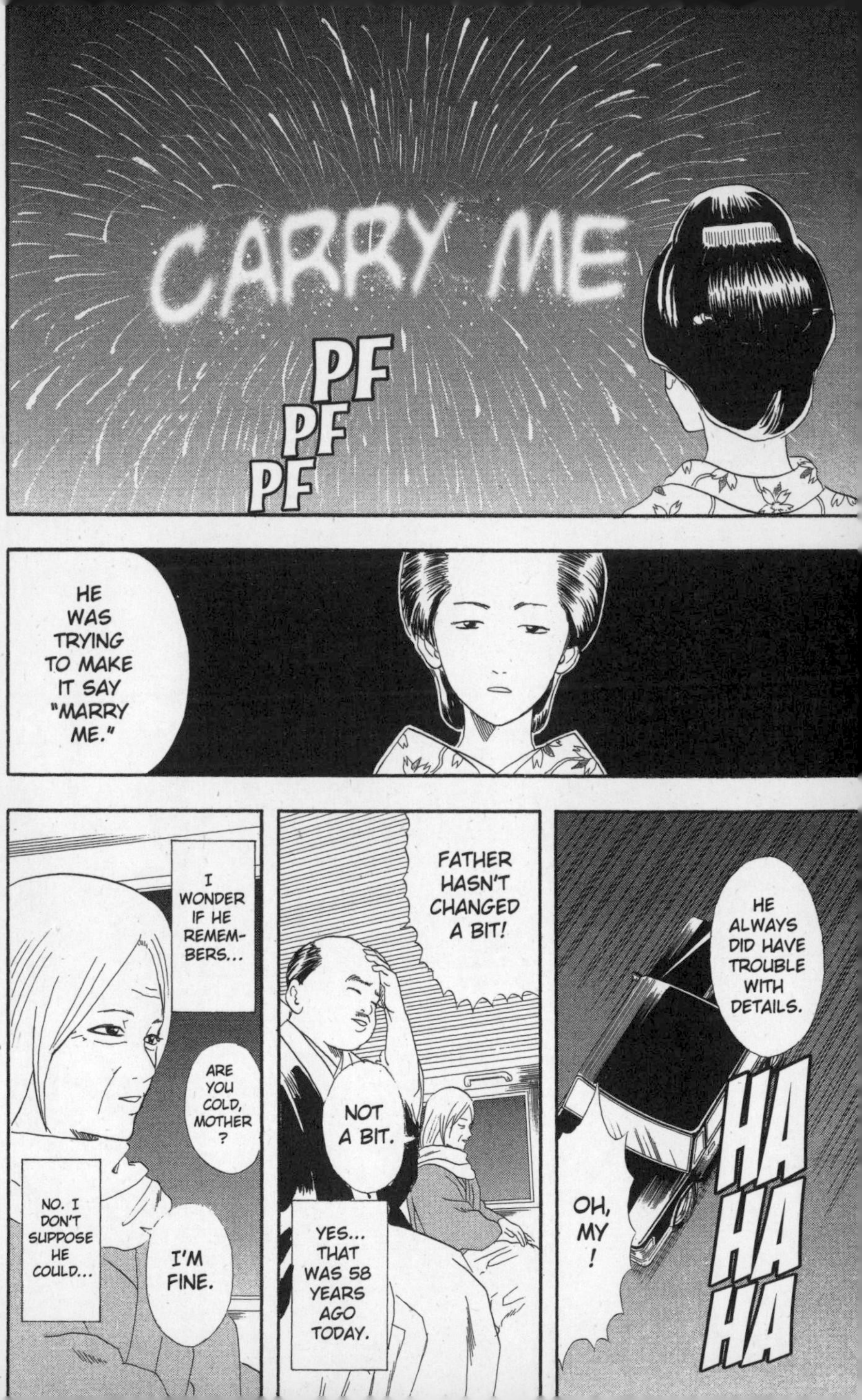
CARRY ME
PF PF PF
HE WAS TRYING TO MAKE IT SAY "MARRY ME."
HE ALWAYS DID HAVE TROUBLE WITH DETAILS.
HA HA HA HA
OH, MY!
FATHER HASN'T CHANGED A BIT!
NOT A BIT.
YES... THAT WAS 58 YEARS AGO TODAY.
I WONDER IF HE REMEMBERS...
ARE YOU COLD, MOTHER?
I'M FINE.
NO. I DON'T SUPPOSE HE COULD...

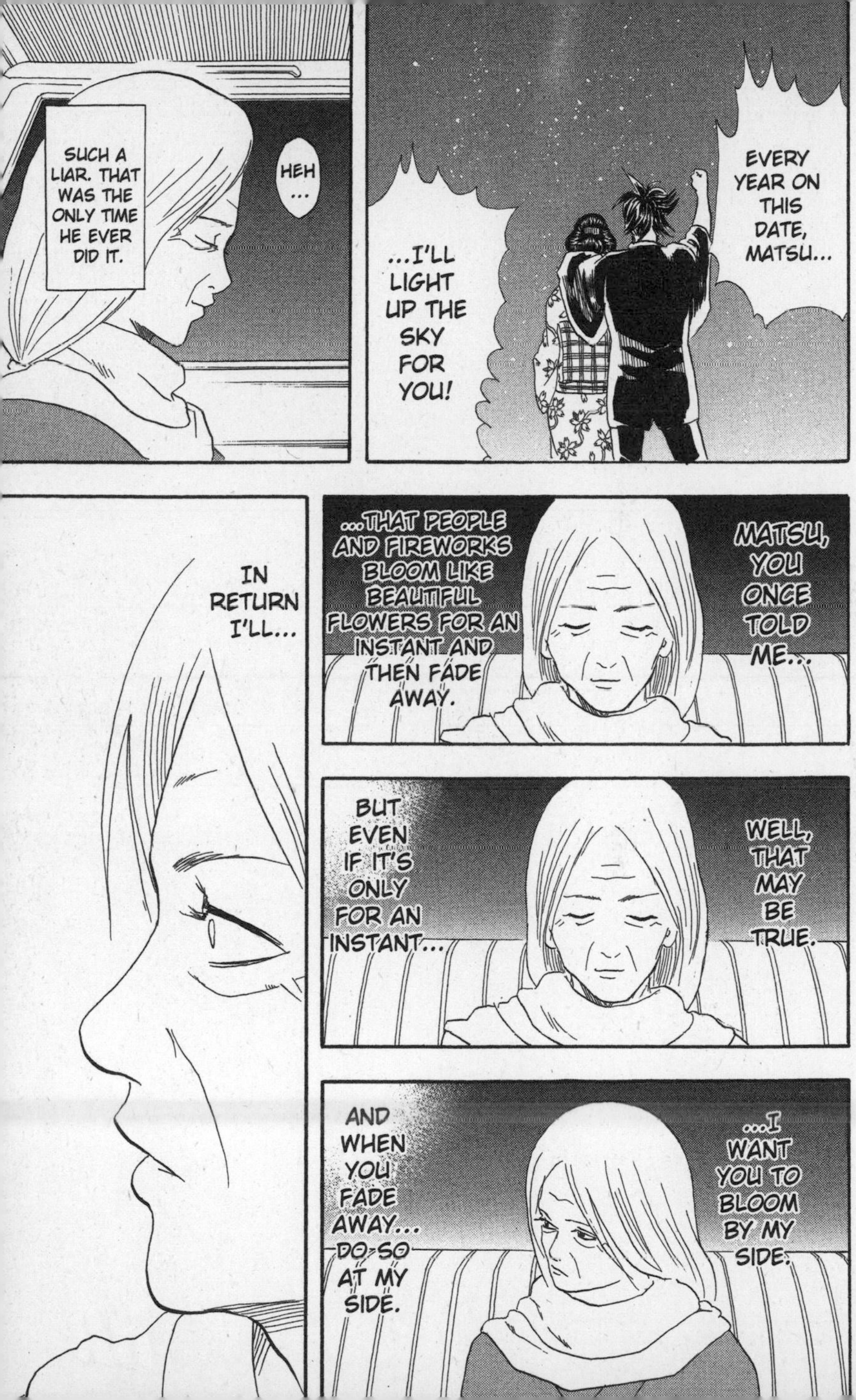
EVERY YEAR ON THIS DATE, MATSU...
...I'LL LIGHT UP THE SKY FOR YOU!
SUCH A LIAR. THAT WAS THE ONLY TIME HE EVER DID IT.
HEH...
MATSU, YOU ONCE TOLD ME...
...THAT PEOPLE AND FIREWORKS BLOOM LIKE BEAUTIFUL FLOWERS FOR AN INSTANT AND THEN FADE AWAY.
WELL, THAT MAY BE TRUE.
BUT EVEN IF IT'S ONLY FOR AN INSTANT...
...I WANT YOU TO BLOOM BY MY SIDE.
AND WHEN YOU FADE AWAY... DO SO AT MY SIDE.
IN RETURN I'LL...

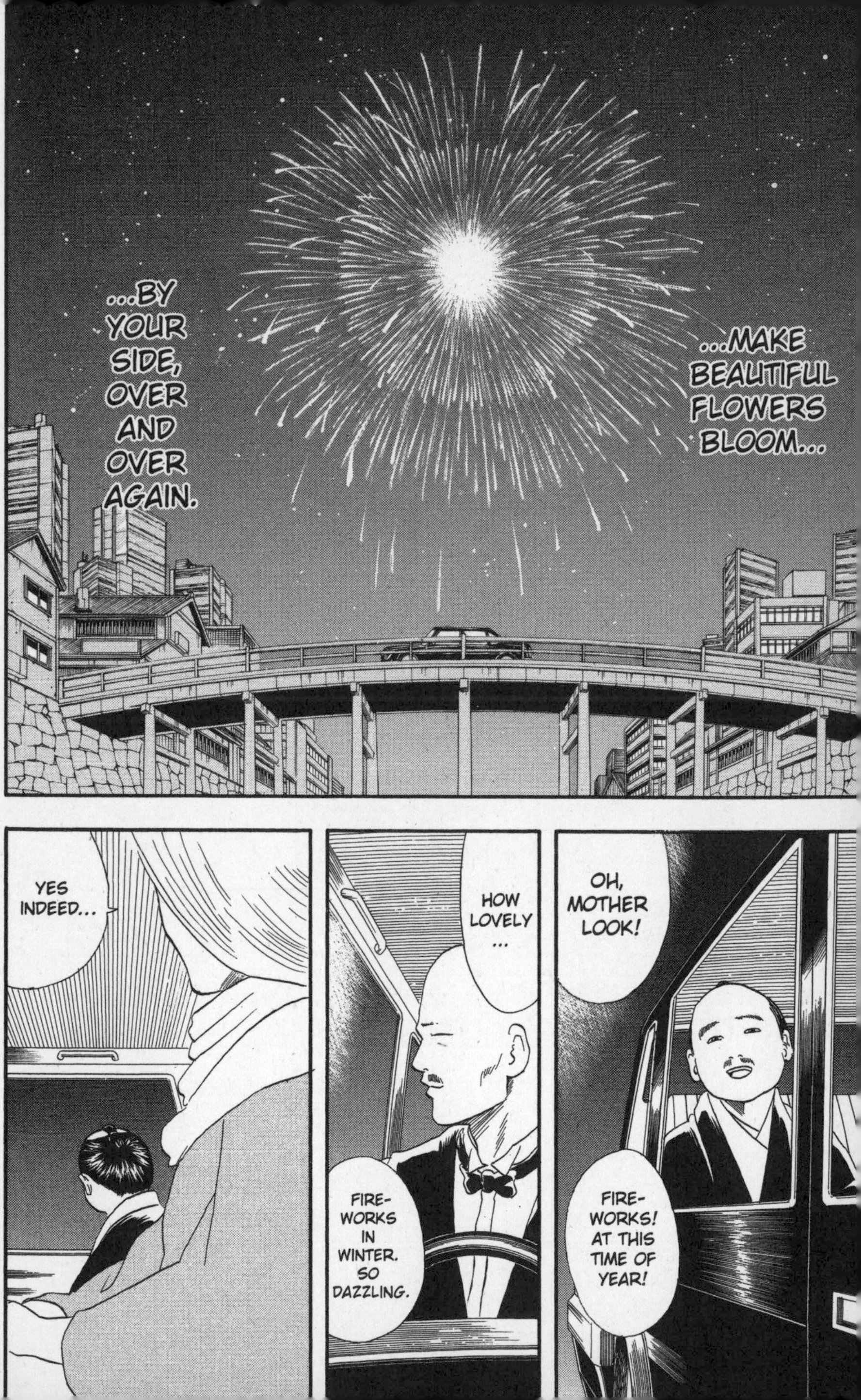
...MAKE BEAUTIFUL FLOWERS BLOOM...
...BY YOUR SIDE, OVER AND OVER AGAIN.
OH, MOTHER LOOK!
FIRE-WORKS! AT THIS TIME OF YEAR!
HOW LOVELY ...
FIRE-WORKS IN WINTER. SO DAZZLING.
YES INDEED...

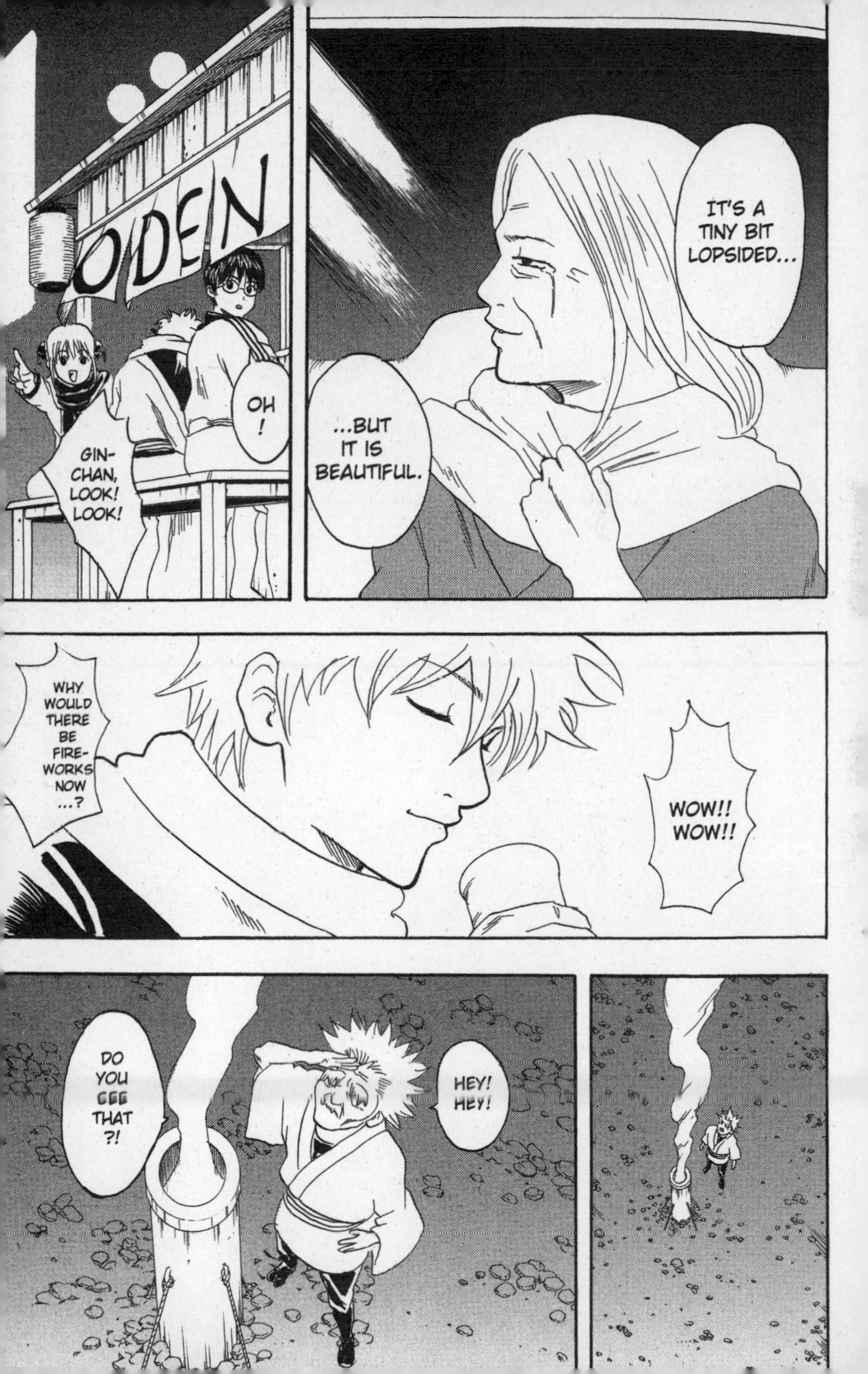
IT'S A TINY BIT LOPSIDED...
...BUT IT IS BEAUTIFUL.
ODEN
OH!
GIN-CHAN, LOOK! LOOK!
WOW!! WOW!!
WHY WOULD THERE BE FIRE-WORKS NOW ...?
HEY! HEY!
DO YOU SEE THAT?!

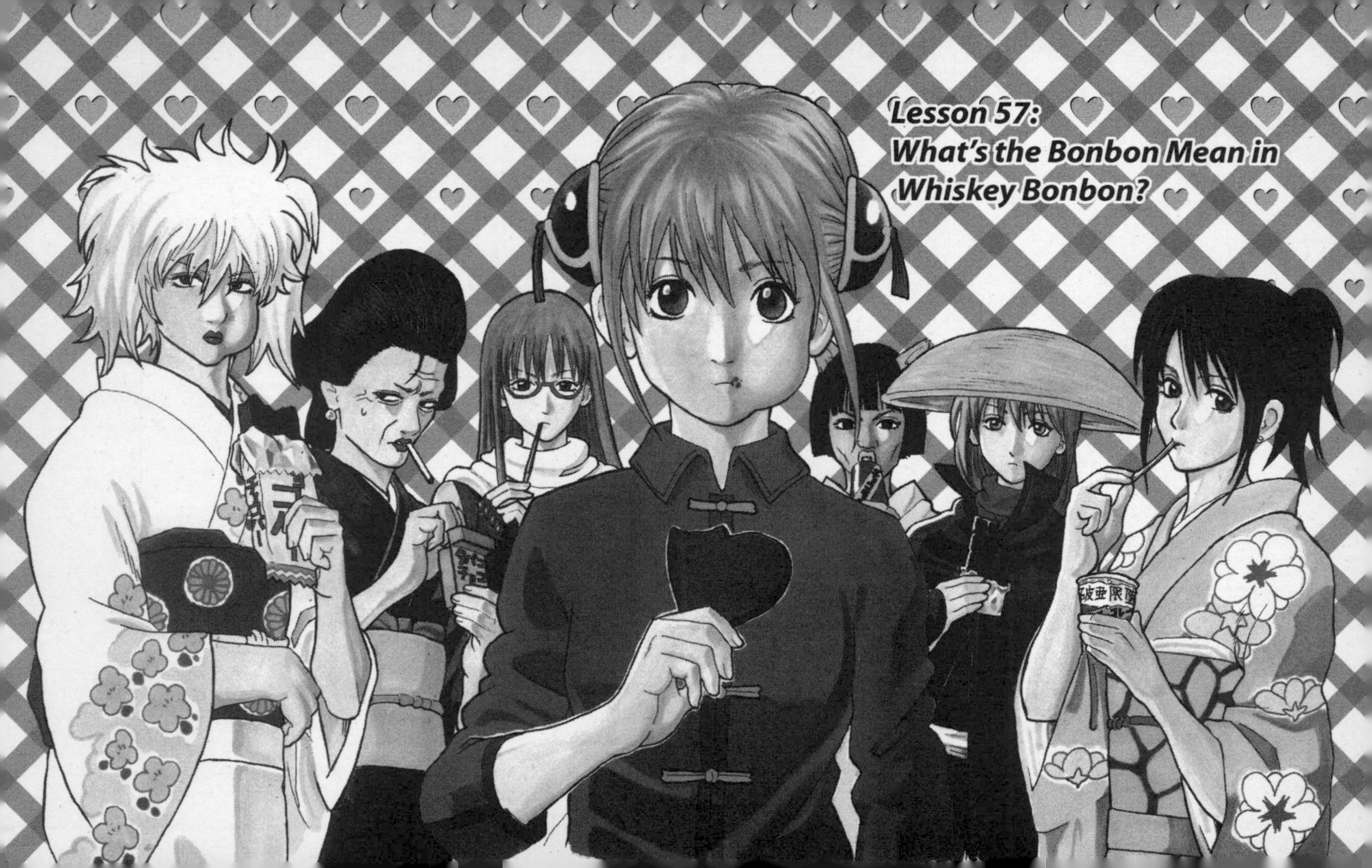
Lesson 57:
What's the Bonbon Mean in
Whiskey Bonbon?

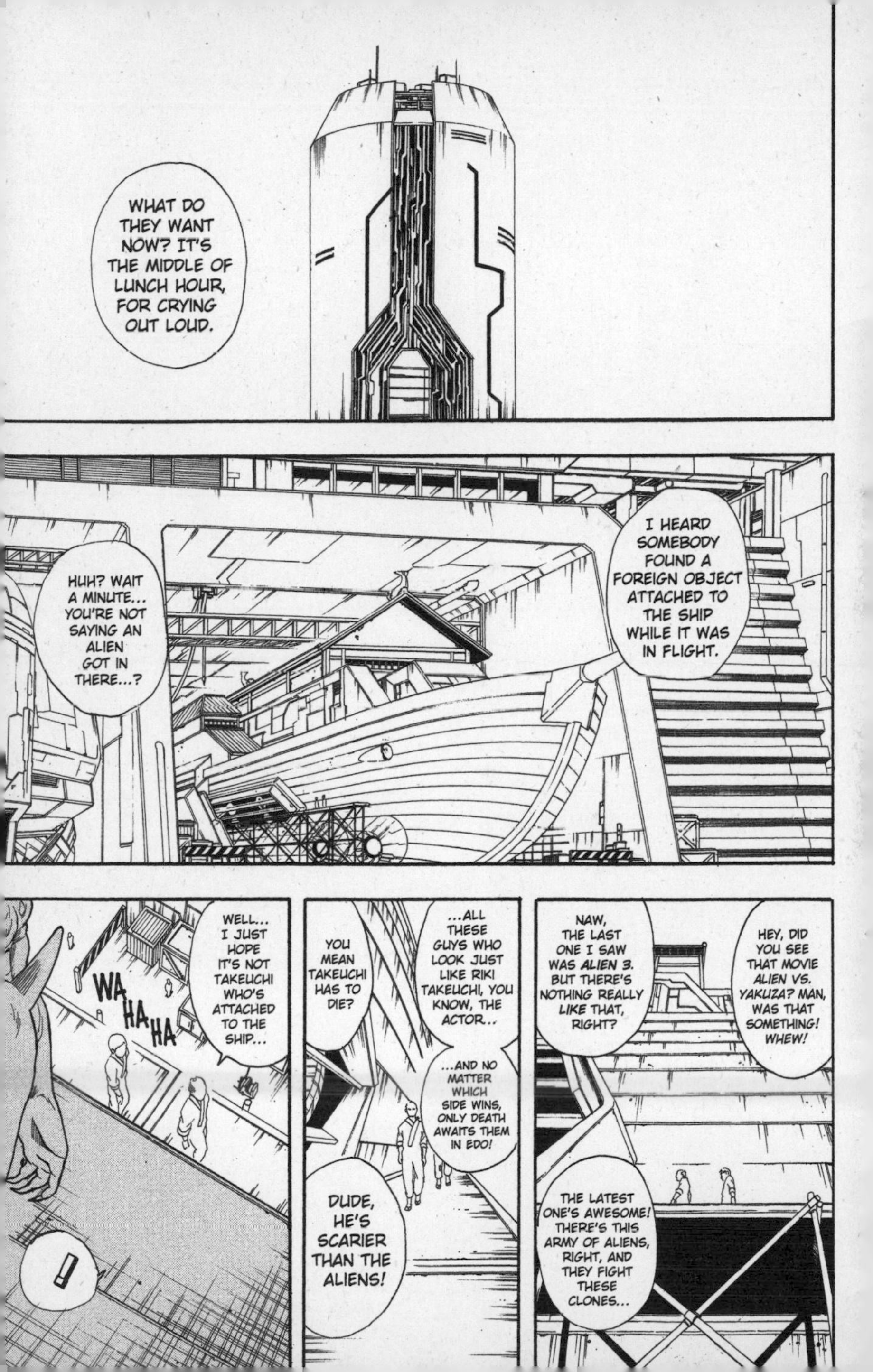
WHAT DO THEY WANT NOW? IT'S THE MIDDLE OF LUNCH HOUR, FOR CRYING OUT LOUD.
I HEARD SOMEBODY FOUND A FOREIGN OBJECT ATTACHED TO THE SHIP WHILE IT WAS IN FLIGHT.
HUH? WAIT A MINUTE... YOU'RE NOT SAYING AN ALIEN GOT IN THERE...?
HEY, DID YOU SEE THAT MOVIE *ALIEN VS. YAKUZA*? MAN, WAS THAT SOMETHING! WHEW!
NAW, THE LAST ONE I SAW WAS *ALIEN 3*. BUT THERE'S NOTHING REALLY *LIKE* THAT, RIGHT?
THE LATEST ONE'S AWESOME! THERE'S THIS ARMY OF ALIENS, RIGHT, AND THEY FIGHT THESE CLONES...
...ALL THESE GUYS WHO LOOK JUST LIKE RIKI TAKEUCHI, YOU KNOW, THE ACTOR...
...AND NO MATTER WHICH SIDE WINS, ONLY DEATH AWAITS THEM IN EDO!
YOU MEAN TAKEUCHI HAS TO DIE?
DUDE, HE'S SCARIER THAN THE ALIENS!
WELL... I JUST HOPE IT'S NOT TAKEUCHI WHO'S ATTACHED TO THE SHIP...
WA HA HA
!

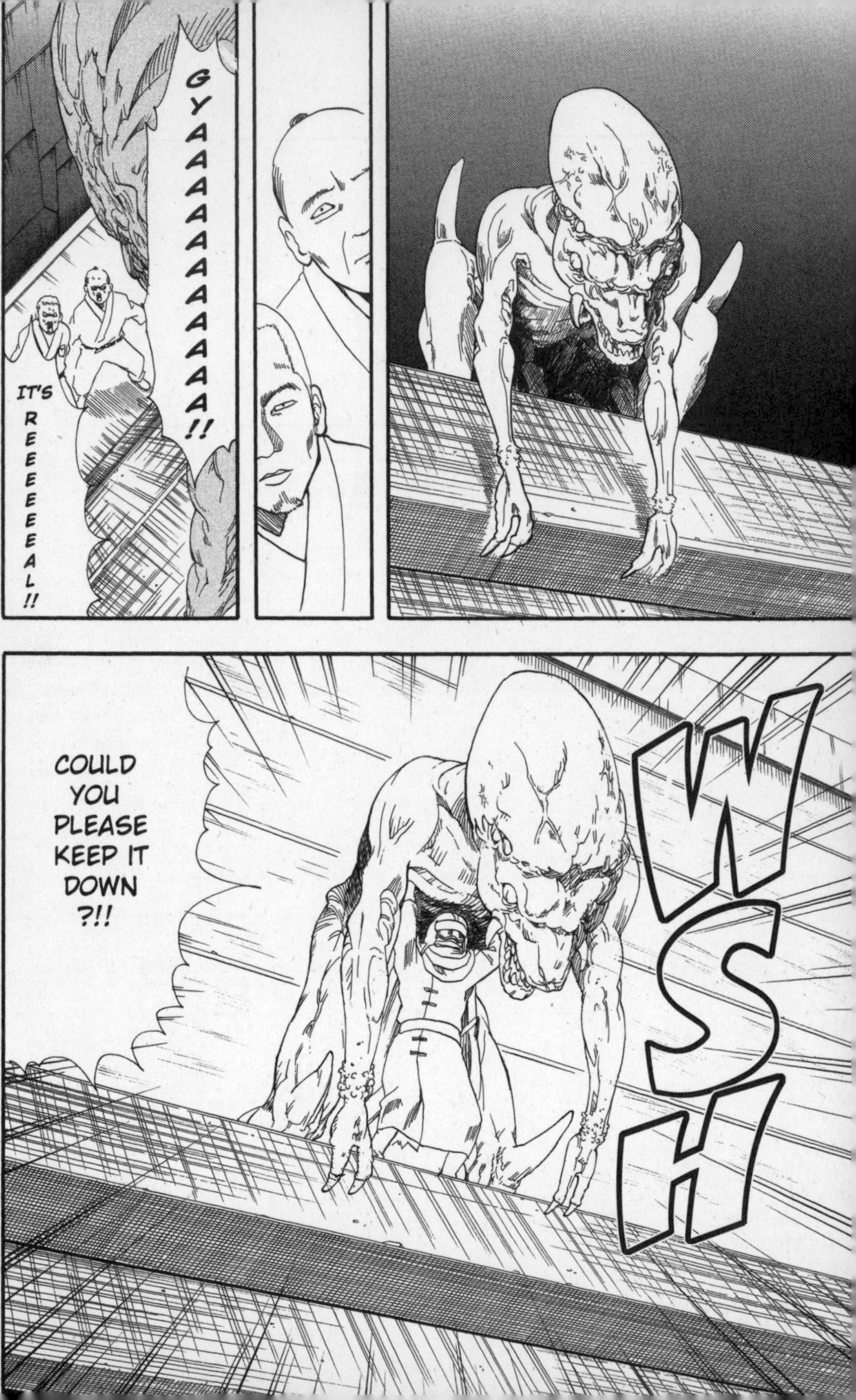
GYAAAAAAAAAAA!!
IT'S REEEEEEEAL!!
COULD YOU PLEASE KEEP IT DOWN?!!
WSH

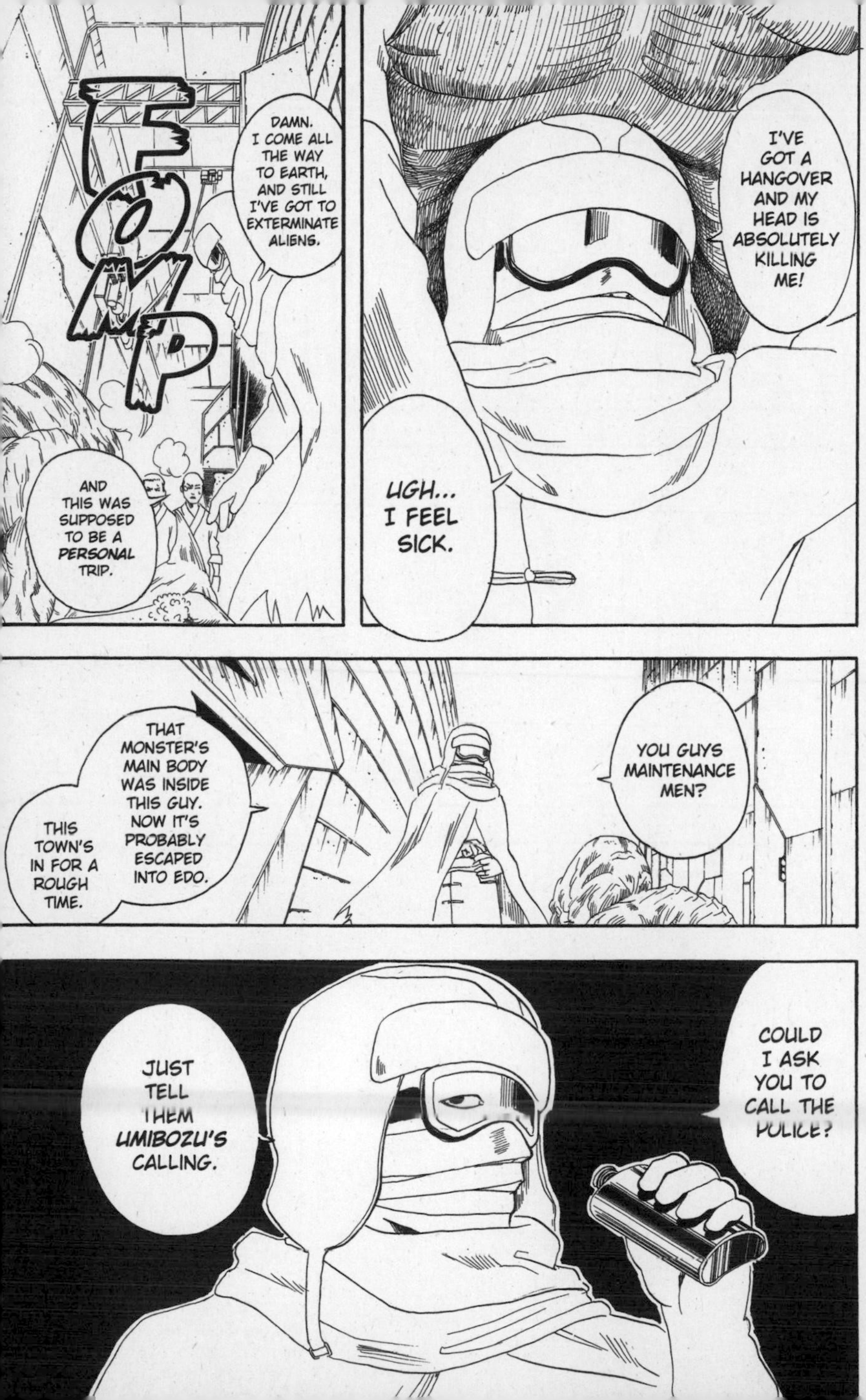
I'VE GOT A HANGOVER AND MY HEAD IS ABSOLUTELY KILLING ME!
UGH... I FEEL SICK.
DAMN. I COME ALL THE WAY TO EARTH, AND STILL I'VE GOT TO EXTERMINATE ALIENS.
FOMP
AND THIS WAS SUPPOSED TO BE A *PERSONAL* TRIP.
YOU GUYS MAINTENANCE MEN?
THAT MONSTER'S MAIN BODY WAS INSIDE THIS GUY. NOW IT'S PROBABLY ESCAPED INTO EDO.
THIS TOWN'S IN FOR A ROUGH TIME.
COULD I ASK YOU TO CALL THE POLICE?
JUST TELL THEM *UMIBOZU'S* CALLING.

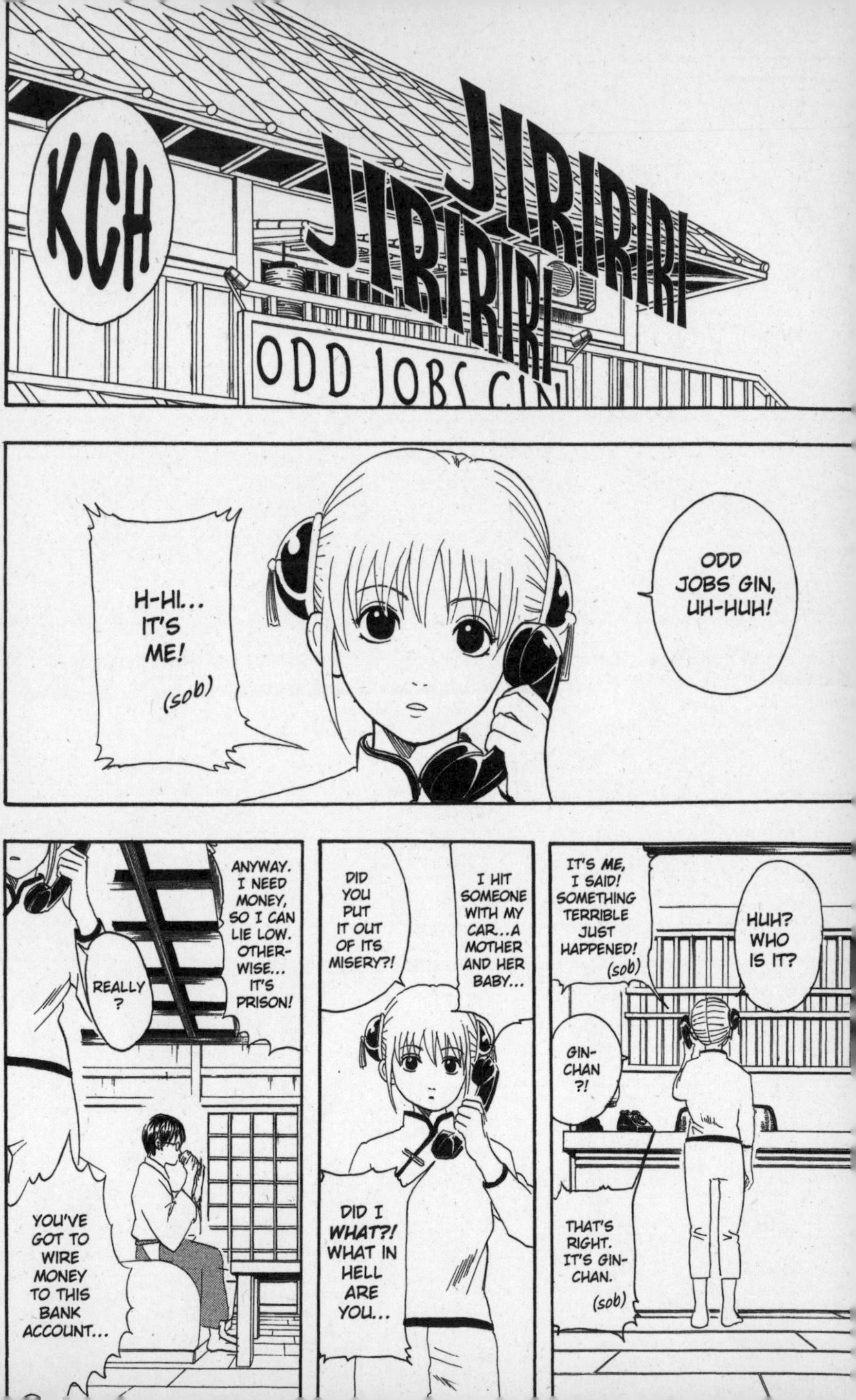
JIRIRIRI
JIRIRIRI
KCH
ODD JOBS GIN
ODD JOBS GIN, UH-HUH!
H-HI... IT'S ME! (sob)
HUH? WHO IS IT?
IT'S ME, I SAID! SOMETHING TERRIBLE JUST HAPPENED! (sob)
GIN-CHAN?!
THAT'S RIGHT. IT'S GIN-CHAN. (sob)
I HIT SOMEONE WITH MY CAR...A MOTHER AND HER BABY...
DID YOU PUT IT OUT OF ITS MISERY?!
DID I WHAT?! WHAT IN HELL ARE YOU...
ANYWAY. I NEED MONEY, SO I CAN LIE LOW. OTHERWISE... IT'S PRISON!
REALLY?
YOU'VE GOT TO WIRE MONEY TO THIS BANK ACCOUNT...

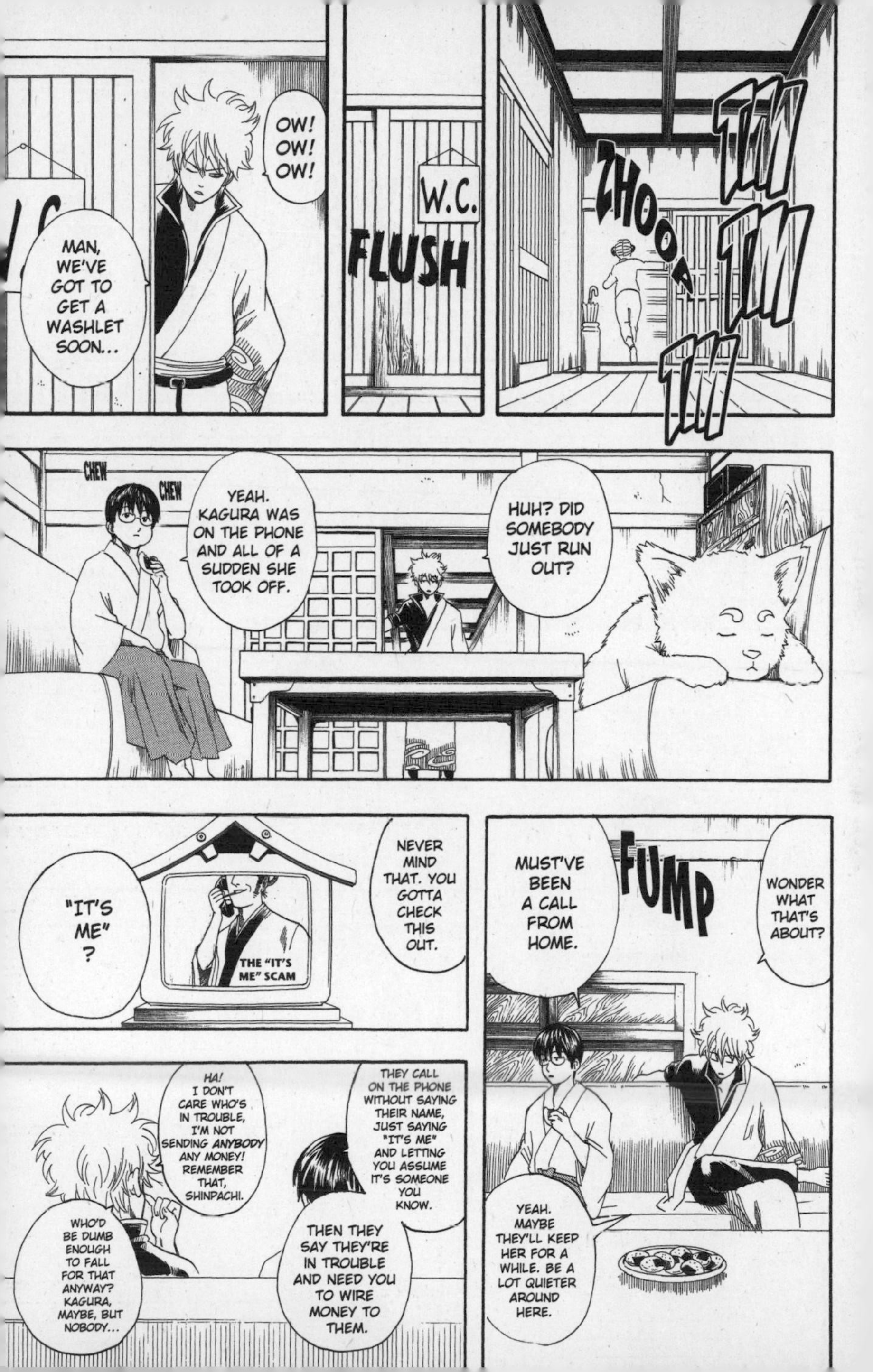
TM TM TM
ZHOOP
W.C.
FLUSH
OW! OW! OW!
MAN, WE'VE GOT TO GET A WASHLET SOON...
HUH? DID SOMEBODY JUST RUN OUT?
YEAH. KAGURA WAS ON THE PHONE AND ALL OF A SUDDEN SHE TOOK OFF.
CHEW
CHEW
WONDER WHAT THAT'S ABOUT?
FUMP
MUST'VE BEEN A CALL FROM HOME.
YEAH. MAYBE THEY'LL KEEP HER FOR A WHILE. BE A LOT QUIETER AROUND HERE.
NEVER MIND THAT. YOU GOTTA CHECK THIS OUT.
"IT'S ME" ?
THE "IT'S ME" SCAM
THEY CALL ON THE PHONE WITHOUT SAYING THEIR NAME, JUST SAYING "IT'S ME" AND LETTING YOU ASSUME IT'S SOMEONE YOU KNOW.
THEN THEY SAY THEY'RE IN TROUBLE AND NEED YOU TO WIRE MONEY TO THEM.
HA! I DON'T CARE WHO'S IN TROUBLE, I'M NOT SENDING *ANYBODY* ANY MONEY! REMEMBER THAT, SHINPACHI.
WHO'D BE DUMB ENOUGH TO FALL FOR THAT ANYWAY? KAGURA, MAYBE, BUT NOBODY...

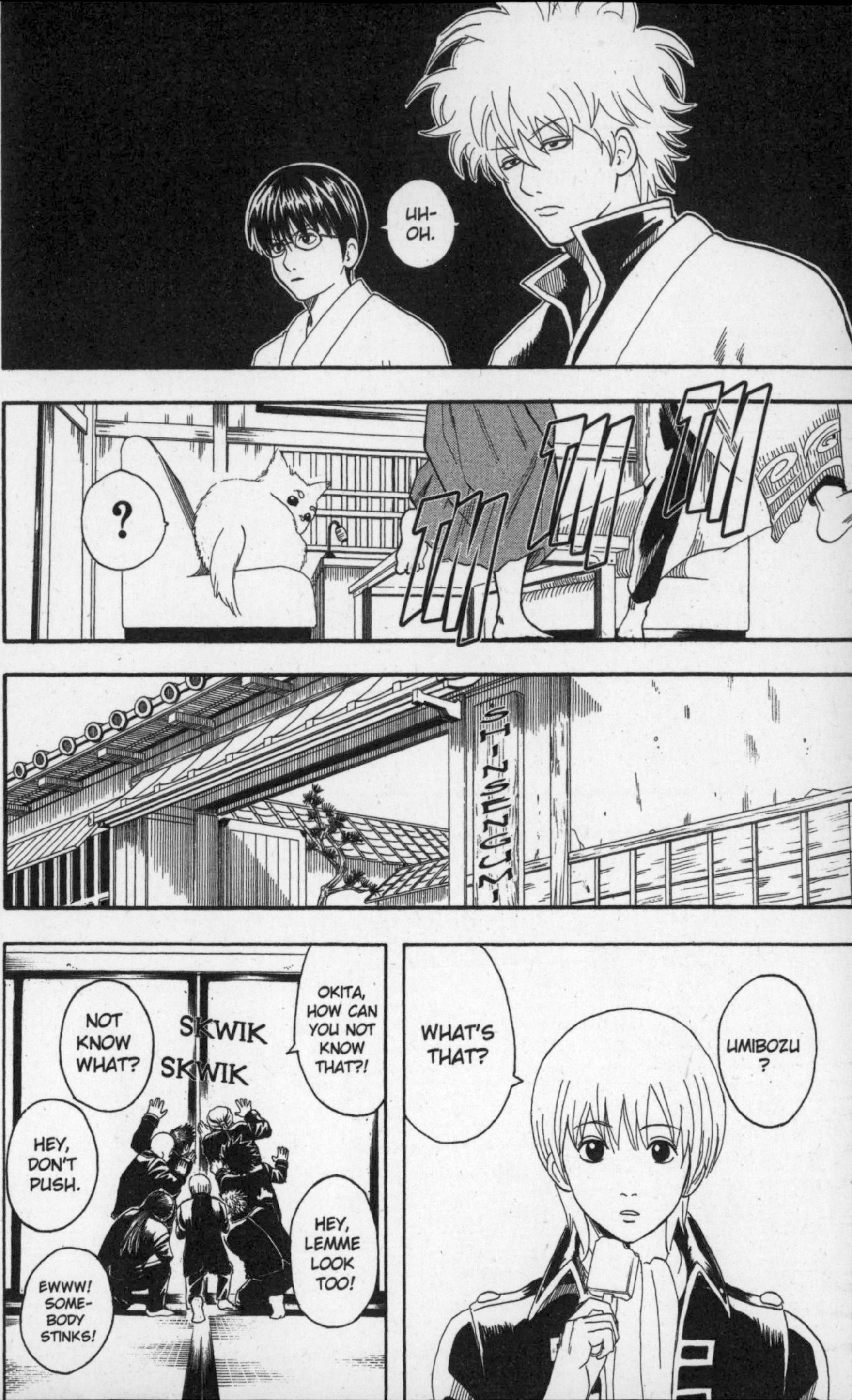

UH-OH.
?
TM TM TM
UMIBOZU?
WHAT'S THAT?
OKITA, HOW CAN YOU NOT KNOW THAT?!
NOT KNOW WHAT?
SKWIK SKWIK
HEY, LEMME LOOK TOO!
HEY, DON'T PUSH.
EWWW! SOMEBODY STINKS!

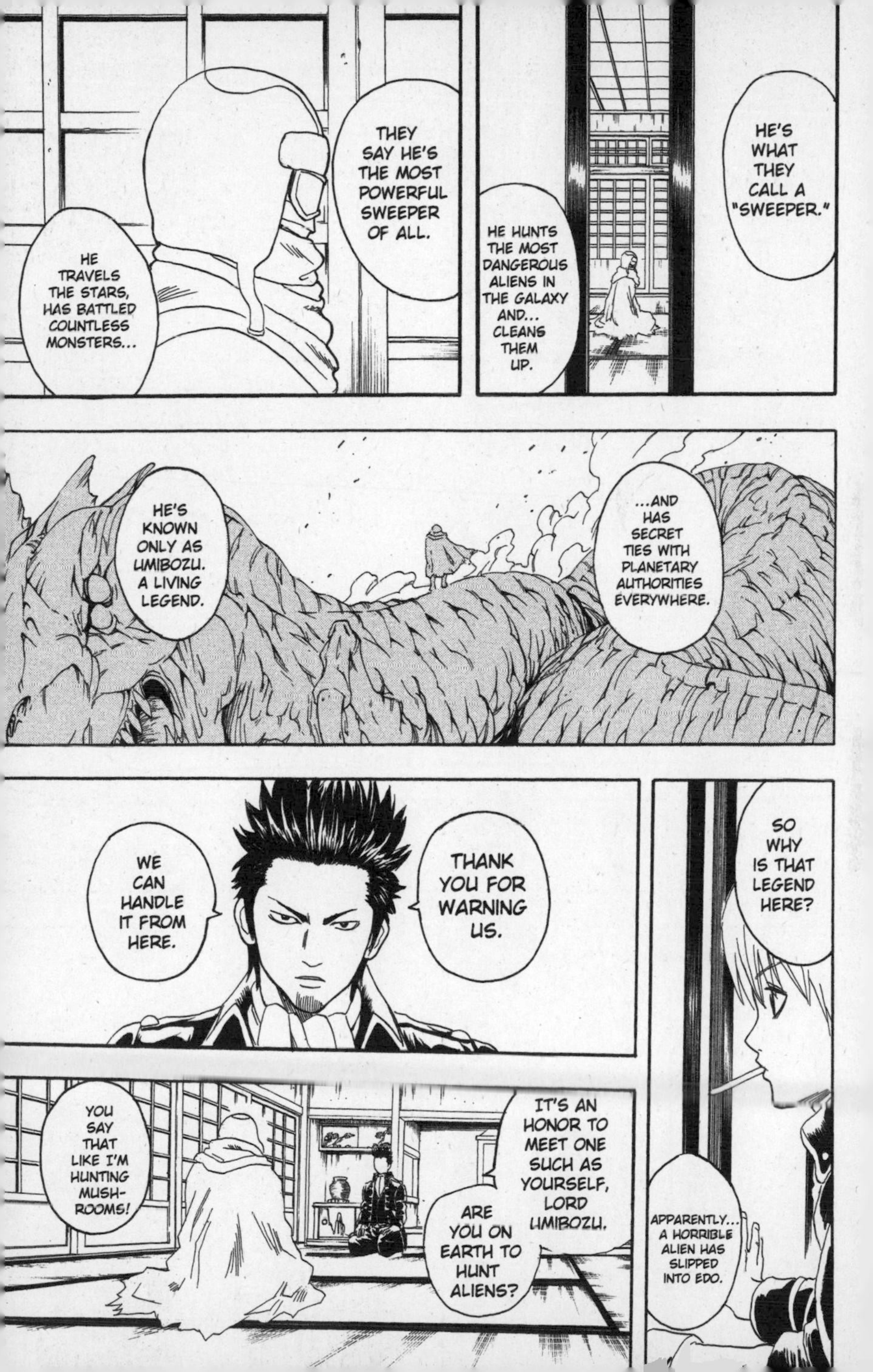
HE'S WHAT THEY CALL A "SWEEPER."
HE HUNTS THE MOST DANGEROUS ALIENS IN THE GALAXY AND... CLEANS THEM UP.
THEY SAY HE'S THE MOST POWERFUL SWEEPER OF ALL.
HE TRAVELS THE STARS, HAS BATTLED COUNTLESS MONSTERS...
...AND HAS SECRET TIES WITH PLANETARY AUTHORITIES EVERYWHERE.
HE'S KNOWN ONLY AS UMIBOZU. A LIVING LEGEND.
SO WHY IS THAT LEGEND HERE?
APPARENTLY... A HORRIBLE ALIEN HAS SLIPPED INTO EDO.
THANK YOU FOR WARNING US.
WE CAN HANDLE IT FROM HERE.
IT'S AN HONOR TO MEET ONE SUCH AS YOURSELF, LORD UMIBOZU.
ARE YOU ON EARTH TO HUNT ALIENS?
YOU SAY THAT LIKE I'M HUNTING MUSH-ROOMS!

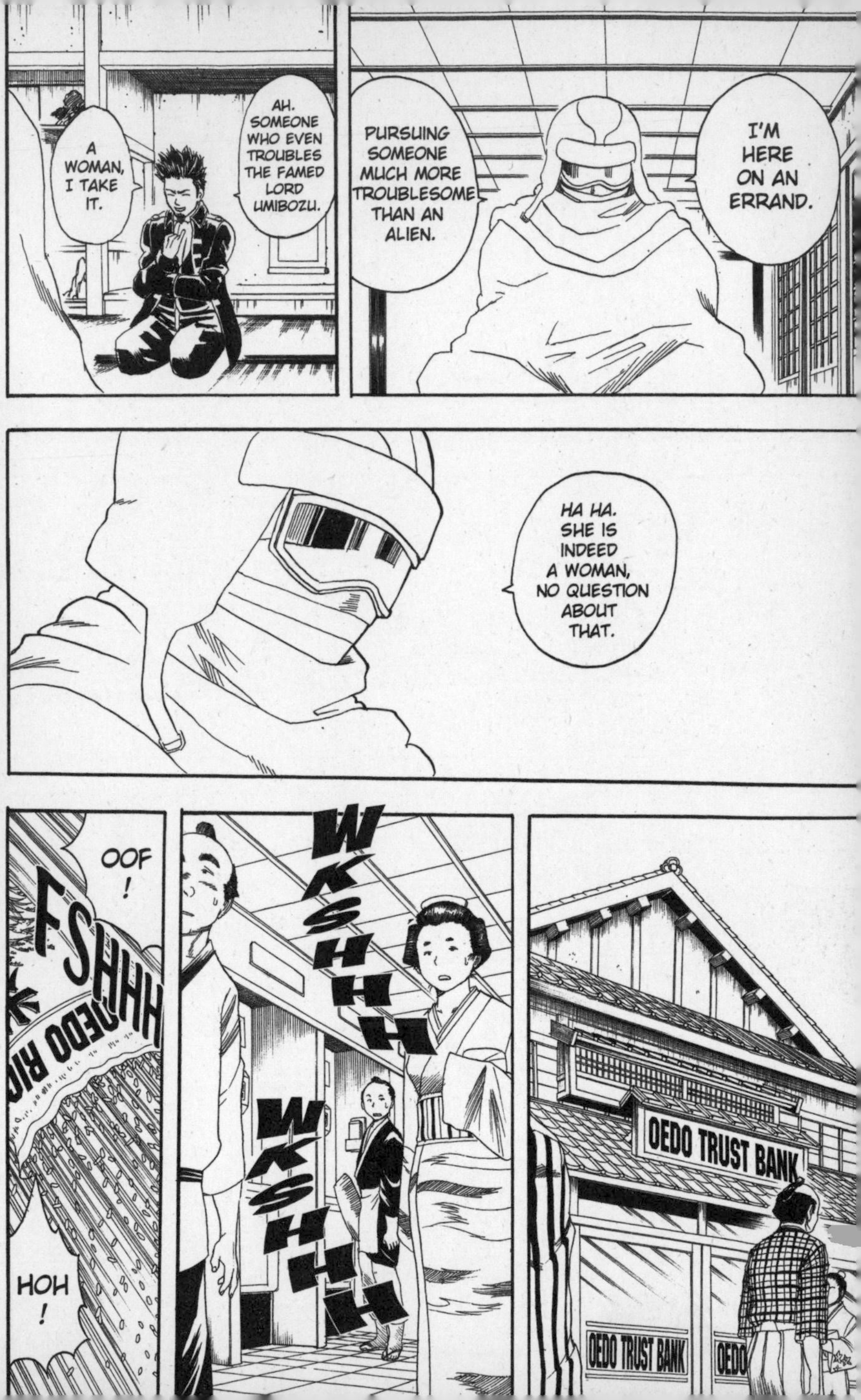
I'M HERE ON AN ERRAND.
PURSUING SOMEONE MUCH MORE TROUBLESOME THAN AN ALIEN.
AH. SOMEONE WHO EVEN TROUBLES THE FAMED LORD UMIBOZU.
A WOMAN, I TAKE IT.
HA HA. SHE IS INDEED A WOMAN, NO QUESTION ABOUT THAT.
OEDO TRUST BANK
OEDO TRUST BANK
WKSHHHH
WKSHHH
OOF!
FSHHH
HOH!

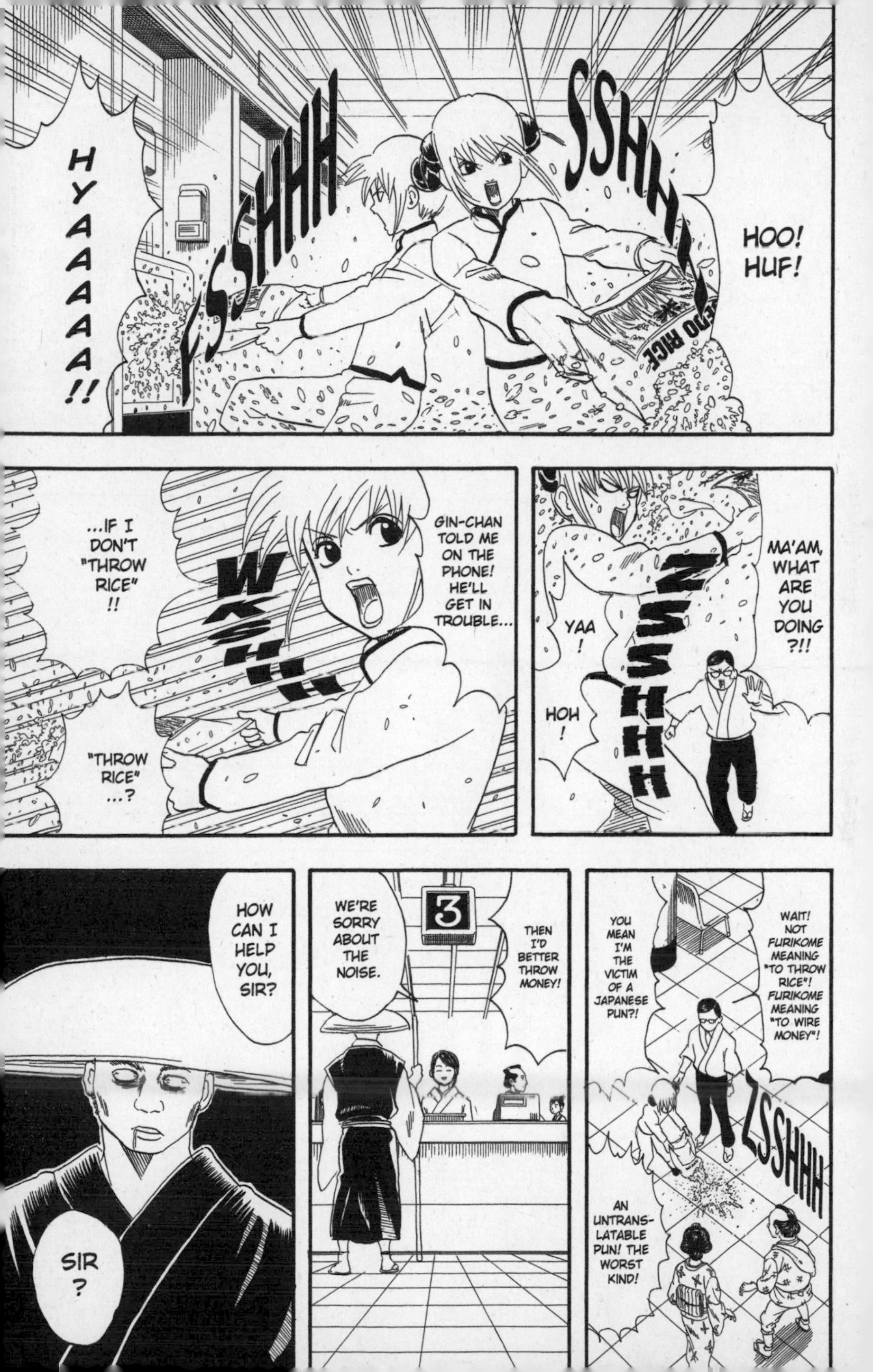
HOO! HUF!
SSHHH
FSSHHH
HYAAAAAA!!
MA'AM, WHAT ARE YOU DOING?!!
YAA!
ZSSHHHH
HOH!
GIN-CHAN TOLD ME ON THE PHONE! HE'LL GET IN TROUBLE...
...IF I DON'T "THROW RICE"!!
WKSHH
"THROW RICE"...?
WAIT! NOT FURIKOME MEANING "TO THROW RICE"! FURIKOME MEANING "TO WIRE MONEY"!
YOU MEAN I'M THE VICTIM OF A JAPANESE PUN?!
ZSSHHH
AN UNTRANS-LATABLE PUN! THE WORST KIND!
THEN I'D BETTER THROW MONEY!
3
WE'RE SORRY ABOUT THE NOISE.
HOW CAN I HELP YOU, SIR?
SIR?

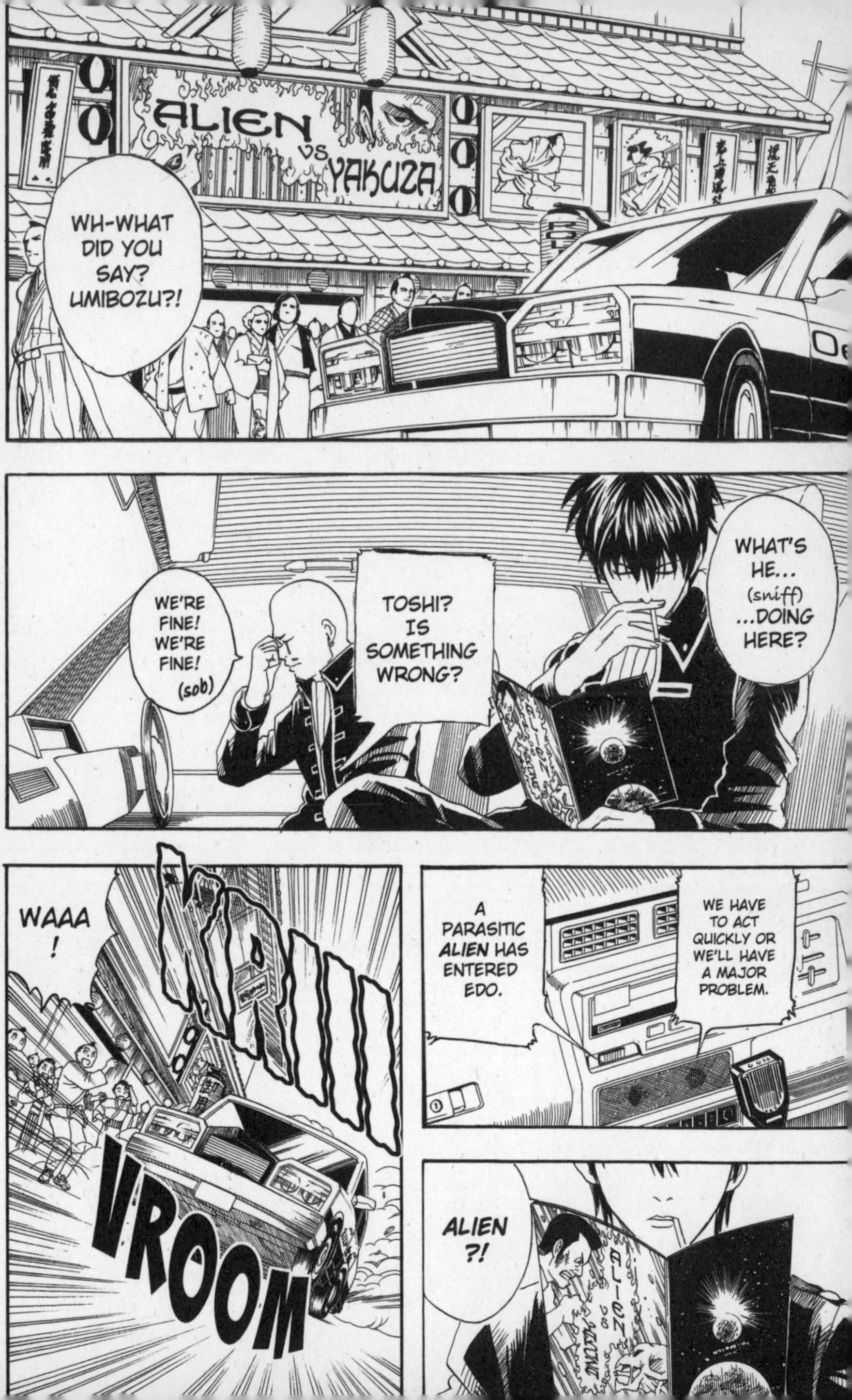
ALIEN VS YAKUZA
WH-WHAT DID YOU SAY? UMIBOZU?!
WHAT'S HE... (sniff) ...DOING HERE?
TOSHI? IS SOMETHING WRONG?
WE'RE FINE! WE'RE FINE! (sob)
WE HAVE TO ACT QUICKLY OR WE'LL HAVE A MAJOR PROBLEM.
A PARASITIC ALIEN HAS ENTERED EDO.
ALIEN ?!
WAAA !
VROOM

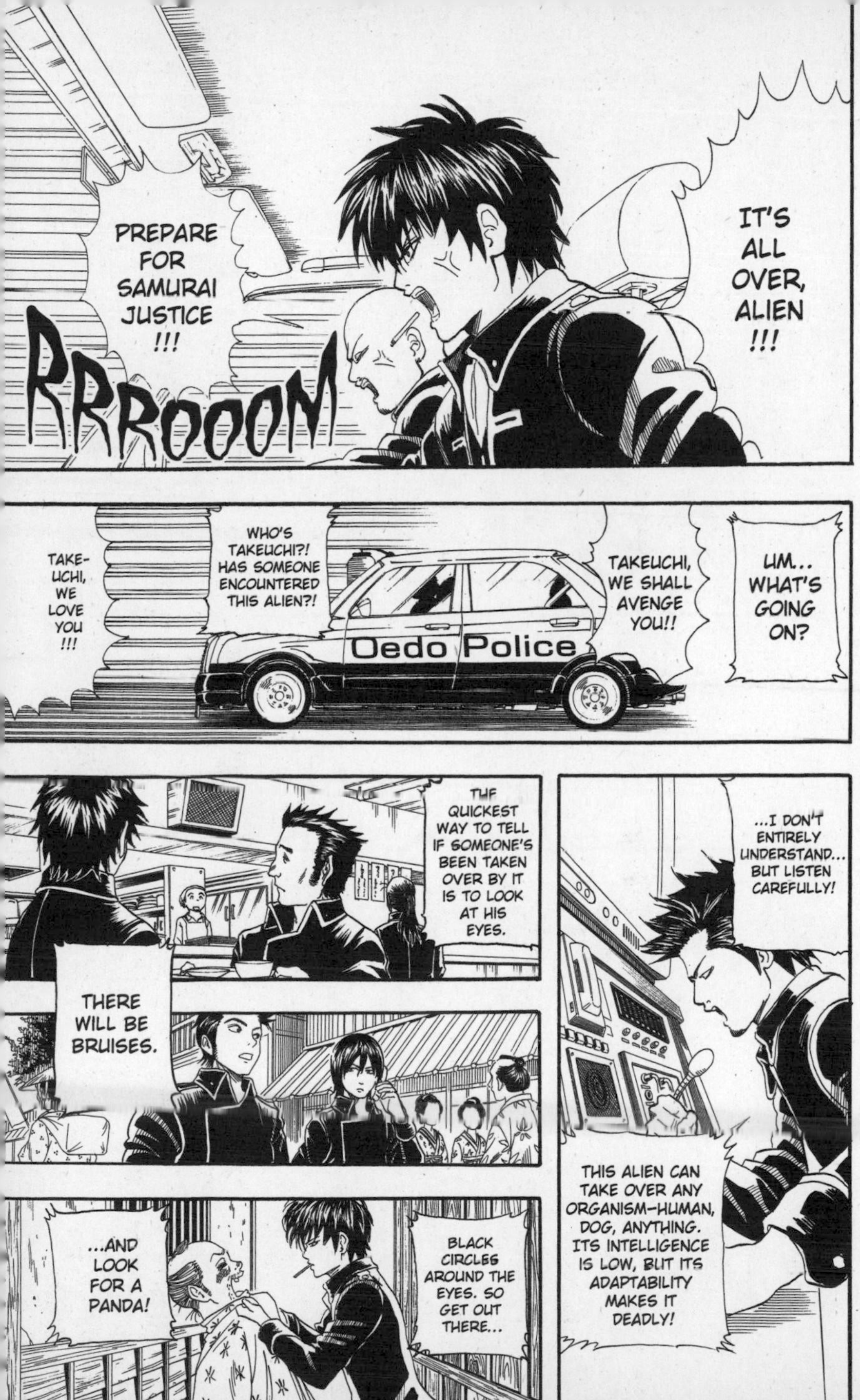
IT'S ALL OVER, ALIEN!!!
PREPARE FOR SAMURAI JUSTICE!!!
RRROOOM
UM... WHAT'S GOING ON?
TAKEUCHI, WE SHALL AVENGE YOU!!
WHO'S TAKEUCHI?! HAS SOMEONE ENCOUNTERED THIS ALIEN?!
Oedo Police
TAKE-UCHI, WE LOVE YOU!!!
...I DON'T ENTIRELY UNDERSTAND... BUT LISTEN CAREFULLY!
THIS ALIEN CAN TAKE OVER ANY ORGANISM—HUMAN, DOG, ANYTHING. ITS INTELLIGENCE IS LOW, BUT ITS ADAPTABILITY MAKES IT DEADLY!
THE QUICKEST WAY TO TELL IF SOMEONE'S BEEN TAKEN OVER BY IT IS TO LOOK AT HIS EYES.
THERE WILL BE BRUISES.
BLACK CIRCLES AROUND THE EYES. SO GET OUT THERE...
...AND LOOK FOR A PANDA!

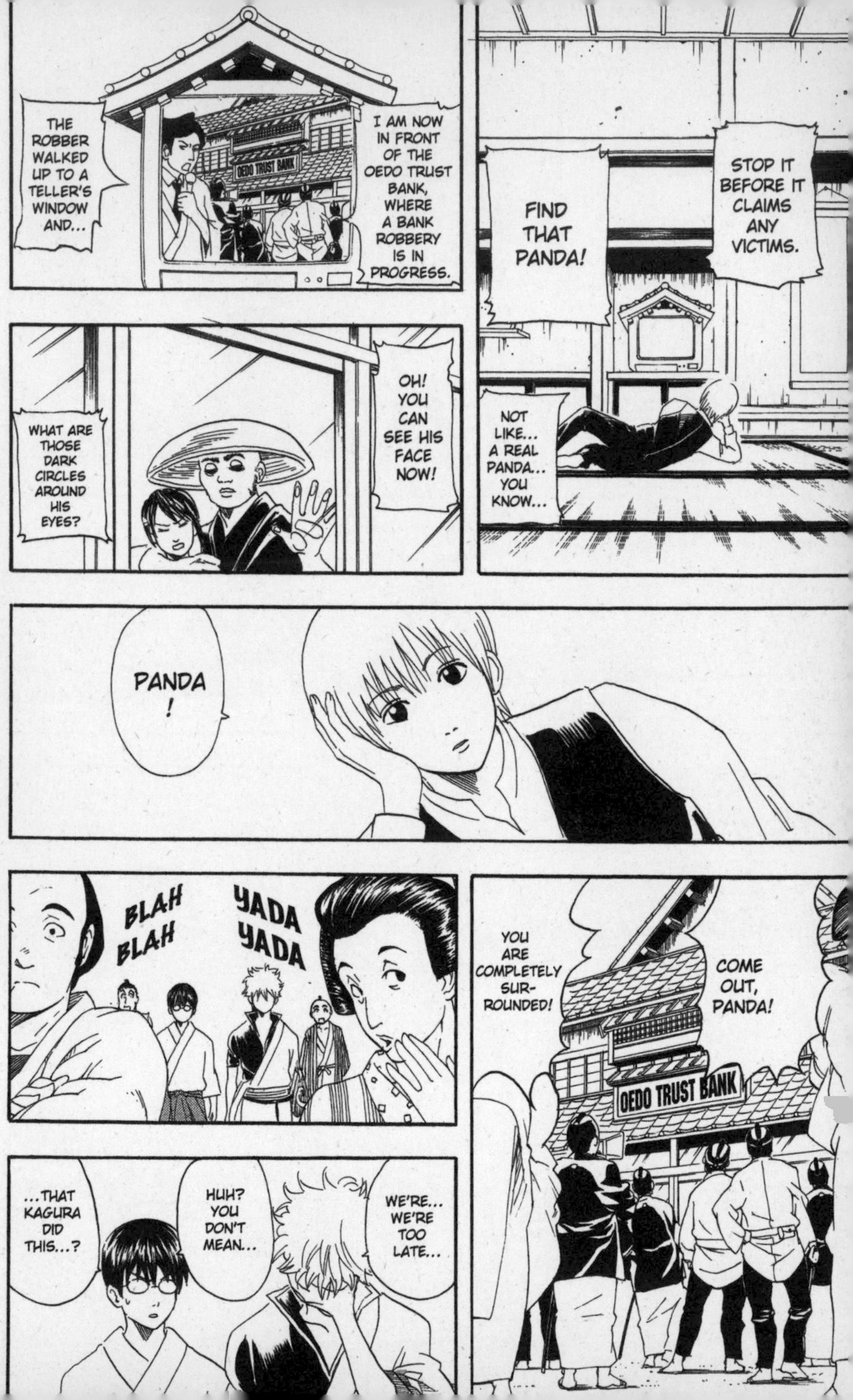
STOP IT BEFORE IT CLAIMS ANY VICTIMS.
FIND THAT PANDA!
NOT LIKE... A REAL PANDA... YOU KNOW...
I AM NOW IN FRONT OF THE OEDO TRUST BANK, WHERE A BANK ROBBERY IS IN PROGRESS.
OEDO TRUST BANK
THE ROBBER WALKED UP TO A TELLER'S WINDOW AND...
OH! YOU CAN SEE HIS FACE NOW!
WHAT ARE THOSE DARK CIRCLES AROUND HIS EYES?
PANDA!
COME OUT, PANDA!
YOU ARE COMPLETELY SUR-ROUNDED!
OEDO TRUST BANK
YADA YADA
BLAH BLAH
WE'RE... WE'RE TOO LATE...
HUH? YOU DON'T MEAN...
...THAT KAGURA DID THIS...?

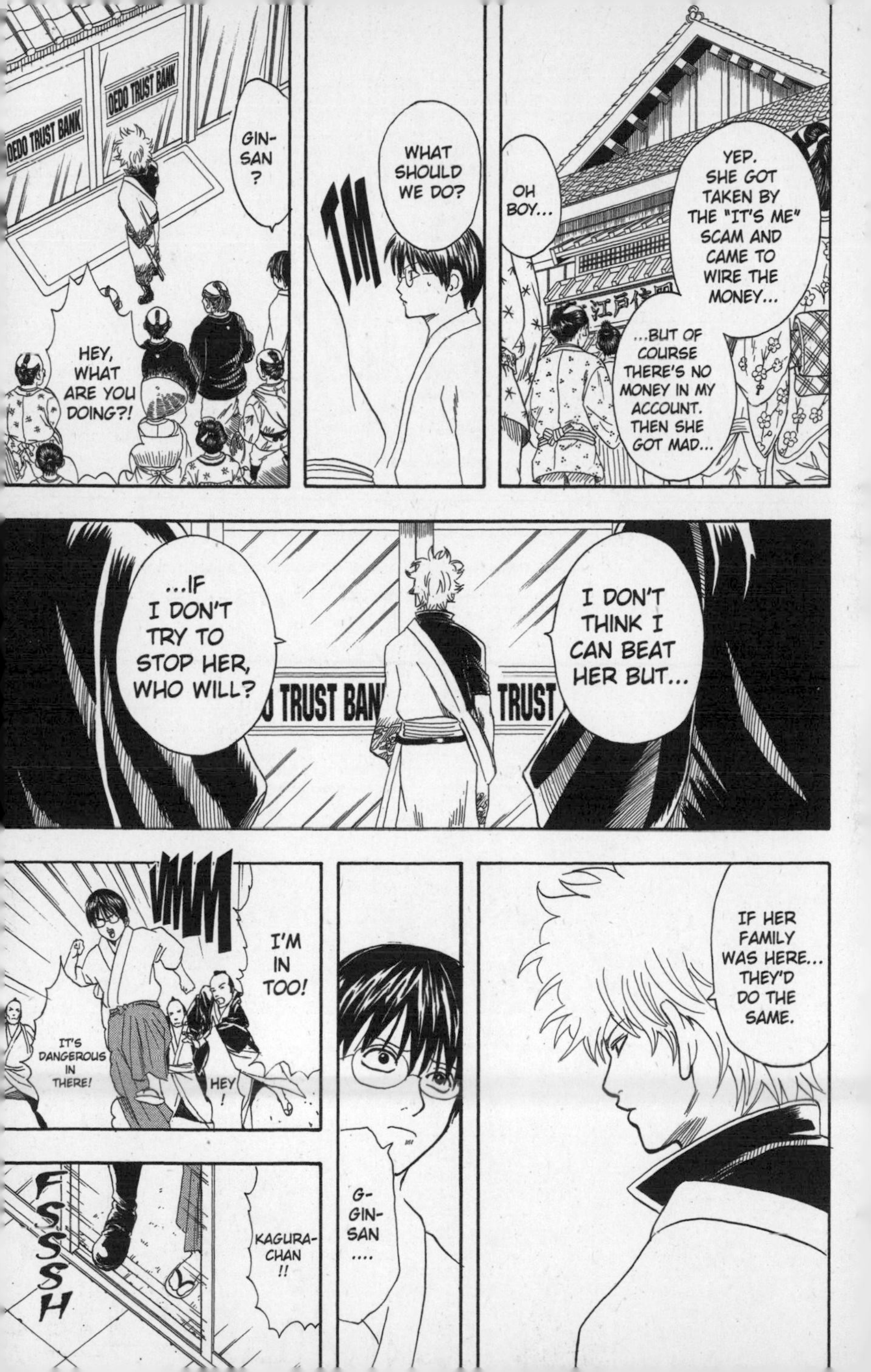
YEP. SHE GOT TAKEN BY THE "IT'S ME" SCAM AND CAME TO WIRE THE MONEY...
...BUT OF COURSE THERE'S NO MONEY IN MY ACCOUNT. THEN SHE GOT MAD...
OH BOY...
WHAT SHOULD WE DO?
TM
GIN-SAN?
OEDO TRUST BANK
OEDO TRUST BANK
HEY, WHAT ARE YOU DOING?!
I DON'T THINK I CAN BEAT HER BUT...
...IF I DON'T TRY TO STOP HER, WHO WILL?
TRUST
O TRUST BAN
IF HER FAMILY WAS HERE... THEY'D DO THE SAME.
G-GIN-SAN....
VMM
I'M IN TOO!
IT'S DANGEROUS IN THERE!
HEY!
FSSSH
KAGURA-CHAN!!

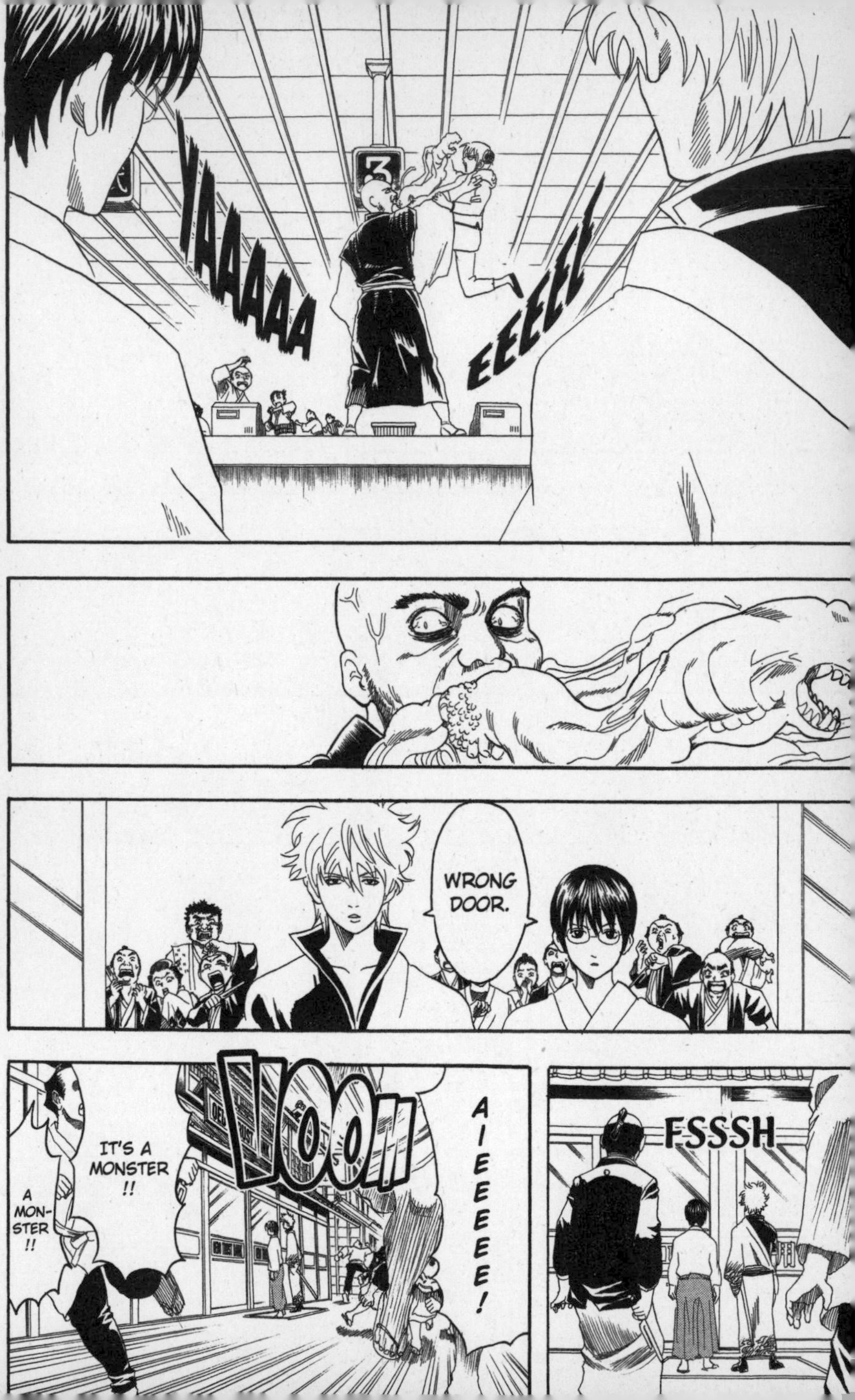
YAAAAAAEEEEE!
WRONG DOOR.
FSSSH
AIEEEEEE!
VOOM
IT'S A MONSTER!!
A MONSTER!!

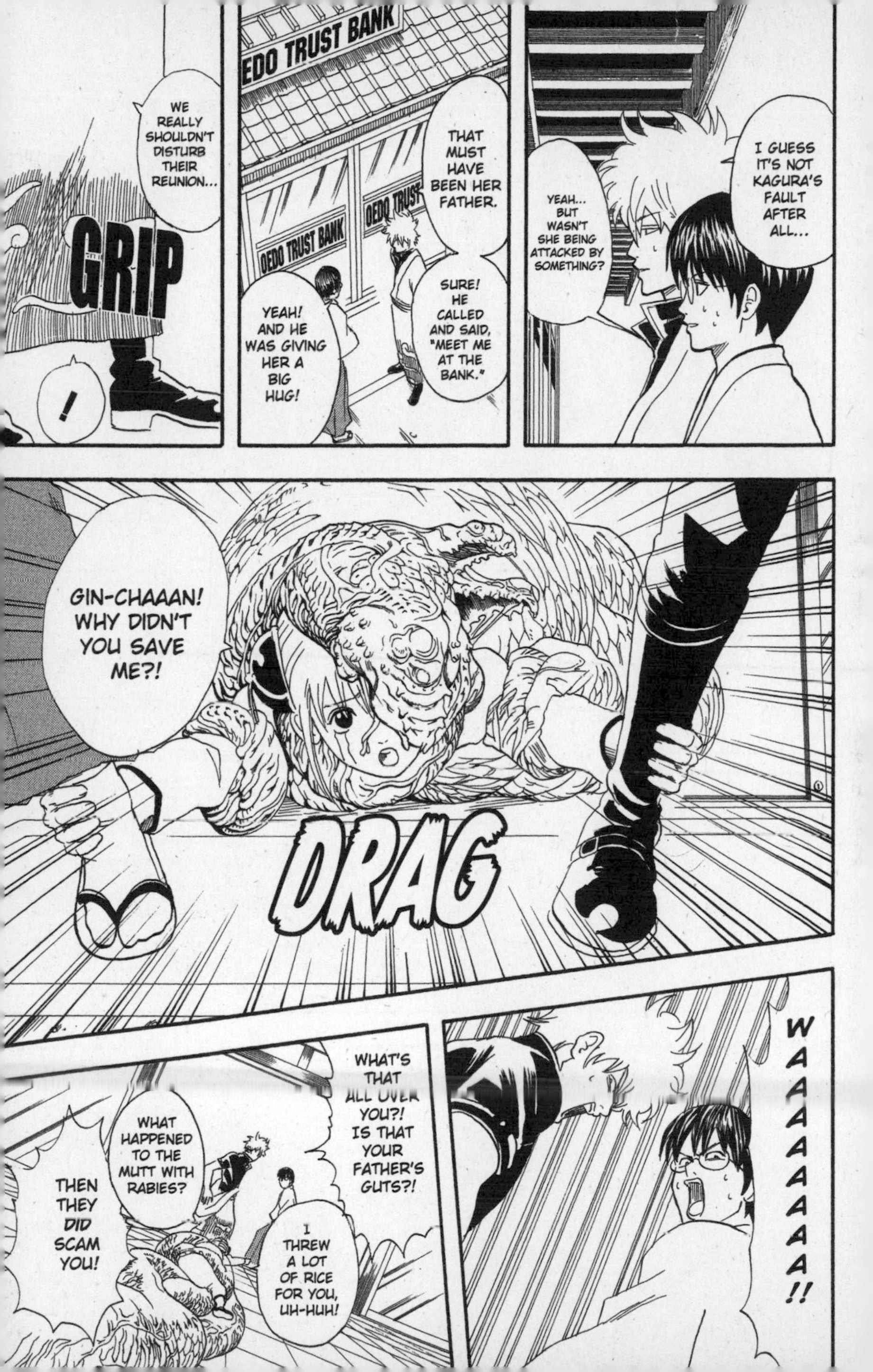
I GUESS IT'S NOT KAGURA'S FAULT AFTER ALL...
YEAH... BUT WASN'T SHE BEING ATTACKED BY SOMETHING?
EDO TRUST BANK
OEDO TRUST BANK
OEDO TRUST
THAT MUST HAVE BEEN HER FATHER.
SURE! HE CALLED AND SAID, "MEET ME AT THE BANK."
YEAH! AND HE WAS GIVING HER A BIG HUG!
WE REALLY SHOULDN'T DISTURB THEIR REUNION...
GRIP
!
GIN-CHAAAN! WHY DIDN'T YOU SAVE ME?!
DRAG
WAAAAAAAAAA!!
WHAT'S THAT ALL OVER YOU?! IS THAT YOUR FATHER'S GUTS?!
I THREW A LOT OF RICE FOR YOU, UH-HUH!
WHAT HAPPENED TO THE MUTT WITH RABIES?
THEN THEY DID SCAM YOU!

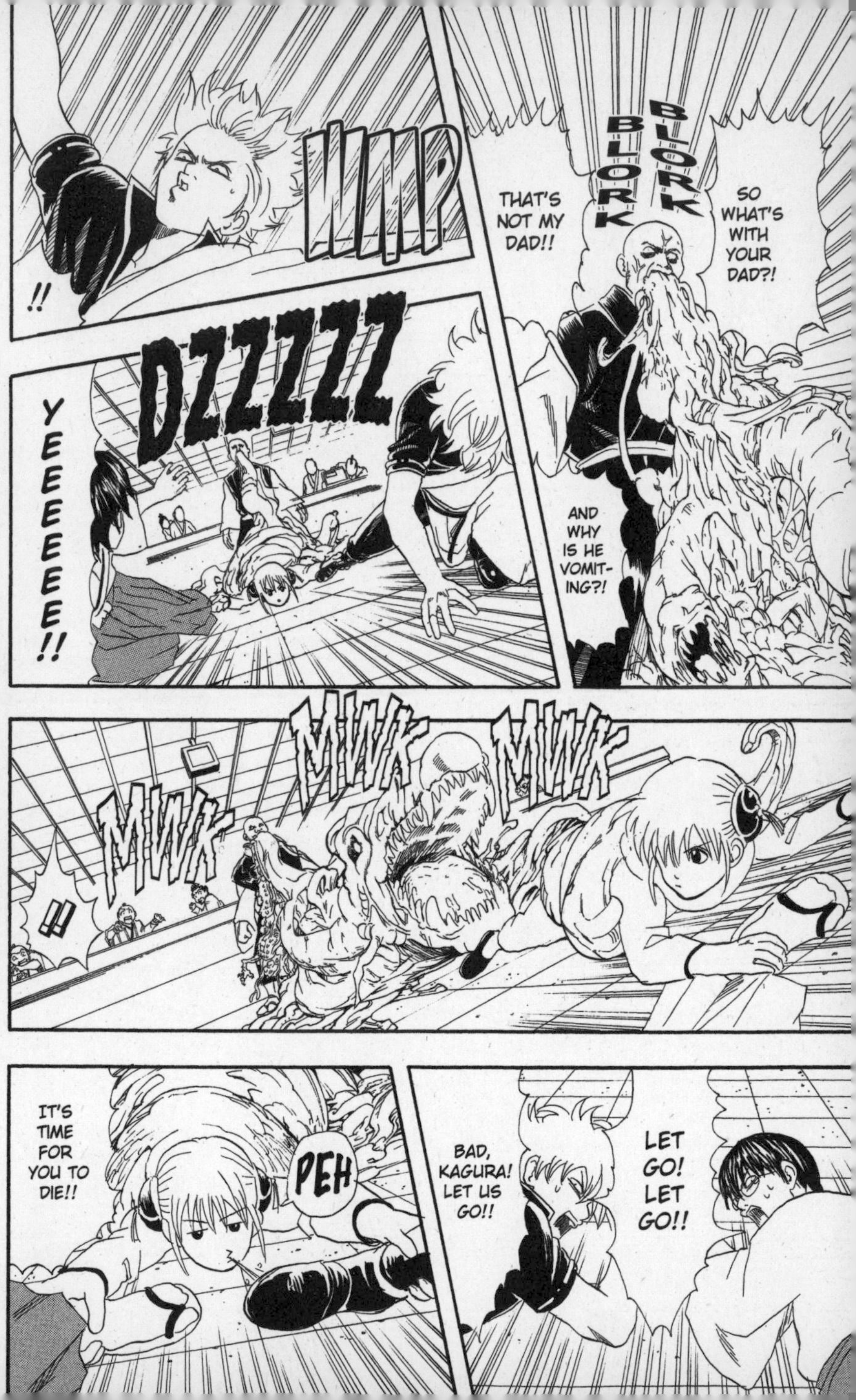
SO WHAT'S WITH YOUR DAD?!
BLORK
BLORK
THAT'S NOT MY DAD!!
AND WHY IS HE VOMIT-ING?!
WMP
!!
DZZZZZ
YEEEEEEEE!!
MWK
MWK
MWK
!!
LET GO! LET GO!!
BAD, KAGURA! LET US GO!!
PEH
IT'S TIME FOR YOU TO DIE!!

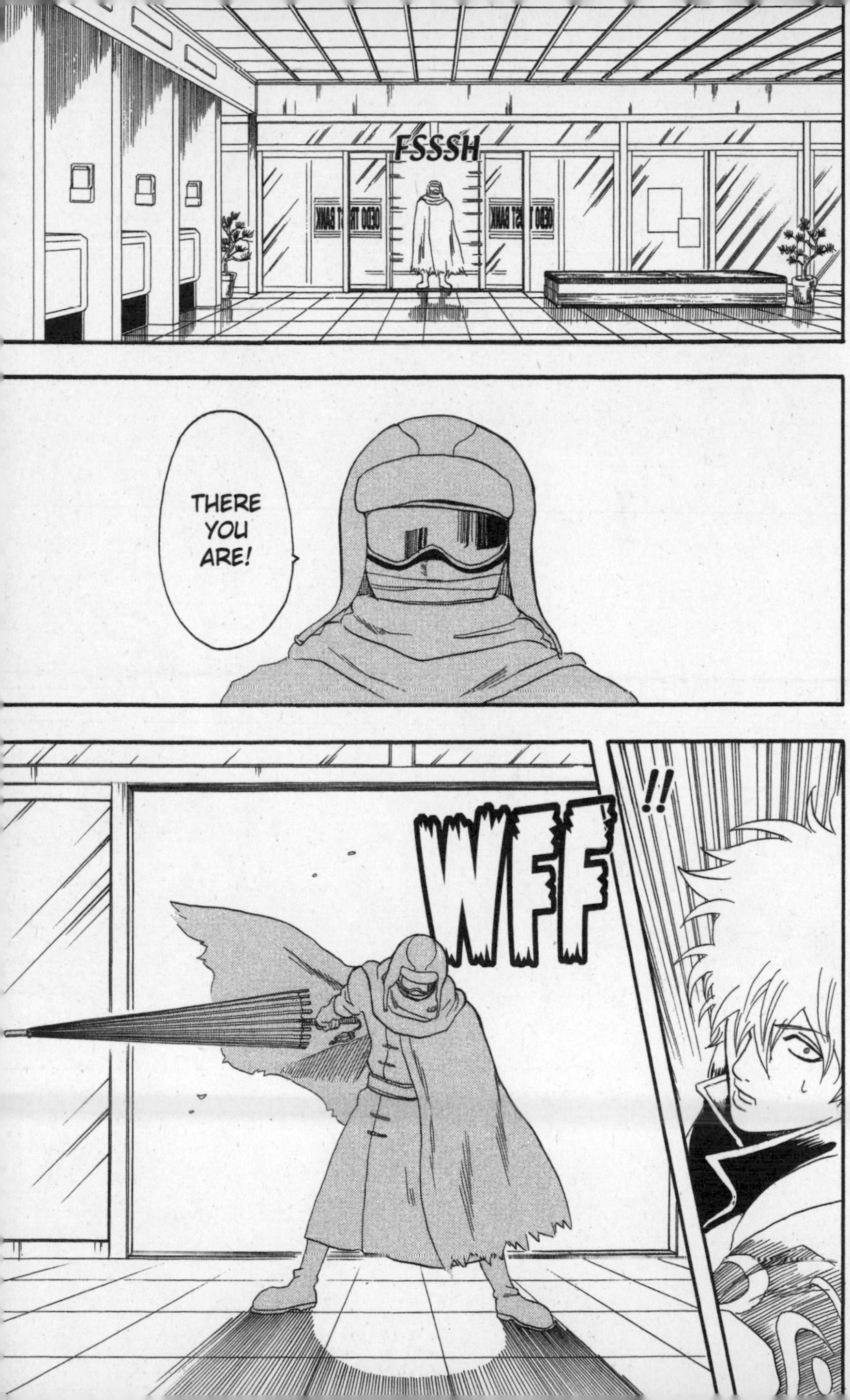
FSSSH
THERE YOU ARE!
!!
WFF

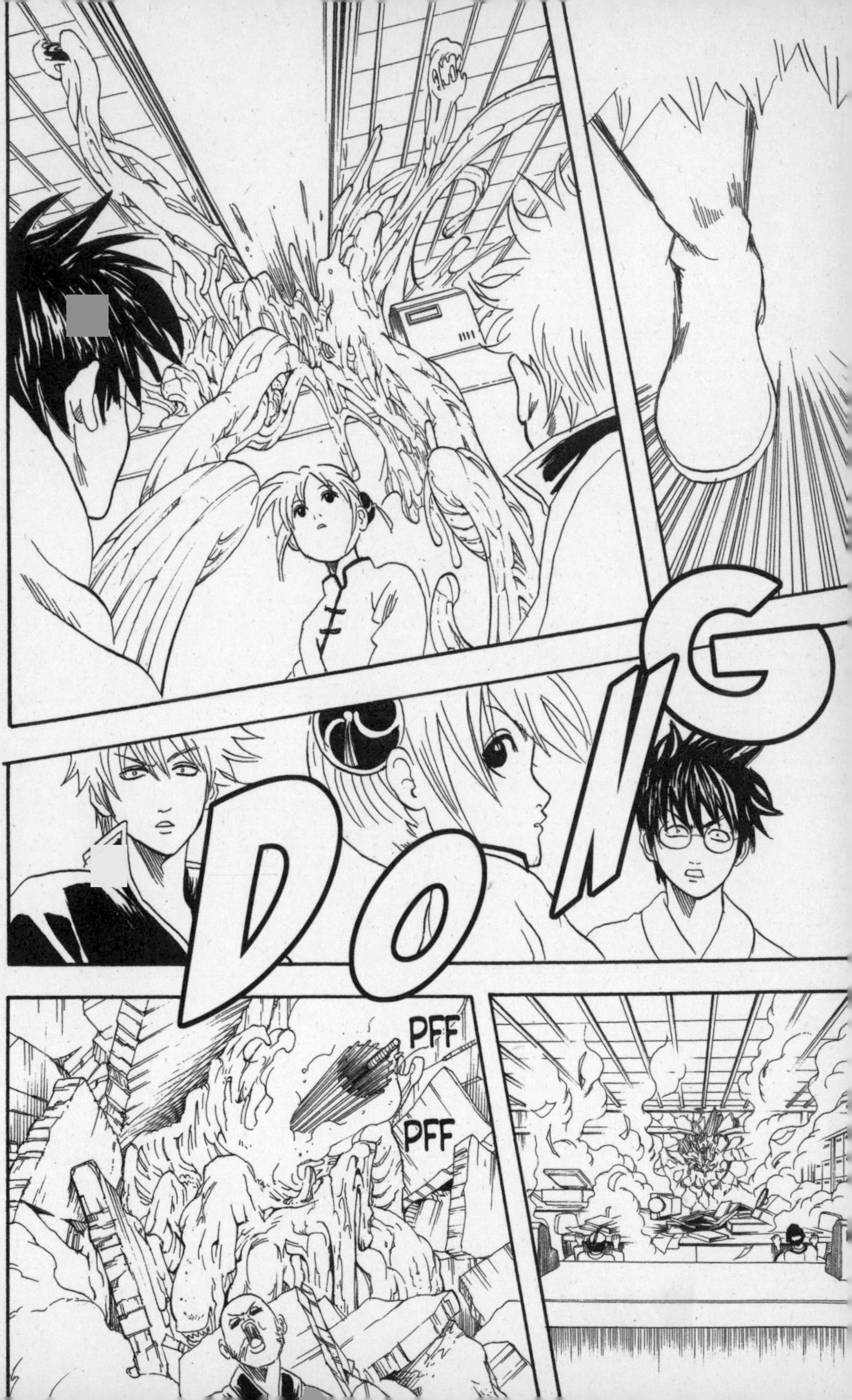
DOING
PFF
PFF

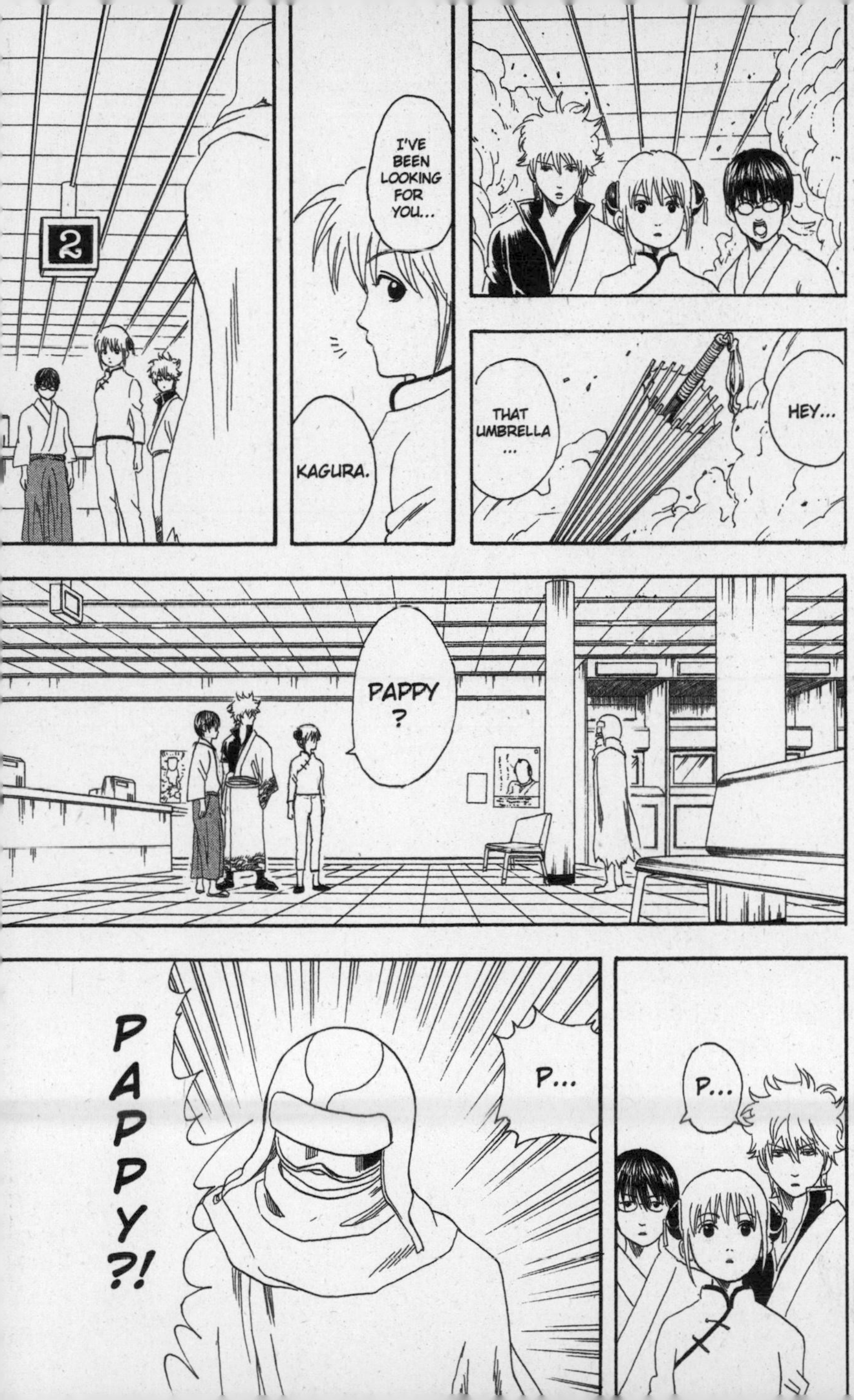
HEY...
THAT UMBRELLA ...
I'VE BEEN LOOKING FOR YOU...
KAGURA.
PAPPY ?
P...
P...
PAPPY ?!

Well, we're wrapping up Volume 7! It's getting pretty repetitive now, don't you think? No, not the manga! These freebie pages! I'm still working hard on the manga! I decided to do something about these pages, so...
Here's the "Please, for God's sake, think up a new alien for me" page!!

Please draw on a postcard an Amanto you've thought up yourself and send it to me. If yours is selected, believe it or not, it'll show up in the main Gin Tama story!! Send it to the same address, written below, same as the address for the Q&A Corner. I'm eagerly awaiting all your creepy drawings!!

Viz Media
ATTN: "I've seen this kind of project somewhere before" Desk
Gin Tama **Editor**
295 Bay Street
San Francisco, CA
94133

※ EDITOR'S NOTE: THIS CONTEST, WHICH RAN IN JAPAN LAST YEAR, HAS ALREADY ENDED. BUT SEND YOUR FAN ART AND LETTERS ALONG TO THE ADDRESS ABOVE IF YOU FEEL LIKE COUGHING UP FOR A STAMP!

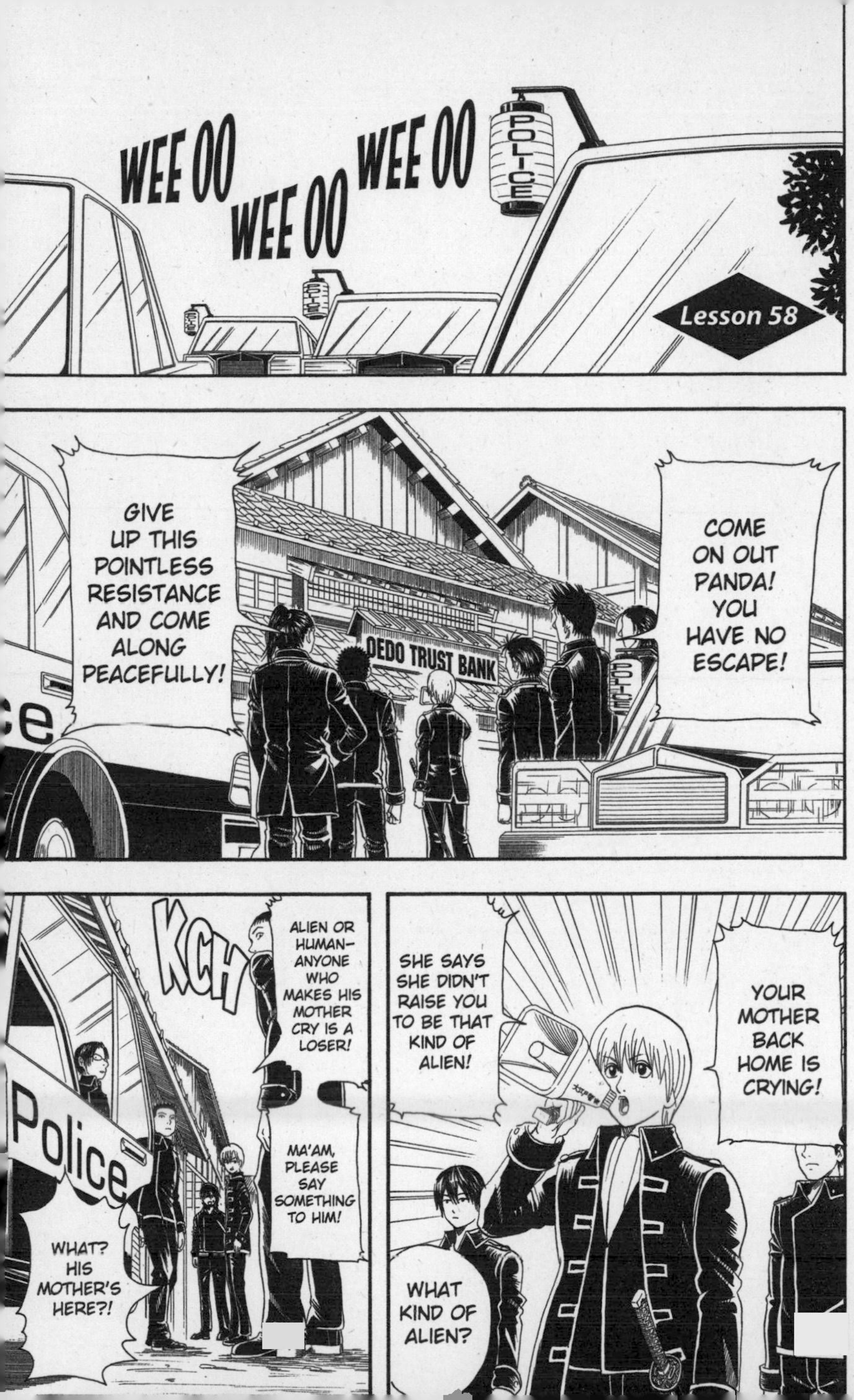
POLICE
Lesson 58
WEE OO
WEE OO
WEE OO
COME ON OUT PANDA! YOU HAVE NO ESCAPE!
OEDO TRUST BANK
GIVE UP THIS POINTLESS RESISTANCE AND COME ALONG PEACEFULLY!
YOUR MOTHER BACK HOME IS CRYING!
SHE SAYS SHE DIDN'T RAISE YOU TO BE THAT KIND OF ALIEN!
WHAT KIND OF ALIEN?
ALIEN OR HUMAN—ANYONE WHO MAKES HIS MOTHER CRY IS A LOSER!
KCH
MA'AM, PLEASE SAY SOMETHING TO HIM!
Police
WHAT? HIS MOTHER'S HERE?!

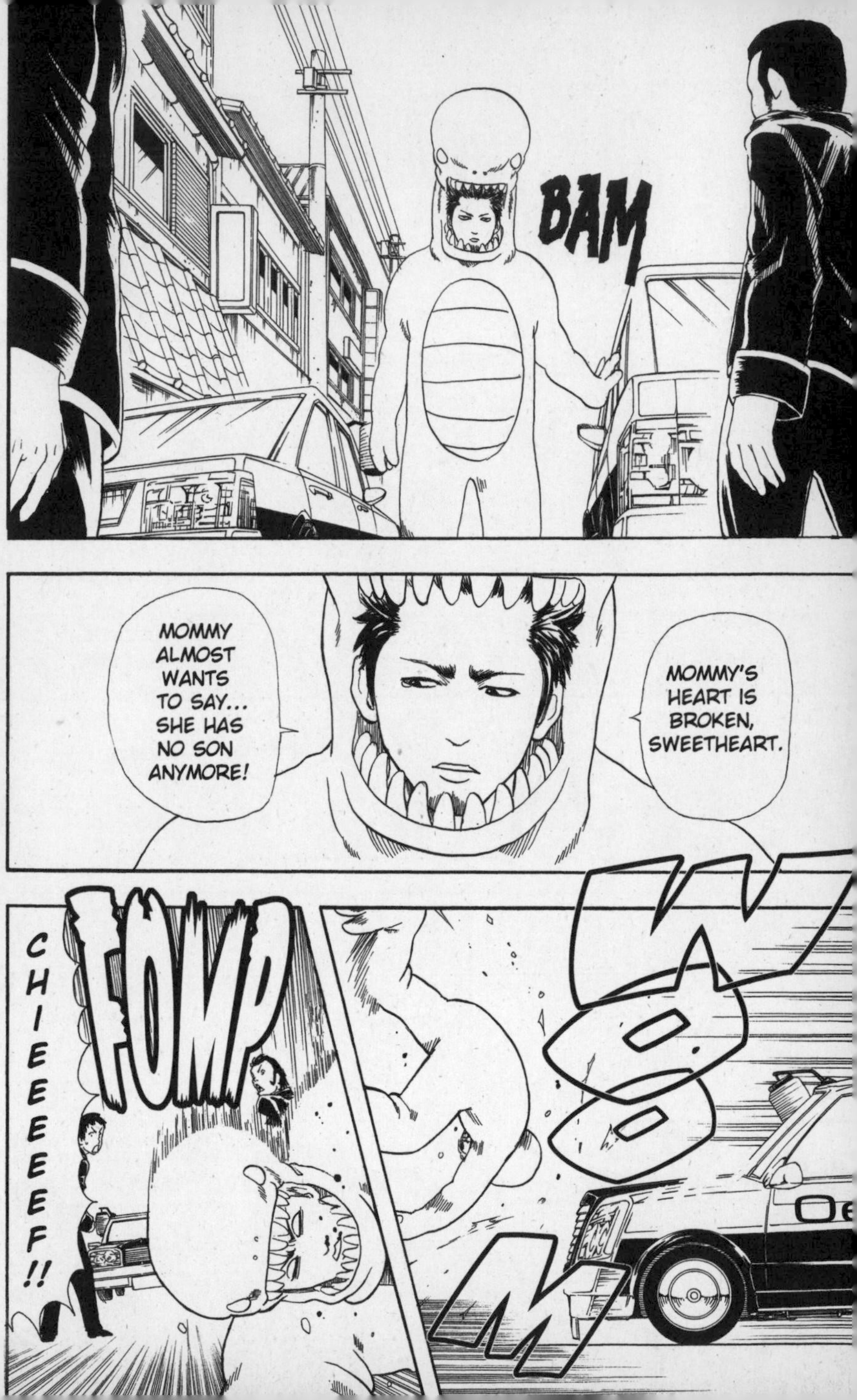
BAM
MOMMY'S HEART IS BROKEN, SWEETHEART.
MOMMY ALMOST WANTS TO SAY... SHE HAS NO SON ANYMORE!
WOOM
FOMP
CHIEEEEEF!!

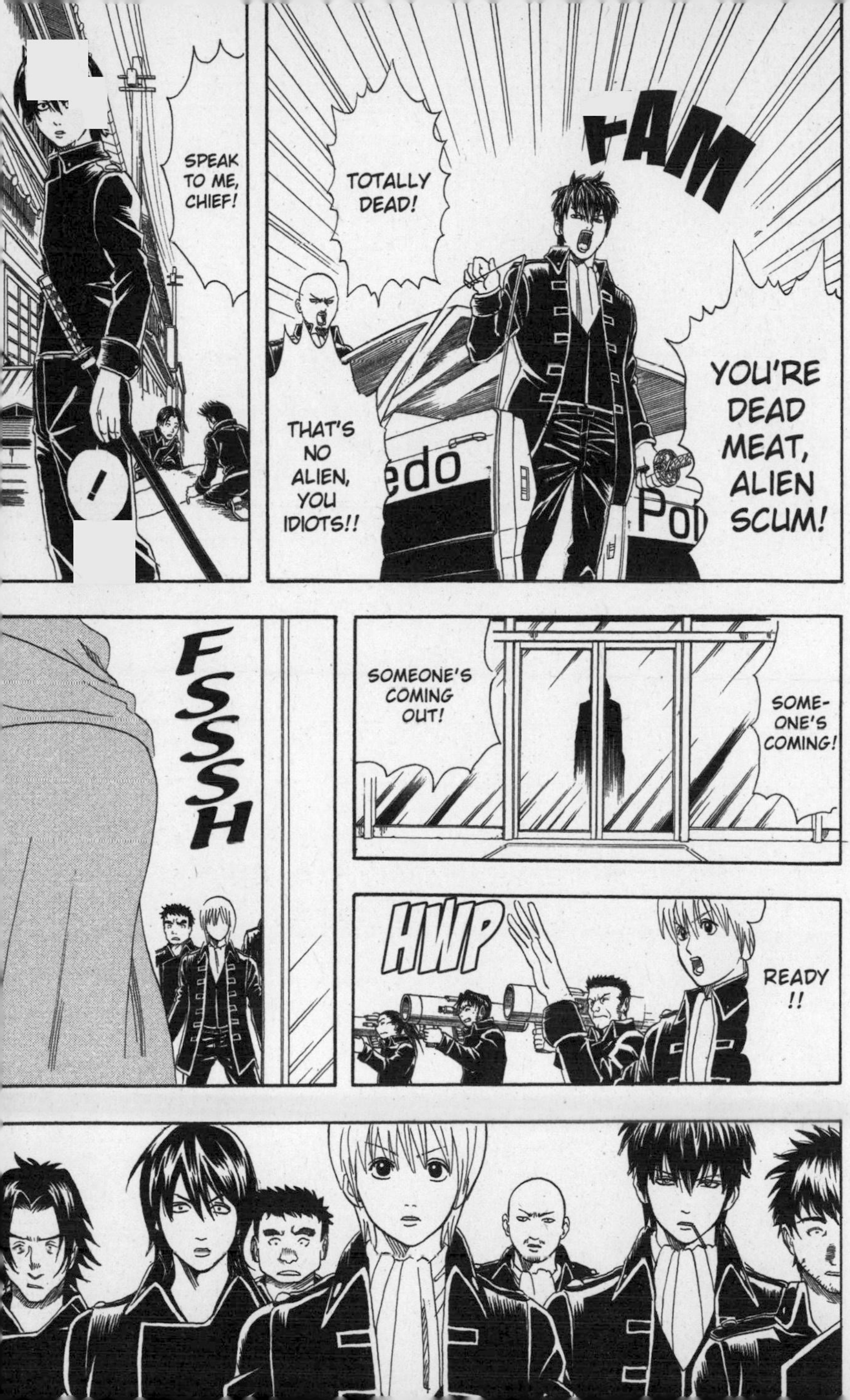
YOU'RE DEAD MEAT, ALIEN SCUM!
TOTALLY DEAD!
THAT'S NO ALIEN, YOU IDIOTS!!
SPEAK TO ME, CHIEF!
!
SOME-ONE'S COMING!
SOMEONE'S COMING OUT!
READY!!
HWP
FSSSH

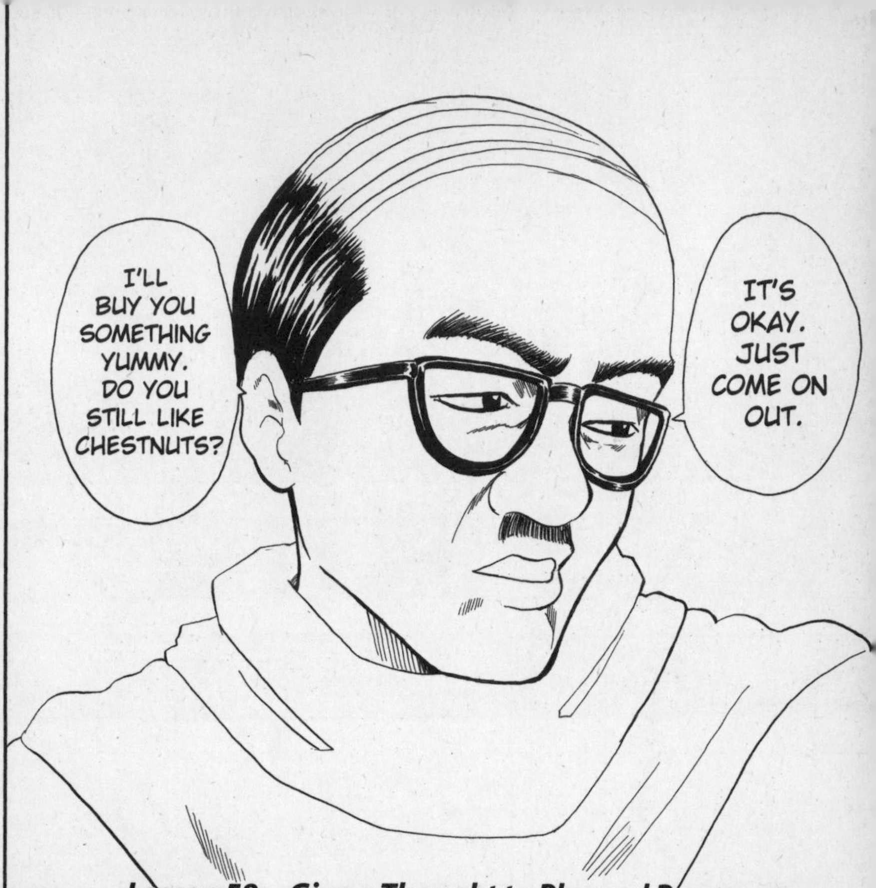
IT'S OKAY. JUST COME ON OUT.
I'LL BUY YOU SOMETHING YUMMY. DO YOU STILL LIKE CHESTNUTS?

Lesson 58: Give a Thought to Planned Pregnancy

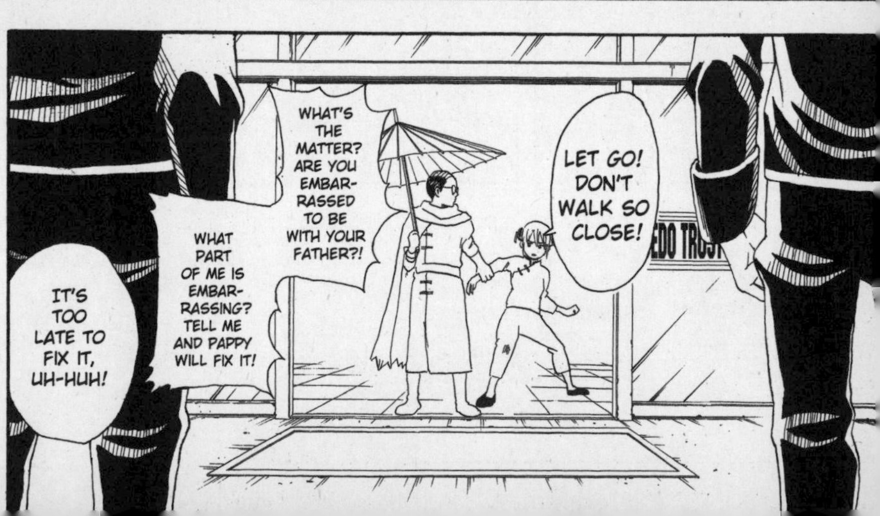
LET GO! DON'T WALK SO CLOSE!
WHAT'S THE MATTER? ARE YOU EMBAR-RASSED TO BE WITH YOUR FATHER?!
WHAT PART OF ME IS EMBAR-RASSING? TELL ME AND PAPPY WILL FIX IT!
IT'S TOO LATE TO FIX IT, UH-HUH!

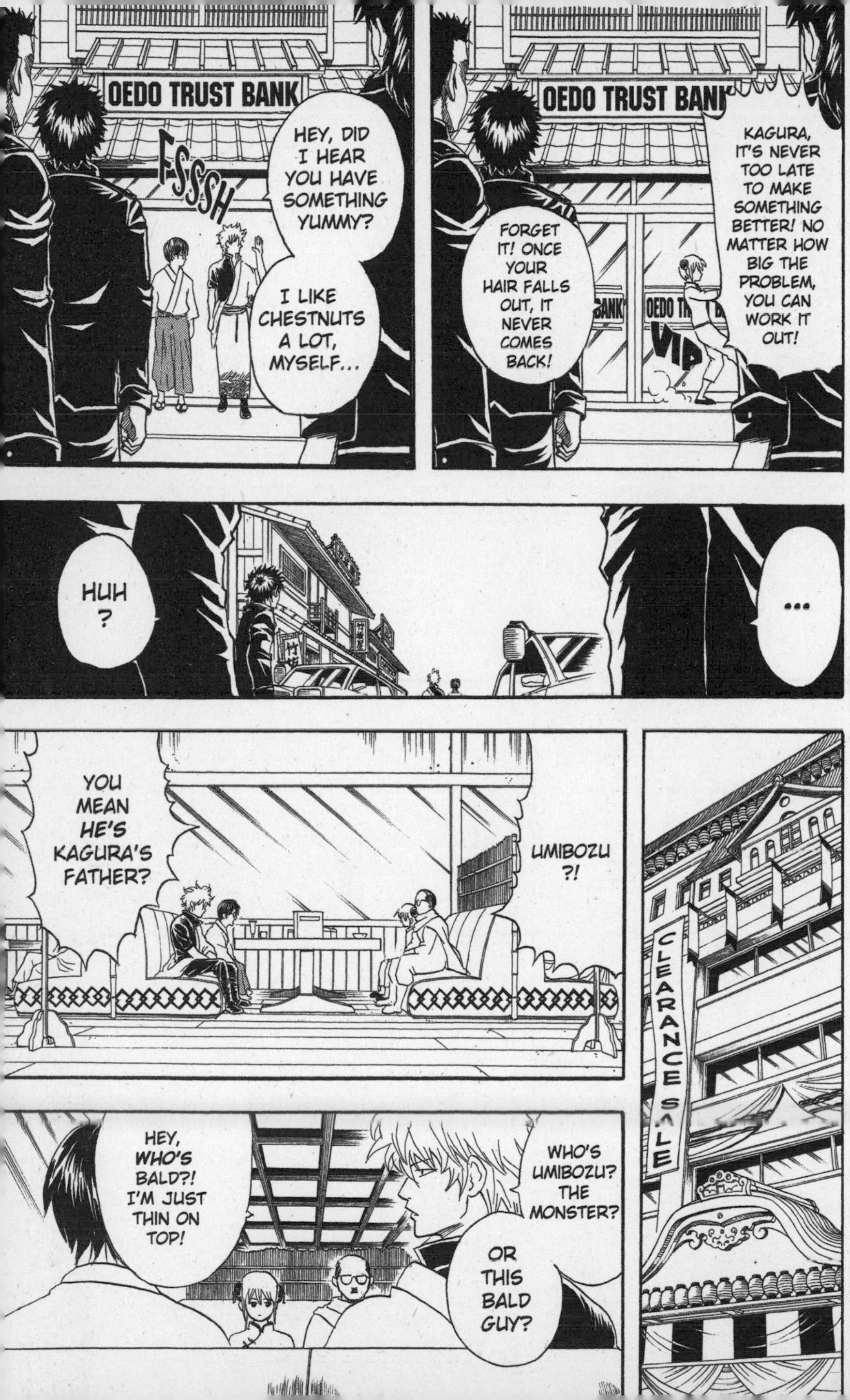
OEDO TRUST BANK
KAGURA, IT'S NEVER TOO LATE TO MAKE SOMETHING BETTER! NO MATTER HOW BIG THE PROBLEM, YOU CAN WORK IT OUT!
FORGET IT! ONCE YOUR HAIR FALLS OUT, IT NEVER COMES BACK!
VIP
OEDO TRUST BANK
FSSSH
HEY, DID I HEAR YOU HAVE SOMETHING YUMMY?
I LIKE CHESTNUTS A LOT, MYSELF...
...
HUH?
CLEARANCE SALE
UMIBOZU?!
YOU MEAN HE'S KAGURA'S FATHER?
WHO'S UMIBOZU? THE MONSTER?
OR THIS BALD GUY?
HEY, WHO'S BALD?! I'M JUST THIN ON TOP!

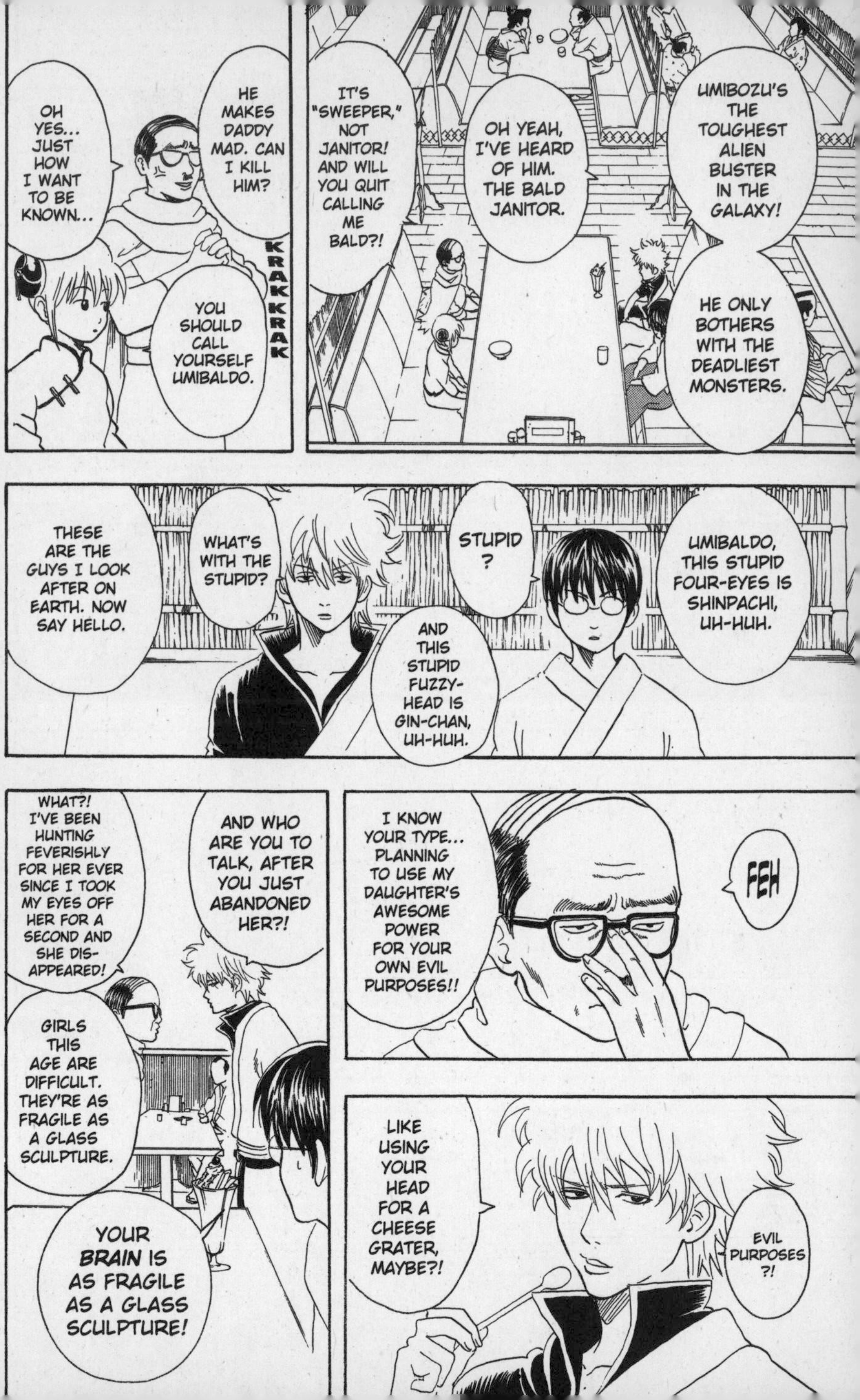
UMIBOZU'S THE TOUGHEST ALIEN BUSTER IN THE GALAXY!
HE ONLY BOTHERS WITH THE DEADLIEST MONSTERS.
OH YEAH, I'VE HEARD OF HIM. THE BALD JANITOR.
IT'S "SWEEPER," NOT JANITOR! AND WILL YOU QUIT CALLING ME BALD?!
HE MAKES DADDY MAD. CAN I KILL HIM?
OH YES... JUST HOW I WANT TO BE KNOWN...
KRAK KRAK
YOU SHOULD CALL YOURSELF UMIBALDO.
UMIBALDO, THIS STUPID FOUR-EYES IS SHINPACHI, UH-HUH.
STUPID?
AND THIS STUPID FUZZY-HEAD IS GIN-CHAN, UH-HUH.
WHAT'S WITH THE STUPID?
THESE ARE THE GUYS I LOOK AFTER ON EARTH. NOW SAY HELLO.
FEH
I KNOW YOUR TYPE... PLANNING TO USE MY DAUGHTER'S AWESOME POWER FOR YOUR OWN EVIL PURPOSES!!
EVIL PURPOSES?!
LIKE USING YOUR HEAD FOR A CHEESE GRATER, MAYBE?!
AND WHO ARE YOU TO TALK, AFTER YOU JUST ABANDONED HER?!
WHAT?! I'VE BEEN HUNTING FEVERISHLY FOR HER EVER SINCE I TOOK MY EYES OFF HER FOR A SECOND AND SHE DIS-APPEARED!
GIRLS THIS AGE ARE DIFFICULT. THEY'RE AS FRAGILE AS A GLASS SCULPTURE.
YOUR BRAIN IS AS FRAGILE AS A GLASS SCULPTURE!

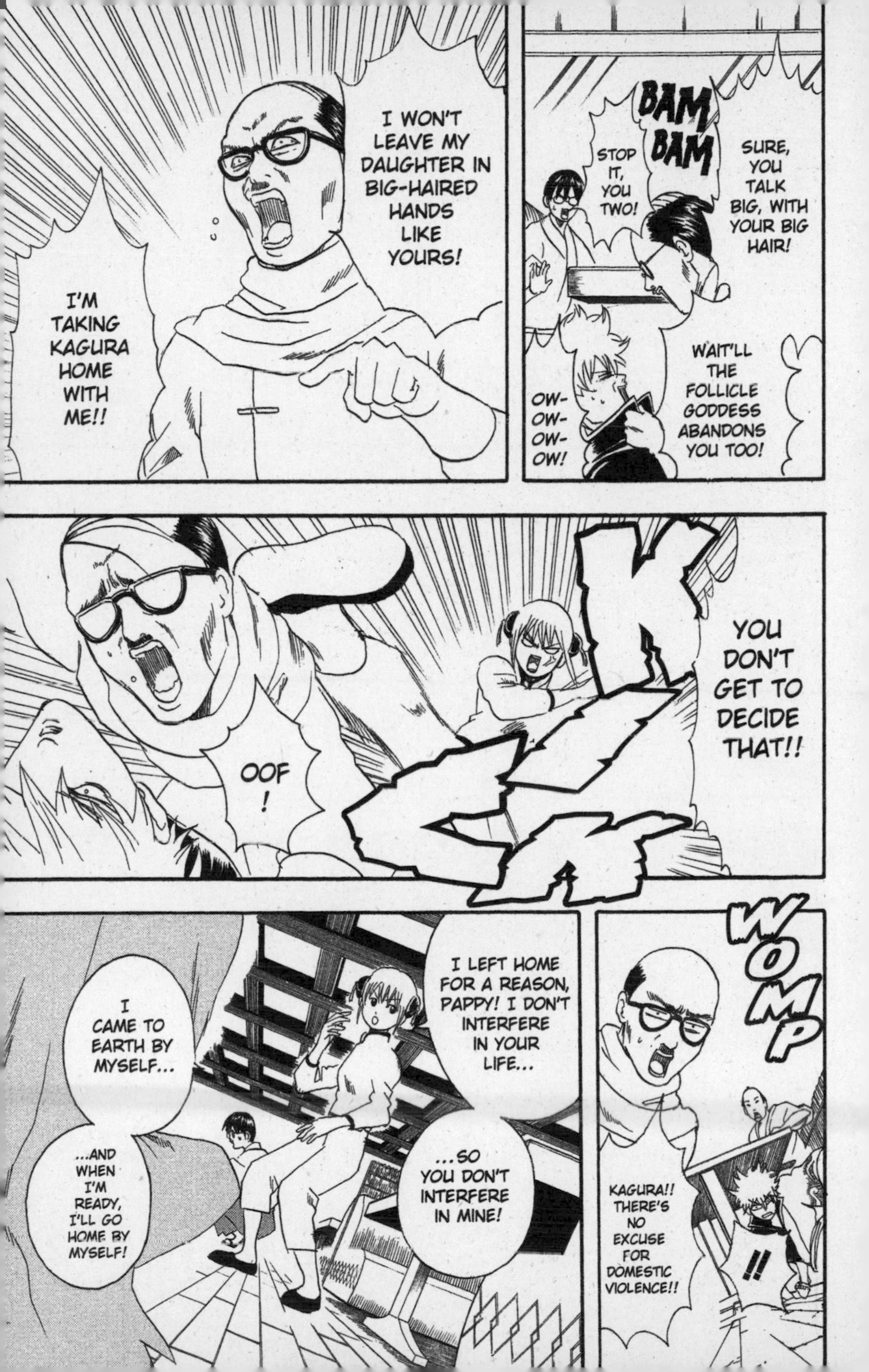
BAM BAM
SURE, YOU TALK BIG, WITH YOUR BIG HAIR!
STOP IT, YOU TWO!
WAIT'LL THE FOLLICLE GODDESS ABANDONS YOU TOO!
OW-OW-OW-OW!
I WON'T LEAVE MY DAUGHTER IN BIG-HAIRED HANDS LIKE YOURS!
I'M TAKING KAGURA HOME WITH ME!!
YOU DON'T GET TO DECIDE THAT!!
OOF!
WOMP
!!
KAGURA!! THERE'S NO EXCUSE FOR DOMESTIC VIOLENCE!!
I LEFT HOME FOR A REASON, PAPPY! I DON'T INTERFERE IN YOUR LIFE...
...SO YOU DON'T INTERFERE IN MINE!
I CAME TO EARTH BY MYSELF...
...AND WHEN I'M READY, I'LL GO HOME BY MYSELF!

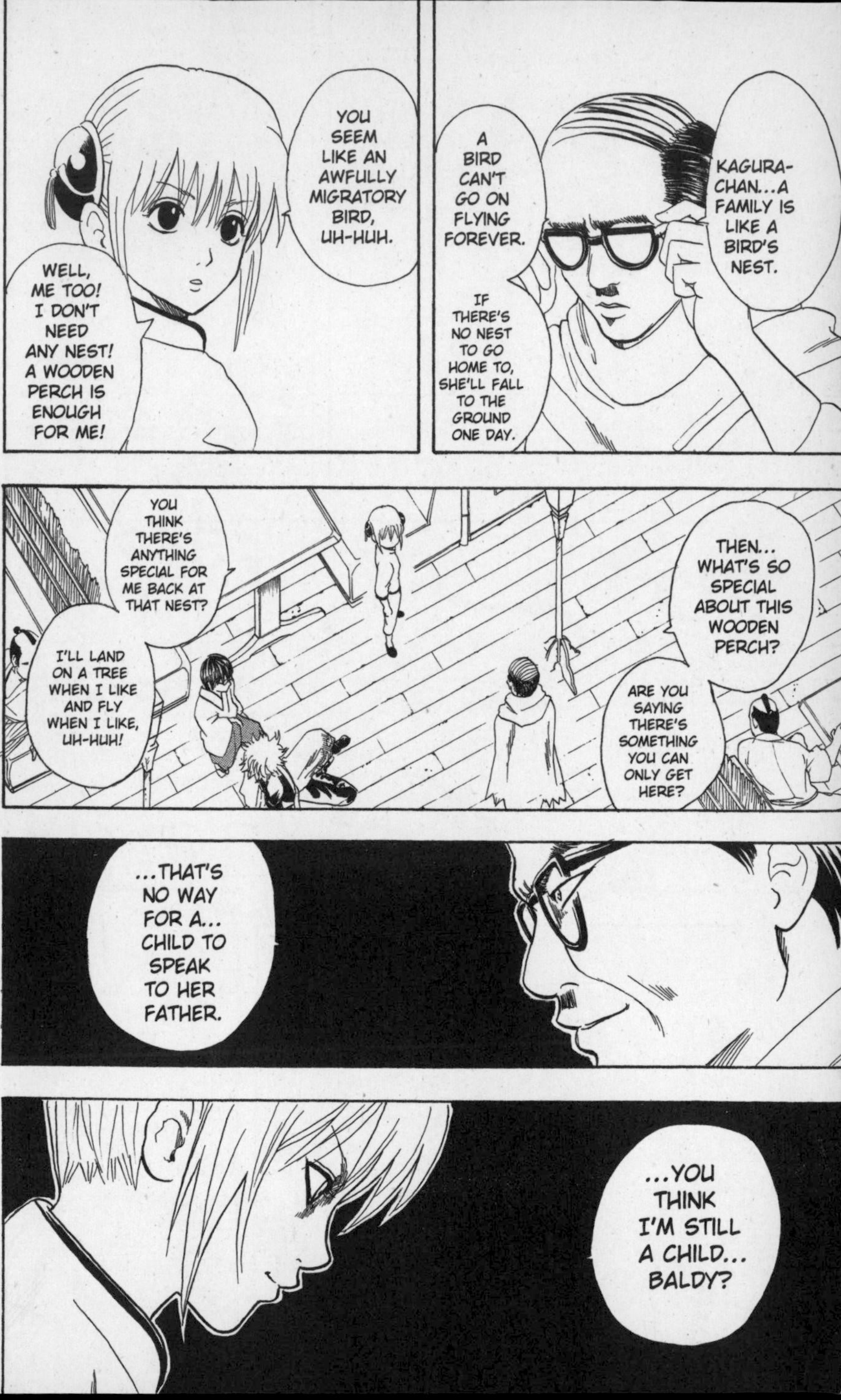
KAGURA-CHAN...A FAMILY IS LIKE A BIRD'S NEST.
A BIRD CAN'T GO ON FLYING FOREVER.
IF THERE'S NO NEST TO GO HOME TO, SHE'LL FALL TO THE GROUND ONE DAY.
YOU SEEM LIKE AN AWFULLY MIGRATORY BIRD, UH-HUH.
WELL, ME TOO! I DON'T NEED ANY NEST! A WOODEN PERCH IS ENOUGH FOR ME!
THEN... WHAT'S SO SPECIAL ABOUT THIS WOODEN PERCH?
ARE YOU SAYING THERE'S SOMETHING YOU CAN ONLY GET HERE?
YOU THINK THERE'S ANYTHING SPECIAL FOR ME BACK AT THAT NEST?
I'LL LAND ON A TREE WHEN I LIKE AND FLY WHEN I LIKE, UH-HUH!
...THAT'S NO WAY FOR A... CHILD TO SPEAK TO HER FATHER.
...YOU THINK I'M STILL A CHILD... BALDY?

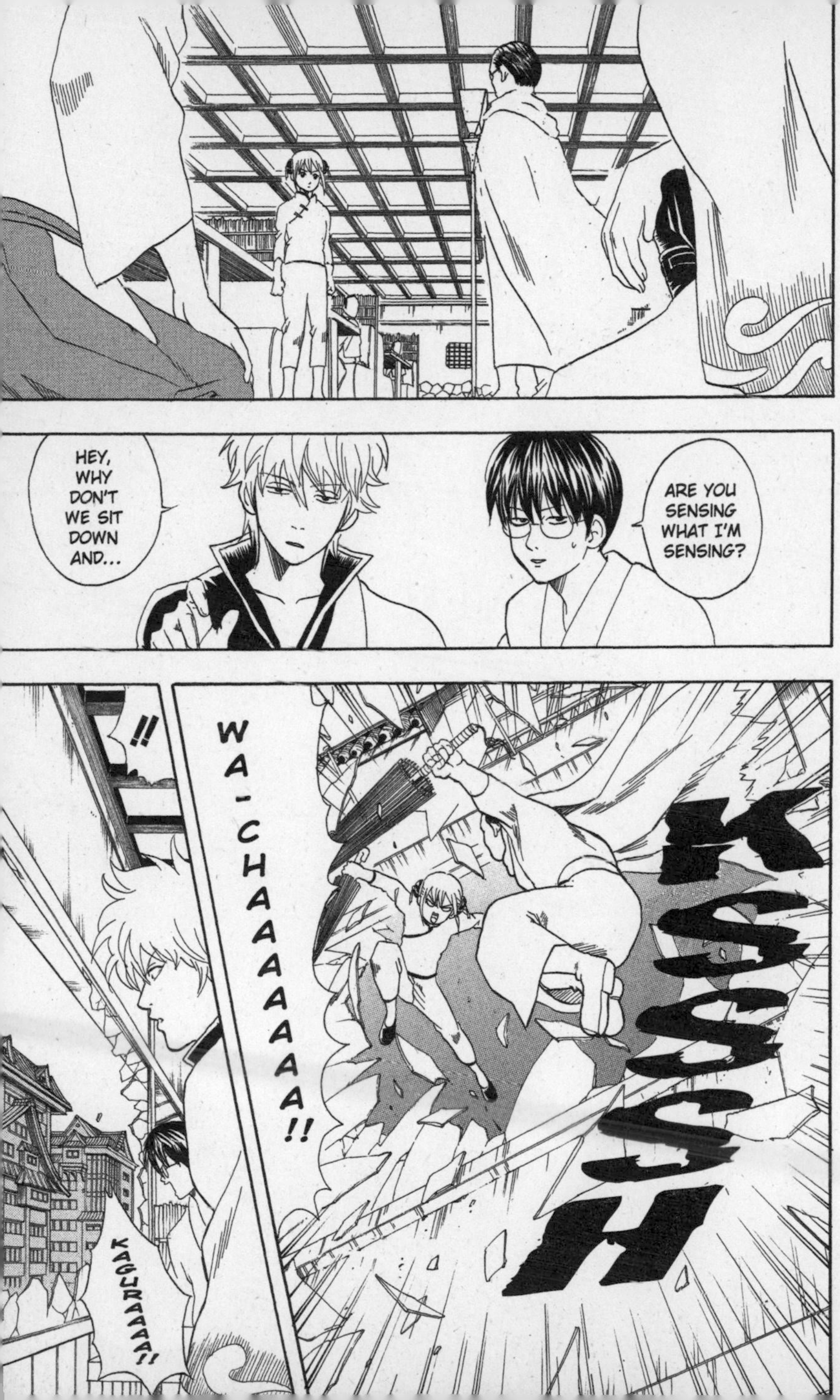
ARE YOU SENSING WHAT I'M SENSING?
HEY, WHY DON'T WE SIT DOWN AND...
KSSSH
WA-CHAAAAAAA!!
!!
KAGURAAAA!!

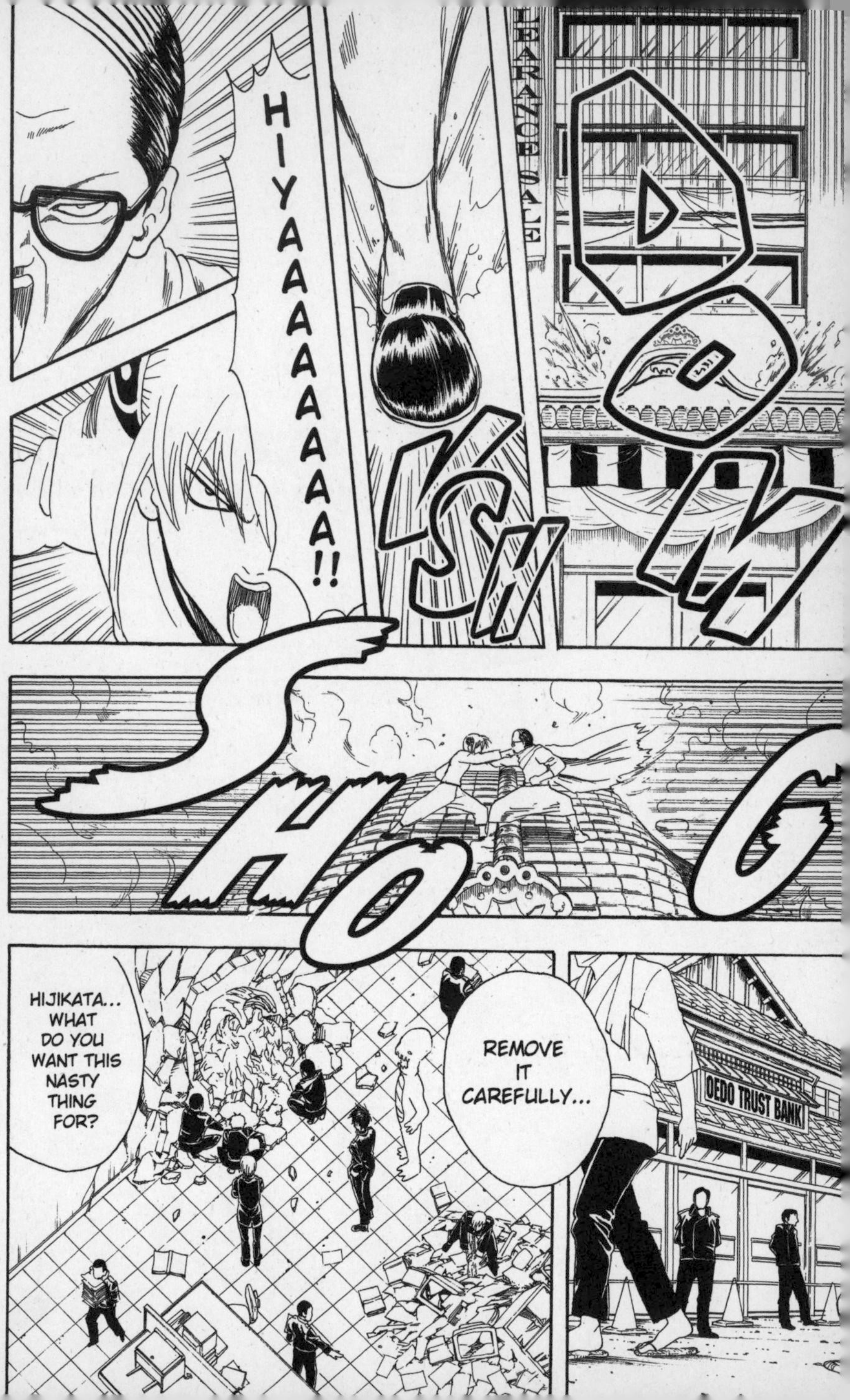
LEARANCE SALE
HIYAAAAAAAAA!!
OEDO TRUST BANK
REMOVE IT CAREFULLY...
HIJIKATA... WHAT DO YOU WANT THIS NASTY THING FOR?

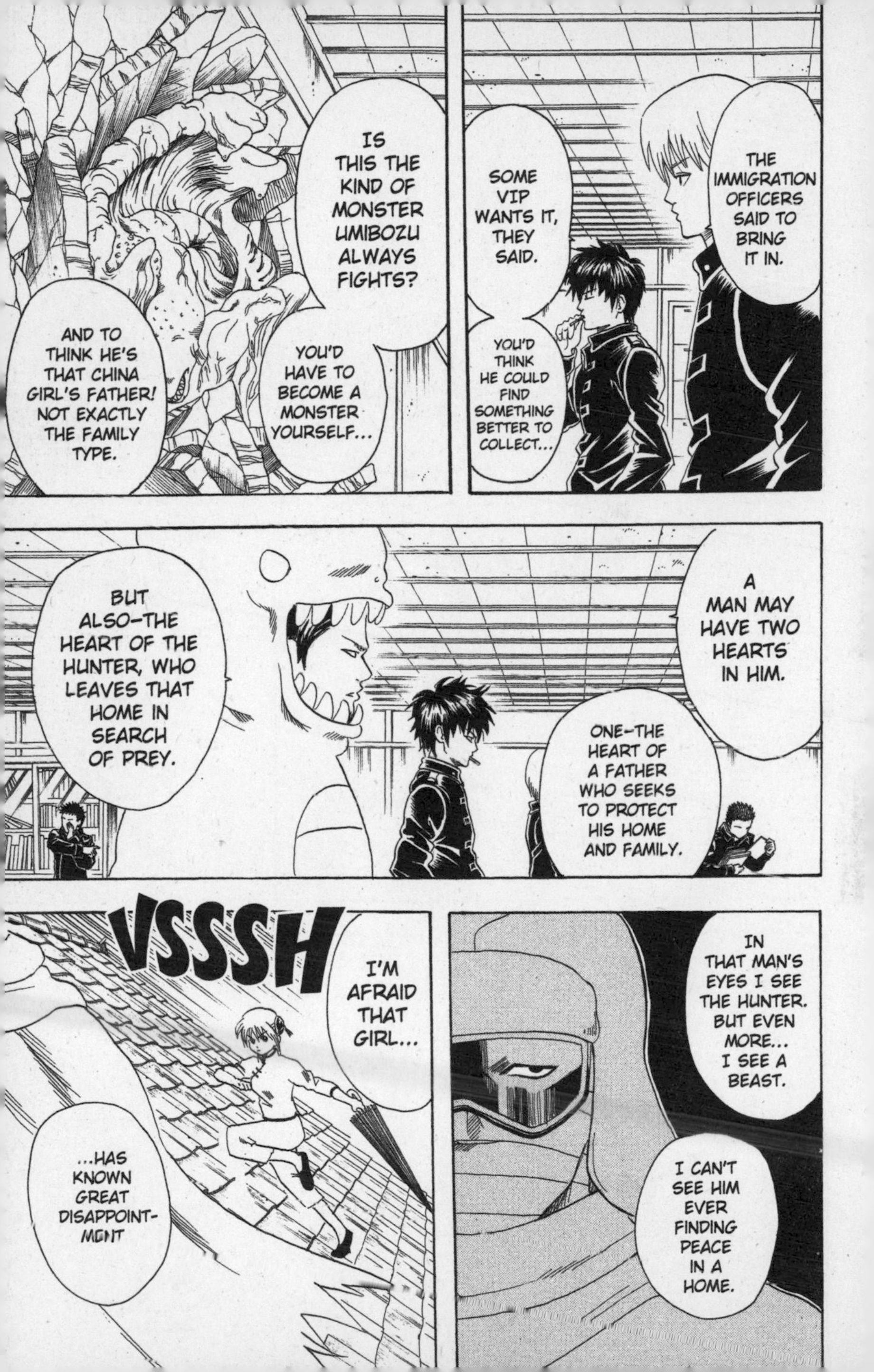
THE IMMIGRATION OFFICERS SAID TO BRING IT IN.
SOME VIP WANTS IT, THEY SAID.
YOU'D THINK HE COULD FIND SOMETHING BETTER TO COLLECT...
IS THIS THE KIND OF MONSTER UMIBOZU ALWAYS FIGHTS?
YOU'D HAVE TO BECOME A MONSTER YOURSELF...
AND TO THINK HE'S THAT CHINA GIRL'S FATHER! NOT EXACTLY THE FAMILY TYPE.
A MAN MAY HAVE TWO HEARTS IN HIM.
ONE—THE HEART OF A FATHER WHO SEEKS TO PROTECT HIS HOME AND FAMILY.
BUT ALSO—THE HEART OF THE HUNTER, WHO LEAVES THAT HOME IN SEARCH OF PREY.
IN THAT MAN'S EYES I SEE THE HUNTER. BUT EVEN MORE... I SEE A BEAST.
I CAN'T SEE HIM EVER FINDING PEACE IN A HOME.
VSSSH
I'M AFRAID THAT GIRL...
...HAS KNOWN GREAT DISAPPOINT-MENT

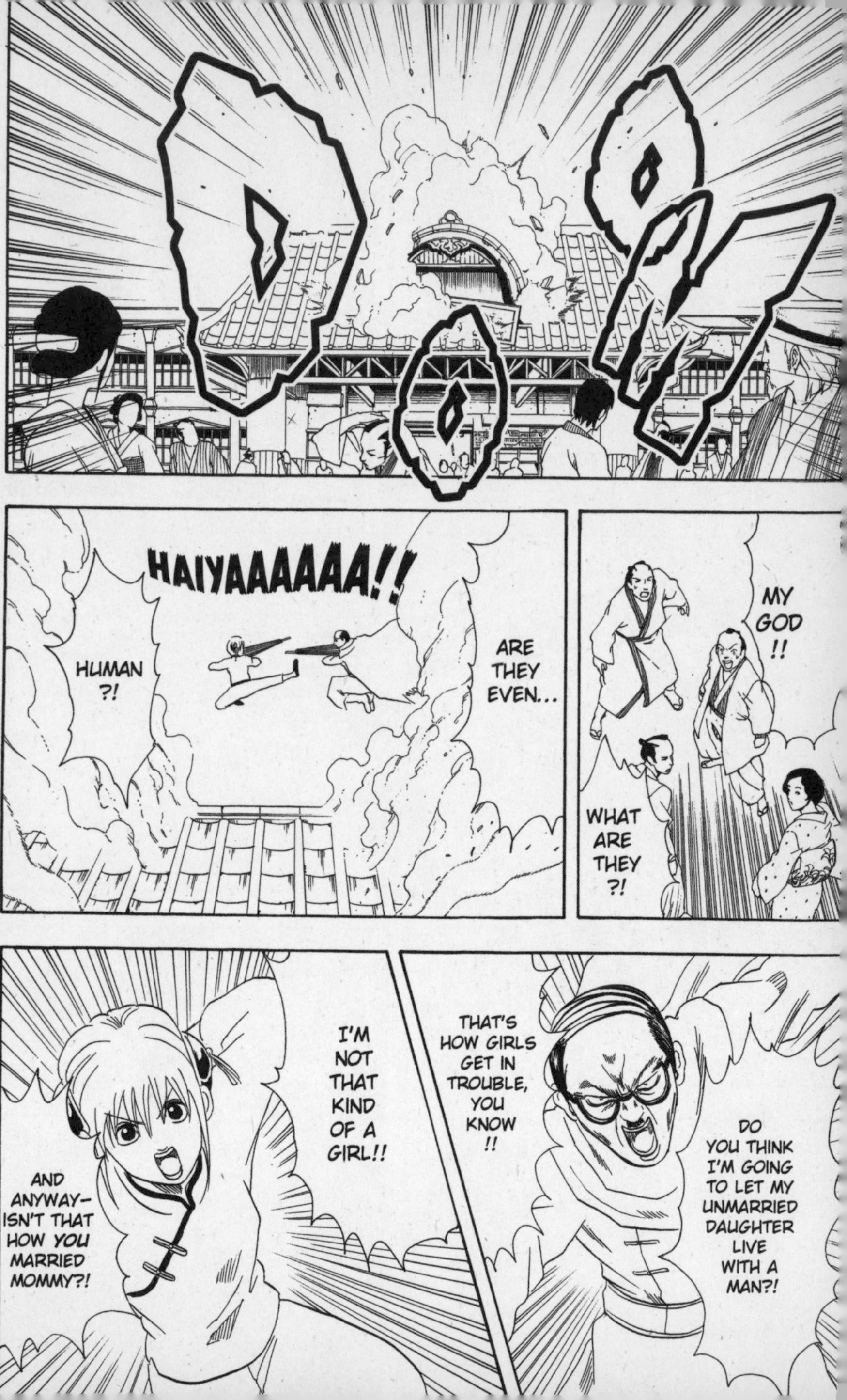
DOOM
MY GOD !!
WHAT ARE THEY ?!
HAIYAAAAAAA!!
ARE THEY EVEN...
HUMAN ?!
DO YOU THINK I'M GOING TO LET MY UNMARRIED DAUGHTER LIVE WITH A MAN?!
THAT'S HOW GIRLS GET IN TROUBLE, YOU KNOW !!
I'M NOT THAT KIND OF A GIRL!!
AND ANYWAY— ISN'T THAT HOW *YOU* MARRIED MOMMY?!

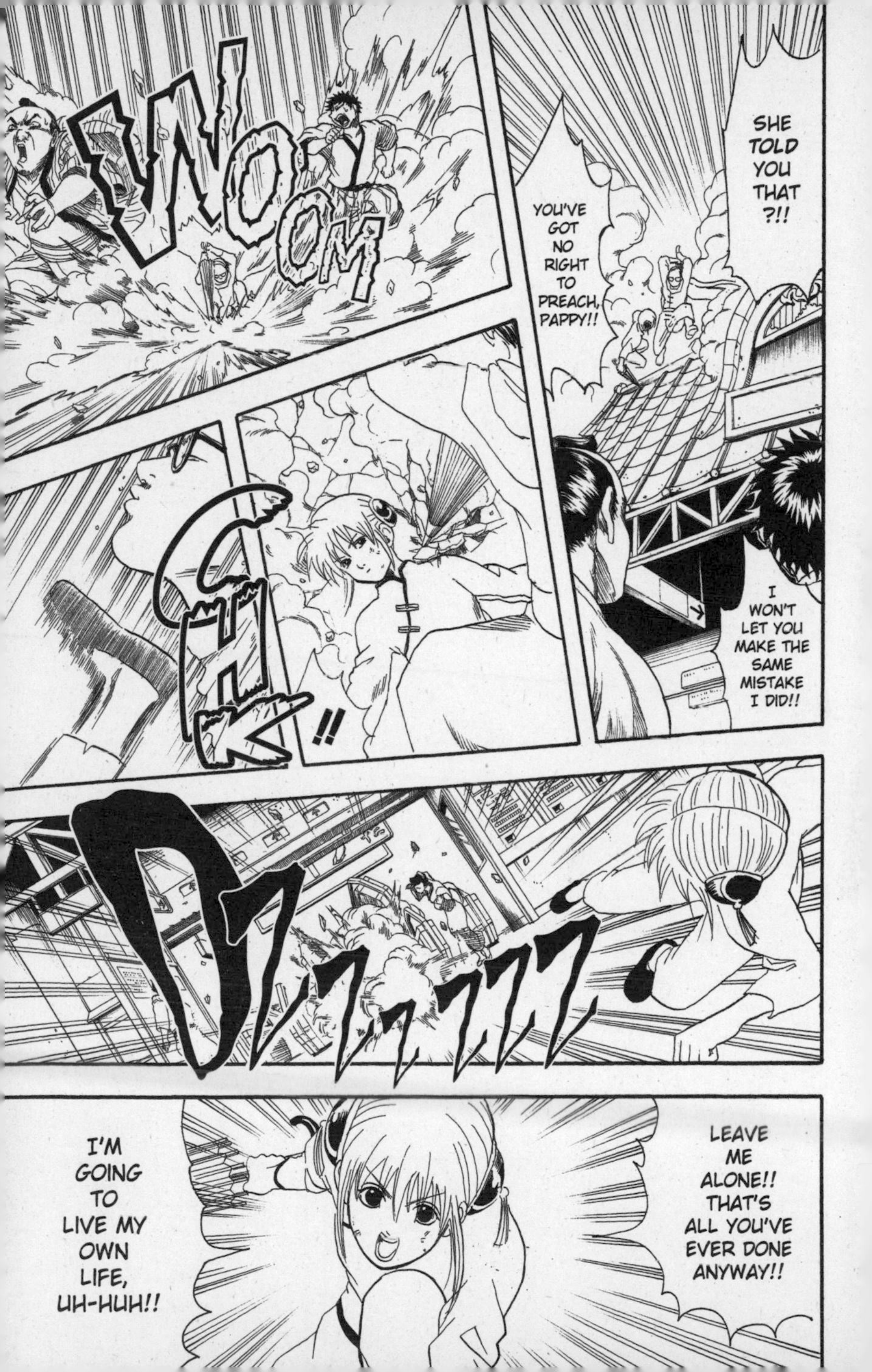
SHE TOLD YOU THAT?!!
YOU'VE GOT NO RIGHT TO PREACH, PAPPY!!
I WON'T LET YOU MAKE THE SAME MISTAKE I DID!!
WOOM
CHK!!
LEAVE ME ALONE!! THAT'S ALL YOU'VE EVER DONE ANYWAY!!
I'M GOING TO LIVE MY OWN LIFE, UH-HUH!!

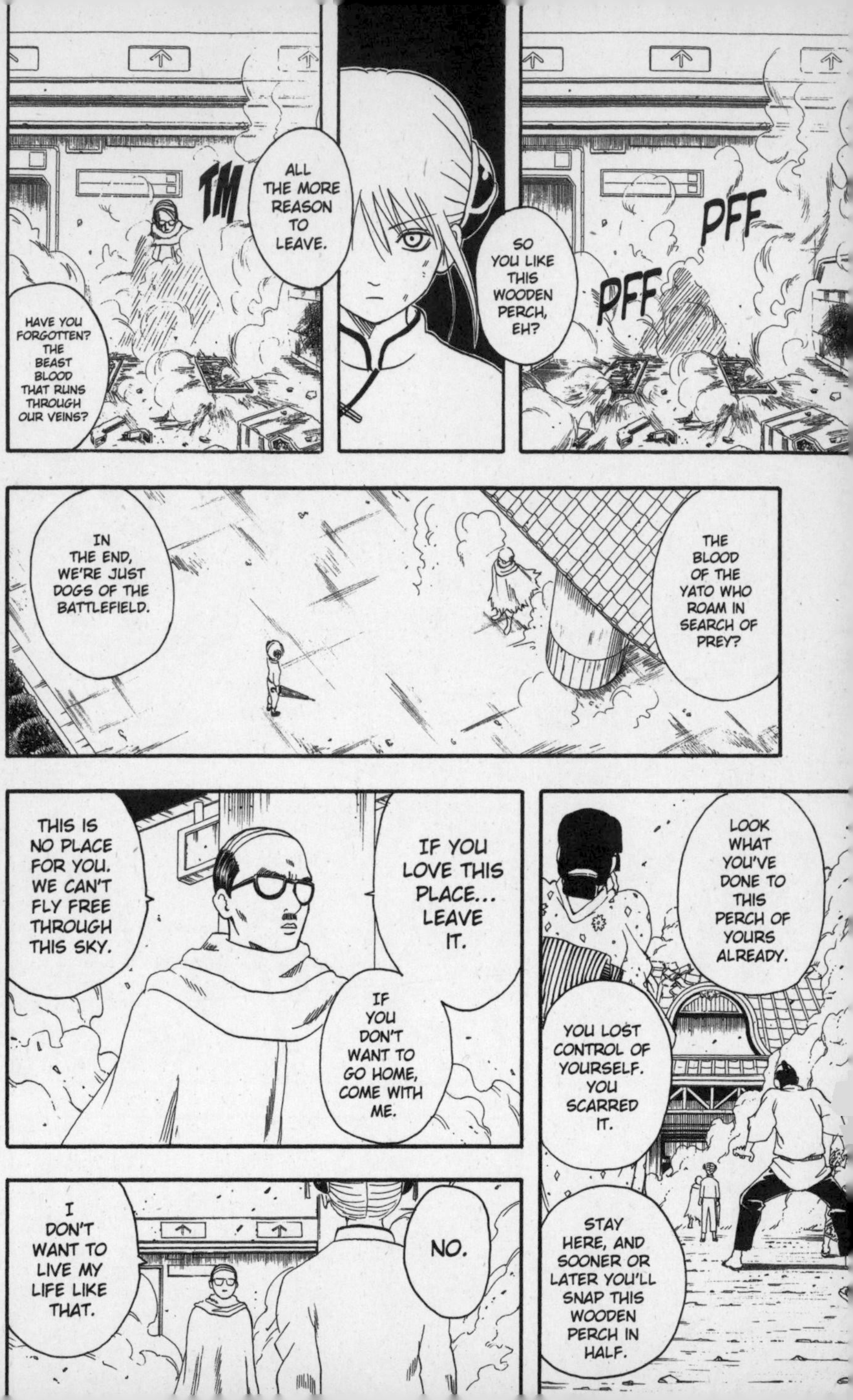
SO YOU LIKE THIS WOODEN PERCH, EH?
PFF
PFF
ALL THE MORE REASON TO LEAVE.
TM
HAVE YOU FORGOTTEN? THE BEAST BLOOD THAT RUNS THROUGH OUR VEINS?
THE BLOOD OF THE YATO WHO ROAM IN SEARCH OF PREY?
IN THE END, WE'RE JUST DOGS OF THE BATTLEFIELD.
LOOK WHAT YOU'VE DONE TO THIS PERCH OF YOURS ALREADY.
YOU LOST CONTROL OF YOURSELF. YOU SCARRED IT.
STAY HERE, AND SOONER OR LATER YOU'LL SNAP THIS WOODEN PERCH IN HALF.
IF YOU LOVE THIS PLACE... LEAVE IT.
THIS IS NO PLACE FOR YOU. WE CAN'T FLY FREE THROUGH THIS SKY.
IF YOU DON'T WANT TO GO HOME, COME WITH ME.
NO.
I DON'T WANT TO LIVE MY LIFE LIKE THAT.

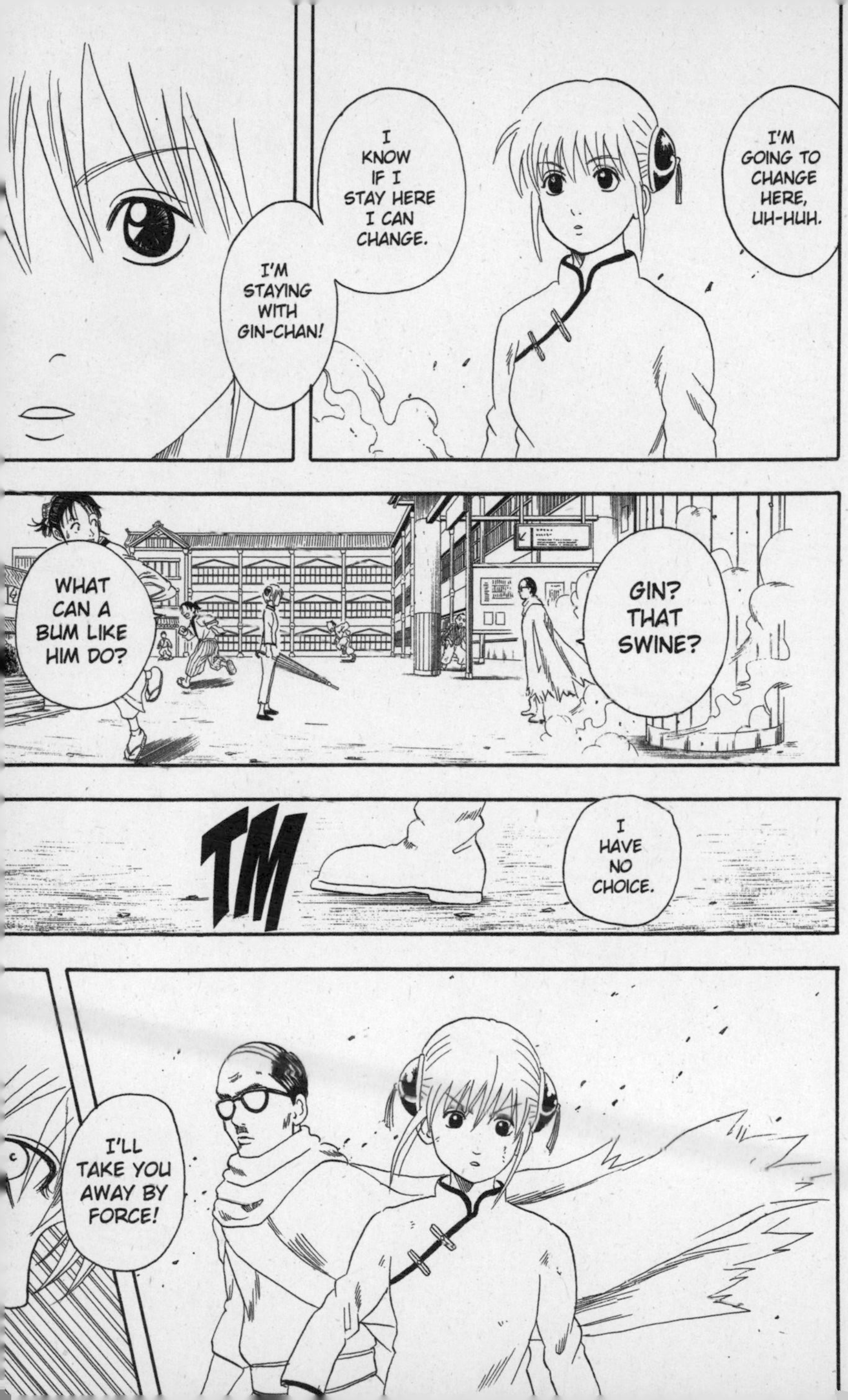
I'M GOING TO CHANGE HERE, UH-HUH.
I KNOW IF I STAY HERE I CAN CHANGE.
I'M STAYING WITH GIN-CHAN!
GIN? THAT SWINE?
WHAT CAN A BUM LIKE HIM DO?
I HAVE NO CHOICE.
TM
I'LL TAKE YOU AWAY BY FORCE!

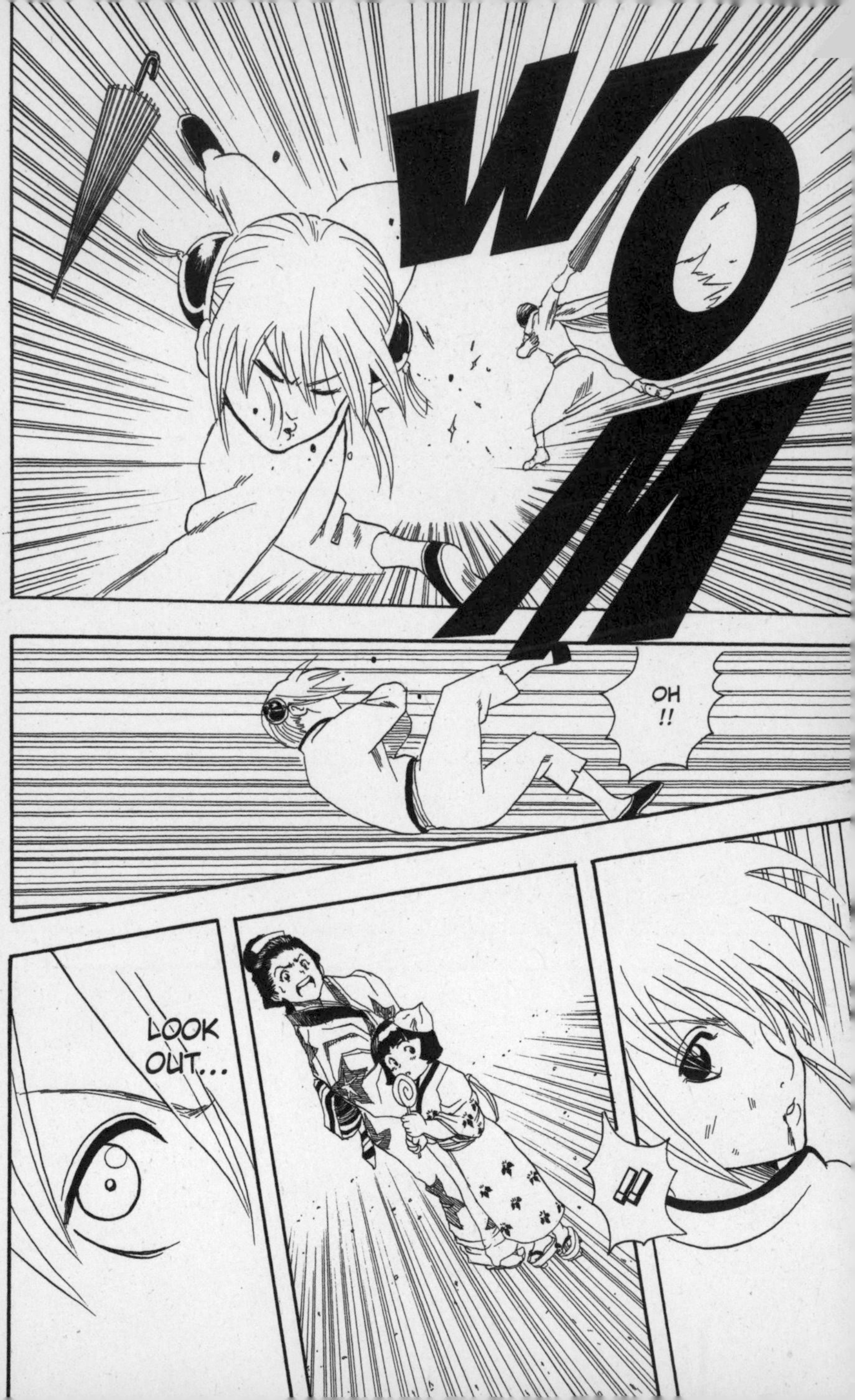
WOM
OH !!
!!
LOOK OUT...

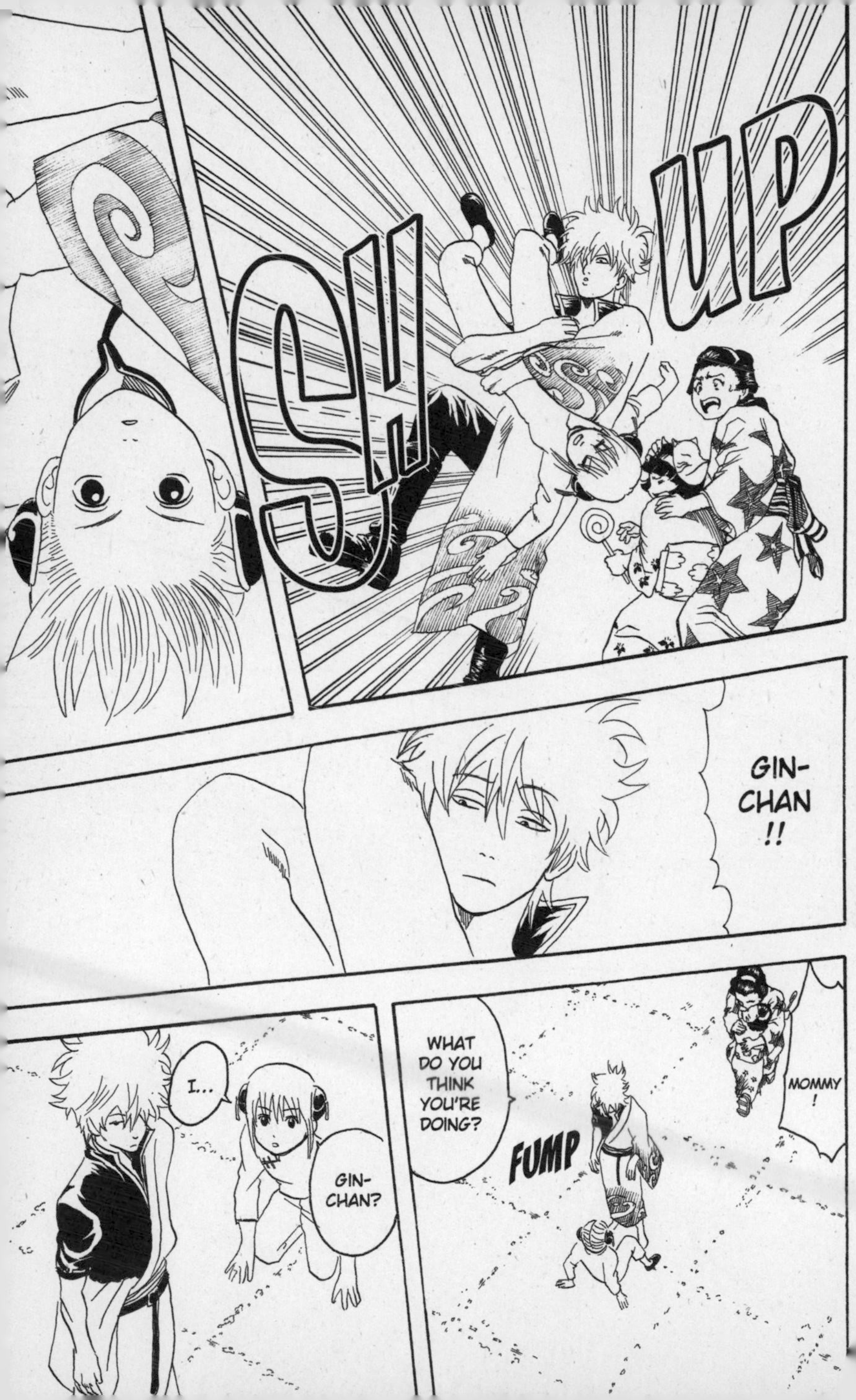
SH
UP
GIN-CHAN!!
MOMMY!
WHAT DO YOU THINK YOU'RE DOING?
FUMP
I...
GIN-CHAN?

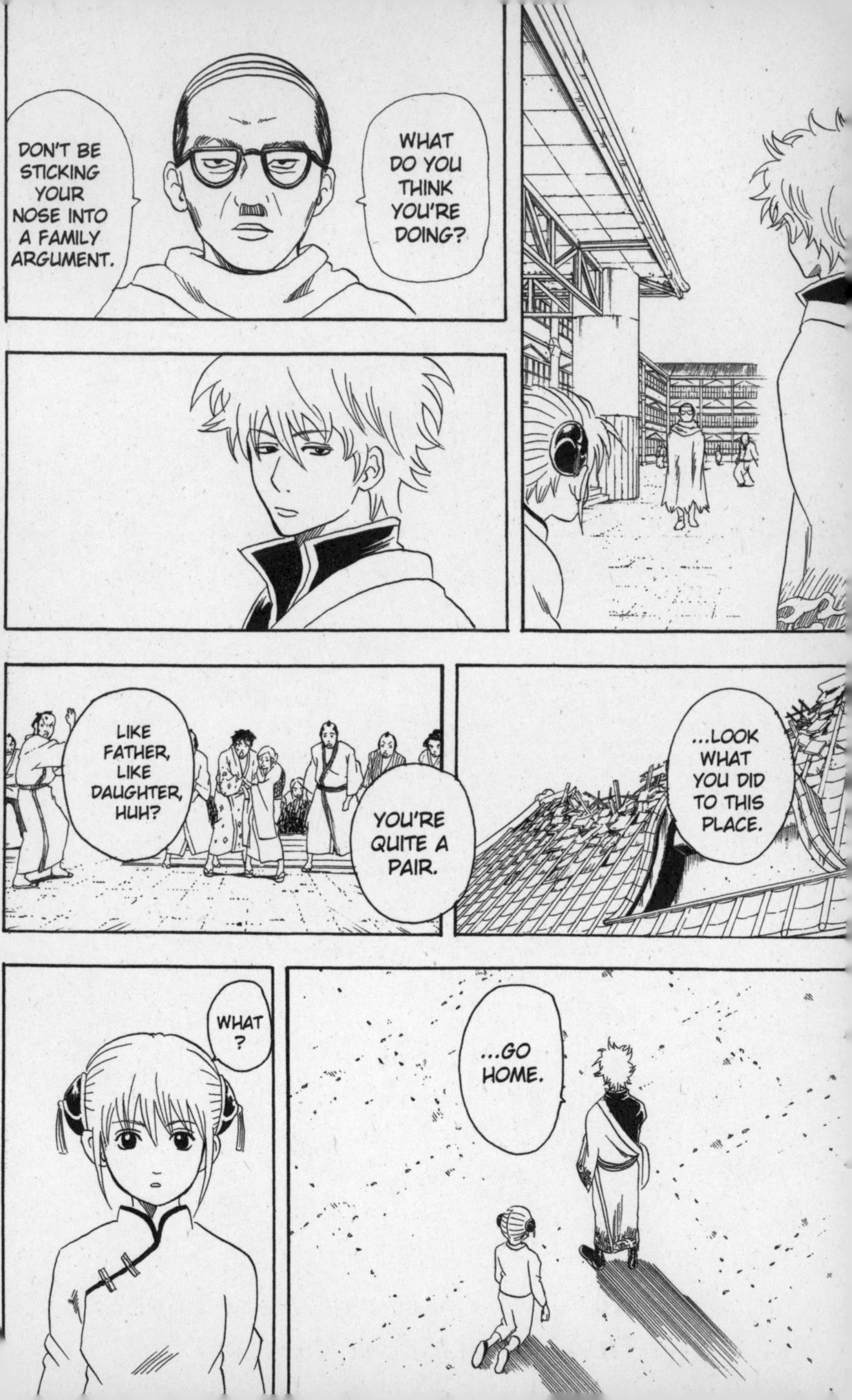
WHAT DO YOU THINK YOU'RE DOING?
DON'T BE STICKING YOUR NOSE INTO A FAMILY ARGUMENT.
...LOOK WHAT YOU DID TO THIS PLACE.
LIKE FATHER, LIKE DAUGHTER, HUH?
YOU'RE QUITE A PAIR.
...GO HOME.
WHAT?

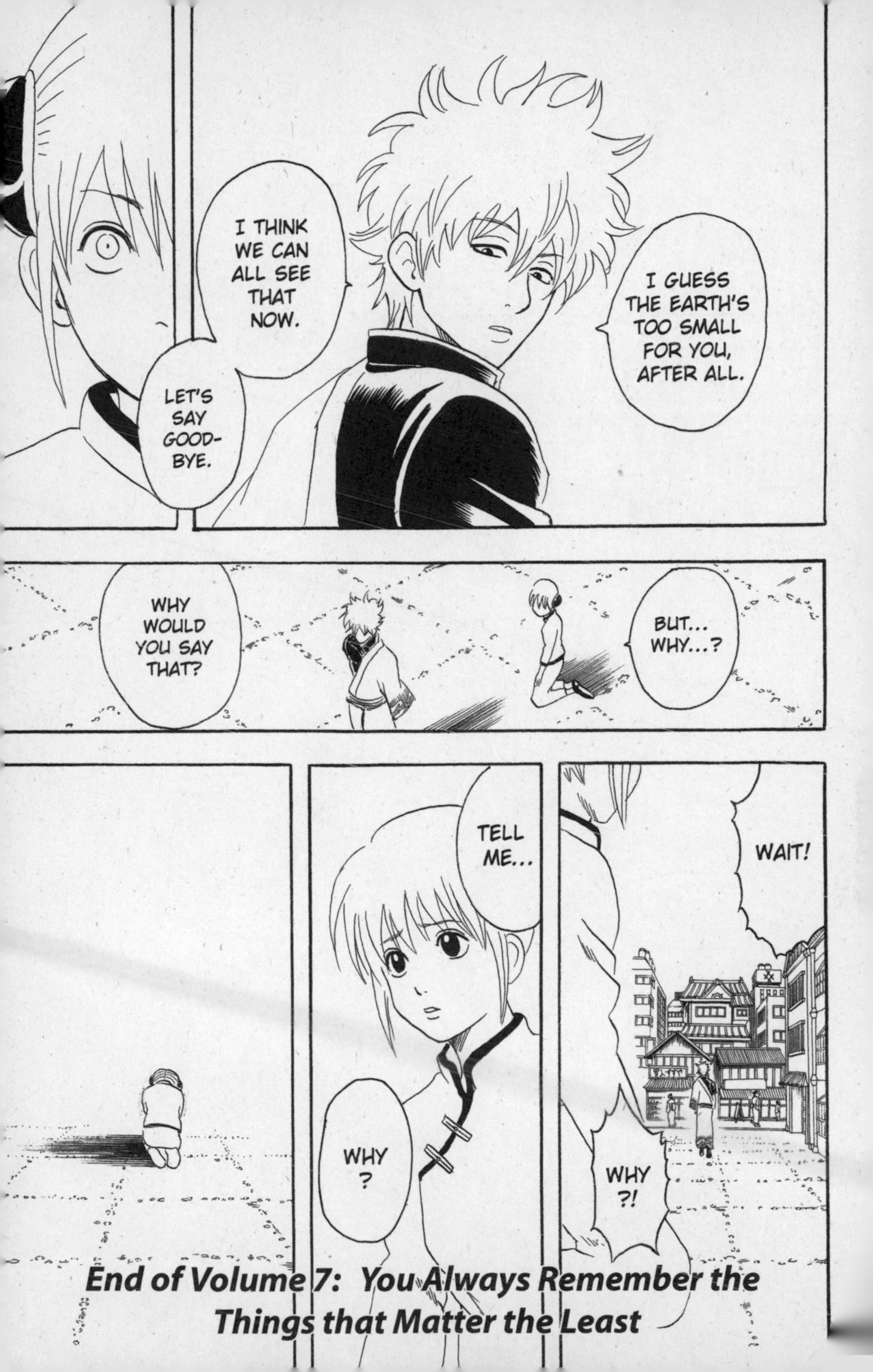
I GUESS THE EARTH'S TOO SMALL FOR YOU, AFTER ALL.
I THINK WE CAN ALL SEE THAT NOW.
LET'S SAY GOOD-BYE.
BUT... WHY...?
WHY WOULD YOU SAY THAT?
WAIT!
WHY ?!
TELL ME...
WHY ?

End of Volume 7: You Always Remember the Things that Matter the Least

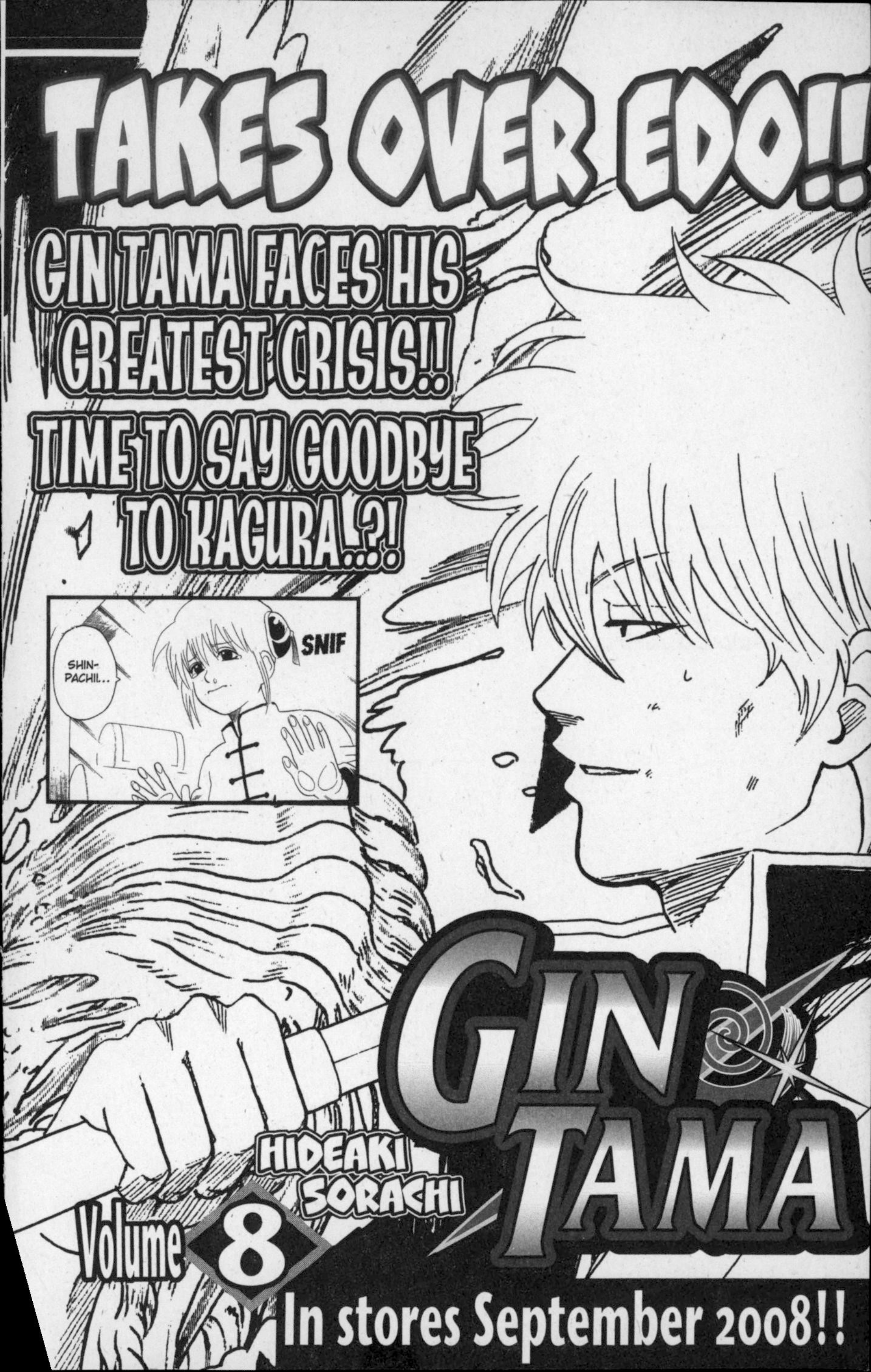

TAKES OVER EDO!!
GIN TAMA FACES HIS GREATEST CRISIS!!
TIME TO SAY GOODBYE TO KAGURA...?!
SNIF
SHIN-PACHII...
GIN TAMA
HIDEAKI SORACHI
Volume 8
In stores September 2008!!

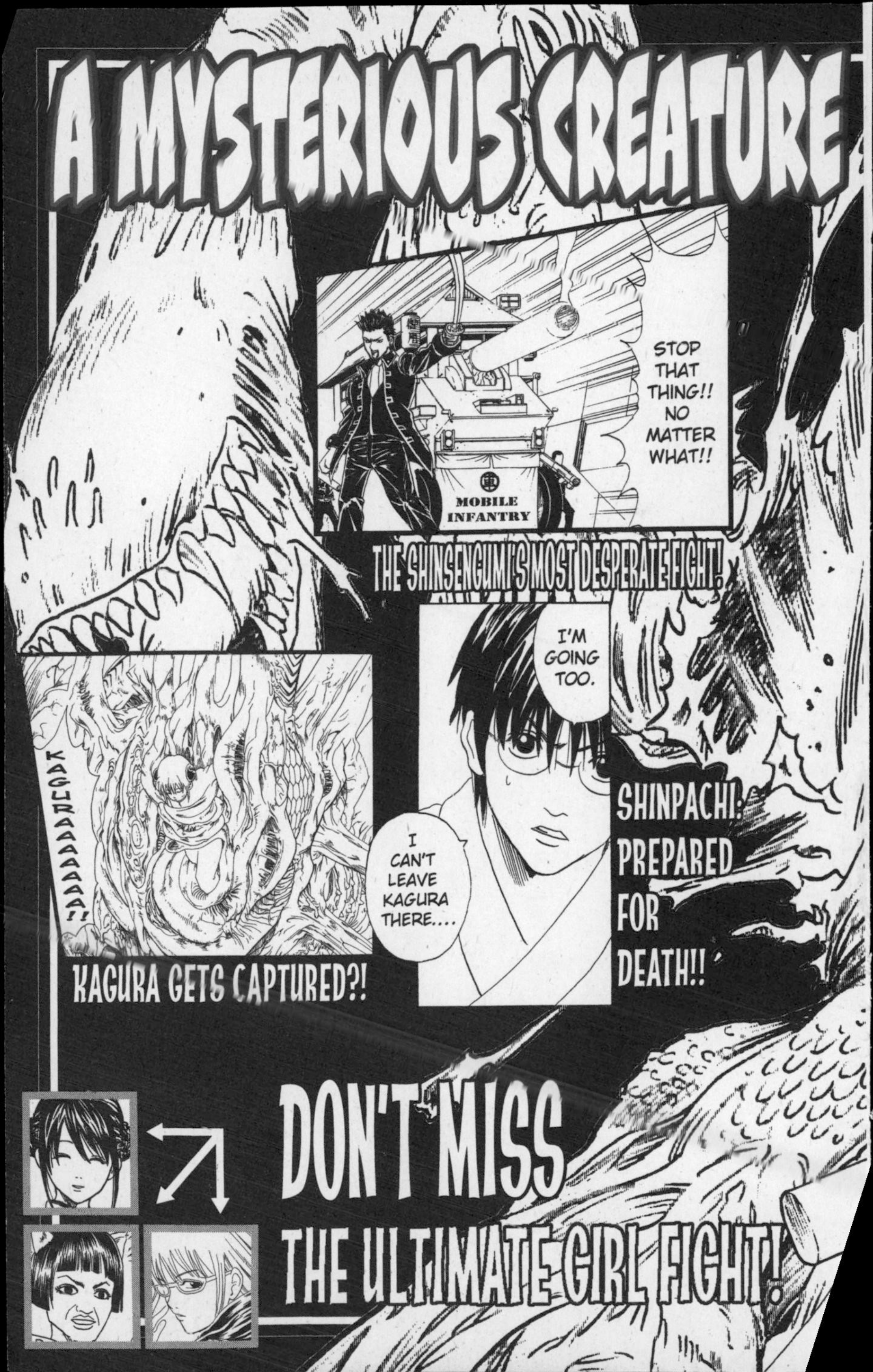
A MYSTERIOUS CREATURE
STOP THAT THING!! NO MATTER WHAT!!
MOBILE INFANTRY
THE SHINSENGUMI'S MOST DESPERATE FIGHT!
I'M GOING TOO.
I CAN'T LEAVE KAGURA THERE....
SHINPACHI! PREPARED FOR DEATH!!
KAGURAAAAAAA!!
KAGURA GETS CAPTURED?!
DON'T MISS
THE ULTIMATE GIRL FIGHT!

Volume 8 Preview

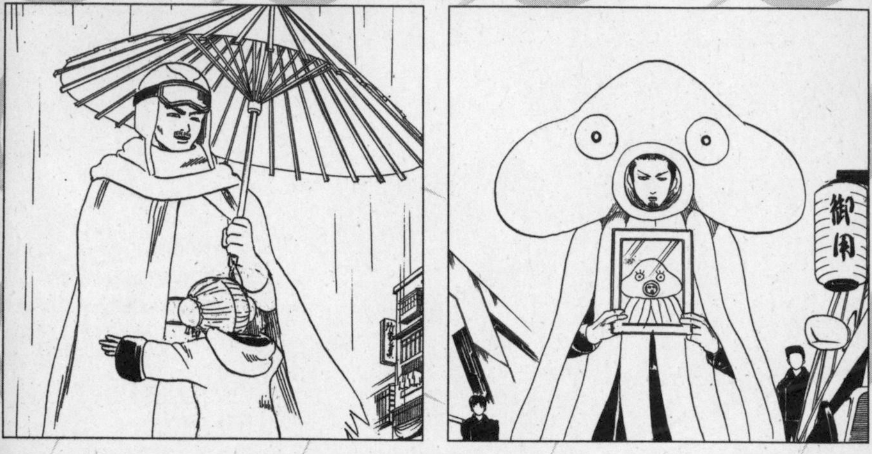
御用

Do's and Don'ts for Daddy-Daughter Day

1. Don't let alien monsters grow exponentially by siphoning energy from space terminals and eat your daughter.
2. Do show your dad you've learned to use your abnormal strength to help others, not break them.
3. Do respect your daughter's planetary preferences, especially when they're in writing.
4. Don't assassinate your daughter's boyfriend.

COMING SEPTEMBER 2008

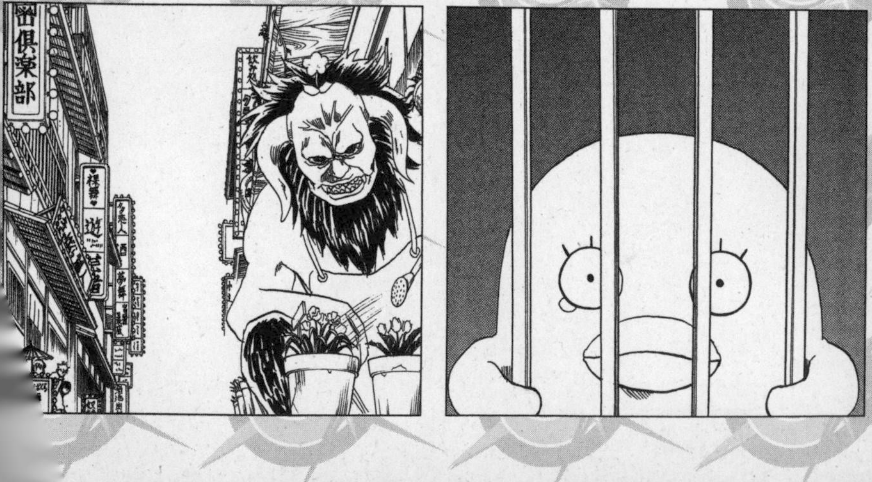

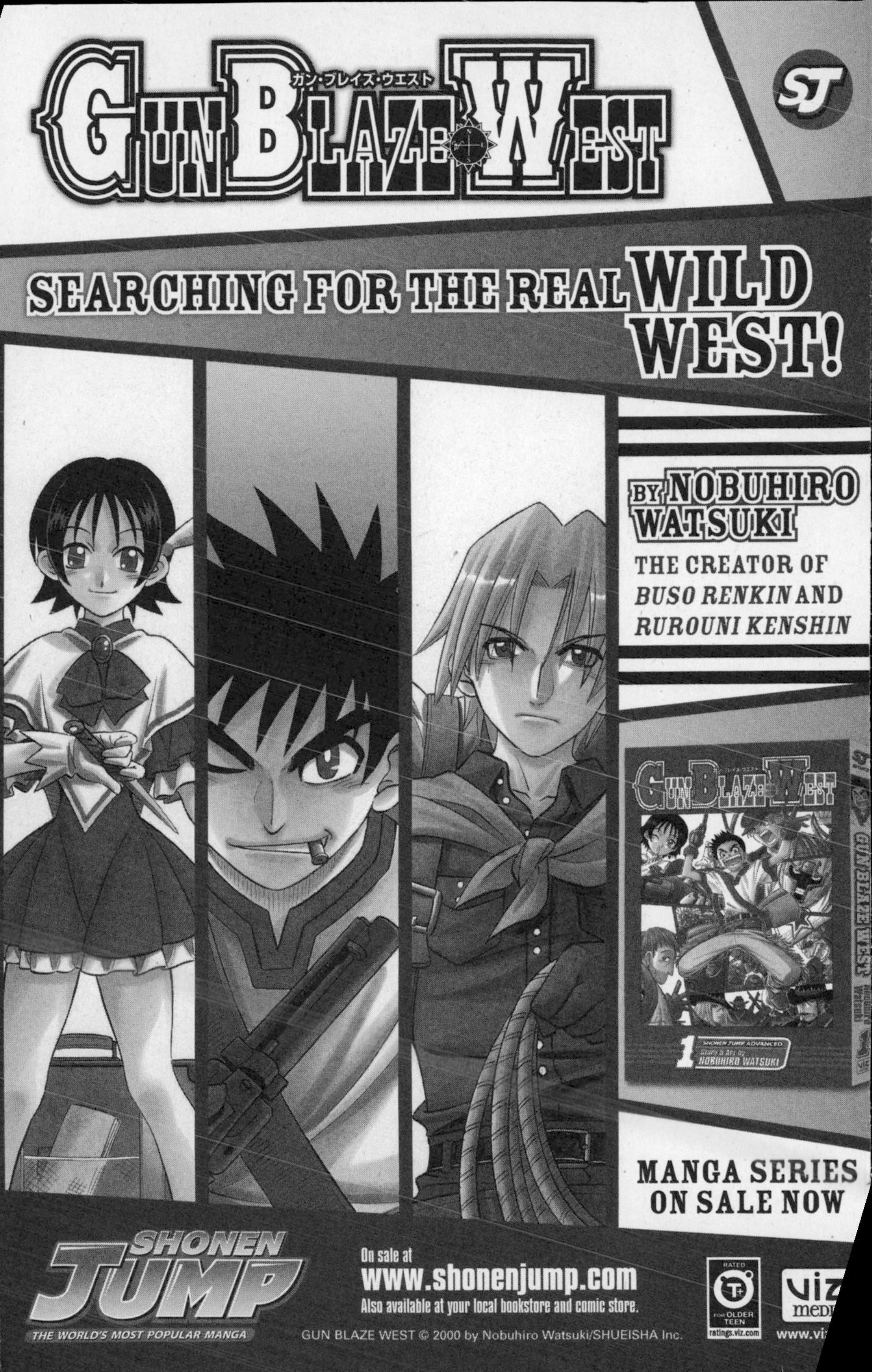
GUN BLAZE WEST
ガン・ブレイズ・ウエスト
SJ
SEARCHING FOR THE REAL WILD WEST!
BY NOBUHIRO WATSUKI
THE CREATOR OF BUSO RENKIN AND RUROUNI KENSHIN
GUN BLAZE WEST
1 SHONEN JUMP ADVANCED
Story & Art by NOBUHIRO WATSUKI
MANGA SERIES ON SALE NOW
SHONEN JUMP
THE WORLD'S MOST POPULAR MANGA
On sale at
www.shonenjump.com
Also available at your local bookstore and comic store.
RATED T+ FOR OLDER TEEN
ratings.viz.com
GUN BLAZE WEST © 2000 by Nobuhiro Watsuki/SHUEISHA Inc.

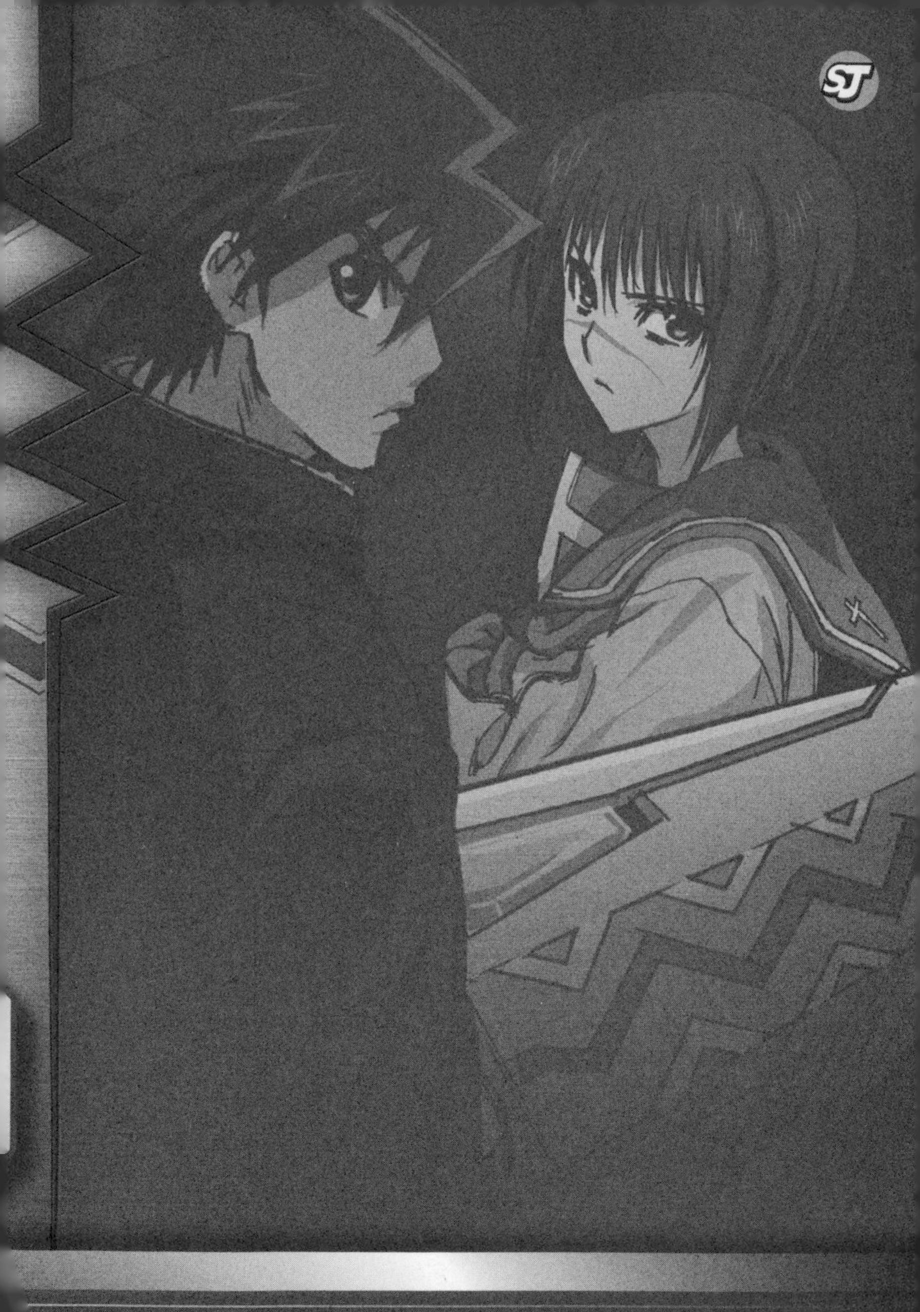

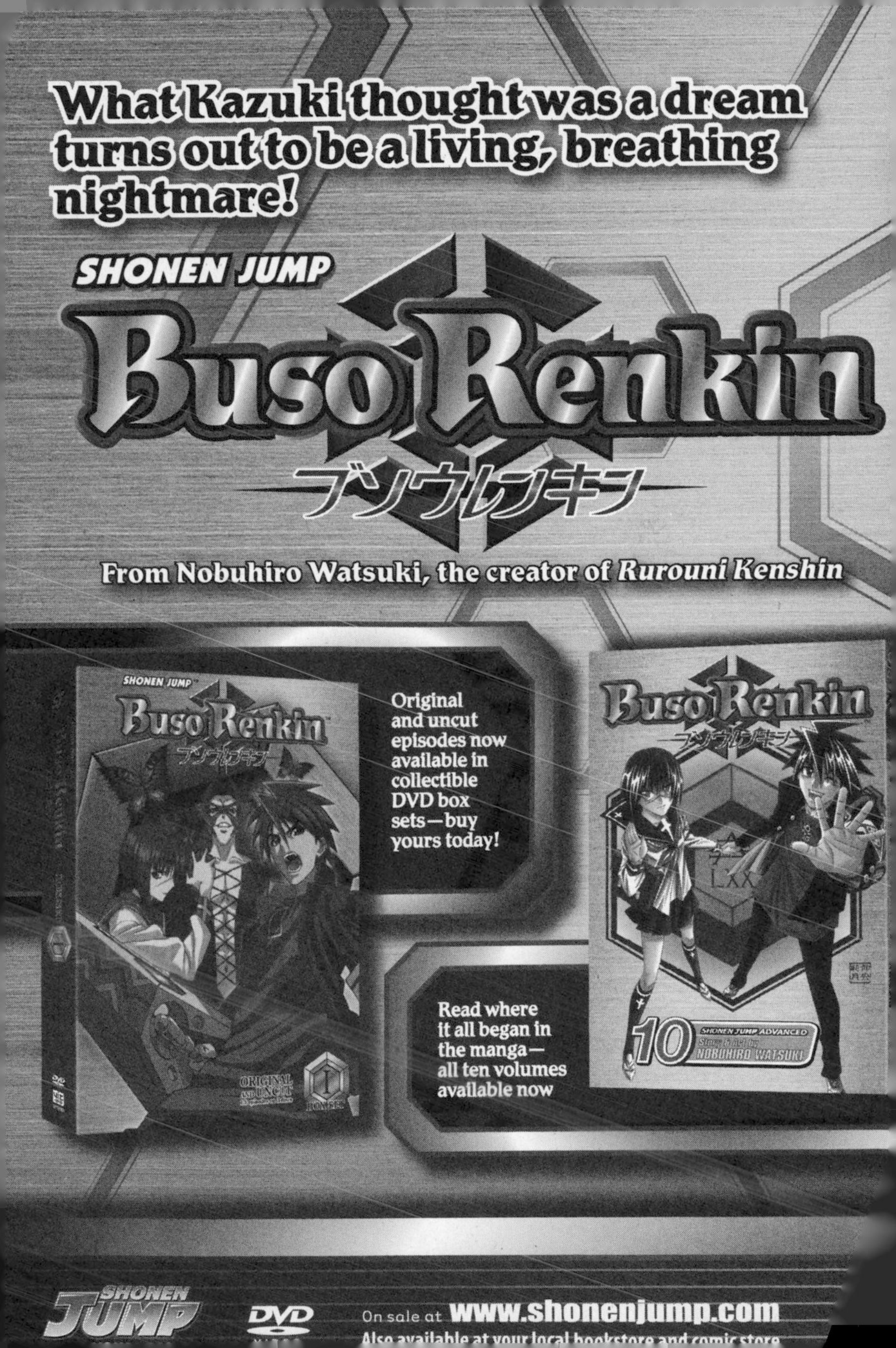

What Kazuki thought was a dream turns out to be a living, breathing nightmare!
SHONEN JUMP
Buso Renkin
ブソウレンキン
From Nobuhiro Watsuki, the creator of Rurouni Kenshin
SHONEN JUMP
Buso Renkin
ブソウレンキン
Original and uncut episodes now available in collectible DVD box sets—buy yours today!
ORIGINAL AND UNCUT
Buso Renkin
ブソウレンキン
LXX
10
SHONEN JUMP ADVANCED
NOBUHIRO WATSUKI
Read where it all began in the manga—all ten volumes available now
SHONEN JUMP
DVD
On sale at www.shonenjump.com
Also available at your local bookstore and comic store

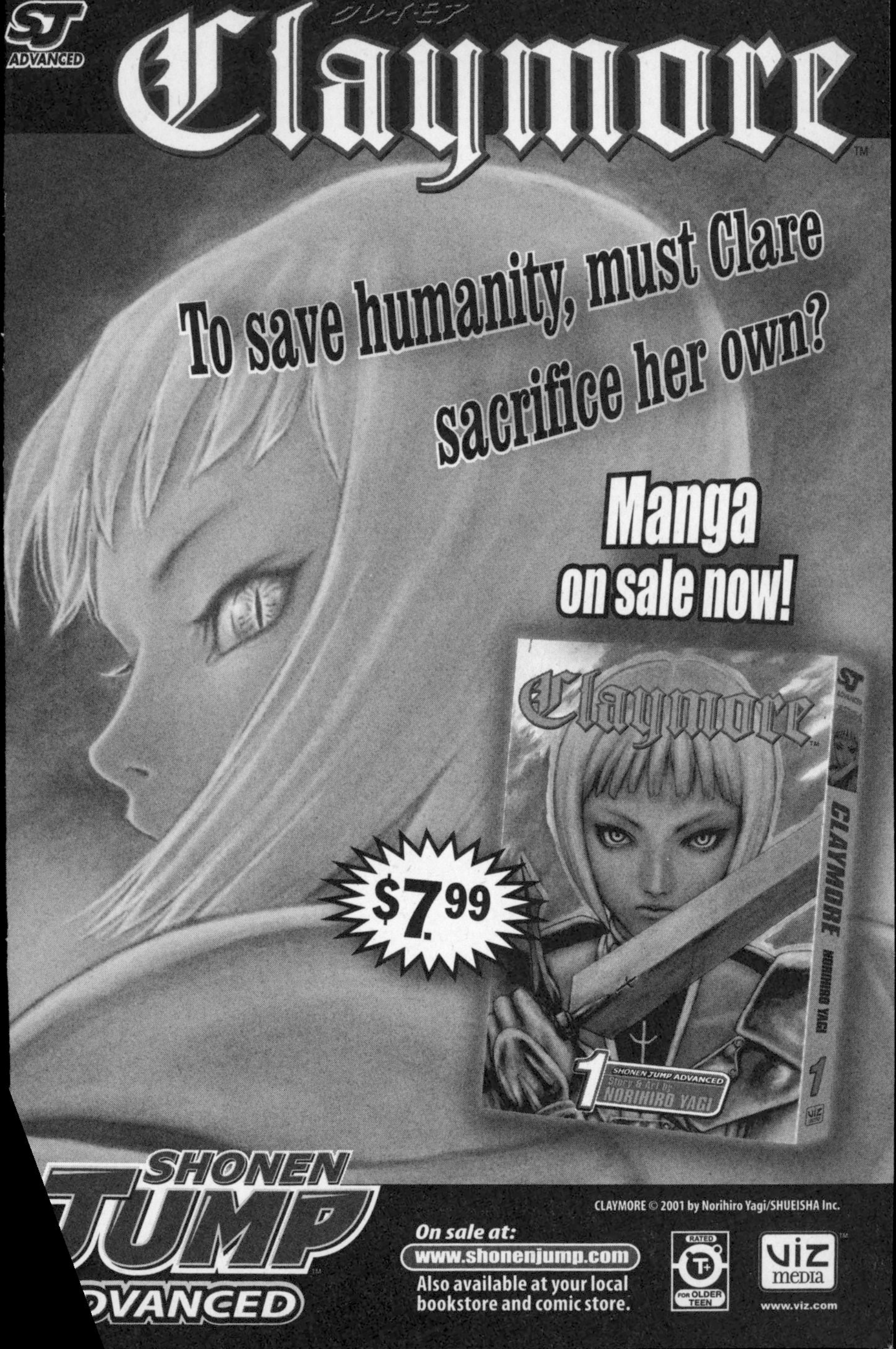

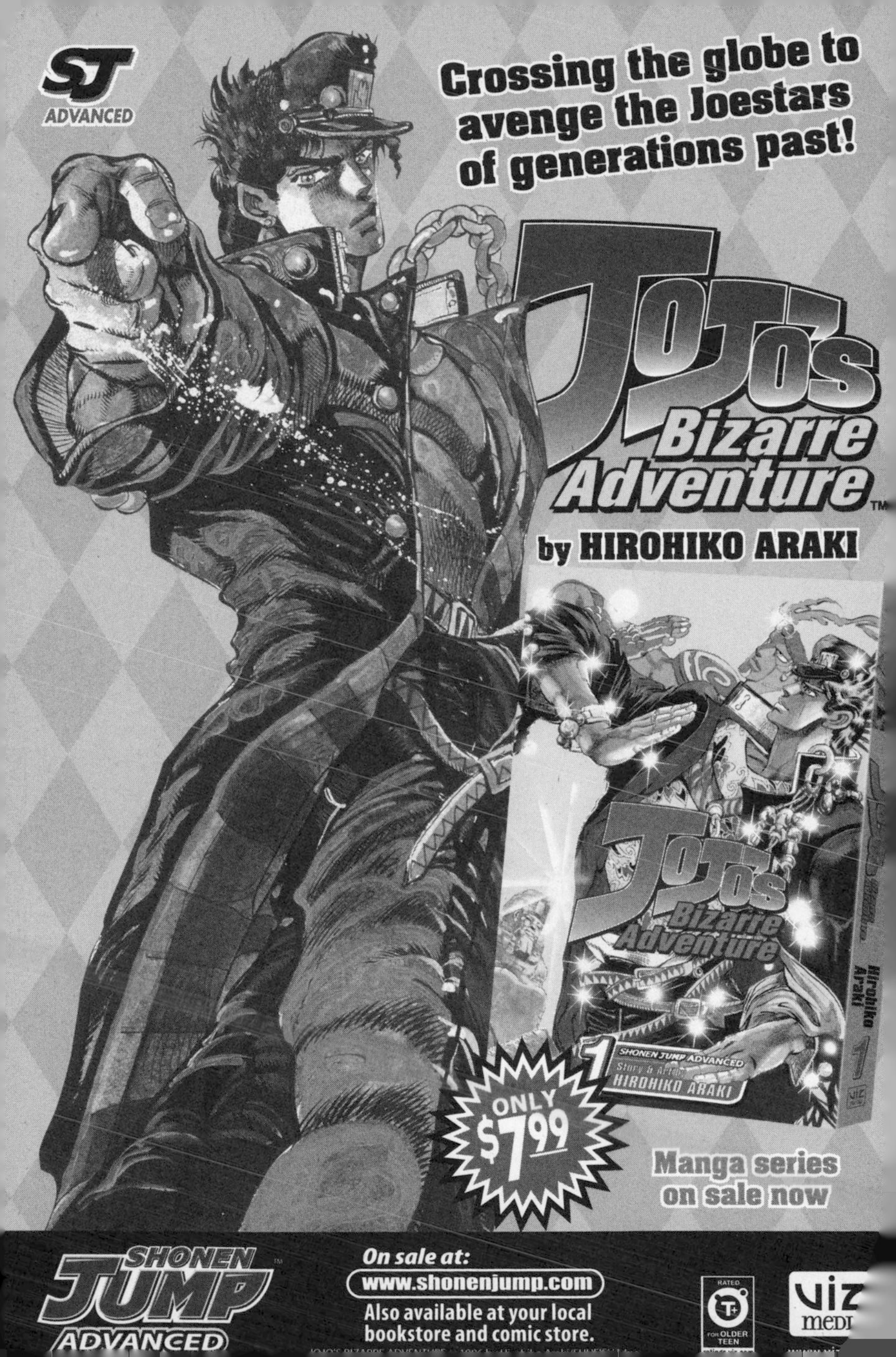

SJ ADVANCED
Crossing the globe to avenge the Joestars of generations past!
JoJo's Bizarre Adventure™
by HIROHIKO ARAKI
JoJo's Bizarre Adventure
1
SHONEN JUMP ADVANCED
HIROHIKO ARAKI
Hirohiko Araki
ONLY $7.99
Manga series on sale now
SHONEN JUMP ADVANCED
On sale at:
www.shonenjump.com
Also available at your local bookstore and comic store.
RATED T+ FOR OLDER TEEN
VIZ MEDIA

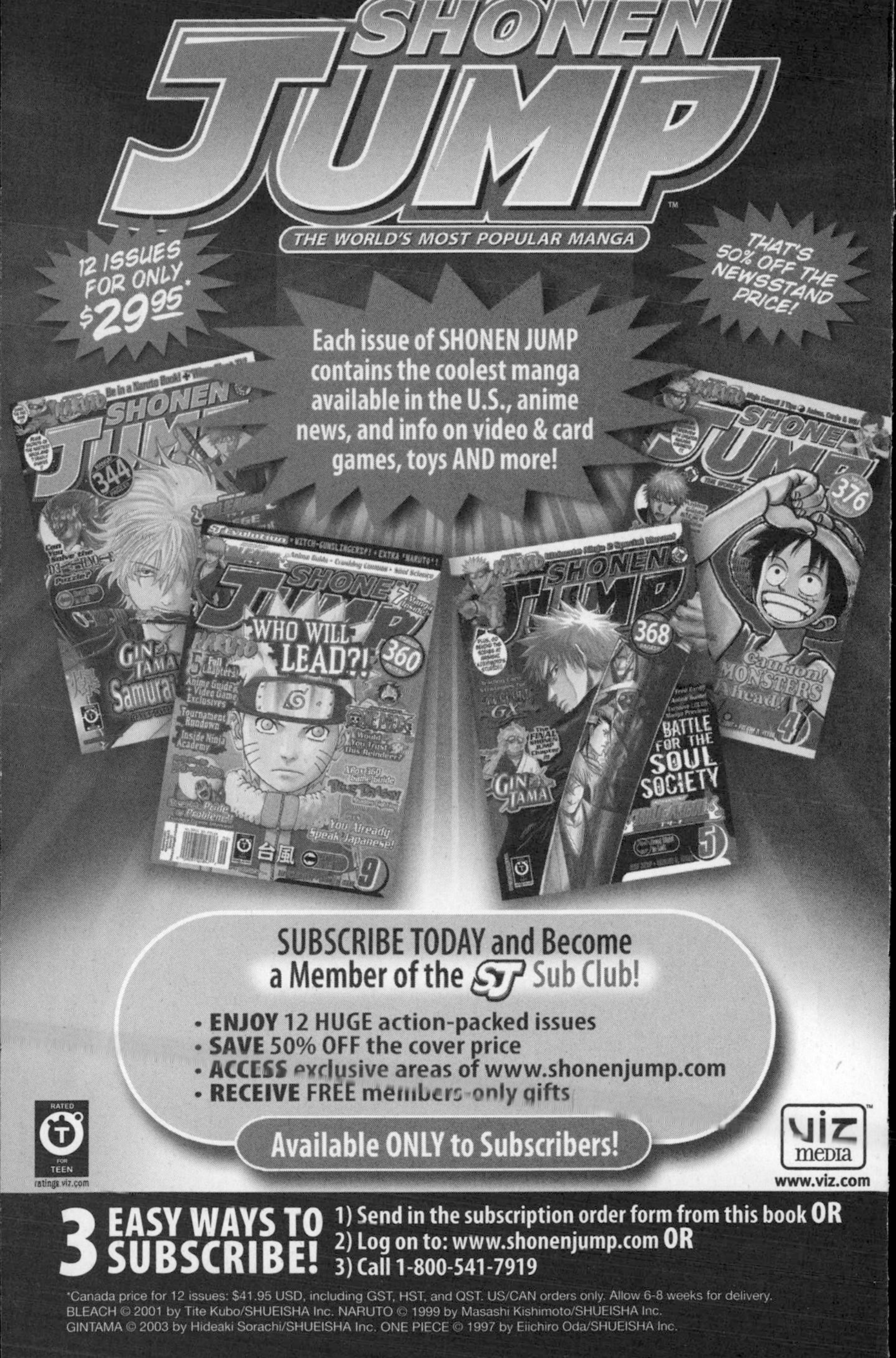
SHONEN JUMP
THE WORLD'S MOST POPULAR MANGA
12 ISSUES FOR ONLY $29.95*
THAT'S 50% OFF THE NEWSSTAND PRICE!
Each issue of SHONEN JUMP contains the coolest manga available in the U.S., anime news, and info on video & card games, toys AND more!
WHO WILL LEAD?!
BATTLE FOR THE SOUL SOCIETY
Caution! MONSTERS Ahead!
SUBSCRIBE TODAY and Become a Member of the SJ Sub Club!
• ENJOY 12 HUGE action-packed issues
• SAVE 50% OFF the cover price
• ACCESS exclusive areas of www.shonenjump.com
• RECEIVE FREE members-only gifts
Available ONLY to Subscribers!
RATED T FOR TEEN
ratings.viz.com
viz media
www.viz.com
3 EASY WAYS TO SUBSCRIBE!
1) Send in the subscription order form from this book OR
2) Log on to: www.shonenjump.com OR
3) Call 1-800-541-7919
*Canada price for 12 issues: $41.95 USD, including GST, HST, and QST. US/CAN orders only. Allow 6-8 weeks for delivery.
BLEACH © 2001 by Tite Kubo/SHUEISHA Inc. NARUTO © 1999 by Masashi Kishimoto/SHUEISHA Inc.
GINTAMA © 2003 by Hideaki Sorachi/SHUEISHA Inc. ONE PIECE © 1997 by Eiichiro Oda/SHUEISHA Inc.

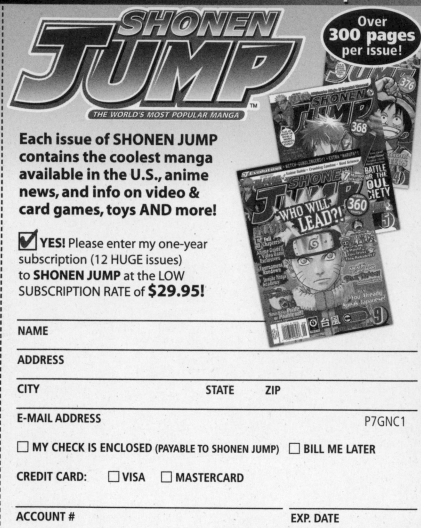